Realizing Children's Rights in a Global Context:

Glocalization of the Reggio Emilia Experience

Marisa Galliano Macy
https://orcid.org/0000-0002-4676-9865
University of Wyoming, USA

Emer Ring
https://orcid.org/0000-0001-8459-8625
University of Limerick, Ireland

Alessandra Landini
https://orcid.org/0000-0001-5954-6030
I.C. Manzoni in Reggio Emilia, Italy

IGI Global
Scientific Publishing
Publishing Tomorrow's Research Today

Vice President of Editorial Melissa Wagner
Director of Acquisitions Mikaela Felty
Director of Book Development Jocelynn Hessler
Production Manager Mike Brehm
Cover Design Jose Rosado

Published in the United States of America by
IGI Global Scientific Publishing
701 East Chocolate Avenue
Hershey, PA, 17033, USA
Tel: 717-533-8845 | Fax: 717-533-7115
Website: https://www.igi-global.com E-mail: cust@igi-global.com

Library of Congress Cataloging-in-Publication Data

LCCN: 2025054466 (CIP Data Pending)
ISBN13: 9798337334318
Isbn13Softcover: 9798337334325
EISBN13: 9798337334332
British Cataloguing in Publication Data
A Cataloguing in Publication record for this book is available from the British Library.

For my husband and daughter, Robert and Adriana, whose passion for reading inspires me to want to write. ~Marisa Galliano Macy

For my grandchildren, Clara, Ava, Dylan and Ethan, that the power of rights threaded through these pages will always be your compass for your magical journeys and adventures ahead. ~Emer Ring

To my father, to you who have always looked at me with love and trust. To my mother, Ilde, the source of my curiosity and creativity. To my husband David, my mate, who supports and encourages me in every project and adventure. For my sons, Francesco and Luca, the motivation behind every aim, question and research. ~Alessandra Landini

Editorial Advisory Board

Kelcie Burke, *University of Nebraska Lincoln, USA*
Kimberlee Tellford, *Buffett Early Childhood Institute, University of Nebraska, USA*
Laurie Catteeuw, *Babilou Family, Bois-Colombes, France*
Linda Madden, *Mary Immaculate College, Ireland*
Lisha O'Sullivan, *Mary Immaculate College, Ireland*
Lori Ryan, *University of Colorado, USA*
Lorraine Diggins, *Early Childhood, Ireland*
Lucia Scipione, *University of Modena and Reggio Emilia, Italy*
Marika Kirvalidze, *Ilia State University, Georgia*
Maurice Harmon, *Mary Immaculate College, Ireland*
Mzia Tsereteli, *Tbilisi State University, Georgia*
Sarah Jackson, *Millersville University, USA*
Sarah Neville, *Mary Immaculate College, Ireland*
Shirley Heaney, *Mary Immaculate College, Ireland*
Sinead Morgan, *National Council for Special Education, Ireland*
Tamar Gagoshidze, *Tbilisi State University, Georgia*
Tracey Hunter-Doniger, *College of Charleston, USA*
Xueyun Su, *East China Normal University, China*

Table of Contents

Detailed Table of Contents

This chapter traces the experimentation of Reggio-inspired playful approaches to learning across diverse contexts. Rooted in the Reggio Emilia philosophy and reinterpreted through local practices and international collaborations, these approaches position play and playfulness as central to creativity, connection, and meaning-making. Learning is viewed as relational and joyful, where curiosity and passion drive development. Inspired by Carla Rinaldi's image of play and learning as "the two wings of a butterfly," the chapter honors her vision of education as a living dialogue among children, teachers, and communities. It argues that play is not only a pedagogical strategy but a fundamental right. Through examples from local and global projects, it makes visible how documentation, teacher-researcher inquiry, and the playfulness of adults nurture play as a participatory, ethical, and relational practice that regenerates education through motivation, passion, and a shared sense of empathy born from listening and co-construction.

This chapter explores the enduring influence of Loris Malaguzzi's socio-constructivist pedagogy and its generative power in inspiring locally rooted yet original educational experiences, such as the San Miniato project. It examines Malaguzzi's vision of children as active, competent protagonists in their own learning, challenging

Chapter 5

This chapter is a comprehensive overview of the potential of the Reggio Emilia approach in diverse settings in South Africa. It traces aspects of the historical legacy of apartheid on education and the ongoing inequalities affecting early childhood education. It highlights ongoing challenges such as limited resources, formalised teaching methods, and disparities related to access. The chapter presents the Reggio Emilia approach as a philosophy of education that focuses on children's rights, agency, creativity, and the significance of learning environments while emphasising the culture of the atelier and the role of the atelierista. Through various case studies of South African schools and communities, it illustrates the transformative potential of this approach, even in under-resourced settings. The chapter underscores the resonance between the Reggio Emilia philosophy and South Africa's aspirations for social justice, advocating for educational reform, and professional development. It acts as a call to action to ensure every child's right to a quality, creative education.

Chapter 6

This chapter explores the ethical and pedagogical dimensions of children's rights within early learning settings, emphasizing the image of the child as a capable, curious, and contributing citizen. Grounded in the principles of the Reggio Emilia philosophy and the United Nations Convention on the Rights of the Child, it examines how democratic participation, documentation, and inquiry-based learning cultivate environments where children's voices and ideas shape the work and projects. Drawing on examples from Acorn School in Toronto, Ontario, the chapter illustrates how everyday encounters with open-ended materials, community rituals, and shared projects become spaces for meaning-making, reflection, and co-construction of knowledge. Through these lived experiences, educators are invited to consider how pedagogy, ethics, and politics intertwine in fostering cultures of listening, belonging, and participation that honor children's rights as lived, relational, and transformative practices.

This chapter explores the Reggio Emilia philosophy as a compelling global model for realizing the child's right to early education, grounded in the UNCRC's principles of access, participation, and benefit. Tracing its post-World War II origins and theoretical lineage through constructivist, sociocultural, and critical pedagogical frameworks, the chapter demonstrates how Reggio operationalises rights in early childhood through democratic learning environments, inclusive practices, and child-led curricula. It critically examines global inequities in access, the participatory mechanisms embedded in Reggio pedagogy, and the multidimensional benefits, i.e., cognitive, social, and emotional, derived from such a rights-based approach. Drawing on comparative international implementations and innovations, it analyses the institutional challenges of embedding Reggio principles in diverse contexts. Finally, the chapter offers policy recommendations and envisions future directions for integrating Reggio-inspired practices into digital, cross-sectoral, and post-pandemic educational landscapes.

This chapter explores how the Reggio Emilia Approach can be re-envisioned through global collaboration among children's key systems of community, school, and family. Grounded in Bronfenbrenner's ecological systems theory and the United Nations Convention on the Rights of the Child, it emphasizes children's rights to participation, voice, and agency. Drawing from a decade of Reggio-inspired study abroad experiences with pre-service and in-service early childhood professionals, the authors propose a new educational partnership that unites parents and teachers through shared experiential learning in Reggio Emilia, Italy. This model seeks to bridge theory and practice, reduce power imbalances between home and school, and strengthen the child's global world by fostering collaborative, rights-based education that values the hundred languages of children.

Foreword

Another World Is Possible

I am pleased to have this opportunity to add a few words to this book, which is another important contribution to the literature about the municipal schools for young children in Reggio Emilia and their practice of early childhood education. The theme of the book is the 'Reggio Emilia Experience' and its embodiment of and contribution to the concept of children's rights. I would like to complement this important theme by adding my own framing of Reggio Emilia, adding some further reasons for the significance of this educational experience.

Over time I have come to understand Reggio Emilia as a local cultural project, a term I once heard used to describe the early childhood education in another Italian city, a reminder that Reggio Emilia is not unique. Rather, it is one example of many from what has been termed Italy's 'municipal school revolution', that time in the 1960s and 1970s when 'municipal councils in the Emilia Romagna area, in particular those controlled by left parties (such as Bologna, Parma, Reggio Emilia, Modena) pre-empted State-run services by starting up their own services for young children' (Catarsi, 2004, p.8). Not only in the region of Emilia Romagna, as the example of the Tuscan town of San Miniato makes clear, whose early childhood education is referred to by Aldo Fortunati, in this book, as 'a community project': a project with some similarities to Reggio's but also with its own distinctive features.

Carlina Rinaldi, one of the first *pedagogistas* in Reggio, has written about 'the construction of the educational project' (Rinaldi, 2021, p.87) in the city. Just as project work plays a central role in Reggio's pedagogy and the process of children co-constructing knowledge, so too we can see Reggio's schools and their pedagogical work as the product of *progettazione*, a collective process of hypotheses (in this case about early childhood education and the school) being co-constructed to be put forward for researching, testing and re-constructing. Moreover, just as project work in the classroom is the product of the particular context of that classroom, so Reggio Emilia's schools and education are the product of that city's particular context – historical, cultural, political and social. Which means it is impossible to copy or emulate Reggio, for like each child Reggio as a community is itself unique: Reggio may have an 'approach' – but that is not a blueprint.

But as the title of the book suggests, Reggio's local project can still have a global role - as a provocateur. We can be provoked by Reggio and its experience, provoked to construct other projects, local and distinctive; provoked to question our assumptions; provoked to imagine and explore alternatives; in sum, provoked to think for ourselves just as the founders of Reggio's project had a 'a vision of children who can think and act for themselves' (Dahlberg, Moss and Pence, 2013. P.13).

Provoked, too, to recognise and value education as, first and foremost, a political practice. The technical, the 'how to', remains important - and we should never lose sight of the intense practicality of Reggio Emilia, the attention paid to the conditions needed for their project to succeed, their acknowledgement of organisation as a value. But the technical, they have understood, must always follow *after* the political for, as Loris Malaguzzi puts it, 'our discourse inevitably is also always a political discourse whether we know it or not. It is about working with cultural choices, but it clearly also means working with political choices' (Malaguzzi, cited in Cagliari et al., 2016, p.267). Political choices necessitated by asking political questions that, unlike technical questions, can have no one right answer. Political questions that start with that most evocative enquiry, 'what is your image of the child?'

To which question, Reggio's choice has been clear and has been the basis for all that has followed, for their project, for their pedagogy, for the provision they have made for their children and families. Their choice has been the 'rich' child, born with a hundred languages, a citizen with rights, a protagonist of unknown potentiality, a potentiality that 'is stunted when the endpoint of their [children's] learning is formulated in advance' (Rinaldi, 1993, p.104). At a time when early childhood education is so dominated by what Malaguzzi called 'prophetic pedagogy', that 'knows everything beforehand...knows everything that will happen... has no uncertainty' (Malaguzzi, cited in Cagliari et al., 2016, p.421), this image of the child is perhaps the greatest of all Reggio Emilia's provocations – a child we cannot reduce to predetermined outcomes and standardised goals, a child that instead instead gives us 'our sense of an unfinished world, a world unknown, a world we ought to know better' (ibid., p.392)

This 'rich' child has a right to education from birth, an education understood as a public good and a public responsibility, delivered by the political expression of the local community, the municipality. Coming from the Anglosphere, where early childhood is dominated by a 'childcare' discourse and provision is increasingly marketized and privatised (Moss and Mitchell, 2024), this assertion of the primacy of education and of the public, of children's rights rather than market choice, is a further and bracing provocation. Not that Reggio ignores the needs of employed parents or indeed the importance of care. Malaguzzi early on recognised that 'schools must adapt to factory hours, progressively opening up to workers' children with improved responses to family needs' (Malaguzzi, cited in Cagliari et al., 2016, p.212); while the women of Reggio Emilia campaigned for municipal schools to meet their needs. But Malaguzzi and the other educators of Reggio got their priorities right, with education, not 'childcare', at the heart of their project, while the women of Reggio Emilia demanded not only their rights but the rights of their children, refusing to see them as in opposition. Reggio's schools for young children may provide 'childcare for working parents' through their opening hours, but 'care' is understood as a universal need and a collective responsibility, a relational ethic that is 'the premise for daily life in Reggio Emilia' (Giamminuti et al., 2024, p.12).

Many years ago the Gramscian scholar, Carl Boggs, wrote a paper on the concept of prefigurative practice, which he described as 'the embodiment within the ongoing political practice of a movement, of those forms of social relations, decision making, culture and human experience that are the ultimate goal' (Boggs, 1977/78, p. 100). Applying this idea to education, Roger Dale (1988, p.17) wrote that '[s]chools should not merely reflect the world of which they are a part, but be critical of it, and show in their own processes that its shortcomings are not inevitable, but can be changed'. Schools, in short, can act as spaces of possibility, showing that there can be alternatives. That, it seems to me, is what the 'Reggio Emilia Experience' as prefigurative practice can teach us: that, indeed, another world is possible.

Peter Moss
University College London, UK

REFERENCES

Boggs, C. (1977/78) 'Marxism, prefigurative communism, and the problem of workers' control', *Radical America, 11.6—12.1*, 99-122.

Cagliari, P., Castagnetti, M., Giudici, C., Rinaldi, C., Vecchi, V., & Moss, P. (Eds.). (2016). *Loris Malaguzzi and the Schools of Reggio Emilia: A selection of his writings and speeches 1945–1993*. Routledge. DOI: 10.4324/9781315778631

Catarsi, E. (2004, March). Loris Malaguzzi and the municipal school revolution. *Children in Europe*, *6*, 8–9.

Dahlberg, G., Moss, P., & Pence, A. (2013). *Beyond Quality in Early Childhood Education and Care: Languages of evaluation* (3rd ed.). Routledge. DOI: 10.4324/9780203371114

Dale, R. (1988) 'Comprehensive Education', Talk given to Madrid Conference, April, unpublished.

Giamminuti, S., Cagliari, P., Giudici, C., & Strozzi, P. (2024). *The Role of the Pedagogista in Reggio Emilia: Voices and ideas for a dialectic educational experience*. Routledge.

Moss, P., & Mitchell, L. (2024). *Early Childhood in the Anglosphere: Systemic failings and transformative possibilities*. UCL Press. DOI: 10.14324/111.9781800082533

Rinaldi, C. (1993). The emergent curriculum and social constructivism. In Edwards, C., Gandini, L., & Forman, G. (Eds.), *The Hundred Languages of Children: The Reggio Emilia approach to early childhood education*. Ablex.

Rinaldi, C. (2021). *In Dialogue with Reggio Emilia: Listening, researching and learning* (2nd ed.). Routledge. DOI: 10.4324/9780367854539

Peter Moss is an Emeritus Professor at Thomas Coram Research Unit, UCL institute of Education, University College London. His research interests include early childhood education, education and democracy, and the relationship between care, gender and employment; much of his work has been cross-national and he is co-founder of the international network on leave policies. His most recent publications include an article on 'The International Early Learning and Child Well-being Study, PISA and the decline of the OECD's testing regime' (with Diana Sousa and Paul Morris) and the books 'Early Childhood in the Anglosphere: Systemic failings and transformative possibilities' and 'Care Leaves and Care Time for All: Towards caring democracies, economies, and worlds' (with Andrea Doucet). . He is currently working on a project on 'Democratic Culture in Early Childhood Education' (with Diana Sousa), drawing inspiration from the democratic tradition and culture in the municipal schools of Reggio Emilia and the Modern School Movement in Portugal.

Preface

A Compass for Navigating Children's Rights

How do people get from one place to another? Navigation. A compass is a tool for navigation that can provide ways for locating places and directions. Navigation endeavors could benefit from a tool, like a compass, to arrive at the chosen destination.

Together with all of our contributors, we perceive this book, *Realizing Children's Rights in a Global Context: Glocalization of the Reggio Emilia Experience,* together with the other volume in this series: *Reggio Emilia-Inspired Pedagogies of Listening and Inclusion: Advancing Children's Rights*, as compasses for navigating a journey of exploration around the rights of babies, toddlers and young children to support readers in arriving at a chosen destination where the rights of all children are realized. Across the chapters, the rights-based philosophy guides early childhood education ideas for babies, toddlers, and young children as seen through the lens from Reggio Emilia, Italy to offer a framework within which children's rights can be realized in practice. Loris Malaguzzi, a pedagogist who led Reggio Emilia early childhood education efforts, referred to the context during which the approach was developed in the period following World War II as, "everything was still violently topsy-turvy" (Gandini, 2011, p. 27). This resonates with the current context globally whereby children may experience uncertainty, volatility, and complexity associated with childhoods affected by the erosion of rights, natural disasters, conflict, poverty, crisis, and the ongoing longitudinal impact of the worldwide health crisis related to COVID-19 (Ring et al., 2022; World Health Organization [WHO], 2020; O'Sullivan & Ring, 2026).

Despite robust research evidence underscoring the benefits of high-quality early childhood experiences on children's immediate and long-term cognitive, health, sociability and education outcomes, underinvestment continues to undermine children's opportunities in this regard (Heckman 2008; 2012; Doyle, 2025). The focus on children's rights and agency reflects the change in our understanding of children and childhood that is mirrored in the provisions of the United Nations Convention on the Rights of the Child [UNCRC] and the United Nations Convention on the Rights of Persons with Disabilities [UNCRPD]. Crucially, this change in our understanding challenges communities globally to assess their policies and practices through a rights-based lens (UN, 1989; 2006).

Where this topic fits in the world today depends on several complex factors. The authors who have contributed to this edited book seek to identify barriers, explore solutions, and strengthen an international commitment to the rights of every child. The book is comprised of an introductory chapter and a collection of eleven chapters that provide interdisciplinary professionals across the globe with an opportunity to reflect on the application of the early childhood education philosophy derived from Reggio Emilia, Italy for realizing the rights of children. The target audience for the book includes but is not limited to: (a) educators and interdisciplinary professionals already in the workforce, (b) pre-service professionals who are in college settings, (c) academics from institutions of higher education (e.g., community colleges and universities), and (d) policy makers.

HOW TO USE THIS BOOK TO NAVIGATE THE RIGHTS OF CHILDREN

This book can in effect be used as a compass to navigate children's rights across the multiple layers of the unique ecosystem that each child inhabits. The chapters can be read as stand alone, or thematically. Over forty authors from across multiple continents have contributed to the two volumes in this series. Four of the authors are from Africa, two from Canada, one from India, six from Ireland, fourteen from Italy, one from Spain, three from Turkey, and twelve from the USA. Authors' locations on the map include:

Figure 1.

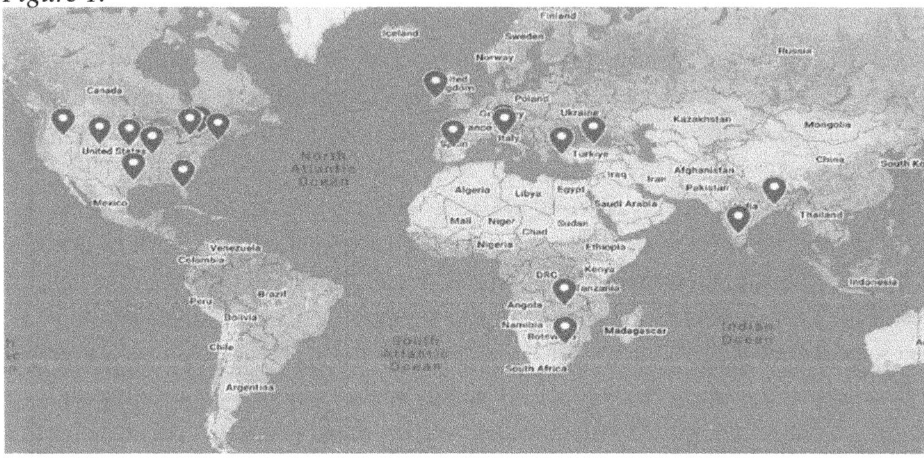

- Bengaluru, India
- Boise, Idaho, USA
- Bornova, Turkey
- Boston, Massachusetts, USA
- Huntsville, Texas, USA
- Johannesburg, South Africa
- Kingston, Ontario, Canada
- Laramie, Wyoming, USA
- Limerick, Ireland
- Lincoln, Nebraska, USA
- Madrid, Spain
- Omaha, Nebraska, USA
- Orlando, Florida, USA
- Reggio Emilia, Italy
- Samsun, Turkey
- San Miniato, Italy
- Toronto, Ontario, Canada
- West Bengal, India
- Zambia, Africa

The introductory chapter and subsequent eleven chapters in this book surface a set of interconnected themes that collectively position the child as a central rights-bearing protagonist. It begins by foregrounding the child's right to play, learn, and develop, emphasizing their agency in shaping their own experiences. This perspective extends into a broader understanding of the child as an active participant within political, social, and natural environments, highlighting their role as an individual with rights in relation to the world around them. Building on this, the discussion turns to the child's right to access, participate in, and benefit from early childhood education, underscoring the importance of equitable and meaningful educational opportunities. The narrative further explores how a Reggio Emilia rights-based approach informs relationships among children, parents, families, teachers, and the wider community. It concludes by emphasizing that children's rights to high-quality services are realized through the ongoing professional development of the early childhood workforce.

CHAPTER OVERVIEW

Introduction~ "Mapping Possibility: True North for Early Childhood Systems"

In the introductory chapter, Marisa Galliano Macy, Emer Ring, and Alessandra Landini question the concept of inclusion and its application to systems of early childhood education. Tracing the evolution of children's rights internationally, the authors identify the rights of young children to access, participate in, and be supported in early childhood education programs. The challenges and opportunities for realizing these rights within existing systems are considered. Based on the authors' experiences, the chapter shares "lessons" for inclusion and participation as viewed through the Reggio Emilia perspective on early childhood education.

CH. 1~ "Two Wings of a Butterfly": Promoting the Right to Play Through a Playful Approach to Learning in Global Contexts"

Lisa Goddard, Maria Barbara Donnici, and Elisa Ferrari remind us that from the outset, the United Nations declarations concerning childhood have referenced education and play as fundamental human rights. Drawing on the Reggio philosophy, the authors demonstrate how the right to play can become tangible in educational practice. Through detailing international projects and collaborations, the chapter explores how Reggio-inspired practices worldwide can translate the values of play as a form of knowledge-making into a fundamental support that cultivates and enables children's rights.

CH. 2~ "Close and Beyond Reggio Emilia. San Miniato and Children's Protagonism in Education"

Aldo Fortunati describes the experience of San Miniato and its idea of "children's education as a community project" in terms of a community-wide commitment that resonates strongly with Reggio Emilia's philosophy. Adopting a socio-constructivist perspective, the author observes how the pedagogy espoused by Malaguzzi embraces changes. The chapter, in a dialogue with an interpretation of Malaguzzi's thought, explains how this experience, even in its specificity, in pursuing children's best interests, can define that children are the most important global priority we face as humanity.

CH. 3~ "Children's Right to Develop Ecological Thinking: The Reggio Emilia Approach in the Era of Environmental Crisis"

In this chapter, Eloisa Di Rocco describes children as active individuals in the environment, capable of encountering the world, and self-supporting their ecological thinking. The chapter defines how children are entitled to enter this public debate, and why Reggio Emilia's pedagogy can be seen as a cultural and ethical posture to redefine the meaning of educating and living in this critical era. The author argues that children have the right to experience other presences as possible encounters and not necessarily as dangers, to feel part of a rich, complex, and vibrant ecosystem that shapes them and that they can shape with harmonious responsibility.

CH. 4~ "Fostering Children's Rights to Literacy Through the Reggio Emilia Approach"

Pamela Beach identifies literacy as a fundamental human right and notes the contribution of being literate to empowerment, and supporting individuals in understanding their rights and responsibilities and enabling them to advocate for justice and equality. The author considers

the vital role of reading in the early childhood years and the potential for core literacy skills to be developed through play and exploration. Located in the principle of the hundred languages, the social construction of knowledge and the environment as the third teacher, the chapter explores the possibilities integral in the Reggio Emilia philosophy for nurturing children's early literacy.

CH. 5~ "An Absolute Possibility: The Reggio Emilia Approach in Diverse Settings in South Africa"

Sarah Browne considers the interpretation of the principles from Reggio Emilia against the historical and current policy background of early childhood education in South Africa. Describing how children's rights are regarded in a South African context and drawing on her own research, the author identifies how Reggio-inspired principles can open up possibilities for educational dialogue and possible reform. South Africa is described by the author as a diverse society with many cultures, economic backgrounds, and twelve official languages.

CH. 6~ "Children's Right in Action at Acorn"

Rosalba Bortolotti shares how the approach developed in Reggio Emilia offers a powerful pedagogical and cultural framework for realizing children's rights in early childhood education, particularly when located within a global context. In considering how children's rights are interpreted in a Canadian context, the author shares her experience of the Acorn School, which she founded and led, and which was deeply influenced by her experience of studying and revisiting the municipal infant-toddler centers and preschools of Reggio Emilia over three decades.

CH. 7~ "Moving beyond Reggio Emilia's 'Special Rights' to a Rights-Based Response for All Children in the Irish Context: Learning from the Reggio Emilia Experience"

Emer Ring and Lisha O'Sullivan reflect on the impact of embedding the Reggio Emilia inspired principles of the image of the child, the hundred languages of children, the pedagogy of listening and the environment as the third teacher in a professional learning program for teachers in Ireland. The authors draw on the principles, not as a model to replicate, but rather as principles to reflect on theory and practice in the specific context of the Irish curriculum framework and cultural context. An analysis of teachers' professional portfolios suggests that these principles support the creation of an inclusive experience for all children.

CH. 8~ "Reimagining Education through Participation, Dialogue, and Listening: Local Communities, Global Perspectives"

Benedetta Melloni, Elisa Ferrari, Mara Davioli, and Alfonso Trillicoso provide insight into an action research project, *Peace Between Cultures*, which took place in a peripheral area of Reggio Emilia. The project confirms how the Reggio Emilia focus on supporting dialogue and the participation of children, teachers, families and the community can be extended outside of the classroom and cultivate shared understandings that mitigate social inequalities. The authors suggest that the school can be positioned as an agent of change that is capable of guiding processes of integration and exchange across cultures and sensitivities.

CH. 9~ "Children's Right to Early Education: Bridging Reggio Emilia Philosophy with Global Educational Practices"

Ashraf Alam situates the evolution of the Reggio Emilia approach in its historical context and examines how the practices developed in Reggio Emilia can potentially address inequities in access and elevate participation as a pedagogical right. Commencing with a genealogical excavation of Reggio Emilia's origins, the chapter explains its emergence as a counter-hegemonic educational movement in post-war Italy. The policy implications of adopting a Reggio-inspired and rights-based approach in diverse contexts is discussed, and future directions suggesting a paradigm shift from education *for* children to education *with* children.

CH. 10~ "Other Worlds and Other Possibilities: Re-envisioning Early Childhood and Children's Rights through Collaboration of a Child's Global World of Community, School, and Family"

Judith Levin, Angela Vatalaro, Kelcie Burke, Suzette Turner, and Marisa Galliano Macy describe a professional development community of practice for early childhood educators. Their chapter focuses on supporting children's rights to a high-quality early childhood education by preparing educators with a study abroad to Reggio

Emilia, Italy. This chapter takes the reader on a journey to discovering alternatives to traditional professional development. The outcomes indicate the value of living and learning in Reggio Emilia that result in shifts in thinking about developmentally appropriate practices and the importance of interaction between community, school, and family.

CH. 11~ "Enacting children's rights through Reggio Emilia–inspired practices in Türkiye: The Quilt-Making Project"

Hatice Inan, Melissa Dawn Gatlin, and Aysenur Gungor-Kircadag map an expedition that weaves together artistic inquiry, cultural heritage, intergenerational knowledge, and the realization of children's rights. Prompted by a conversation with children about the difference between art and craft, a spontaneous, multi-week, child-led exploration of this question through dialogue, artistic experimentation and research culminated in the quilt-making project. The project exemplifies how the right to express views, the right to play, and the right to participate in cultural and artistic life can be integrated into everyday learning for young children.

TREASURE MAP

Place matters. Cultural and linguistic factors are considered from Reggio Emilia that situate pedagogical practices at the local level, and will impact how early childhood education can be realized depending on the place, resources, and rights of children and their local context. Through exploring how the Reggio-inspired philosophy can inform the rights of children, we hope this book will contribute to positioning children's rights as the global priority for our times and signal how these responsibilities can be realized in practice. In the age of globalization, early childhood education systems around the world are exposed to and influenced by multiple curriculum philosophies, theories, pedagogies, policies, and practices (Bautista et al., 2021; Li & Chen, 2023).

Glocalization occurs when global influences merge with local practices across different cultural contexts (Andrian et al., 2025; Krengel, 2021; Ødegaard, 2015; Yang et al., 2021; Yang & Li, 2022). As evidenced across the chapters in this book, the interpretation of the Reggio Emilia Approach is an example of how glocalization in early childhood education can be realized in practice (Li & Chen, 2023). The Reggio Emilia Approach has been embraced, experimented with, and adapted to varying degrees across a range of cultural contexts (Su & Edwards, 2016; Zhang et al., 2025). This publication and the other volume in this series entitled, *Reggio Emilia-Inspired Pedagogies of Listening and Inclusion: Advancing Children's Rights,* provide a window into how the Reggio Emilia experience has inspired early childhood education and the experiences of young children in contexts across Canada, Italy, Ireland, India, South Africa, Spain, Turkey, Zambia, and the United States.

Each chapter highlights the Reggio Emilia Approach as a child-centered philosophy where the child has rights, is viewed as an active constructor of knowledge in a context where knowledge is socially constructed and involves multiple forms of knowing (Edwards et al., 2011; Rinaldi, 2012; Ring, 2018). While a range of Reggio-inspired philosophies, theories, pedagogies, policies and practices are shared in this publication, these cannot be equated with the Reggio Emilia Approach itself. As editors and authors, we are very clear that the Reggio Emilia Approach is the preserve and exclusive asset of Reggio Emilia's municipal preschools and infant-toddler centers. The Reggio Emilia Approach is rooted in a specific cultural, historical, social and political context that cannot be imposed on, or transferred in its entirety to another context. While experiences in this publication have all been influenced and inspired by the Reggio Emila Approach, they do not purport to replicate the approach, nor can they be equated with the approach itself. Rather the ideas represent an interpretation in a range of distinctive cultural, social, and political contexts that have their own unique history and identity (Nissinen et al., 2025; Varner et al., 2021).

The book is an invitation for you to journey into reflection on the variety of chapters written by authors from around the world. These authors seek to highlight the importance of embedding the principles of reciprocity, the protection of childhood as an important period and agency in teacher preparation practices that build teachers' competencies and places a premium value on teachers' professionalism. We trust that across the chapters, which are located in a robust theoretical framework comprised of empirical and philosophical strands in underrepresented contexts, professionals will be supported in their quest to craft a responsive inclusive pedagogy related to their own specific contexts (Landini & Colacino, 2023; Ring et al., 2022; O'Sullivan & Ring, 2023; Ring & O'Sullivan, 2025).

While the approach at Reggio Emilia supports children up to the early years and more recently in its application to children in primary school, its principles resonate with the global rights-based agenda and have applicability for all children and young people in a variety of contexts (Gandini, 2011; Landini & Macy, 2025; Ring & O'Sullivan, 2025; UN, 1989; 2006; Macy et al., 2025). Specifically, the principles of adults as co-learners, authentic assessment, a view of childhood as an important period, the promotion of a rights-based approach to children's lives have the potential to contribute to the transformation of how children and young people experience childhood globally.

Maps assist us in discovering new places and ideas. We hope this book together with the other volume in this series: *Reggio Emilia-Inspired Pedagogies of Listening and Inclusion: Advancing Children's Rights* serve as compasses for readers to begin a voyage into thinking about children's rights to education in the early years of their life and beyond. When you wander into each chapter, notice what authors share about orienting ideas into spaces for reflection. Determine a course for navigation that is uniquely your own. "*La vita e un lungo cammino, dove sei maestro e studente. Qualche volta insegni, ma ogni giorni impari.*" This Italian phrase translates into: "Life is a long journey where you are teacher and student. Sometimes you teach, but every day you learn." Like the many visionaries involved in the establishment of the "People's Nursery School" at Villa Cella near Reggio Emilia in the aftermath of the Second World War (Edwards et al., 2012), we invite you to travel through each chapter as though this book is a treasure map to discover new things about the rights of children on a voyage of discovery.

Marisa Galliano Macy
University of Wyoming, USA

Emer Ring
Mary Immaculate College, Ireland

Alessandra Landini
I.C. A. Manzoni of Reggio Emilia, Italy & University of Modena and Reggio Emilia, Italy

REFERENCES

Andrian, N., Valenza, E., & Zucchi, A. (2025). Taking care: A GloCal service-learning experience with teacher and parent education in northeast Brazil. *Education Sciences, 15*(12), 1652. DOI: 10.3390/educsci15121652

Bautista, A., Bull, R., Ng, E. L., & Lee, K. (2021). "That's just impossible in my kindergarten." Advocating for "glocal" early childhood curriculum frameworks. *Policy Futures in Education, 19*(2), 155–174. DOI: 10.1177/1478210320956500

Doyle, O. (2025) *The age 14 follow-up of the preparing for life study. Technical report.* University College Dublin. https://www.preparingforlife.ie/wp-content/uploads/2025/06/PFL_Age14_Technical_Report_Final.pdf

Edwards, C., Gandini, L., & Forman, G. (Eds.). (2012). *The hundred languages of children: The Reggio Emilia experience in transformation* (3rd ed.). Praeger.

Gandini, L. (2011) History, ideas and basic principles: An interview with Loris Malaguzzi. In C. Edwards, L. Gandini, & G. Forman (Eds.), *The hundred languages of children: The Reggio Emilia experience in transformation* (3rd ed.) (pp. 27-71). Praeger.

Heckman, J. J. (2008) *Schools, skills and synapses.* Institute for the Study of Labor. https://heckmanequation.org/wp-content/uploads/2017/01/Schools_Skills_Synapsis.pdf

Heckman, J. J. (2012) *The Heckman equation. Invest in early childhood development: Reduce deficits, strengthen the economy.* https://heckmanequation.org/wp-content/uploads/2013/07/F_HeckmanDeficitPieceCUSTOM-Generic_052714-3-1.pdf

Krengel, F. (2021). "Glocal education" through virtual exchange? Training pre-service EFL teachers to connect their local classrooms to the world and back. *Global Education Review (2379-8998), 8*(2/3 part 2), 138–153.

Landini, A., & Colacino, M. (2023). Inclusion and policies for the enhancement of the individual: From the international perspective to the context of the city of Reggio Emilia. In *Annali online della Didattica e della Formazione Docente*, Vol. 15, n. 25/2023, ISSN 2038-1034, Ferrara, Italy, 117-131.

Landini, A., & Macy, M. (2025). Early childhood inclusion in Italy. *Infants and Young Children, 38*(4), 322–333. DOI: 10.1097/IYC.0000000000000302

Li, P. H., & Chen, J. J. (2023). *The glocalization of early childhood curriculum.* Routledge.

Macy, M., Harshbarger, D., Burke, K., & Neukirch, E. (2025). Experiential learning in Reggio Emilia, Italy: Reflections from in-service and pre-service professionals. *Journal of Early Childhood Teacher Education*, •••, 1–23. DOI: 10.1080/10901027.2025.2493175

Nissinen, S., Vartiainen, H., Vanninen, P., Pöllänen, S., & Kokko, S. (2025). How to shoe an elk? Teachers' reflections on creating a glocal learning community. *Research and Practice in Technology Enhanced Learning*, *20*, 1–25. DOI: 10.58459/rptel.2025.20004

Ødegaard, E. E. (2015). "Glocality" in play: Efforts and dilemmas in changing the model of the teacher for the Norwegian national framework for kindergartens. *Policy Futures in Education*, *14*(1), 42–59. DOI: 10.1177/1478210315612645

O'Sullivan, L., & Ring, E. (2026). *Play from the inside out: Theory, research and practice perspectives.* Peter Lang.

Rinaldi, C. (2012). The pedagogy of listening: The listening perspective from Reggio Emilia. In C. Edwards, L. Gandini, & G. Forman (Eds.), *The hundred languages of children: The Reggio Emilia experience in transformation* (3rd ed.) (pp.233-246). Praeger.

Ring, E. (2018). Harnessing the Reggio Emilia concept of the environment as the 'third teacher' for children with autism spectrum difference. In E. Ring, P. Daly, and E. Wall, E. (Eds.), *Autism from the inside out: Signposts for parents, early childhood, primary, post-primary and special school settings* (pp. 181-198). Peter Lang.

Ring, E., & O'Sullivan, L. (2025). *Play, learning and teaching in a redeveloped primary curriculum.* National Council for Curriculum and Assessment. https://ncca.ie/en/resources/play-learning-and-teaching-in-a-redeveloped-primary-curriculum/

Ring, E., O'Sullivan, L., & Harmon, M. (2022). The concept of the child, pedagogy, curriculum and accountability in early childhood education for a post-covid 19 world: Insights from Dewey's philosophy. In J. Ávila, A.G. Rud, L. Waks, and E. Ring (Eds.), *The contemporary relevance of John Dewey's theories on teaching and learning: Deweyan perspectives on standardization, accountability, and assessment in education* (pp. 284-298). Routledge.

Su, G., & Edwards, C. P. (2016). *Reggio Emilia inspiration for early education in China: The case of Zhejiang Province.* University of Nebraska.

United Nations. (1989). *Convention on the rights of the child.* https://www.ohchr.org/sites/default/files/crc.pdf

United Nations. (2006). *Convention on the rights of persons with disabilities.* https://treaties.un.org/doc/Publication/CTC/Ch_IV_15.pdf

Varner, K., Markides, J., Schrader, P. G., Gerlach, D., & Opić, S. (2021). Glocal challenges to teacher education and a glocally sustaining pedagogical framework. *Global Education Review*, *8*(2), 8–20.

World Health Organization. (2020). *Improving early childhood development.* https://iris.who.int/server/api/core/bitstreams/af368e00-83fc-44e4-aa10-fd4b467c2904/content

Yang, W., & Li, H. (2022). Curriculum hybridization and cultural glocalization: A scoping review of international research on early childhood curriculum in China and Singapore. *ECNU Review of Education*, *5*(2), 299–327. DOI: 10.1177/20965311221092036

Yang, W., Li, H., & Ang, L. (2021). Early childhood curriculum policies and practices in Singapore: The case of glocalisation. Policy Futures in Education, 19(2), 131–138. https://doi-org/DOI: 10.1177/1478210320987689

Zhang, Q., Yin, J., & Jiang, K. (2025). Glocalization of early childhood curriculum: An ethnographic study on the integration of the Reggio Emilia approach into the Chinese Kindergarten curriculum. *Asia Pacific Education Review*, *26*(1), 49–60. DOI: 10.1007/s12564-023-09851-3

Acknowledgment

We wish to thank the children around the world who inspire this book, as well as their families and professionals who serve children. Thank you to Prof. Peter Moss for writing the foreword of the book. We are grateful to Elizabeth Barrantes, Melissa Wagner, and their team at IGI Global who have been extremely helpful with bringing this book to fruition. It is with immense gratitude that we acknowledge the contributions of the members of our Editorial Advisory Board who reviewed chapters of this book.

Introduction

Mapping Possibility: True North for Early Childhood Systems

"The fact that the rights of children are recognized as the rights of all children is the sign of a more accomplished humanity."

~ Loris Malaguzzi, Founder of the Reggio Emilia Approach (Malaguzzi, 1995, p. 67)

For the first time, in 1948, the Universal Declaration of Human Rights [UDHR], pronounced the basic human rights that required protection with the purpose of setting a common standard for all peoples and nations to aspire to and realize (United Nations [UN], 1948). The right to education is expressly articulated in Article 26, which unequivocally states that "everyone has the right to education" (UN, 1948). There is no express reference to early childhood or preschool education in Article 26, nonetheless, a right to free education is envisaged "at least in the elementary and fundamental stages." Despite the UDHR not being categorized as an international treaty, its significant contribution to the promotion of global rights and freedoms is widely acknowledged (Glendenning, 2023).

Subsequently, children's right to education has been articulated in three pivotal human rights treaties: (a) the International Covenant on Economic: Social and Cultural Rights [ICESCR], (b) the UN Convention on the Rights of the Child [UNCRC], and (c) the UN Convention on the Rights of Persons with Disabilities [UNCRPD] (UN, 1966; 1989: 2006). These treaties have been ratified by many countries globally, with ratifying countries committing to aligning their domestic law with the provisions of these agreements (UN, n.d.). While there is an explicit commitment to the right to primary and secondary education articulated in these treaties, early childhood education is not referenced, however there is an expectation that signatories to the treaties move progressively towards providing education across the continuum including early childhood programs (O'Mahony, 2006; O'Sullivan & Ring, 2026).

Despite the incontrovertible evidence that high-quality early childhood education has a potentially transformative impact on children's lives from education, health, social and economic perspectives (Heckman, 2012; 2013; UN, 2022: Doyle 2025), currently, approximately only 4 in every 10 preschool children, or less than half, attend early childhood preschool programs around the world (United Nations Children's Fund [UNICEF], 2025). In essence, the significance of high-quality early childhood education for children is not always acknowledged or understood across education systems, which leads to grossly inadequate policy development and investment. This chapter provides ideas for mapping the landscape of children's rights to early childhood education. We share ideas to map inclusion and use the Reggio Emilia story to illustrate arriving at a destination where early childhood education becomes the fulcrum of the right to education.

MAPPING INCLUSION

Inclusion as a concept in education has a range of meanings that continue to shift and change over time as we continue our journey to creating an inclusive education system where each child can thrive and achieve their potential. There are few who would oppose inclusion as an ideology promoting social justice, human rights, and equity of educational opportunity and yet neurodivergent children have experienced exclusion from early childhood education opportunities (Bricker et al., 2013; Guralnick & Bruder, 2025; Long & Guo, 2023; Odom et al., 2004; Soares & Serrano, 2014). Exclusion as the converse of inclusion emerges as an obstacle to realizing the rights and potential of each child (Guralnick, 2023; Nutbrown & Clough, 2004; UNICEF, 2025; Zinsser et al., 2022).

The perils of the absence of an infrastructure and a general commitment to advocate for quality inclusive programs are well substantiated (Guralnick, 2020; UNICEF, 2020; World Health Organization [WHO] et al., 2018; WHO & UNICEF 2023). Inclusion is a fundamental human right; however, children and their families report experiencing challenges in navigating opportunities related to accessing, participating in, and deriving benefit from early childhood education (Bruder, 2010; Gilliam, 2005; Harris, 2019; McWilliam, 2010; UNICEF, 2020; WHO & UNICEF, 2023).

According to Loris Malaguzzi, inclusive education involves typically developing and neurodivergent children attending school together (Malaguzzi, 1987). This resonates with the WHO and UNICEF's position that, "Inclusion means promoting the full participation of individuals and groups in all aspects of community life. Whether at school or work, in clubs or playgrounds, at the health center or the supermarket, the right to inclusion requires the removal of barriers and social structures which impede participation" (2023, p. 62).

While there is no one universally agreed definition of inclusion, the contributors to this publication equate inclusion in early childhood education as the cultivation of an environment where each child is welcomed; feels they belong and are enabled to achieve their full potential. In the chapters of this book, inclusion is framed within a child's rights framework that probes how children's right to access, participate in, and be supported in high-quality early childhood settings can be progressively vindicated as envisaged in the provisions of the ICESCR, the UNCRC and the UN-CRPD (UN, 1966; 1989; 2006). Agreeing a shared understanding of what constitutes children's right to access, participation and supports is a fundamental step towards building high-quality inclusive early childhood systems that cultivate a sense of belonging for all children.

Children's Right to *Access* Early Childhood Education

Making early childhood education accessible is a way to realize the right to an inclusive early childhood education (Division for Early Childhood Education [DEC] of the Council for Exceptional Children & the National Association for the Education of Young Child [NAEYC], 2009; Symeonidou et al., 2022; WHO, 2020). The WHO and UNICEF (2023) acknowledge the significance of *access* in their global report on children with developmental disabilities as encapsulated in the statement that: "Early learning opportunities and education are key factors in the promotion of children's development and well-being. Schools and other learning environments should provide *access* to nurturing relationships, opportunities to participate in educational and recreational activities with their peers, *access* to school health interventions and socio-emotional learning" (p.33). Accessibility to a wide array of developmental and learning activities involves removing barriers for children. Access offers multiple ways for children to learn and develop in a range of early learning environments that may include their early childhood setting, community, and their home (Levin & Towson, 2025; Macy, 2023; Macy & Marks, 2024; Sannipoli, 2023). According to DEC and NAEYC (2009), "Providing access to a wide range of learning opportunities, activities, settings, and environments is a defining feature of high-quality early childhood inclusion" (p.2).

Promoting *access* to high-quality early childhood education depends on a cohesive universal system of access based on the principle of equitable opportunity (Bricker, 1995; European Agency for Special Needs and Inclusive Education [EASNIE], 2017a; 2017b; 2017c; 2017d; O'Sullivan and Ring, 2023). As summarized by Guralnick (2005), "Inclusion would certainly be maximized if the point of access were part of a broader system of community-based child development supports and services to which all children had access" (p. 61).

The struggle to include neurodivergent children has undergone a paradigm shift over the past five decades from working for *access* to inclusive services and programs, toward creating *quality* inclusive services and programs (Bricker, 2000; Guralnick & Bruder, 2025; Hanline et al., 2024; Ianes et al., 2020; Landini & Colacino, 2023; Odom et al., 2012; Olusanya et al., 2023; Ring et al., 2021a; Steed et al., 2024; United Nations Educational, Scientific and Cultural Organization [UNESCO], 2021). Many places around the world now have accessible early childhood education, however maintaining quality early childhood inclusion continues to present challenges for systems more broadly (Bricker, 1995; Dionne et al., 2021; Odom et al., 2002; Ring & O'Sullivan, 2019; Shonkoff, 2010). Enabling participation and providing requisite support have been identified as key to reducing the barriers to quality early childhood programs that children and families continue to experience (Ring et al., 2021a).

Children's Right to *Participate* in Early Childhood Education

High-quality education is more than just being included in a space, but also involves high-quality participation for children to engage in the fullest way possible. Children are described as "powerful, active, competent protagonists of their own growth…protagonists in society, bearing the right to be listened to and to participate" (Edwards, 2012, p. 150). Social inclusion is consonant with the right of children to participate in their community (Dionne et al., 2021; Landini & Macy, 2025; Macy, 2024; Long & Guo, 2023).

This construct resonates with a human rights-based philosophy that rejects the image of the child as passive and submissive in favor of viewing childhood as a distinctive period and each child as a human being, global citizen, and unique individual with their own undeniable rights. Article 12 of the UNCRC specifically articulates children's right to express their views in all matters affecting them, and these views listened to and given due weight, subject to the age and maturity of the child (UN, 1989).

In essence Article 12 highlights the central importance of children's participation and aligns with the literature confirming the positive impact of prioritizing children's participation on their resilience, autonomy, independence and social competence (Ring et al., 2021b). A democratic early childhood system places children's voices at the center and demonstrates a commitment to meaningfully and authentically include children's hundred-plus voices in the acoustic of the early childhood setting (Rinaldi, 2012; Ring et al., 2021b).

Ensuring the participation of all children is a way to realize the right to an inclusive early childhood education (DEC & NAEYC, 2009; Guralnick & Bruder, 2025; Landini & Macy, 2025; Ring & O'Sullivan, 2019; Steed & Barla, 2025). Making participation for children in early childhood education the norm is reflected in the DEC and NAEYC (2009) position statement on inclusion, "Even if environments and programs are designed to facilitate access, some children will need additional individualized accommodations and supports to participate fully in play and learning activities with peers and adults" (p. 2). Participation happens when children have opportunities to learn at their own pace, in accordance with their unique needs and abilities, using teaching and assessment strategies that are responsive to each child (Bagnato & Macy, 2010; Bronfenbrenner, 2005; Landini et al., 2025; Macy & Marks, 2024; Macy et al., 2023; Pool, 2025).

Providing opportunities for children to participate in learning activities, play, and daily routines that are respectful and promote active engagement with familiar adults and peers further consolidates children's meaningful participation (McWilliam, 2010; O'Sullivan & Ring, 2026; Ring & O'Sullivan, 2025; Steed & Barla, 2025). Promoting *participation* in high-quality early childhood education programs means creating universal designs that facilitate the inclusion of all children. Families are also empowered when their children are participating to the fullest extent possible (Imms et al., 2017; Lin et al., 2024; McWilliam, 2010).

Children's Right to *Supports* for Early Childhood Education

High-quality early childhood education involves universal and targeted supports that ensure each child receives individualized support for cultivating their abilities and meeting their needs (Dionne et al., 2021; Macy & Bricker, 2007; Ring & O'Sullivan, 2025). Acknowledging the necessity of appropriate and adequate *supports* for children and their families represents another landmark in building inclusive, high-quality early childhood education systems (Lazzari et al., 2020; Long & Guo, 2023; Rinaldi, 2006; Tyler Krings & Dibbern Manhart, 2025). Support refers to wider aspects of the system at macro and micro levels that may include, but are not limited to: robust and responsive policy development and enactment, service delivery and collaboration among families and professionals. However, without support for workforce development whereby educators are provided with responsive professional development opportunities, developments at macro and micro levels will have negligible impact (Bruns & Mogharrenban, 2007; D'Agostino & Douglas, 2021; Ring, 2024).

Neurodivergent children are often placed into early childhood programs where the professional may have limited professional development in working with diverse groups of children (Ring et al., 2021a). Without access to educators with the requisite knowledge, disposition and competencies, children's rights to high-quality education becomes compromised and ultimately denied. Researchers have found extensive variability in the way specialized instruction and supports are addressed in early childhood programs (Odom et al., 2002; Rakap et al., 2017). Supports in inclusive settings requires professional development, which could include experiential learning (Macy et al., 2025; Vatalaro et al., 2015), and individualizing instruction for neurodivergent children in inclusive environments (Bricker, 1995; Dionne et al., 2021; Koller et al., 2026; Ring, 2018; Ring et al., 2021a). Quality inclusive early childhood education involves professionals who use effective teaching strategies and supports designed to maximize development for all children (Ring et al., 2021a).

According to DEC & NAEYC, "Family members, practitioners, specialists, and administrators should also require ongoing access to professional development and support to acquire the knowledge, skills, and dispositions required to implement effective inclusive practices" (p.2). When mapping inclusion onto existing early childhood programs, we can consider the unique journey each child and family experiences. The Reggio Emilia experience that is interpreted across all of the chapters in this book, provides us with lessons for inclusion and participation that can support systems globally in ensuring access, participation and supports are key principles that are key for all children.

"Lessons" for Inclusion and Participation from Reggio Emilia, Italy

The authors suggest that the wider idea of participation and democracy articulated by the philosophy of Reggio Emila can be harnessed to provide for a systematic and globally shared commitment to the inclusion of children in early childhood education. In the 2008 communication, "Improving Competences for the 21st Century: an Agenda for European Cooperation on Schools," the European Commission identified the goal of providing, as soon as possible and from early childhood, support for children with special educational needs by integrating individualized teaching and a holistic approach to the individual, through a perspective that promoted the concept of lifelong learning (Landini & Colacino, 2023). International laws from the UDHR in 1948 to the present highlight how, in the European continent and beyond, there has been an effort to establish what the inalienable rights of young children are, and how this can be realized in inclusive systems, despite differing educational and political infrastructures.

A discernible theme across all the chapters in this book is the potential of the Reggio Emilia philosophy to support participation and democracy across multiple levels of each child's unique ecosystem. Acknowledging that the concepts of participation and democracy can be considered for political or ideological purposes, the aim of this project is to rediscover the deeper and natural significance of the concepts by relating them to that of inclusion. According to Reggio Children, "Participation is the educational strategy that is constructed and lived in encounter and relations day after day. Participation valorizes and makes use of the hundred languages of children and human beings, understood as plurality of points of view and of cultures. Participation generates and informs the feelings and culture of solidarity, responsibility and inclusion, and produces change and new cultures" (Reggio Children, 2025). The definition can provide ways and routes for locating core concepts related to children's rights in a global context. Furthermore, it suggests how individuals and their relations, environments and their institutions could define new common directions to take. Access, participation, and support early childhood education and education in general is a "lesson" that Reggio Emilia can teach or at least propose.

It is possible to ground a parallel between school and society, reversing in the discourse the famous analogy introduced by Dewey in his work, "Democracy and Education" in which the life in schools, with pairs and adults, mirrors, like a microcosm, the broader society (Dewey, 1916). Comparatively, we advocate that Loris Malaguzzi's vision of education and school could inspire our societies in lessons from Reggio Emilia, Italy. Could our global society aim to become a source of "lovable, industrious, livable" relationships, like Malaguzzi expressed as a fundamental value? How do communities invest in research that lead to routes to children's rights and well-being? The Reggio Emilia perspective can add *insight* into children's education and could serve as a stimulus for our discussion on children's rights. It has, among few other examples, "Throughout history [...] achieved levels of 'legendary' quality" (Gardner, 2001).

During the last years of his life, Loris Malaguzzi left important traces of his views on education and children's rights in a global context: advocating for children, for the attentiveness of politicians to educational issues, and for the necessity of democratic citizenship. He stated, among other things that, "what is lost in the global vision that would allow the political world to have all the elements necessary, integrated and related to each other, to enable it to understand what is happening to the future conditions of citizens to come" (Malaguzzi, 1992, in Cagliari et al, 2016, p. 421). The lessons from Reggio Emilia can foster further reflections on the role of children in our communities, their participatory capacity and ability to learn, their competencies, and how these can be an integral part of a discourse on our societies.

CONCLUSION

Participation and the provision of adequate and appropriate support systems are signposts for mapping the landscape of children's rights to early childhood education. Children and their families deserve early childhood education. Through focusing on these three elements (i.e., access, participation, and supports) as a first step, it is suggested that people can create early childhood education systems for their communities where children's rights are recognized and realized.

In essence, we are suggesting that the true north for early childhood systems safeguards the rights of children to *access*, *participation*, and *supports*. The Reggio Emilia story, which is explored in this chapter and throughout all the chapters in this book, has the potential to deepen our understanding of inclusion in education for all children through its focus on the concepts of participation and democracy across all levels of each child's unique ecosystem.

REFERENCES

Bagnato, S., & Macy, M. (2010). Authentic assessment in action: A "R-E-A-L" solution. *NHSA Dialog*, *13*(1), 1–4. DOI: 10.1080/15240750903458121

Bricker, D., Macy, M., Squires, J., & Marks, K. (2013). *Developmental screening in your community: An integrated approach for connecting children with services.* Brookes Publishing.

Bricker, D. D. (1995). The challenge of inclusion. *Journal of Early Intervention*, *19*(3), 179–194. DOI: 10.1177/105381519501900301

Bricker, D. D. (2000). Inclusion: How the scene has changed. *Topics in Early Childhood Special Education*, *20*(1), 14–19. DOI: 10.1177/027112140002000103

Bronfenbrenner, U. (2005). *Making human beings human: Bioecological perspectives on human development.* Sage Publications Ltd.

Bruder, M. B. (2010). Early childhood intervention: A promise to children and families for their future. *Exceptional Children*, *76*(3), 339–355. DOI: 10.1177/001440291007600306

Bruns, D. A., & Mogharrenban, C. C. (2007). The gap between beliefs and practices: Early childhood practitioners' perceptions about inclusion. *Journal of Research in Childhood Education*, *21*(3), 229–241. DOI: 10.1080/02568540709594591

D'Agostino, S. R., & Douglas, S. N. (2021). Early childhood educators' perceptions of inclusion for children with autism spectrum disorder. *Early Childhood Education Journal*, *49*(4), 725–737. DOI: 10.1007/s10643-020-01108-7

Dewey, J. (1916). Nationalizing education. *Journal of Education*, *84*(16), 425–428. DOI: 10.1177/002205741608401602

Dionne, C., Paquett, A., Lemire, C., Rousseau, M., Dugas, C., Squires, J., Macy, M., Chen, C.-I., Schonhaut, L., Pomes, M., Arias Beccerra, N. J., & Moratto Vasquez, N. S. (2021). *Inclusive early childhood care and education: From commitment to action.* UNESCO. https://unescdoc.unesco.org/ark:/48223/pf0000378076

Division for Early Childhood of the Council for Exceptional Children & National Association for the Education of Young Children. (2009). *Early childhood inclusion: A joint position statement of the Division for Early Childhood (DEC) and the National Association for the Education of Young Children (NAEYC).* Authors. https://www.naeyc.org/sites/default/files/globally-shared/downloads/PDFs/resources/position-statements/ps_inclusion_dec_naeyc_ec.pdf

Doyle, O. (2025). *The age 14 follow-up of the preparing for life study. Technical report*. University College Dublin. https://www.preparingforlife.ie/wp-content/uploads/2025/06/PFL_Age14_Technical_Report_Final.pdf

Edwards, C. (2012). Teacher and learner, partner and guide: The role of the teacher. In C. Edwards, L. Gandini, & G. Forman (Eds.) *The hundred languages of children: The Reggio Emilia experience in transformation* (3rd ed.) (pp. 147-172). Praeger.

European Agency for Special Needs and Inclusive Education. (2017a). *Inclusive early childhood education: Literature review* (Bellour, F., Bartolo, P., & Kyriazopoulou, M., Eds.). Author., https://www.european-agency.org/sites/default/files/IECE%20Literature%20Review.pdf

European Agency for Special Needs and Inclusive Education. (2017b). *Inclusive early childhood education: New insights and tools – Contributions from a European study. (M. Kyriazopoulou, P. Bartolo, E. Björck-Åkesson* (Giné, C., & Bellour, F., Eds.). Author., https://www.european-agency.org/sites/default/files/IECE_Synthesis_Report_2017.pdf

European Agency for Special Needs and Inclusive Education. (2017c). *Inclusive early childhood education: New insights and tools – Final summary report. (M. Kyriazopoulou, P. Bartolo, E. Björck-Åkesson* (Giné, C., & Bellour, F., Eds.). Author., https://www.european-agency.org/sites/default/files/IECE-Summary-ENelectronic.pdf

European Agency for Special Needs and Inclusive Education. (2017d). *Inclusive early childhood education environment self-reflection tool. (M. Kyriazopoulou, P. Bartolo, E. Björck-Åkesson* (Giné, C., & Bellour, F., Eds.). Author., https://www.european-agency.org/resources/publications/inclusive-early-childhood-education-environment-self-reflection-tool

European Commission. (2008). *Improving competencies for 21st century: An agenda for European cooperation in schools*. Communication of the European Commission, 3 July 2008 COM(2008) 425. European Commission. https://www.european-agency.org/sites/default/files/commission-communication.pdf

Gardner, H. (2001). *The pursuit of excellence through education*. Routledge.

Gilliam, W. S. (2005). *Prekindergarteners left behind: Expulsion rates in state prekindergarten systems*. Yale University Child Study Center.

Glendenning, D. (2023). *Education and the law* (3rd ed.). Bloomsbury Professional. DOI: 10.5040/9781526514448

Guralnick, M. J. (2005). Inclusion as a core principle in the early intervention system. In Guralnick, M. J. (Ed.), *The developmental systems approach to early intervention* (pp. 59–69). Brookes.

Guralnick, M. J. (2020). Applying the developmental systems approach to inclusive community-based early intervention programs: Process and practice. *Infants and Young Children*, *33*(3), 173–183. DOI: 10.1097/IYC.0000000000000167

Guralnick, M. J. (2023). A framework for the design of inclusive community-based early childhood intervention programs. *Infants and Young Children*, *36*(4), 270–284. DOI: 10.1097/IYC.0000000000000251

Guralnick, M. J., & Bruder, M. B. (2025). Inclusion in preschool as a catalyst to enhance the quality of comprehensive community-based early childhood programs. *Infants and Young Children*, *38*(4), 262–279. DOI: 10.1097/IYC.0000000000000304

Hanline, M. F., Eldridge, J. N., & Robbins, A. (2024). Meta-synthesis of qualitative studies: Inclusion in the early childhood years. *Infants and Young Children*, *37*(4), 284–315. DOI: 10.1097/IYC.0000000000000274

Harris, H. A. (2019). Parental choice and perceived benefits of Reggio Emilia inspired programs. *Early Child Development and Care*, *191*(1), 123–135. DOI: 10.1080/03004430.2019.1608194

Heckman, J. J. (2012). *The Heckman equation. Invest in early childhood development: Reduce deficits, strengthen the economy*. https://heckmanequation.org/wp-content/uploads/2013/07/F_HeckmanDeficitPieceCUSTOM-Generic_052714-3-1.pdf

Heckman, J. J. (2013). *Giving kids a fair chance*. Massachusetts Institute of Technology Press.

Ianes, D., Demo, H., & Dell'Anna, S. (2020). Inclusive education in Italy: Historical steps, positive developments, and challenges. *Prospects*, *49*(3-4), 249–263. DOI: 10.1007/s11125-020-09509-7

Imms, C., Granlund, M., Wilson, P. H., Steenbergen, B., Rosenbaum, P. L., & Gordon, A. M. (2017). Participation, both a means and an end: A conceptual analysis of processes and outcomes in childhood disability. *Developmental Medicine and Child Neurology*, *59*(1), 16–25. DOI: 10.1111/dmcn.13237

Koller, D., Matthiesen, A., Oulton, A., & Murphy, E. (2026). "It isn't the same for everyone": Early childhood educators' lived experiences with cultivating social inclusion. *Journal of Early Childhood Teacher Education*, *47*(1), 1–24. DOI: 10.1080/10901027.2025.2450794

Landini, A., Bedogni, E., Domenichini, G., Reggiani, C., Trillicoso, A., & Altiero, T. (2025). Walking among trees: Scientific, naturalistic and narrative itineraries. A playful-expressive approach for Citizen Science and the Heritage Curriculum. In Berti, F., & Seitz, S. (Eds.), *The primary school as a playful space. Theories and practices in an international perspective* (pp. 357–374). Bozen Bolzano University Press.

Landini, A., & Colacino, M. (2023). Inclusion and policies for the enhancement of the individual: From the international perspective to the context of the city of Reggio Emilia. In Landini, A., & Colacino, M. (Eds.), *Annali online della Didattica e della Formazione Docente* (pp. 117–131). University of Ferrara.

Landini, A., & Macy, M. (2025). Early childhood inclusion in Italy. *Infants and Young Children*, *38*(4), 322–333. DOI: 10.1097/IYC.0000000000000302

Lazzari, A., Balduzzi, L., Van Laere, K., Boudry, C., Rezek, M., & Prodger, A. (2020). Sustaining warm and inclusive transitions across the early years: Insights from the START project. *European Early Childhood Education Research Journal*, *28*(1), 43–57. https://doi-org.uwyo.idm.oclc.org/10.1080/1350293X.2020.1707361. DOI: 10.1080/1350293X.2020.1707361

Levin, J., & Towson, J. (2025, September). Global rights for children with disabilities and "special rights" of children in Reggio Emilia. Paper presented in Symposium entitled, *The rights of children: Reggio Emilia's influence in a global context*, with Macy, M., Levin, J., Pool, J., Tyler Krings, A., Towson, J., & Dibbern Manhart, J. International Society for Early Intervention & Eurlyaid international conference in Lisbon, Portugal.

Lin, C. L., Lin, H. Y., & Wang, P. J. (2024). Association between mastery motivation, executive function, and daily participation of young children with and without global developmental delays. *Children (Basel, Switzerland)*, *11*(2), 1–13. DOI: 10.3390/children11020220

Long, T., & Guo, J. (2023). Moving beyond inclusion to belonging. *International Journal of Environmental Research and Public Health*, *20*(20), 6907. DOI: 10.3390/ijerph20206907

Macy, M. (2023). Authenticity of assessment in inclusive spaces. *Head Start Dialog: The Research-to-Practice Journal for the Early Childhood Field*, *26*(2), 100–106. DOI: 10.55370/hsdialog.v26i2.1632

Macy, M. (2024). Promoting social inclusion of children and their families with experiential learning. *The International Journal of the Inclusive Museum*, *17*(2), 33–50. DOI: 10.18848/1835-2014/CGP/v17i02/33-50

Macy, M., Bagnato, S., & Ring, E. (2023, July). Interdisciplinary exploration of authentic assessment purposes & practices. *18th World Congress for the World Association for Infant Mental Health*. Dublin, Ireland.

Macy, M., & Bricker, D. (2007). Embedding individualized social goals into routine activities in inclusive early childhood classrooms. *Early Child Development and Care*, *177*(2), 107–120. DOI: 10.1080/03004430500337265

Macy, M., Harshbarger, D., Burke, K., & Neukirch, E. (2025). Experiential learning in Reggio Emilia, Italy: Reflections from in-service and pre-service professionals. *Journal of Early Childhood Teacher Education*, •••, 1–23. DOI: 10.1080/10901027.2025.2493175

Macy, M., & Marks, K. (2024). Core concepts and resources for community-based, developmental-behavioral screening. *Young Exceptional Children*, *27*(1), 29–41. DOI: 10.1177/10962506231194040

Malaguzzi, L. (1987). *The hundred languages of children. The hundred languages of children* (I cento linguaggi dei bambini. Exhibition catalogue) 16-21. Reggio Children.

Malaguzzi, L. (1995). A charter of rights. In Children, R. (Ed.), *A journey into the rights of children*. Reggio Children.

McWilliam, R. A. (Ed.). (2010). *Working with families of young children with special needs*. Guilford Press.

Nutbrown, C., & Clough, P. (2004). Inclusion and exclusion in the early years: Conversations with European educators. *European Journal of Special Needs Education*, *19*(3), 301–315. DOI: 10.1080/0885625042000262479

O'Mahony, C. (2006). *Educational rights in Irish law*. Thomson Round Hall.

O'Sullivan, L., & Ring, E. (2023). On the path to developing a high-quality inclusive preschool system in the Irish context: Outcomes from a systemic focus on structural and process quality dimensions. In Şenol, H. (Ed.), *Recent perspectives on preschool education and care*. IntechOpen., DOI: 10.5772/intechopen.113764

O'Sullivan, L., & Ring, E. (2026). *Play from the inside out: Theory, research and practice perspectives*. Peter Lang.

Odom, S. L., Buysse, V., & Soukakou, E. (2012). Inclusion for young children with disabilities: A quarter century of research perspectives. *Journal of Early Intervention*, *33*(4), 344–356. DOI: 10.1177/1053815111430094

Odom, S. L., Vitztum, J., Wolery, R., Lieber, J., Sandall, S., Hanson, M. J., Beckman, P., Schwartz, I., & Horn, E. (2004). Preschool inclusion in the United States: A review of research from an ecological systems perspective. *Journal of Research in Special Educational Needs, 4*(1), 17–49. DOI: 10.1111/J.1471-3802.2004.00016.x

Odom, S. L., Wolery, R. A., Lieber, J., & Horn, E. (2002). Social policy and preschool inclusion. In Odom, S. L. (Ed.), *Widening the circle: Including children with disabilities in preschool programs* (pp. 120–136). Teachers College Press.

Olusanya, B. O., Storbeck, C., Cheung, V. G., & Hadders-Algra, M. (2023). Disabilities in early childhood: A global health perspective. *Children (Basel, Switzerland), 10*(1), 1–11. DOI: 10.3390/children10010155

Pool, J. (2025, September). Observation, documentation, and authentic assessment from Reggio Emilia perspective. Paper presented in Symposium entitled, *The rights of children: Reggio Emilia's influence in a global context,* with Macy, M., Levin, J., Pool, J., Tyler Krings, A., Towson, J., & Dibbern Manhart, J. International Society for Early Intervention & Eurlyaid international conference in Lisbon, Portugal.

Rakap, S., Cig, O., & Parlak-Rakap, A. (2017). Preparing preschool teacher candidates for inclusion: Impact of two special education courses on their perspectives. *Journal of Research in Special Educational Needs, 17*(2), 98–109. DOI: 10.1111/1471-3802.12116

Reggio Children. (n.d.). Values. Reggio Children. https://www.reggiochildren.it/en/reggio-emilia-approach/valori-en/

Rinaldi, C. (2006). Listening, researching, and learning. In Dahlberg, G., & Moss, P. (Eds.), *The Space of childhood: Contesting early childhood series.* Routledge Taylor & Francis Group.

Rinaldi, C. (2012). The pedagogy of listening: The listening perspective from Reggio Emilia. In C. Edwards, L. Gandini, & G. Forman (Eds.), *The hundred languages of children: The Reggio Emilia experience in transformation* (3rd ed.) (pp.233-246). Praeger.

Ring, E. (2018). Harnessing the Reggio Emilia concept of the environment as the 'third teacher' for children with autism spectrum difference. In E. Ring, P. Daly, and E. Wall, E. (Eds.), *Autism from the inside out: Signposts for parents, early childhood, primary, post-primary and special school settings* (pp. 181-198). Peter Lang.

Ring, E. (2024). *Special education in an independent Ireland 1922-2022. Insights from a journey through the century*. National Council for Special Education., ncse .ie/wp-content/uploads/2024/09/Emer_Ring_Special_Education_Independent _Ireland_NCSE2024.pdf

Ring, E., Harte, P., & Harmon, M. (2021b). Making children's right to participate visible and children's voices distinct in the acoustic of early childhood education. In Ring, E., O'Sullivan, L., Ryan, M., & Daly, P. (Eds.), *Leading inclusion from the inside out: A handbook for parents and early childhood teachers in early learning and care, primary and special school settings* (pp. 31–60). Peter Lang. DOI: 10.3726/b15063

Ring, E., & O'Sullivan, L. (2019). Creating spaces where diversity is the norm. *Childhood Education, 95*(2), 29–39. DOI: 10.1080/00094056.2019.1593758

Ring, E., & O'Sullivan, L. (2025). *Play, learning and teaching in a redeveloped primary curriculum*. National Council for Curriculum and Assessment.

Ring, E., O'Sullivan, L., Ryan, M., & Daly, P. (Eds.). (2021a). *Leading inclusion from the inside out: A handbook for parents and early childhood teachers in early learning and care, primary and special school settings*. Peter Lang. DOI: 10.3726/b15063

Sannipoli, M. (2023). Early childhood services as inclusive contexts. Opportunities to support families. *Rivista Italiana Di Educazione Familiare, 22*(1), 77–88. https://doi-org.uwyo.idm.oclc.org/10.36253/rief-14515

Shonkoff, J. P. (2010). Building a new biodevelopmental framework to guide the future of early childhood policy. *Child Development, 81*(1), 357–367. DOI: 10.1111/j.1467-8624.2009.01399.x

Soares, E. M., & Serrano, A. M. (2014). Peer relations: The challenges of children with special needs. *Revista de Investigacion En Logopedia, 4*(1), 67–92. DOI: 10.5209/rlog.58662

Steed, E. A., & Barla, M. A. (2025). Inclusion and belonging in an early childhood program: A mixed methods case study. *Early Childhood Education Journal*. Advance online publication. DOI: 10.1007/s10643-025-01947-2

Steed, E. A., Strain, P. S., Rausch, A., Hodges, A., & Bold, E. (2024). Early childhood administrator perspectives about preschool inclusion: A qualitative interview study. *Early Childhood Education Journal, 52*(3), 527–536. DOI: 10.1007/s10643-023-01448-0

Symeonidou, S., Loizou, E., & Recchia, S. (2022). The inclusion of children with disabilities in early childhood education: Interdisciplinary research and dialogue. *European Early Childhood Education Research Journal*, *31*(1), 1–7. DOI: 10.1080/1350293X.2022.2158632

Tyler Krings, A., & Dibbern Manhart, J. (2025, September). Inclusive Reggio Emilia-inspired program for children who are deaf or hard of hearing. Presented in Symposium entitled, *The rights of children: Reggio Emilia's influence in a global context, w*ith Macy, M., Levin, J., Pool, J., Tyler Krings, A., Towson, J., & Dibbern Manhart, J. International Society for Early Intervention & Eurlyaid international conference in Lisbon, Portugal.

United Nations. (1948). *Universal declaration of human rights*. Author. https://www.un.org/en/about-us/universal-declaration-of-human-rights

United Nations. (1966) *International covenant on economic, social and cultural rights*. Author. https://www.ohchr.org/en/instruments-mechanisms/instruments/international-covenant-economic-social-and-cultural-rights

United Nations. (1989). *Convention on the rights of the child.* Author. https://www.ohchr.org/sites/default/files/crc.pdf

United Nations. (2006). *Convention on the rights of persons with disabilities*. Author. https://treaties.un.org/doc/Publication/CTC/Ch_IV_15.pdf

United Nations. (n.d.). *Status of ratification interactive dashboard*. Author. https://indicators.ohchr.org/

United Nations Children's Fund. (2020). *Children with disabilities: Ensuring their inclusion in COVID-19 response strategies and evidence generation.* Author. https://data.unicef.org/resources/children-with-disabilities-ensuring-inclusion-in-covid-19-response/

United Nations Children's Fund. (2025). *Too few children are attending pre-school programmes*. Author. https://data.unicef.org/topic/early-childhood-development/early-childhood-education/

United Nations Educational, Scientific and Cultural Organization. (2021). *Inclusive early childhood care and education: From commitment to action.* Author. https://unescdoc.unesco.org/ark:/48223/pf0000378076

Vatalaro, A., Szente, J., & Levin, J. (2015). Transformative learning of pre-service teachers during study abroad. *The Journal of Scholarship of Teaching and Learning*, *15*(2), 42–55. DOI: 10.14434/josotl.v15i2.12911

World Health Organization. United Nations Children's Fund, & World Bank Group (2018). *Nurturing care for early childhood development: a framework for helping children survive and thrive to transform health and human potential.* Authors. https://www.who.int/publications/i/item/9789241514064

World Health Organization. (2020). *Improving early childhood development.* Author. https://iris.who.int/server/api/core/bitstreams/af368e00-83fc-44e4-aa10-fd4b467c2904/content

World Health Organization & the United Nations Children's Fund. (2023). *Global report on children with developmental disabilities: from the margins to the mainstream.* Authors. https://www.unicef.org/media/145016/file/Global-report-on-children-with-developmental-disabilities-2023.pdf

Zinsser, K. M., Silver, H. C., Shenberger, E. R., & Jackson, V. (2022). A systematic review of early childhood exclusionary discipline. *Review of Educational Research, 92*(5), 743–785. DOI: 10.3102/00346543211070047

Chapter 1

"Two Wings of a Butterfly": Promoting the Right to Play Through a Playful Approach to Learning in Global Contexts

Lisa Goddard
http://orcid.org/0009-0003-3997-6959
University of Modena and Reggio Emilia, Italy

Maria Barbara Donnici
http://orcid.org/0009-0005-3886-1863
Fondazione Reggio Children, Italy

Elisa Ferrari
http://orcid.org/0009-0008-6834-8878
Fondazione Reggio Children, Italy

ABSTRACT

This chapter traces the experimentation of Reggio-inspired playful approaches to learning across diverse contexts. Rooted in the Reggio Emilia philosophy and reinterpreted through local practices and international collaborations, these approaches position play and playfulness as central to creativity, connection, and meaning-making. Learning is viewed as relational and joyful, where curiosity and passion drive development. Inspired by Carla Rinaldi's image of play and learning as "the two wings of a butterfly," the chapter honors her vision of education as a living dialogue among children, teachers, and communities. It argues that play is not only a pedagogical strategy but a fundamental right. Through examples from local and global projects, it makes visible how documentation, teacher-researcher

DOI: 10.4018/979-8-3373-3431-8.ch001

inquiry, and the playfulness of adults nurture play as a participatory, ethical, and relational practice that regenerates education through motivation, passion, and a shared sense of empathy born from listening and co-construction.

INTRODUCTION

Since the first United Nations declarations concerning childhood, both education and play have been acknowledged as fundamental human rights. The 1959 Declaration of the Rights of the Child affirmed in its seventh principle that "The child shall have full opportunity for play and recreation," positioning play alongside education as central to the full development of the child (United Nations, 1959). This notion was later reaffirmed in Article 31 of the 1989 United Nations Convention on the Rights of the Child (UNCRC), which calls on governments to recognize every child's right to rest, leisure, and play (United Nations, 1989). These declarations recognize play, not as a privilege or extracurricular pastime but as a condition of justice and equity in childhood.

Yet in recent decades, early childhood education has been shaped by increasing pressures of "schoolification," the encroachment of formal schooling practices, standardized assessment, and prescriptive curricula into spaces once focused on holistic, play-based learning (Broström, 2017; Moss, 2015). In this context, reasserting the right to play takes on renewed urgency. Play is itself a form of knowledge-making that stokes children's curiosity about the world they currently live in. Dewey (1938) argued that focusing solely on the future undermines meaningful learning. He believed that understanding and engaging fully with present experiences is what truly prepares individuals for what lies ahead. Learning, he wrote, must be driven by "the desire to go on learning," cultivated through curiosity, motivation, and passion (p. 48). Play is a space that brings those dimensions together.

Malaguzzi and the educators of Reggio Emilia rejected the reduction of childhood to preparation for school or adulthood. They positioned children as full citizens with rights in the present, including the right to learn and express themselves through the "hundred languages," to explore and inquire freely, and to encounter environments that respect and expand their imaginative capacities. In Reggio contexts, play is a primary mode through which children build relationships, investigate the world, and create meaning (Edwards et al., 2012). Reggio educators have long emphasized that play is entwined with democratic participation and knowledge production (Edwards et al., 2012; Moss, 2019). As Rinaldi (2006) argued, listening to children means taking their ideas, theories, and playful encounters seriously as contributions to a shared culture of learning. Documentation, project work, and the design of environments are pedagogical strategies that make visible the right to play by giving value to children's playful meaning-making. Similarly, Vecchi (2010) highlighted the aesthetic and imaginative dimensions of play as vital forms of knowledge and expression, inseparable from education.

In this sense, the Reggio Emilia Approach offers a vision of quality education in which play is the engine of creativity and democratic life (Dahlberg et al., 2013; Moss, 2019). By recognizing play as a serious and essential way of knowing, Reggio educators defend children's rights by reminding us that the future of education depends on promoting play as a fundamental human right (United Nations Committee on the Rights of the Child, 2013). As Malaguzzi (1990) said in his speech at the international conference on the rights and potentials of children and adults regarding new preschool guidelines:

> *...This means we must rein in the non-rules of play, the freedom of play, the fertility of play, the great capacity of all games for being played from different points of view. Without even giving children a chance to improvise. If this came true the human species would die out, because if the human species does not continue to play with the unforeseen, with chance, with probability and improbability, if it stopped improvising . . ., then it would be a very poor, much poorer, species. I do not know if we would even continue to exist. (Malaguzzi, pp. 396–397)*

OUTLINE OF THIS CHAPTER

This chapter examines the enduring legacy of the Reggio Emilia educational project and its ongoing evolution across local, national, and international contexts through research collaborations, professional networks, and community-based educational movements. It situates this legacy within the broader discourse on playful learning and democratic education, highlighting how the Reggio approach continues to serve as a living model of pedagogical innovation and ethical practice (Edwards et al., 2012; Moss, 2019).

In particular, the chapter honors the life and vision of Carla Rinaldi, whose recent passing marks a moment of collective reflection on her extraordinary contribution to educational thought. Rinaldi's (cited in The LEGO Foundation, 2017a) conceptualization of play and learning as "the two wings of a butterfly" (p. 11) captures the interdependence of imagination, inquiry, and emotion at the heart of human development. Her work has profoundly shaped contemporary understandings of education as an aesthetic and participatory act. Drawing on this intellectual and pedagogical heritage, the chapter reaffirms that play is not only a pedagogical strategy, but a fundamental right of every child (Rinaldi, 2006; UNCRC, 2013).

In this chapter, we explore how the Reggio Emilia Approach and Reggio-inspired practices worldwide translate the values of play and playfulness into educational action. It examines how children's right to play is recognized and supported within early childhood education and beyond. Drawing on collaborations between Fondazione Reggio Children (FRC), the MIT Media Lab's Lifelong Kindergarten group, the LEGO Foundation, and other international partners, the chapter situates play within a human rights framework and emphasizes its role in fostering inclusion and educational quality.

We also address the growing pressures of schoolification, showing how standardized curricula can limit playful learning. In contrast, the Reggio Emilia–inspired playful approach to learning positions play at the heart of pedagogy and demonstrates how research and international collaboration can renew the meaning of playfulness in diverse contexts. Ultimately, the chapter argues that upholding children's right to play is both an ethical and practical imperative for democratic and inquiry-based education.

By weaving together historical insight, legal foundations, and living examples, we aim to show how children are present protagonists in shaping a more just and playful world. In doing so, we hope to inspire readers to protect and promote the right to play for all, both children and educators alike.

PLAY AND PLAYFULNESS

> *"Playfulness is a more important consideration than play. The former is an attitude of mind; the latter is a passing outward manifestation of this attitude" (Dewey, 1910, p. 162).*

Dewey's distinction between play and playfulness marks a foundational contribution to educational philosophy. By asserting that playfulness is "an attitude of mind" and play is merely its "outward manifestation," Dewey reframes play beyond an isolated activity as a disposition toward experience. Playfulness, for Dewey, represents an exploratory and imaginative orientation to learning and to the world, one that encourages curiosity and openness to the unexpected.

This interpretation resonates strongly with later thinkers in education and creativity research. Schön (1983) described reflective practice as a "conversation with the situation," a process that depends on playful experimentation with ideas (p. 76). Similarly, Sutton-Smith (1997) argued that the rhetoric of play is central to human adaptability and meaning-making, emphasizing that playfulness allows individuals to reframe problems and envision alternatives.

In contemporary educational theory, Resnick (2017) extended Dewey's insight by defining playfulness as a lifelong mindset for creative learning, a willingness to take risks, test boundaries, and explore possibilities. This attitude, rather than any specific form of play activity, is what sustains creativity and innovation across all ages and contexts. Thus, the importance of playfulness lies in its epistemological power: it transforms learning into a reflective process of discovery and imaginative reconstruction of experience, precisely the kind of education Dewey envisioned as the foundation of a democratic society.

FRC RESEARCH APPROACH

The concept of research carries many meanings, shaped by context, culture, and purpose. Within the work of FRC, research represents a living, evolving encounter between two complementary worlds: the everyday research that takes place in schools, through observations, hypotheses, and discoveries—of children and teachers—and the systematic, theory-driven inquiry that characterizes academic research.

In the educational experience of Reggio Emilia, research is the very heartbeat of pedagogy. It is woven into the daily life of schools, where children explore the world. This kind of research begins with children's questions rather than adult-imposed objectives; it unfolds through multiple languages, and it is sustained by documentation, interpretation, and exchange among educators. As Rinaldi (2006) wrote, "research" describes both individual and collective journeys that lead toward "new universes of possibility" (p. 101). To consider learning as research means to recognize every child and every teacher as a researcher, an explorer of meaning and relationship.

Academic research, as conducted in universities and research institutions, tends to follow more formal and systematic protocols: formulating hypotheses, collecting data, analyzing results, and producing generalizable knowledge. This kind of inquiry seeks to establish evidence and contribute to disciplinary understanding through rigor and peer review. Both forms of research are indispensable, yet they serve different epistemological and ethical purposes. FRC seeks to build a bridge between them, creating a hybrid space of research where pedagogical inquiry and academic investigation can meet on equal terms. The spontaneous and imaginative explorations of children and educators become sources of legitimate and generative knowledge that can dialogue with and challenge academic theory. Conversely, academic research can offer languages, frameworks, and validation that help make this living form of inquiry more visible and recognized.

This convergence does not aim to standardize or reduce either form of research but, rather, to acknowledge their shared potential: to expand what counts as knowledge, who can produce it, and how it can serve the collective good. In many ways, this conception of research echoes the quality of playfulness: openness, curiosity, agency, joy and intrinsic motivation. Research, like play, unfolds through experimenting, inviting participants to construct meaning together in ways that remain close to the everyday experiences of children and teachers. In this sense, this research approach aligns with what Cochran-Smith and Lytle (2009) described as "inquiry as stance," a form of teacher research that is not only methodological but also profoundly political and ethical. It situates educators as active producers of knowledge whose inquiries both reflect and reshape the contexts in which they work.

EDUCATION AND PLAY AS HUMAN RIGHTS

The recognition of play as a fundamental human right has a long, complex history within the international legal framework on childhood. The Universal Declaration of Human Rights (1948) made its first implicit reference to play in Article 24, affirming the right of all individuals to rest and leisure and it was primarily directed toward workers and adults, rather than specifically addressing the needs of children. A more explicit recognition appeared with the Declaration of the Rights of the Child (1959) which, in Principle 7, affirmed that "[t]he child shall have full opportunity for play and recreation, which should be directed to the same purposes as education; society and the public authorities shall endeavour to promote the enjoyment of this right" (United Nations General Assembly, 1959). In this statement, play is placed on the same level as education, both being recognized as necessary for children's growth and both entrusted to the responsibility of families, society, and public institutions.

A decisive shift occurred with the adoption of the United Nations Convention on the Rights of the Child (UNCRC, 1989), in which play was recognized as a right in its own terms. Article 31 recognizes "the right of the child to rest and leisure, to engage in play and recreational activities appropriate to the age of the child and to participate freely in cultural life and the arts" (United Nations General Assembly, 1989). The explicit inclusion of play as a right, distinct yet parallel to education, marked a turning point in the international discourse on childhood. The separation of education (Article 28) and play (Article 31) highlights that both are essential rights but operate within distinct domains.

Despite this legal recognition, the implementation of Article 31 remains uneven. Play has frequently been described as "the forgotten right," as it is often underrepresented in State Party reports to the Committee on the Rights of the Child and in monitoring mechanisms more broadly. This gap between legal affirmation and everyday realization reflects a broader tension within rights-based education frameworks. While children's rights are widely endorsed in policy, their enactment in educational settings is frequently constrained by adult-defined priorities, accountability pressures, and institutional demands. As a result, the right to play may be acknowledged in principle while remaining limited in practice, particularly in contexts shaped by school readiness agendas and standardized outcomes (Lundy et al., 2024).

In response to these persistent challenges, advocacy organizations and international bodies have sought to strengthen the visibility and protection of play. The International Play Association had already declared in its Declaration on the Child's Right to Play (1977), revised in 1982 and in 1989, that play is as essential to children as food, shelter, health, and education. The declaration urged governments to safeguard conditions for play and has since served as a reference point for advocacy worldwide (International Play Association, 1989).

Recognizing persistent gaps in implementation, the UNCRC (2013) issued General Comment No. 17 to clarify the scope of Article 31. This authoritative document highlights the obligations of countries to ensure that children have adequate time, space, and opportunities to play, and it explicitly frames play as indispensable for children's health, well-being, and cultural participation. General Comment No. 17 thus reinforces that play is a nonnegotiable right to be upheld in law and practice.

At the European level, the Charter of the Rights of the Child (1992) and the UNESCO's International Charter of Physical Education, Physical Activity, and Sport (UNESCO, 2015b) reinforced the right to play within broader agendas of cultural participation and equity. National initiatives have further advanced the recognition of play as a fundamental right. In this context, for example, in 2002 the Welsh Assembly Government established the "play policy." Following the development of this policy, a series of implementation strategies were crafted to ensure its effective execution. This policy culminated in the introduction of a statutory obligation, positioning Wales as the first country in the world to legally safeguard children's right to play through the "play sufficiency duty."

In addition, in several countries such as Australia, Canada, Denmark, New Zealand, Scotland, and Sweden, educational policies for children aged 0 to 8 years mandate learning through play as part of early childhood curricula. This approach is officially embedded in national frameworks and guidelines (Parker & Thomsen, 2019).

Taken together, these documents and initiatives show that the right to play has moved from implicit recognition to explicit codification, supported by advocacy and evolving legislation. At the same time, they highlight an enduring tension between rights as articulated in legal and policy texts and the conditions under which those rights are realized in everyday educational practice. As Bobbio (2007) argued, guaranteeing the right to play requires more than allocating time for recreational activity; it demands recognition of play as a cultural practice through which children express agency and belonging. This understanding positions play not only as a developmental necessity, but as a collective and cultural dimension of childhood that must be actively promoted within educational and social systems. (p. 89).

SCIENTIFIC EVIDENCE ON THE CENTRALITY OF PLAY

Alongside its legal recognition, a large body of scientific research has documented the centrality of play in children's development. Developmental psychology, pedagogy and, more recently, neuroscience have all confirmed that play contributes to cognitive growth by experimenting, taking risks, and making new connections (Diamond, 2013; Pellis & Pellis, 2009; Thibodeau et al., 2016); development of executive functions, including perception, motor control, language, and evaluation (Brown & Vaughn, 2009); social competence, when children negotiate rules, resolve conflicts, and develop empathy (Gray, 2013; Trawick-Smith, 2014; Weisberg et al., 2013); and emotional well-being (Bodrova & Leong, 2015; Ginsburg, 2007; Lillard et al., 2013; Whitebread et al., 2012) .

Although only a limited number of studies establish a direct causal link between play deprivation and developmental deficits, the evidence is convincing enough to raise concern. Children who are given limited opportunities for free, active, and outdoor play tend to display higher levels of stress, lower resilience, and weaker socio-emotional skills (Brussoni et al., 2015; Burghardt, 2011; Lester & Russell, 2008). Moreover, the global trend toward reducing spaces and times for play, whether due to safety concerns or the over-scheduling of children's lives, exacerbates the risk of neglecting this fundamental dimension of childhood.

As some scholars have noted, when opportunities for play are denied, children lose access to one of the primary means through which they develop social understanding and resilience. As Lester and Russell (2010) noted, play supports "a repertoire of social behaviors that enable the player to cope with stress, particularly humiliation and powerlessness" (p. 42). In an ever-changing world, the denial of play can thus be read not only as a pedagogical loss but also as a violation of children's rights, with implications for health, citizenship, and democracy (United Nations Committee on the Rights of the Child, 2013).

Despite this evidence, contemporary educational systems often fail to safeguard the right to play. In many countries, play is increasingly marginalized in early years curricula and almost disappears altogether as children advance through compulsory schooling. This tension between what research affirms and what practice enforces is captured by the concept of the schoolification of early childhood and beyond (Broström, 2017; Moss, 2019; Wood, 2014).

SCHOOLIFICATION AND MARGINALIZATION OF PLAY

In recent decades, early childhood education has undergone a process often described as the *schoolification* of early years (Broström, 2017; Moss, 2015).

Schoolification refers to the growing adoption of formal school structures and practices within preschool and kindergarten settings, including academic curricula and standardized assessments. These approaches mark a departure from previous traditions of early childhood education that emphasized play and social development. This shift has been largely driven by policy initiatives focused on school readiness and improved academic outcomes. Policies such as No Child Left Behind (United States, 2001), the Common Core State Standards (United States), the Early Years Learning Framework (Australia), and the *Early Years Foundation Stage* framework (United Kingdom) were developed, often with a focus on disadvantaged populations, to support school readiness and improve long-term academic outcomes. As a result, play-based learning is often constrained or justified mainly in terms of its contribution to specific academic objectives.

Although these policies are frequently framed as strategies to reduce educational inequities, research indicates that play-based approaches are at least as effective as more formal instructional methods in supporting later academic achievement (Barblett et al., 2016; Hirsh-Pasek, 2009). In contrast, early exposure to formal academic instruction has been associated with higher levels of anxiety, less positive attitudes toward school, and reduced creativity (Chafel, 1991). This evidence raises important questions about the increasing dominance of school-like practices in early childhood education.

Scholars such as Dahlberg et al. (2013) argue that this trend reflects a broader neoliberal orientation, in which education is reframed as preparation for the labor market, emphasizing measurable outcomes and accountability. Within this paradigm, play risks being either marginalized or instrumentalized, valued only insofar as it can be shown to enhance academic readiness. What is lost in this process is precisely what makes play irreplaceable: its open-endedness, unpredictability, and capacity to generate meaning beyond predetermined outcomes. This is in direct tension with Article 31 of the Committee on the Rights of the Child. If play is treated as a luxury, a reward, or a tool for academic preparation, then educational systems are not fulfilling their responsibility to uphold children's rights. To honor the right to play means resisting schoolification trends and creating environments where children's curiosity and creativity are central features of learning.

The tension between learning and play becomes even more evident when we move beyond the early childhood years and consider compulsory schooling. Primary school (ages 6–10) in Italy still preserves some traces of the combination between play and learning, but the daily structure of school life increasingly separates the two. Play is usually confined to recess, while the majority of the day is spent sitting at individual desks, facing the teacher.

Middle and high school (ages 11–18) represent an even sharper break. Within these settings, play has virtually disappeared from the school day. Except for a few isolated initiatives, play is absent from curricula and spaces and is often perceived as something to avoid, incompatible with the seriousness of "real" learning. Even students themselves tend to internalize this view: Play becomes associated with younger children, and adolescents often feel "too old" to admit that they play (Association for Middle Level Education, 2023).

This progressive disappearance of play across the schooling trajectory reflects a deep cultural divide: the widespread idea that school is for work, not for play. Work/study and play are frequently imagined as two opposite activities, mutually exclusive in both time and space. Yet, as many scholars have pointed out, play is itself a strategy for learning, an activity that fosters problem solving, imagination, collaboration, and resilience (Johnston et al., 2023; Webb-Williams et al., 2021). By excluding play from school, education systems deny children and adolescents a right recognized by international law (United Nations Committee on the Rights of the Child, 2013) and impoverish the very processes of knowledge construction and personal growth that they claim to promote.

If legislation and science affirm play as essential, but school practice continues to marginalize it, the question becomes: How can children's right to play be effectively realized?

THE REGGIO EMILIA APPROACH

The Reggio Emilia Approach offers a distinctive contribution to this question. Emerging from the community's reconstruction after World War II, Reggio schools anticipated the legal codification of play as a right by building educational environments where play is not supplementary but constitutive of learning (Edwards et al., 2012). For Malaguzzi (1993) and the Reggio Emilia educators, the right to play was never an abstract declaration: It was a daily practice embedded in the design and organization of space and time, and in the pedagogical ethos of "nothing without joy."

This intuition anticipates today's scientific evidence that joy and curiosity are not accessories but conditions of learning (Brown & Vaughan, 2009; Panksepp, 2010). Play is the context in which children negotiate meaning, test hypotheses, and construct knowledge together. In the Reggio schools, the atelier, piazza, and open, relational architecture are designed to guarantee the right to play in rich and plural ways, ensuring that play and playfulness extend beyond leisure time and permeate the entire educational experience (Strong-Wilson & Kind, 2013).

For Loris Malaguzzi and the Reggio Emilia community, the child holds rights from birth, including the right to play. The Reggio Emilia Approach does not separate what legislation and research often distinguish, play and learning. Instead, it insists that play is itself a form of culture and knowledge, inseparable from children's right to participate in society (Dahlberg et al., 2013). Play is recognized as a form of research and democratic participation. This positioning directly challenges schoolification; it affirms that childhood has an intrinsic value.

Thus, while much of the international debate reveals tensions between the rhetoric of rights and the reality of practice, the experience of Reggio Emilia offers a living example of how the right to play can be realized in an educational community. Its vision finds resonance in contemporary frameworks such as the LEGO Foundation's concept of learning through play (Zosh et al., 2017) and the "OECD Learning Compass 2030" (Organization for Economic Cooperation and Development, 2019), both of which emphasize agency, creativity, collaboration, and joy as essential to lifelong learning and human flourishing.

PROMOTING THE RIGHT TO PLAY: FROM LOCAL TO GLOBAL CONTEXTS

In projects promoted by FRC, playfulness is considered central to fostering a creative, empathetic, and transformative view of the world. In this section, we share a selection of projects developed with a Reggio-inspired approach to playful learning that show how from local contexts to global communities, FRC projects promote and sustain the right to play.

THE LOCAL CONTEXT - REGGIO EMILIA

La Palestra delle Domande *(the Questions Playground)*

Among the experimental initiatives developed within the Play Explore Research project, *La Palestra delle Domande* (the Questions Playground), developed in Reggio Emilia, has offered a distinctive professional learning opportunity designed to reconnect educators with the playful foundations of inquiry and creativity. In collaboration with the PhD in Reggio Childhood Studies, this FRC pilot action-research invited teachers, educators, and doctoral students to attend workshop's activities to explore the question: *How can we cultivate creativity and give space to the competences of children in formal and informal educational contexts?*

The theoretical principle guiding this research was the inseparability of play and learning, two dimensions often artificially divided in educational discourse. As in the metaphor of the butterfly, the wings of play and learning move independently yet interdependently, creating the dynamism that enables flight.

The workshops were conceived as a professional "playground" to exercise the muscle of curiosity, and drew inspiration from the values of the Reggio Emilia pedagogical experience, research on creative learning by the MIT Lifelong Kindergarten group, the LEGO Foundation's framework for learning through play, and the Pedagogy of Play project at Harvard's Project Zero. Participants were encouraged to understand open-ended questioning as a strategy that opens their work with children to playfulness; open-ended questions, such as "What have you noticed about the moon?" rather than "What are the phases of the moon?", were offered as invitations to curiosity and divergent thinking (Mardell et al., 2023, p. 79). By framing the act of asking open-ended questions as a playful and communal endeavor, the pilot research sought to understand how educators can regain the sense of creativity and possibility that underlies all meaningful learning.

WHY OPEN-ENDED QUESTIONS?

Open-ended questions play a central role in sustaining the right to play because they create conditions of freedom and imagination. Closed questions, instead, tend to define boundaries and expected outcomes, reducing the learner's voice and creativity. As children are seen as protagonists in their own learning, capable of directing their inquiries and shaping knowledge through relationships (Edwards et al., 2012; Rinaldi, 2006), when educators pose open-ended questions, they are affirming this right to self-determination and agency, and keep open spaces of possibility and experimentation (Bateson & Martin, 2013; Sutton-Smith, 1997). And importantly, they position the educator as someone who is also curious.

Open-ended questions are one of the primary tools of pedagogical listening - *ascolto* - which is a core element of the Reggio Emilia philosophy. To listen deeply is to be open to difference, to resist imposing one's own meanings, and to recognize the value of multiple perspectives (Rinaldi, 2006; Moss, 2019). Listening sustains the right to play because it acknowledges play as a language, through which children learn about the world around them and express themselves (Edwards et al., 2012; Vecchi, 2010), and asks educators to use multiple senses to "listen" to children's points of view.

ON THE QUESTIONS PLAYGROUND

Each workshop, conducted with up to 20 participants, followed a common structure while allowing space for spontaneous emergence and reflection. After a brief introduction sharing the conceptual notes and metaphors that inspired the project, participants were invited to work in pairs and move throughout the space. Materials, architectural features, and everyday details became provocations for inquiry. Their task was to find a context or material that could inspire them to formulate open-ended questions that might awaken curiosity, invite multiple interpretations, or provoke a sense of wonder.

At the conclusion of the pilot experience, participants were invited to complete a questionnaire about their experience. The responses offer insight into how the practice of questioning can shape educational reflection and classroom practice. Several participants reported transferring elements of the experience into their everyday work with children. One respondent described how the encounter with the space and materials during the first meeting prompted a shift in her pedagogical approach:

After the experience of the first meeting, being questioned by the space of the former Caffarri building and by the many materials present, I tried to introduce some of the questions shared by the participants to my class, in relation to ongoing research projects… It was very stimulating: the children were engaged by the questions and developed many hypotheses and graphic representations.

Many described a renewed sense of attentiveness and openness, noting how stepping into a playful mode of exploration changed not only the kinds of questions they asked but also their way of perceiving the world around them. This suggests that questioning functioned as both a pedagogical and perceptual shift, influencing how educators framed learning processes.

Another participant highlighted the collective and dialogical dimension of the experience:

"I find the way reflection on 'questions' is proposed very interesting, especially the opportunity to share and listen to the hypotheses of others."

A further response emphasized the relevance of questioning as a pedagogical theme within the broader school context:

"Asking questions is a valuable topic for ... the school context, and I am sure that if there is a way I can share the journey of the research in the school, others will be interested."

The feedback indicates that La Palestra delle Domande supported participants in understanding questioning not merely as a didactic strategy, but as an epistemological stance. The pilot experience appears to have fostered reflective processes and encouraged the transfer of inquiry-based approaches into educational settings.

The action-research dimension focused on how educators' ability to formulate open, inclusive, and generative questions can foster richer learning processes for children and young people. To ask well is to play well: Both involve attentiveness, risk-taking, and responsiveness. *La Palestra delle Domande* is an example of how research and professional learning can become an act of advocacy for the right to play (UNCRC, 2013). By reintroducing playfulness as a legitimate and necessary mode of thinking and being for educators, it challenges the persistent assumption that play belongs only to early childhood (Bateson & Martin, 2013; Sutton-Smith, 1997). It echoes Dewey's (1910) conception of playfulness as an attitude of mind, and aligns with Resnick's (2017) argument that playfulness represents a lifelong mindset for creative learning. Through this lens, research and professional learning become a space for experimentation and curiosity, qualities central to reflective and innovative educational practice (Claxton, 2008; Schön, 1983). Ultimately, the project reaffirms the value of play as a lifelong human competence and advocates for the cultivation of playful and creative learning among adults as a prerequisite to meaningfully supporting playful learning experiences of children (Craft, 2013; Whitebread et al., 2012).

NATURA DIGITALE: TO SEE LIKE A BEE

The *Natura Digitale* (Digital Nature) project was part of an action-research program involving five primary schools of the Istituto Comprensivo Einstein in Reggio Emilia. The project affirmed that play is not only a right of the youngest children but a lifelong right and a fundamental condition for meaningful learning across ages and disciplines. Yet as children move through school, opportunities for play often diminish. *Natura Digitale* challenged this tendency, affirming that science, technology, engineering, and mathematics (STEM) learning can be strengthened by the "hundred languages", the many ways children think, explore, learn, represent, and communicate. By integrating movement, dialogue, drawing, and play, the project invited students to investigate scientific and technological ideas through multiple expressive modes, creating a learning environment where different ways of knowing co-exist and enrich one another.

A central initiative, To See Like a Bee (Figure 1), enacted a playful learning approach (Paoli & Ronzoni, 2025) with 4th- and 5th-grade children and their teachers to explore scientific ideas through curiosity-driven, hands-on experiences. The project aimed to strengthen competences in STEM through playful, integrative methods. Rather than receiving information about bees, color perception, or vision from textbooks or lectures, children investigated these phenomena through open-ended questions and creative experimentation. The focus on bees emerged from the children themselves, who had noticed bees in their schoolyard.

Figure 1. Natura Digitale Initiative: To See Like a Bee

Note. Photo from Ca' Bianca school.

The inquiry began with the question: "Have you ever wondered how a bee sees your school garden?" Their investigations included experimenting with camera filters to explore color perception, using drones to simulate bee flight, and comparing how vision differs across species. Technology became a means of experiencing perspective and spatial awareness in an embodied way, merging scientific reasoning with artistic expression. Through these playful experiences, abstract scientific ideas became tangible, understood through experimentation, dialogue, and imagination.

While To See Like a Bee centered on children's learning, it equally focused on teachers' professional development. Educators participated in 20 hours of collaborative training, including site visits, co-design sessions, and classroom facilitation with researchers and *atelieristas*. This experience involved teachers as co-learners. They participated in the same explorations as the children: observing, questioning, experimenting, and reflecting together. This hands-on approach helped teachers rediscover the joy of learning and the creative potential within their practice. Working with technology, nature, and children's ideas, they experienced how play can make complex subjects accessible and engaging for both children and adults. They saw how open-ended exploration fosters curiosity and participation. As one teacher reflected, "I learned that in a group you can do even what seems very difficult. Children always amaze us; they are a source of ideas and energy." This reflected the belief that teachers, too, have the right to learn through play and experimentation.

The project also modeled how playful learning integrates disciplines. One teacher remarked, "What I enjoyed most was the interdisciplinarity of the project.

I'd like to change STEM into STEAM, where art and images become protagonists." This transdisciplinary vision linking art, science, and technology mirrors real-world inquiry, where curiosity and creativity are essential for understanding complexity.

In the words of one child, "Are we sure that the world we see is the world our eyes see?" This question, born from playful investigation, captures the spirit of *Natura Digitale*: learning as an open-ended process of wondering and imagining. To See Like a Bee reminds us that play is not only a child's right but an educational necessity. When schools make space for play, they create conditions for creativity and deep learning to flourish. By extending Reggio-inspired, inquiry-based practices into primary classrooms and teacher training, the project shows how playful learning can transform teaching and learning for both students and teachers. *Natura Digitale* demonstrated that play and learning are partners, much like the two wings of a butterfly.

THE NATIONAL CONTEXT - ITALY

Abitare il Paese – La Cultura della Domanda *(Living the Country: Building a Culture of Awareness)*

Abitare il Paese – La Cultura della Domanda is an educational and cultural initiative promoted by the National Council of Architects, Planners, Landscape Architects, and Conservators and implemented in collaboration with FRC and realized with the participation of local orders of architects within the Italian school system. The project seeks to introduce students to the culture of quality architecture and urban design, fostering an awareness of architecture as a collective, civic resource and emphasizing critical reflection on the built environment.

Since its first edition, the project has reached over 9,000 young people, involving 67 local orders of architects, more than 200 tutor-architects and teacher-tutors, and over 200 schools across different educational levels. It includes multiple activities such as co-design sessions with local professionals, classroom-based workshops exploring themes related to architecture and the territory, and collective reflection on the meaning of the city as a space of relationships, encounters, and everyday life. In this context, children often articulate with striking clarity the link between social life and urban form. As one child in the project observed, "Cities change because people change." By situating learning within real-world contexts, *Abitare il Paese* exemplifies a pedagogy that values participation, dialogue, and inquiry by transforming the school and local community into a shared space for knowledge co-construction, emphasizing the role of architecture not only as a technical or aesthetic discipline but as an ethical and civic practice.

A playful approach is also evident: Children, educators, architects, and communities are involved in a process that goes beyond rethinking public spaces, to imagining and designing an environment that responds to the needs of all individuals, within a logic of active participation. As Malaguzzi (1975) stated, “environments are defined as an integral part of the overall project of educational experience and play a decisive role for the co-existence, coherency and intensity of response to the request of children to be and to do, and the request of workers to be and to do”, suggesting that physical and relational spaces are in constant interaction, shaping and being shaped by educational experience. According to Malaguzzi (1996), space is a language and, consequently, an integral part of the formation of thought. The structures, the choice of materials, and the inviting way in which they are made available to children constitute an invitation to exploration that comes from the environment itself. Everything is conceived with the intention of fostering exchange among people, as well as connections between people and things, within a network of possible combinations and constructions.

As Pignataro (2014) noted, “A pedagogy based on relationships must be realized in spaces that allow for a certain permeability. . . . Space must provide opportunities for exploration, invention, and freedom of choice” (p. 91). Architecture, in this sense, must provide opportunities for relationships and openness. Malaguzzi (1996) used a powerful image to describe educational environments: “the environment should be like an aquarium in which the ideas, ethics, attitudes, and cultures of those who live in it are reflected. We have tried to move in this direction” (p. 40).

Abitare il Paese positions playfulness as a fundamental component of participatory design processes where play and playfulness, in all their forms, become a strategy for exploration, inquiry, and the construction of shared knowledge that allows participants, children and adults alike, to construct and represent ideas of public and private space, community, and belonging. Children’s questions often become powerful critical devices, capable of revealing contradictions in the use of public space, as when one child asked: “Excuse me, but why are they called a piazza [square] if they are used as parking lots?”

Play, by placing relationships with others at its center, allows access to new and unexpected points of view. In territorial projects, play is the most widely adopted method for exploring and discovering cities; the spaces that host playful investigations support the ideas and creativity of their inhabitants. Extended time and autonomy, grounded in trust, are essential elements of play at any age. (Paoli, 2023)

This consideration generated within the project also embodies reflections on the “right to live and inhabit a place” (Moreno, 2025).

The playful approach of the project intertwines with a series of other strategies (narration, listening, tentative design, tactical urbanism, street art) that invite participants to engage with the city and its spaces through different languages, each contributing to the collective reflection on the urban environment. These research strategies operate on multiple levels, allowing for both creative expression and critical engagement. They become tools of connection and transformation.

INTERNATIONAL CONTEXTS

The Right To Play in Reggio-Inspired Pedagogical Contexts Abroad: An Example From Boston, Massachusetts, United States

The Boston Area Reggio Inspired Network (BARIN), officially established in 2016, provides workshops, grants, and networking opportunities that sustain and evolve Reggio-inspired practices in local communities. Recently, BARIN has funded the formation of inquiry groups that come together to reflect on and deepen their teaching practice through shared inquiry.

Like FRC's approach to research, Baker and Salas Davila (2018) argued that inquiry itself can be understood as a form of play when it is taken up by adults with curiosity and imagination. They highlighted how the iterative processes of wondering, experimenting, documenting, and reflecting mirror the generative qualities of children's play. Adult inquiry as play also aligns with the human right to lifelong learning (UNESCO, 2015a). By cultivating environments where adults learn through play, Reggio-inspired practices not only sustain children's right to play but also affirm that play and creativity are fundamental dimensions of learning at all stages of life.

Building on this, Baker and Ryan (2021) reported empirical evidence that playful participatory research can shift teachers' mindsets and professional identities toward more playful, experimental, and risk-accepting stances. Their study of long-term teacher research groups documents how adults become more comfortable modeling playfulness and uncertainty in their practice through engaging in playful inquiry. These teacher shifts are important because adult dispositions toward playfulness can significantly shape whether children's play is nurtured and taken seriously as a way of knowing (Baker & Ryan, 2021).

PLAi Inquiry Group

This insight has informed several BARIN-supported inquiry groups, including Playing in the Anthropocene (PLAi; 2023–present), which convenes educators from around the world to explore how adult playfulness can support children's right to play in complex ecological times.

Among the various topics taken up by these inquiry groups, play is the central focus of PLAi. Each monthly meeting includes time for the adult participants to play (Figure 2). Through collaborative, creative activities, building with natural materials, experimenting with drawing and movement, or improvising with found objects, the group practices inhabiting a playful mindset. This enactment of adult play mirrors children's processes of meaning-making and reinforces the idea that sustaining children's right to play requires adults to nurture their own capacities for curiosity, openness, and creativity.

Figure 2. Play! Screenshots from the Play! segment of a PLAi meeting held remotely through Google Participants engaged in a body movement activity

Note. Screenshots from the Play! segment of a PLAi meeting held remotely through Google

Documentation also serves as a fundamental reflective practice in the inquiry group. Educators share traces of children's play across diverse contexts, using photographs, transcripts, videos, and artifacts to provoke new insights and to make visible the "hundred languages" through which children express meaning. Using a thinking protocol Looking Playfully at Documentation (Figure 3), educators ask questions, role play, and offer suggestions for ways the children's play might be extended or supported. In this way, documentation becomes both a method of collaborative study and a catalyst for rethinking how adults might listen to and support children's right to play in a time of increased schoolification, which has resulted in less time for play, particularly outdoor play (D'Souza, 2024).

Figure 3. Looking playfully at documentation

Note. Screenshot from the Looking Playfully at Documentation segment of a PLAi meeting held on Google Meet, in which one educator shared documentation of children playing with a water jug and pump.

Reflecting on their involvement in the PLAi group, educators shared in a survey that they found it valuable to take the time to engage in play. One educator shared that she enjoyed having "'play time' within adult meetings," as it was "really powerful to have the time and space to play." Another stated that the experience "challenge[d] the idea that play is separate from serious issues,instead, it frames play as a critical way of engaging with complexity." Crucially, one educator emphasized that being part of the group helped them to "take play seriously as a right."

By engaging in playful processes themselves, educators experienced firsthand the generative and imaginative qualities of play. This not only deepened their appreciation of play as integral to children's lives but also reoriented their professional practice; they began to recognize play as a right that requires safeguarding, time, and space. In this way, PLAi demonstrates how adult play sustains children's right to play by cultivating dispositions of openness and attentiveness in educators, qualities that are essential for creating environments where children's play is honored, expanded, and made central to educational practice. By modeling playful inquiry and collaborative study, PLAi affirms that quality education cannot be reduced to content delivery or assessment metrics, as is occurring with schoolification. Rather, it requires pedagogical cultures that honor play as central to learning. PLAi serves as a reminder that adults must play, too, if children's right to play is to be promoted.

FROM RIGHTS TO PRACTICE: REINTERPRETING RIGHTS TO QUALITY EDUCATION AND PLAY THROUGH P.E.R. INNOVATIONS

P.E.R. is an international research project promoted by FRC in collaboration with the LEGO Foundation as a global platform of exchange and collaboration among diverse cultural, economic, social, and geographical contexts. The main goal of P.E.R. is to promote the rights to quality education and play for children across different continents through four areas:

- convening educators: gathering educators and researchers worldwide to share ideas on playful learning and innovative educational strategies (Fondazione Reggio Children, 2024);
- research: supporting emerging scholars in disseminating research globally on learning through play and the Reggio Emilia Approach;
- shared projects: opening a new Research Center to host free educational activities and pilot workshops, connecting local initiatives with international conference-actions;
- management, monitoring, and evaluation: assessing the educational and social impact of the P.E.R. initiative to ensure its ongoing effectiveness and accountability.

P.E.R. can be considered an example of how a Reggio-inspired playful approach to learning gave life to an innovative way of implementing public gatherings following the values of participation and democratic educational practice through listening.

As Rinaldi (2006) explained, "To be a citizen from birth means to be the bearer of rights, to be part of a community that recognizes and values the child's capacity to think and to learn" (p. 108). In this view, learning is not the transmission of knowledge but a shared process of meaning-making, sustained through dialogue and participation in a community of learners (Edwards et al., 2012; Rinaldi, 2006).

In the organization of the P.E.R. events, the same concept was applied to partner organizations embracing a vision of education as an evolving process where creativity and participation converge. Guided by the pedagogy of listening, this approach recognizes that every voice, of children, educators, researchers, and communities, contributes to the collective construction of knowledge (Rinaldi, 2006), and that for education to be democratic, it must remain an open space for dialogue and interpretation where learning emerges through relationships and mutual trust (Bruner, 1996; Dewey, 1938). Therefore, every partner organization contributed to the co-design and implementation of activities, sharing plenary sessions and offering workshop activities. This kind of participation is central to every stage of educational practice and research (Dahlberg et al., 2013; Malaguzzi, 1993).

For this reason it was necessary to also create a new concept for the events that, instead of being indicated as conferences or seminars, have been called *conference-actions.*

It is through conference-actions that reflection and practice intertwine, that ideas are tested, shared, and reimagined in real time, and listening becomes both an ethical and epistemological stance, a way of recognizing the other as a co-constructor of meaning and knowledge (Freire, 1970; Rinaldi, 2001). As co-designers, partner organizations act as active contributors, shaping contexts, tools, and meanings alongside educators and researchers. This collaborative process nurtures innovation that is both context-sensitive and ethically grounded.

The project crossed different continents and territories, offering in each one a specific focus of study, as shown in Table 1.

Table 1. Play Explore Research Conference-Actions

City/Country	Event title	Main themes and description
São Paulo, Brazil	Play and Learning: Community Educational Practices	Focused on community educational practices and explored how play and learning can become shared civic actions that strengthen local networks and promote inclusive, culturally responsive education.
Johannesburg, South Africa	Playful Parenting and Caring for Childhood	Examined the role of playful parenting and caregiving and highlighted how families and communities can co-construct environments that affirm childhood as a time of creativity, agency, and belonging.
Denver, United States	Growing Worlds Together Through Natural Digital Dialogues	Focused on the relationship between nature and digital media as interconnected dimensions of learning.
Nairobi, Kenya	Empowering Communities: Shaping Resilient Pillars for Quality Education	Emphasized community empowerment and the creation of resilient educational ecosystems.
Hanoi, Vietnam	Nurturing Well-Being: The Intersection of Play, Education, and Research	Centered on *well-being* as a vital outcome of the intersection between play and learning.
Billund, Denmark	The Future of Learning	Examining emerging perspectives on learning, with particular emphasis on the interrelations among play, learning, and research. Relaunch for future research.

Promoting playful learning meant rethinking the very idea of a conference, giving time, space, and protagonism to local organizations, not only to keynote speakers or academic experts. All conference-actions were organized through a co-design process that involved local stakeholders, public and private research institutions, local school systems, Italian authorities abroad, nongovernmental organizations, and individual citizens.

Each conference-action was structured around three phases:

1. Before: This phase was dedicated to getting to know the partners, sharing values and experiences, and co-designing the event program collaboratively.
2. During: This phase included the implementation of the conference-action itself, emphasizing interaction, participation, and reflective practice.
3. After: This phase focuses on maintaining dialogue with local partners to explore possibilities for developing long-term collaborations and educational initiatives.

CONFERENCE-ACTION AS SITE OF PLAYFUL PARTICIPATION

In the innovative spirit that animates the P.E.R. project, the conference-actions seek to cultivate a playful and generative atmosphere, where curiosity, experimentation replace the formality of conventional academic exchange. They are designed as opportunities for reciprocal learning, occasions where diverse perspectives can interact and spark new ideas. In this sense, each conference-action becomes a living laboratory of playful learning, capable of bringing inspiration back to the community while fostering an international dialogue on creativity and the right to play.

Each edition took place in a different location, designed and adapted to the specific cultural and social context of the host community. At the heart of these events was exchange among peers. Participants contributed dynamically during panels and workshops, engaging in collective reflection, experimentation, and dialogue. The co-design approach echoes the principles of participatory action research, where knowledge is co-created rather than transferred, and innovation emerges from dialogical processes among diverse agents (Borda, 2001; Kemmis et al., 2014). Through interactive workshops and collaborative activities, the conference-actions promoted the circulation of knowledge, encouraging participants to learn not only from experts but also from one another. This process fostered shared responsibility, mutual trust, and collective empowerment in learning.

Importantly, several conference-actions also included family-oriented sessions where children, parents, and educators engaged together in playful and creative activities. These moments highlighted the pedagogical and social value of play as a vehicle for connection and learning, both within families and in broader educational settings.

THE ROLE OF PHD STUDENTS

A distinctive innovation in the design and implementation of the conference-actions was the active involvement of students from the Reggio Childhood Studies doctoral program. With diverse international backgrounds and research interests spanning multiple educational and cultural contexts, these doctoral researchers have played a crucial role in linking theory and practice.

In some cases, their direct familiarity with local contexts proved invaluable for fostering relationships with partners and navigating cultural dynamics. In others, they took on organizational and operational roles, facilitating communication and supporting on-site coordination. Their contributions, both academic and practical, demonstrate how doctoral research can become an instrument of social engagement and pedagogical transformation.

Acting as mediators between institutions, researchers, and communities, PhD students embodied the principles of participation and co-responsibility at the core of the P.E.R. innovation framework. Their engagement highlights how doctoral education can cultivate relational research competencies, fostering a new generation of scholars capable of combining critical inquiry with participatory practice (Biesta, 2011).

The reflections of some of the participating doctoral students further attest to the transformative potential of participatory doctoral work where learning, research, and action intersect to create living examples of democratic education in practice:

As a Kenyan student of the Reggio approach, collaborating in the planning and execution of two P.E.R. projects, in Johannesburg and Nairobi, has [...] expanded my understanding of project planning, collaboration, and action-based dialogue in real-world settings. [...] Unlike traditional conferences that often revolve around presentations and formalities, the conference-actions opened a window into the lived experiences of partners, communities, and schools, bridging gaps between theory and practice. (Frashia Ndungu, on South Africa and Kenya conference-actions)

The value of the P.E.R. project's conference-actions lies in their ability to activate an authentic dialogue among those who live education every day, across the most diverse contexts: teachers, educators, families, children, experts, policymakers, and NGO practitioners. [...] The possibility of physically entering the spaces and observing them in their everyday use represents a fundamental added value compared to theoretical study or indirect narration. (Laura Berni, on Kenya conference-action)

DEMOCRACY IN ACTION

The evolution of the conference-action model represents a compelling example of how educational innovation can be aligned with the Reggio Emilia values and grounded in the pedagogy of listening. By integrating co-design, peer exchange, playful learning, and the active engagement of doctoral researchers, the P.E.R. initiative outlines education as living democracy. Through these practices, the conference-actions have become a methodology of participation, a living laboratory of collaborative learning where theory and practice are continuously redefined. In doing so, they reaffirm the idea that innovation in education is not necessarily the pursuit of novelty, but the collective construction of meaning, responsibility, and shared transformation.

DISCUSSION

The values of the Reggio Emilia–inspired playful approach to learning can actively promote and support children's right to play and playfulness while remaining responsive to diverse social and cultural contexts. The initiatives described in this chapter offer illustrative examples of how playful learning is valued and enacted in different settings, rather than an exhaustive account of play across cultures. Together, they show that playful learning serves as a powerful avenue for inquiry and participation for both children and adults, and for advancing children's right to play as recognized internationally.

While international rights frameworks such as the United Nations Convention on the Rights of the Child provide an important foundation for recognizing children's right to play and participation, scholars have noted that these frameworks require careful interpretation in practice. When applied without attention to local histories, cultures, and material conditions, rights-based discourses risk relying on generalized assumptions about childhood and participation that may not fully reflect children's lived experiences in different contexts (Dar, 2025). The initiatives presented in this chapter respond to this challenge by illustrating how the right to play can be meaningfully interpreted and enacted in situated ways, attending to local relationships, cultural values, and pedagogical traditions rather than assuming a one-size-fits-all model.

At the local level in Reggio Emilia, we see how the *Natura Digitale* and *La Palestra delle Domande* projects support children's right to play in public school settings by ensuring that adults are equipped to foster curiosity and experimentation to make explicit the connection between play as a right and play as a vehicle for learning.

They help to reposition teachers as lifelong learners through playful interventions, reinforcing the idea that play and learning go hand in hand.

At the national level in Italy, projects such as *Abitare il Paese* demonstrate how play is not just about exploration but also about engagement in participatory design processes. In *Abitare il Paese*, children and communities (teachers and architects) work together to reimagine public spaces that reflect their collective needs and aspirations, demonstrating that playful inquiry is integral to civic engagement. This project exemplifies the call by Article 12 of the CRC for children to have access to spaces where they can express themselves freely and engage with their environment.

At the international level, the global P.E.R. project and the Boston-area teacher inquiry group further demonstrate how adult play is crucial to sustaining children's right to play. Educators engaging in playful participatory research not only model curiosity and creativity but also affirm that play is a lifelong right. This reflects a holistic view of education, where both children and educators learn and grow together, establishing a community of learners. PLAi demonstrates how adult play sustains children's right to play by cultivating dispositions of openness and curiosity in educators. P.E.R. also clearly shows how playfulness is not just an incidental part of education but a cross-cutting dimension that permeates every aspect of the learning process, from curriculum design to classroom interaction, and even professional development for educators. This aligns with the Reggio Emilia emphasis on reciprocal relationships and the co-construction of knowledge (Rinaldi, 2006).

Collectively, these examples reveal that play is an active, transformative force within education, and the weaving together of play with the values of the Reggio Emilia Approach creates conditions for lifelong learning and creativity. The projects documented show how play and playfulness are essential for deep learning, for democratic participation, and for fostering a sense of belonging and agency within communities. At the same time, they represent only a partial view of how playful learning is understood and enacted across different cultural and educational contexts. A more sustained cross-cultural comparison of playful learning practices would offer valuable insights, but such an analysis lies beyond the scope of this chapter.

CONCLUSIONS

Across the projects discussed in this chapter, a shared thread emerges: Each initiative extends the pedagogical sensibilities of FRC to support educators in sustaining and protecting children's right to play. Whether through digital explorations, international collaborations, or playful teacher research, these projects show how

Reggio-inspired practices create the conditions for play to thrive as a serious and joyful form of learning.

What makes the Reggio Emilia educational experience so uniquely suited to this work is its deep alignment with the principles that underpin meaningful play. At its foundation lies a strong image of the child as capable, curious, and full of potential. The concept of the hundred languages of children, that children learn, think, and communicate through many expressive forms, further supports this vision. By welcoming this multiplicity, play becomes a legitimate means of knowledge construction and a space where diverse cultural and personal ways of knowing can co-exist. Central, too, is the role of the teacher as researcher and co-player. In the projects outlined here, teachers are long-life learners participating in inquiry, observing, documenting, reflecting and learning alongside children.

In this way, Reggio-inspired approaches make the right to play visible and actionable in educational practice. They remind us that curiosity, imagination, and exploration are not culturally marginal or developmentally expendable, but widely recognized values that must be continually supported across contexts. While the examples in this chapter provide only a glimpse into the many ways playful learning is valued around the world, they point toward the importance of continued dialogue and research on how play can be nurtured and enacted across diverse educational and cultural landscapes.

We end this chapter with an invitation offered by Carla Rinaldi, in one of her last speeches:

> *The future of education will be there if there is childhood.*
> *And so today our task is above all political.*
> *And now, the floor is yours, my friends.*
> —Rinaldi, 2025

REFERENCES

Association for Middle Level Education. (2023). *Middle schoolers must play*. https://www.amle.org/middle-schoolers-must-play/

Baker, M., & Ryan, J. (2021). Playful provocations and playful mindsets: Teacher learning and identity shifts through playful participatory research. *International Journal of Play*, *10*(1), 6–24. DOI: 10.1080/21594937.2021.1878770

Baker, M., & Salas Davila, G. (2018). Inquiry is play: Playful participatory research. *YC Young Children*, *73*(5), 64–71. https://www.naeyc.org/resources/pubs/yc/nov2018/inquiry-is-play-playful-participatory-research

Barblett, L., Knaus, M., & Barratt-Pugh, C. (2016). The pushes and pulls of pedagogy in the early years: Competing knowledges and the erosion of play-based learning. *Australasian Journal of Early Childhood*, *41*(4), 36–43. DOI: 10.1177/183693911604100405

Bateson, P., & Martin, P. (2013). *Play, playfulness, creativity and innovation*. Cambridge University Press. DOI: 10.1017/CBO9781139057691

Biesta, G. J. (2011). *Learning democracy in school and society: Education, lifelong learning, and the politics of citizenship*. Springer Science & Business Media. DOI: 10.1007/978-94-6091-512-3

Bobbio, A. (2007). *I diritti sottili del bambino. Implicazioni pedagogiche e prospettive formative per una nuova cultura dell'infanzia*. Armando Editore.

Bodrova, E., & Leong, D. J. (2015). Vygotskian and post-Vygotskian views on children's play. *American Journal of Play*, *7*(3), 371–388.

Borda, O. F. (2001). Participatory (Action) Research in Social. *Handbook of action research: Participative inquiry and practice*, 27.

Broström, S. (2017). Curriculum in preschool: Adjustment or a possible liberation? *Nordic Journal of Studies in Educational Policy*, *3*(1), 19–28.

Brown, S., & Vaughan, C. (2009). *Play: How it shapes the brain, opens the imagination, and invigorates the soul*. Avery.

Bruner, J. (1996). *The culture of education*. Harvard University Press. DOI: 10.4159/9780674251083

Brussoni, M., Gibbons, R., Gray, C., Ishikawa, T., Sandseter, E. B. H., Bienenstock, A., & Tremblay, M. S. (2015). What is the relationship between risky outdoor play and health in children? *International Journal of Environmental Research and Public Health, 12*(6), 6423–6454. DOI: 10.3390/ijerph120606423 PMID: 26062038

Burghardt, G. M. (2011). Defining and recognizing play. In Pellegrini, A. D. (Ed.), *The Oxford handbook of the development of play* (pp. 9–18). Oxford University Press.

Chafel, J. A. (1991, April). The play of children: Developmental processes and policy implications. []. New York: Kluwer Academic Publishers-Human Sciences Press.]. *Child and Youth Care Forum, 20*(2), 115–132. DOI: 10.1007/BF00756693

Claxton, G. (2008). *What's the point of school? Rediscovering the heart of education*. Oneworld.

Cochran-Smith, M., & Lytle, S. L. (2009). *Inquiry as stance: Practitioner research for the next generation*. Teachers College Press.

Craft, A. (2013). Childhood in a digital age: Creative play. *British Journal of Educational Studies, 61*(1), 123–141.

D'Souza, K. (2024, October 18). *Nature's classroom: Why preschoolers need more time outdoors*. EdSource. https://edsource.org/2024/learning-amid-the-leaves-why-preschoolers-need-more-time-outdoors/720758#:~:text=Yet%2C%20that's%20the%20exception%20to,attention%20spans%20and%20frayed%20nerves

Dahlberg, G., Moss, P., & Pence, A. (2013). *Beyond quality in early childhood education and care: Languages of evaluation* (3rd ed.). Routledge. DOI: 10.4324/9780203371114

Dar, A. (2025). A critical perspective on children's right to play. In Llobet, V., Reynaert, D., Imoh, A.T.-D., & Vandenhole, W. (Eds.). *Critical Children's Rights Studies: A Research Companion (1st ed.)*, 255-267. Routledge. DOI: 10.4324/9781003510284-18

Dewey, J. (1910). *How we think*. D.C. Heath & Co. DOI: 10.1037/10903-000

Dewey, J. (1938). *Experience and education*. Macmillan.

Diamond, A. (2013). Executive functions. *Annual Review of Psychology, 64*(1), 135–168. DOI: 10.1146/annurev-psych-113011-143750 PMID: 23020641

Edwards, C., Gandini, L., & Forman, G. (Eds.). (2012). *The hundred languages of children: The Reggio Emilia experience in transformation* (3rd ed.). Praeger.

Fondazione Reggio Children. Play Explore Research Reggio Emilia conference proceedings, 2024, Reggio Emilia, Edizioni Junior

Freire, P. (1970). *Pedagogy of the oppressed.* Herder and Herder.

Ginsburg, K. R. (2007). The importance of play in promoting healthy child development and maintaining strong parent–child bonds. *Pediatrics, 119*(1), 182–191. DOI: 10.1542/peds.2006-2697 PMID: 17200287

Hirsh-Pasek, K. (2009). A mandate for playful learning in preschool: Applying the scientific evidence.

International Play Association. (1989). *Declaration of the Child's Right to Play.* International Play Association.

Johnston, O., Wildy, H., & Shand, J. (2023). Teenagers learn through play too: Communicating high expectations through a playful learning approach. *Australian Educational Researcher, 50*(3), 921–940. DOI: 10.1007/s13384-022-00534-3

Kemmis, S., Heikkinen, H. L., Fransson, G., Aspfors, J., & Edwards-Groves, C. (2014). Mentoring of new teachers as a contested practice: Supervision, support and collaborative self-development. *Teaching and Teacher Education, 43*, 154–164. DOI: 10.1016/j.tate.2014.07.001

Lester, S., & Russell, W. (2008). *Play for a change: Play, policy and practice: A review of contemporary perspectives.* Play England.

Lester, S., & Russell, W. (2010). *Children's right to play: An examination of the importance of play in the lives of children worldwide.* Bernard van Leer Foundation.

Lillard, A. S., Lerner, M. D., Hopkins, E. J., Dore, R. A., Smith, E. D., & Palmquist, C. M. (2013). The impact of pretend play on children's development: A review of the evidence. *Psychological Bulletin, 139*(1), 1–34. DOI: 10.1037/a0029321 PMID: 22905949

Lundy, L., Murray, C., Smith, K., & Ward, C. (2024). Young children's right to be heard on the quality of their education: Addressing potential misunderstandings in the context of early childhood education. *British Educational Research Journal, 00*, 1–15. DOI: 10.1002/berj.3968

Malaguzzi, L. (1990). Speech at the international conference on the rights and potentials of children and adults. In P. Cagliari, M. Castagnetti, C. Giudici, C. Rinaldi, V. Vecchi, & P. Moss (Eds.), *Loris Malaguzzi and the schools of Reggio Emilia* (pp. 396–397). Routledge.

Malaguzzi, L. (1993). For an education based on relationships. *Young Children, 49*(1), 9–12.

Malaguzzi, L. (1996). *The hundred languages of children: The Reggio Emilia approach—Advanced reflections* (C. Edwards, L. Gandini, & G. Forman, Eds.). Ablex Publishing.

Mardell, B., Ryan, J., Krechevsky, M., Baker, M., Schulz, T. S., & Liu-Constant, Y. (2023). *A pedagogy of play: Supporting playful learning in classrooms and schools*. Project Zero.

Moreno, C. (2025). *La città dei 15 minuti: Per una cultura urbana democratica.* ADD Editore.

Moss, P. (2015). *Transformative change and real utopias in early childhood education: A story of democracy, experimentation and potential.* Routledge.

Moss, P. (2019). *Alternative narratives in early childhood: An introduction for students and practitioners.* Routledge.

Organisation for Economic Cooperation and Development. (2019). *OECD learning compass 2030: A series of concept notes.* Organisation for Economic Co-operation and Development. https://www.oecd.org/education/2030-project/learning-compass-2030/

Panksepp, J. (2010). The affective neuroscience of play: The joyful discovery of self. *American Journal of Play, 2*(3), 315–337, 245–277.

Paoli, E. S. (2023). Comunità/gioco. In Consiglio nazionale degli architetti, pianificatori, paesaggisti e conservatori (Eds.), *Abitare il Paese – La cultura della domanda. Attivare comunità educanti: Nuove generazioni, partecipazione, città* (Anno scolastico 2023/2024). CNAPPC.

Paoli, E. S., & Ronzoni, R. (2025). Come un'ape. Dialoghi tra naturale e digitale per una visione ecologica in ambito educativo. *FRC news, 1*, 28–29.

Parker, R., & Thomsen, B. S. (2019). *Learning through play at school: A study of playful integrated pedagogies that foster children's holistic skills development in the primary school classroom.* LEGO Foundation.

Pellis, S. M., & Pellis, V. C. (2009). *The playful brain: Venturing to the limits of neuroscience.* Oneworld.

Pignataro, P. (2014). *La pedagogia relazionale di Loris Malaguzzi.* FrancoAngeli.

Resnick, M. (2017). *Lifelong kindergarten: Cultivating creativity through projects, passion, peers, and play.* MIT Press. DOI: 10.7551/mitpress/11017.001.0001

Rinaldi, C. (2001). A pedagogy of listening: The listening perspective from Reggio Emilia. *Innovations in Early Education: The International Reggio Exchange*, *8*(4), 1–4.

Rinaldi, C. (2006). *In dialogue with Reggio Emilia: Listening, researching and learning*. Routledge.

Rinaldi, C. (2025, April 10). Open Questions on Education [Conference Keynote]. Retrieved from https://www.frchildren.org/en/news-and-events/news/post/carla-rinaldis-open-questions-education

Schön, D. A. (1983). *The reflective practitioner*. Basic Books.

Strong-Wilson, T., & Kind, S. (2013). *Reggio Emilia, the image of the child and the child's voice in the classroom.* Routledge.

Sutton-Smith, B. (1997). *The ambiguity of play*. Harvard University Press.

The LEGO Foundation. (2017a). *What we mean by: Learning through play (Version 1.2).* Billund: The LEGO Foundation. https://cms.learningthroughplay.com/media/vd5fiurk/what-we-mean-by-learning-through-play.pdf

The LEGO Foundation. (2017b). *Learning through play: What does it mean?* Billund: LEGO Foundation. https://www.lego.com/cdn/cs/sustainability/assets/blt7aaec03836d94291/LtP_What_Is_It_-_Parents_PDF.pdf

Thibodeau, R. B., Gilpin, A. T., Brown, M. M., & Meyer, B. A. (2016). The effects of fantastical pretend-play on the development of executive functions: An intervention study. *Journal of Experimental Child Psychology*, *145*, 120–138. DOI: 10.1016/j.jecp.2016.01.001 PMID: 26835841

Trawick-Smith, J. (2014). The physical play and motor development of young children: A review of literature and implications for practice. In Roopnarine, J. L., & Johnson, J. E. (Eds.), *Approaches to early childhood education* (6th ed., pp. 213–234). Pearson.

UNESCO. (2015a). *Recommendation on Adult Learning and Education*. UNESCO.

UNESCO. (2015b). *International Charter of Physical Education, Physical Activity, and Sport*. UNESCO.

United Nations Committee on the Rights of the Child. (2013). *General comment No. 17 on the right of the child to rest, leisure, play, recreational activities, cultural life and the arts (Article 31) (CRC/C/GC/17).* United Nations. https://digitallibrary.un.org/record/778539?ln=en

United Nations General Assembly. (1959). *Declaration of the Right of the Child.* UN General Assembly.

United Nations General Assembly. (1989). *Convention on the Rights of the Child.* United Nations.

Vecchi, V. (2010). *Art and creativity in Reggio Emilia: Exploring the role and potential of ateliers in early childhood education.* Routledge. DOI: 10.4324/9780203854679

Webb-Williams, J., Kennedy-Behr, A., & Graham, A. (2021). *Play in early adolescence.* University of South Australia. https://www.unisa.edu.au/research/.../play-in-early-adolescence/

Weisberg, D. S., Hirsh-Pasek, K., & Golinkoff, R. M. (2013). Guided play: Where curricular goals meet a playful pedagogy. *Mind, Brain and Education : the Official Journal of the International Mind, Brain, and Education Society*, *7*(2), 104–112. DOI: 10.1111/mbe.12015

Whitebread, D., Basilio, M., Kuvalja, M., & Verma, M. (2012). *The importance of play: A report on the value of children's play with a series of policy recommendations.* University of Cambridge.

Wood, E. (2014). The play–pedagogy interface in contemporary debates. In L. Brooker, M. Blaise, & S. Edwards (Eds.), *The SAGE handbook of play and learning in early childhood* (pp. 145–156). SAGE. DOI: 10.4135/9781473907850.n15

Zosh, J. M., Hopkins, E. J., Jensen, H., Liu, C., Neale, D., Hirsh-Pasek, K., Solis, S. L., & Whitebread, D. (2017). *Learning through play: a review of the evidence (white paper).* The LEGO Foundation.

Chapter 2
Close and Beyond Reggio Emilia:
San Miniato and Children's Protagonism in Education

Aldo Fortunati
http://orcid.org/0009-0008-5319-2380
La Bottega di Geppetto, Italy

ABSTRACT

This chapter explores the enduring influence of Loris Malaguzzi's socio-constructivist pedagogy and its generative power in inspiring locally rooted yet original educational experiences, such as the San Miniato project. It examines Malaguzzi's vision of children as active, competent protagonists in their own learning, challenging traditional "funnel" models of education that suppress diversity. Through attention to documentation, reflection, and community involvement, pedagogy becomes a shared process of change engaging educators, families, and the local context. The San Miniato experience, while distinct from Reggio Emilia, demonstrates how Malaguzzi's ideas can foster innovative, community-based curricula centred on relationships, diversity, and the continuous co-construction of knowledge and identity.

DOI: 10.4018/979-8-3373-3431-8.ch002

SAN MINIATO, THE RIGHT TO EDUCATION AND CHILDREN'S PROTAGONISM

The Long – and Unfinished – Road to the Affirmation of Children's Rights

A quote that aligns perfectly with the theme of this chapter's first section is one that Malaguzzi himself reported in a private correspondence, made public several years after his death: "*Reggio Emilia, January 3, 1994 – Dear Aldo, as you can see, life is an unfinished sketch always – shamelessly and wonderfully – fresh. A warm hug. Loris*" (L. Malaguzzi, personal communication. January 3, 1994).

To begin, as the title of this chapter suggests, the central theme of this contribution concerns highlighting the relationship between Malaguzzi's pedagogy and the educational experience developed in San Miniato, a Municipality located in the very heart of Tuscany and internationally renowned as a social community deeply committed to children's right to high-quality education[1].

In this regard, it is appropriate to recall some aspects that more generally concern, precisely as this volume seeks to explore, the theme of the affirmation of children's right to education as a global and current challenge (Rinaldi, 2022).

Remembering that more than 35 years have passed since the United Nations approved the Convention on the Rights of the Child (hereinafter referred to as the Convention), it can be useful to reflect upon some of the statements regarding children's rights in this text (United Nations, 1989).

Perhaps three words can help us understand the perspective outlined by the Convention itself and these words are also very relevant to the theme of this volume: participation, listening, education.

Let's start with the first one: "participation". It is not necessary to recall how the UN Committee, in monitoring the implementation of the Convention on the Rights of the Child, has repeatedly highlighted to Italy the need to create conditions for a better implementation of this right, noting the weakness of the actions carried out to date in this direction[2] (UN Committee on the Rights of the Child, 2019).

However, beyond these observations, it is worth considering here that a common misconception is to confuse the gradual acquisition of adult responsibilities with the necessity of respecting children's voices. These are distinct issues: the lack of legal rights, such as voting or working, does not diminish the relevance of a child's point of view. The relevance of respecting children's thought must be recognized as a fundamental right, independent of the transition to adulthood.

The fact is that often, in the end, granting spaces for participation becomes the pretense of anticipating the forms that correspond to the structure of democratic representative bodies. On the contrary, it would be far more interesting and useful to welcome and take into account the perspectives of children and young people by paying them widespread attention and considering, first and foremost, the contexts in which they normally live and experience their sociality.

Participation – in short – is not the context for clearing adults' guilty consciences through ritualized celebration. Like listening, participation is not something that can be fully realized in artificially constructed situations. Under such conditions, spontaneous and sincere expression is unlikely to occur. Instead, participation should be understood as a habitual relational posture adopted by adults. It should not be conceived as a concession limited to specific, prearranged circumstances.

While the theme of participation, as proposed by the Convention, seems to mainly concern youth and not younger children, another issue – that of listening – helps us calibrate our reflections by including them in those that concern very young children.

Regarding the issue of "listening", the Convention – as is well known – obliges us, with Article 12[3], to consult children in all proceedings, whether judicial or administrative, that concern them (United Nations, 1989). This aspect, without contradicting what has just been said about participation as a widespread necessity and opportunity, reminds us of the importance of children and young people being mandatorily involved when decisions need to be made that specifically affect them.

Rather, it is the ways in which this happens that deserve reflection[4], from a double point of view (D.Lgs. n.149, 2022):

- on the one hand, because a child – like anyone else – never tells the truth unless they feel comfortable in a situation. This, of course, has nothing to do with their capacity for discernment, but rather with the quality of the contexts offered to children for expression and the competence and relational sensitivity of their adult interlocutors who listen. As we will argue later, educational contexts offered at an early age and based on a project that recognizes children's identity and role are essential – and certainly beneficial – for embracing children's perspectives;
- on the other hand, and specifically when considering the capacity for discernment, we are faced with a topic where the time limit tends to decrease and, over time, the age at which it is considered necessary to consult a child tends to decrease. This consequently offers food for thought: considering that today's children are the same as those of yesterday, what changes is not so much their capacity for discernment; rather, what tends to change – fortunately – is our ability to discern their thoughts and feelings. This certainly includes the awareness that children listen to each other not only by speaking to us, but also in many other ways, as observational research has long highlighted, particularly those who have had the privilege of observing children in well-

organized educational settings open to their experience in the earliest years of life (Gardner, 1993).

Thus, even in the case of the issue of listening, it seems we are facing an inexorable frontier of progressiveness in its affirmation, considering that attention to the topic diminishes the younger the child. The issue on which, however, the process of affirming the rights of the very young seems to be even slower is precisely the one closest to the focus of this volume: we are talking about the right to education as a prerequisite for the affirmation of a right to citizenship that is directly and concretely due and guaranteed from the moment a child is born.

Regarding the right to "education", while it is well known that it is mentioned in Article 28 of the Convention[5], it would not be inappropriate to also recall that in that context the Convention is responsible for calling on States to guarantee access to primary education, making the right to education coincide with access to compulsory schooling (United Nations, 1989).

Yet international literature has unraveled the issue – at least in words – for a long time, since the end of the last century when people began to talk about the growth and development of childhood by combining the words "education and care"[6] in a complementary pairing. Overcoming an assistance-based perspective, this means there is no care without education and – to avoid precocious attractions towards schoolification – that there is no education without care (OECD, 2001).

But in the meantime, as we await for the concrete realization of the "education and care" binomial, childhood remains "in the lurch": according to Eurostat, the spread of educational opportunities for children aged 3 to 5 years across the European Union is close to universal coverage, even though it is not included in compulsory schooling, while the coverage rate for children aged 0-2 years is still stuck at 27%, compared to a defined target for the 0-2 year old of 45% by 2030 (Eurostat, 2025).

But beyond the aggregate data just mentioned, below the general averages, the data paint a European picture in which the right to education for children aged 3-5 has a very different confirmation in the facts than what happens in the case of the right to education for the youngest, those aged 0 to 2.

Schools for children aged 3 to 5 represent a largely universally available opportunity, to the point where it is uncommon for a child not to attend. Their widespread availability directly results in the "common sense" that they are a natural and expected opportunity that families can rely on to manage their children's educational responsibilities: a right exercised also becomes a right embraced as such by all, and this circumstance should help us understand how the dissemination of educational opportunities at an early age is a key element in shaping the social representation of children's rights.

Indeed, when we turn our attention to the situation for children aged 0-2, the scenario changes significantly, and the limited coverage of opportunities – rarely exceeding one-third and almost never reaching half – recalls what we have long described as the slow increase in rights for younger children.

This situation highlights a clear pattern: the younger the children, the less policies guarantee sufficiently adequate opportunities, both quantitatively and qualitatively, to meet families' free choice to utilize them. In some cases, the complete lack of supply even nullifies the expression of demand.

While parental leave, especially in the earliest years of life, is an integral part of the framework for raising and caring for children, two considerations remain central. First, parental leave is not always available to parents in precarious employment or in self-employment. Second – and more crucially – the fundamental families' right to choose among different options cannot be realized when there is a lack of available opportunities from which to freely choose.

Taken together, these circumstances effectively lead to a situation in which the right to education for very young children is highly dependent on local circumstances and is not yet part of a universal policy mandate.

This presents two emblematic critical elements. The first is that the age-old question of whether the education of a young child is a matter of public interest rather than a private matter concerning the family has been raised – or remains open. The second, related to the previous one, is that educational services for children aged 0-2 are not free for families but require the payment of a fee.

The Italian context, beyond the peaks of excellence such as Reggio Emilia and San Miniato and several other local experiences mainly in central and northern Italy, exemplifies the coexistence of local experiences of the highest quality and the lack of a National policy effectively aligned with the concrete affirmation of children's rights (Fortunati, 2010b; 2010c).

Thus, for example, the recent Italian 0-6 educational system reform (D.Lgs. 65, 2017) states that *"Girls and boys, from birth to six years of age... are guaranteed equal educational opportunities... overcoming inequalities and geographic, economic, ethnic and cultural barriers"*[7].

In this general framework, the Italian guidelines for infant school (for children aged 3 to 5) are built around the idea of preparing children for primary education. At the same time, the youngest children (aged 0 to 2) continue to access educational services on an individual basis and for a fee, as if the problem of their education was a private matter and not of public interest and as if the only way to promote accessibility to services, rather than making them free as already happens for infant school, was to give families a subsidy – or a "bonus" – to reduce the burden of the fees they have to pay[8] (Legge 232, 2016).

Yet, in truth, these two words – education and care – are the essential foundation for a full and active citizenship. They represent the way a social community welcomes new citizens, offering them care – that is, quality relationships – as well as quality educational opportunities capable of recognizing and valuing identities as naturally different.

Only in this way, in fact, the literacy process can be oriented not toward constructing conforming identities that merely reproduce the existing; rather as the process through which the basis for a critical citizenship capable of imagining, planning, and building its own future is established (Fortunati, 2010a; 2016; Fortunati & Tognetti, 2017).

There is, indeed, a close correlation between the affirmation – updated with respect to the text of the Convention – of the right to education as a right that arises with childhood and the issue of recognizing the most fundamental rights of full citizenship for all girls and boys. Early childhood, from this perspective, undoubtedly represents the point on which we must focus our attention, in the knowledge that any lack of attention in the early years of life will not be remedied later, not even at a significant cost (Heckman, 2013).

From this point of view, we might reflect – and we would urge this – on the fact that even in the literal text of the Convention, which has suffered from a lack of updates since its approval over 35 years ago, the call for protection and safeguarding – although entirely appropriate then as it is today – does not provide adequate space for the promotion of rights, identifying them as a perspective to be pursued rather than a necessity to be affirmed here and now (United Nations, 1989).

The resulting idea is that children must be protected as representatives of citizens of the future. Whereas it is obvious that the lack of adequate attention – and above all adequate educational opportunities – in early childhood ends up frustrating the possibility of fully realizing citizenship rights. These rights, as in the case of education, must be affirmed from birth as a specific commitment and responsibility in the public interest. (Fortunati & Pagni, 2018; UNICEF & UNESCO, 2007).

Beneath these commentary considerations lies not only the perception of the realism with which, in a world where children's rights are still far from being fully recognized, the Convention has decided to prioritize the fundamental rights to life and health above all others. It also highlights the fact – which should be overcome and which finds its bulwark precisely in the push for the dissemination of quality educational services during childhood – that we are ultimately creating a sort of hierarchy of rights, with some coming first and others following, as if it were possible to distinguish within a category that admits no difference: rights either exist or they don't.

These considerations bring us to the topic discussed in the following section: the image of the child and their social representation. This topic greatly impacts our ability to embrace educational responsibility for children, and it is also strongly influenced by the quantitative and qualitative level of our investments in children's education. This means that the more children suffer from a weak social representation, the weaker their educational opportunities will be, while the stronger the educational opportunities for children, the higher their image and social representation will be.

To examine this more systemically, this conceptual shift leads directly to a necessary re-examination of how the very identity of the child is perceived and legally recognized within the educational framework.

BETWEEN CHILDREN'S IDENTITY AND THE RECOGNITION OF THEIR RIGHTS

Again, the tribute Malaguzzi paid to San Miniato during one of his many visits to its ECEC services are those that best introduce this second part of the present chapter: "*San Miniato, March 22, 1991 – I am well aware of the bond of love that ties things, words, actions, hard work and intelligence to an endeavor that, combining the heart and mind, honors San Miniato, your ECEC services and the culture of children. Loris Malaguzzi"* (L. Malaguzzi, personal communication. March 22, 1991).

At this point in our discussion, approaching the central theme of this chapter, it would be appropriate to focus our attention on the theme that most closely shared Malaguzzi's pedagogy and its original reworking in the context of the San Miniato's experience: the reflection on children's identity and its reflection in the design of educational projects for childhood (Fortunati, 2014; Malaguzzi, 2016).

It is true that today we all agree in speaking of children as individuals with rights. However, many stereotypical and questionable representations lie within the views that our social perception often attributes to boys and girls in the first years of life.

When we see a newborn child, rarely do we truly perceive her/him as a person, rather than an organism that will become a person only after passing through childhood. This is a time we not only don't always consider useful for education, but often consider a time when the only useful thing is "taking care": as if children were shadows that precede the emergence of a person's identity.

Curiously – usually immediately after the transition to the onset of verbal communication has taken place – the idea gains ground that children rapidly become capable of accelerated learning, and always earlier than we were accustomed to thinking.

This also includes the bizarre idea that everything is further accelerated by the fact that children today are often called "digital natives". It is as if the quick reaction children show to the friendly cues offered by digital tools was equivalent to the ability to use them effectively and exploit their true potential. Perhaps, when adults will learn to use these tools less sloppily, they will say fewer stupid things about how children use them.

In any case, whether it's traditional learning or digital tools, the idea is that children are true “sponges” who absorb everything. We fail to reflect on the fact that considering them as such is a false compliment, because we always end up considering them receptive, but not proactive and constructive.

And so the two images of the newborn dependent on his/her caregiver and the child open to early learning are both based on an idea of an empty childhood that someone must take charge of filling.

A real mess and a major problem when considering educational strategies, because if and as long as the idea of child as weak and needy gains prominence, it will be even more difficult to establish educational experiences that focus on recognizing children's identity, competences, and potential as the cornerstone of a new way of conceiving education.

In this regard, it would be appropriate to recall that both neuroscience and the recent global focus on the so-called “first 1.000 days of life” (OECD 2021) state that children are biologically predisposed toward curiosity and exploration of both the physical world and social relationships. This is the foundation of their intelligence and their direct and active engagement in the processes that accompany their growth and the development of their relationships, knowledge, and learning.

However, to fully embrace this representation of children as persons, we must not only affirm it by recognizing them as holders of rights, but above all by demonstrating the capacity to recognize their identity as persons and, right from the very beginning, as intelligent persons.

From this perspective, children's schools must change their traditional paradigm, according to which the educational process is accomplished by a unidirectional transfer of skills from the adult who possesses them to the child who still lacks them. Instead, they must adopt the principle of starting from the recognition of children's identity as active and constructive individuals, building a new concept and practice of school around this.

Let us now see what the founding ingredients of this new idea of education are, which can be found in Malaguzzi's pedagogy (Edwards et. al., 2011; Malaguzzi, 2016).

Perhaps it is the love for intelligence, combined with the curiosity of capturing a child’s first forays into becoming active, constructive – and passionate – that constitutes the greatest innovation – and the extraordinary potential – of Loris Malaguzzi’s thinking (Fortunati, 2006).

Another profound belief of Malaguzzi is that in many educational theories and teaching practices, the “funnel” system results in diversity being diluted or suppressed in the cause of literacy. The idea is that the notion behind education is that of creating the conditions so that this will occur, before actually thinking about where it will lead. In truth, what is needed is for the "funnel" view of education to be turned on its head.

The new vision sees the importance of taking into account children as unique and diverse individuals, allowing such kind of diversity to be cultivated as an intrinsic human value and as a valuable objective for an educational program. The aim is to create people who are curious about possibilities and capable of attributing value and potential to the encounter between diversities. These children must be considered for who they are, valued as the key foundation of a capacity to extend our horizons, and not on the basis that any presumed notion of normality might want them to be, a way of distinguishing who is ahead and who stays behind.

It is hard to define the "magic" that enables all this to take shape – otherwise we would not have spoken of magic – but in our opinion, it is clear that from this standpoint, the metaphor of the "hundred languages" appears to be only an approximation, a sort of first cue, to direct the heart and mind towards the complexity of the questions over which we must hover simultaneously, so as to create the best and most fertile conditions to sustain the adventure of education.

In a first analysis, considering what Malaguzzi defined as a "socio-constructivist perspective", many different principles can be detected (Malaguzzi, 2016). Indeed, Malaguzzi's pedagogy – like the Reggio experience – brings together a series of characteristics:

- attention to space and the idea that the context must have a link with the relations of whoever occupies it;
- the idea that families are inside the school and not outside;
- the idea that paying attention to processes involves listening and a capacity for reflection;
- the idea that documentation is a fundamental ingredient to sustain the challenging interpretation of experiences;
- the idea that educational work is an adventure to be shared in a group, bringing individuality into play and maintaining a dialogue.

It is not easy to give a brief explanation of something that is inherently difficult to define or pin down. But we might say that all these things exist side by side, and together make up a whole that immediately becomes different than the sum of its parts. This is not a contradiction: we are moving in a complex field, but at least we can begin to understand why the sensation is that there is some magic involved.

It does however remain true – and this can be seen by looking at the extraordinary suggestive power of the situation in Reggio and by the way it is sometimes unfortunately misrepresented around the world – that Malaguzzi's thinking does not exist in a vacuum. On the contrary, it is inextricably woven into the fabric of Reggio, where it first took shape and flourished.

This leads to the observation of an important factor that takes on a general significance: high-quality pedagogy requires a specific context – more precisely, a community – in order to build its school. And since the ecologies of communities are inherently diverse, the theme of diversity cannot be avoided, because there is no point in attempting to simplify what is fundamentally complex.

Child pedagogy – including that of Malaguzzi which has made this a fundamental tenet of his philosophy – does not depend on guidelines. Nor should it anxiously strive to be reproduced. Instead, it requires interpretations that are deeply rooted in their specific context.

The pedagogy of Malaguzzi has certainly always been hungry for exchanges, relationships, enrichment and other original and differently contextualized interpretations, with which to compare itself and continue its own construction and development (Rinaldi, 2009).

This aspect is for sure at the heart of the natural complexities of the Reggio project and the way it draws sustenance from exchanges and comparisons with other experiences. It once led Malaguzzi to describe the best strategy to adopt by taking the example of the rake used by the croupier at the end of a round of bets. He gathers up the chips remaining on the table and puts them together again. It was a way of saying that pedagogy requires original and constructive interpretations, like those that it seeks to favor in the experiences it offers to children.

The pedagogy of Malaguzzi eschews stasis and places every resource and action involved in a dimension and perspective of change. Upon closer inspection, this is hardly surprising, given that education is clearly a process that involves change. It is not strange, but it is actually slightly more complex than that. The scope of the change described by Malaguzzi is not simply or mainly related to children. It also involves educators, teachers, parents and the school itself, along with the range of opportunities that the latter offers, together with all that surrounds it, starting with the local community.

Pedagogy takes on a historic dimension that is nourished by the inter-connected roles played by various actors, engendering a social memory and a starting point from which to explore and construct new perspectives and experiences.

Thus, between experience and memory, a reflective dimension finds a place in which everyone is involved. This is a philosophy which, far from simply evaluating and checking how much children have learned – activities to which normal schools continue to dedicate energy as part of a banal interpretation of the experiences and bureaucracy of the processes that underlie them – embraces an openness to the unexpected. It equally encourages comparison and discussion as the road map for interpreting and understanding the individuality of each child.

It is no coincidence that – bringing together the factors of complexity, change and the need for context – the pedagogy of Malaguzzi shuns the idea of identifying targets, instead constantly opting for possibilities and problematization for the future (Fortunati, 2016a; Malaguzzi, 2016).

It could be said that Malaguzzi's is a pedagogy in which the wealth of opportunities brought into play, in terms of human and material resources, is inversely proportional to the attention paid to determining beforehand what will happen in the future: this is the element of magic, so extraordinarily suggestive, original and unique that it cannot be fragmented and reassembled somewhere else, but can only be the object of other different interpretations.

It should be made clear from the start that the issue of the connection with Reggio is not simply or mainly about what can be taken: above all, it is about how to invent a new interpretation.

On the contrary, anyone unable to delve below the surface of the Reggio experience, and grasp the inextricable links with the community and the history that generated it and sustained its development and evolution, will therefore remain constrained by impractical ideas, unable to regenerate new and different experiences (Rinaldi, 2009).

To move beyond these "impractical ideas" and effectively regenerate such experiences, it is necessary to shift the focus from mere educational contents to the specific pedagogical conditions that allow children to emerge as true protagonists.

SHIFTING FROM CONTENTS TO CONDITIONS, STARTING WITH CHILDREN AS PROTAGONISTS

As we reach the opening of the final part of this chapter and address the theme of children's protagonism in education, it is interesting to recall the first stanza of a poem that, in the very same period when Malaguzzi wrote his famous poem on the "hundred languages of children," proposes a child-centered idea strongly rooted in the recognition of their potential: "*San Miniato, September 17th 1990 – Toward an idea of a rich child, at the crossroads of possible worlds that lie in the present and transform the present into future. Aldo Fortunati*" (Fortunati, 1998, p.1).

As we have repeatedly evoked, San Miniato – and its idea of "children's education as a community project" – is an experience that resonates strongly with that of Reggio, but it is also very different and independent from it. Perhaps for this very reason it may be valuable to show the generative potential of Malaguzzi's pedagogy in sustaining the development of original projects and experiences, ones that are not simply variations of a single and unique model (Edwards et al., 2011).

What is certain is that the meeting of the head and the heart, of cognition and emotion, acknowledges one of the key prerequisites in the experience of the San Miniato 0 to 2 ECEC services. Malaguzzi himself referred to this in the brief quotation given at the beginning of the second section of this chapter. This prerequisite involves the capacity and habit – or at least the effort – of combining the firm definition of the organizational framework with the substantial freedom given to the processes of experience.

Within what we might call the fabric of the project, there are clear differentiating features, as well as others that show a strong continuity between San Miniato and Reggio (Fortunati, 2014).

If we want to identify the main ones, there are three that immediately come to mind for each field:

- regarding differences and autonomy:
    - San Miniato focuses on medium to small-sized ECEC services (from 18 to 45 children), while Reggio has a ECEC service system mainly based on larger numbers (more than 60 children);
    - San Miniato organizes groups placing children of different ages together, while Reggio organizes groups on the basis of four different age ranges;
    - San Miniato proposes the idea of the laboratory as an opportunity that is external to the group and which is offered in a quantity that corresponds to the number of the groups, while Reggio aims for a single workshop within the service and for mini-workshops within each section;
- regarding factors that reflect strong convergence:
    - the theme of children as protagonists is central to the San Miniato program and this echoes many of Malaguzzi's observations about renewing the image of children and the idea of constructing children's schools around this new representation of his or her identity and potential;
    - the theme of documentation and memory led San Miniato to set up a Center for Research and Documentation for Childhood, based on research experiences from its ECEC services, in order to bear witness and give visibility to the notion of children as protagonists. Instead of conducting child pedagogy based on written theory, this new philosophy involves using the documented evaluation of children's experiences as a starting point;
    - the idea that families are an integral part of the San Miniato educational service program is a core feature of the project, as is the idea that the community as a whole must bear its own share of responsibility for the education of children. In this respect, the San Miniato project re-launch

the Reggio theme of the importance of social management of children's schools.

Seen from outside – and especially when viewed in a superficial manner – there appears to be considerable differences between the two experiences, so much so as to limit the prospects of any significant reciprocal consistency:

- the different size of the communities of children that are grouped together would seem to indicate variations in the potential for achieving experiences in small groups, perhaps favored by social dimensions that are smaller in scale;
- the separation – at least at the organizational level – of the groups could give the impression of a regressive step in the school's choice, and also of a "worry" for the youngest ones, whether the idea of letting children of different ages constantly meet in a natural manner may seem a gentler way of getting diverse individuals to meet each other;
- the choice of a core workshop and other mini-workshops within the group could be read as offering fewer opportunities for exchanges and encounters, compared with the option of offering children from the different groups a wide variety of different opportunities among themselves that are interchangeable over time.

As for a "proof of reality", it is a question of differences that identify stories rather than choices, and also stories whose different circumstances probably resulted in different choices being made when it came to the organization of ECEC services.

The Reggio project started at least 10 years earlier and developed the theme of the 0 to 2 ECEC services after having built up extensive experience in its own 3 to 5 schools. That of San Miniato emerged during a time when attitudes towards the smallest children were generally less worried and were already more open to acknowledge the value of relationships between children of different ages.

We believe that the theme of conducting good pedagogy in ECEC services does not concern the development of single models, but rather lies in maintaining some consistency, in different conditions, in aspects that are truly fundamental.

The most important point here is marking the difference between taking, or failing to take into account, the identity of children, their capacity to live experiences as protagonists and therefore to be the real protagonists in the process of their own growth and development of their relationships, knowledge and learning; this does not depend on one or other specific organizational choice, but rather on making an ECEC service work as a system.

This must be a system whereby different opportunities, which are simultaneously available in terms of potential, can be accessible to all children, underlining the sense and value of the ecology of opportunities and relations that the service takes on as a whole.

In exploring this point, the theme of renewing the image of children's identity is without doubt central to the pedagogy of Malaguzzi. This means to rethink as a positive "pre-judgement" the child as an active, competent and constructive individual together with the idea that the practice of working with children and families leads to a regeneration of the social representations of the needs of children (Malaguzzi, 2016).

San Miniato strongly advocates this aspect, considering all the resources that it brings into play. The sum of these resources includes the spaces, furnishings, materials, wall coverings and also the children and educators and the various initiatives involved. These are features that can construct useful links and unleash energies and strategies for encouraging identities to emerge as protagonists. These will be based on experiences that the program of an educational service must above all stimulate in their individual diversity, rather than seeking to compare them against any given norm.

The idea that seeing children as protagonists is not just a concept to be evoked, but is also a potential on which conditions and opportunities can be based, leads to the conclusion that a primary aim for early childhood pedagogy should be encouraging the flourishing of this identity as protagonists.

Such a philosophy would help to compensate for children's lack of visibility as persons and should also lead us to – in the words of Malaguzzi – make a mental leap beyond the wall of prejudice, indifference and systematic devaluation and underestimation of children's identity (Edwards et al., 2011).

The central role of the theme of documentation seen in the San Miniato experience loudly echoes the value that Malaguzzi himself attributed to documentation as a strategy for helping a child to emerge as a competent protagonist, shaking the sensibility of adult culture and engendering in the child a new sense of respect and recognition of his or her identity as a person.

Finally, it is clear that the concept of social management, introduced in the plan to make ECEC services more widespread in Italy as codified in Italian legislation from the 1970s (Legge 1044, 1971), had its roots in the experiences of Reggio. These were based on family participation in the creation of ECEC services and the development of their experiences within the community.

San Miniato – as appears in a somewhat generalized perspective within the so-called Tuscan approach to children's education (Fortunati & Catarsi, 2012; Fortunati & Pucci, 2019) – reinterprets this root, assigning the participatory nature of the family with the role of encouraging ECEC services to become not so much part of children or of families, but rather part of the community.

This paves the way for seeing ECEC services differently: not just as places that welcome and encourage families to participate and be protagonists alongside the children, but also as places that welcome situations of comparison and exchange between parents, as part of a renewed focus on the theme of family education.

Turning our attention to the features that define the San Miniato's philosophy to children's education, we can single out what is without doubt a core theme, around which the whole program is structured and articulated: this is the notion of recognizing and giving value to the identity of children as protagonists.

This theme is central to:

- a focus on children's learning processes;
- an evaluation of the environment as a relational resource;
- the radical affirmation of the open and collegial nature of educative work;
- the investment in memory as a strategy for making the identity of children as protagonists become visible;
- a recognition that the participation of the family is not only a duty, but is also a vital prerequisite for the program of an educational service.

If, however, we try to make a more direct link between the theme of children as protagonists and the curriculum, the experience in San Miniato brings us back to an idea, which is powerful and central to the pedagogy of Malaguzzi: the idea that the theme of the curriculum should be developed by considering that the base represents opportunities, the means are the processes and the results are "stories of diversity" (Fortunati, 2016a; Fortunati & Tognetti, 2017).

It is certain that a predictable child frees the educator from a great many problems. Such a child has little possibility of actively and constructively expressing him or herself and is therefore certain never to surprise anyone with his or her behavior. Above all, this frees the educator from any responsibility of having to listen to anything that has not previously been fashioned by a supposed knowledge of what to do and for what purpose.

A closer examination reveals that in this way, not only do all declarations about the potential of childhood and its treasures become purely rhetorical and not only does the educational profession become banal and mechanical.

But, going on this way, with lightning speed, all the old images of childhood begin to re-emerge, with the paucity of attributes they give to children and their repositories of instructions of how to tap adult wisdom to fill the original incompleteness of childhood: as if nature had given the human species potential that is inherent in immaturity, with the sole purpose that education can free children of this immaturity as fast as possible.

In truth, attributing and recognizing an identity as protagonist in children requires a corresponding shift in the role of the adult.

Actions must be geared more towards organizing structural backgrounds than towards the idea of offering direct stimulus to children's behavior. Far more emphasis needs to be placed on the capacity to recognize and expand diversities of behavioral styles in children than on steering them towards precise and predefined performances. Far more focus needs to be given to the process of behaving as an expression of an evolutionary strategy than on the frenzy for certifying the stage of development obtained within supposed general parameters: the dimension that emerges is one of dialogue, sharing, exchange and comparison.

It is for this reason that educators in San Miniato are committed, not so much to designing pathways and targets, as to organizing opportunities and support for the experiences of children.

Indeed, when considering the processes of growth, learning and the development of experience, children should be involved in discussions and evaluated beyond the boundaries of common expectations. The worth of predefined results should also be called into question, so as to avoid applying them indiscriminately, without taking account of the context and individual motivations.

Not only does this perspective leave no place for predetermined results. It calls directly the concept of the curriculum, understood as "a pre-established program of action to produce previously known and defined results," an idea and a practice that is widespread across the board in childhood educational services worldwide (Dahlberg & Moss, 2005; Dahlberg et al., 2013).

The "new idea of the curriculum" attributes a pivotal role to the concept of "strategic planning action". Traditionally, the "curriculum" involves following predetermined operations so as to produce predetermined results. Instead, the "strategy" requires the ability to take advantage of, and work with, the opportunities and connections that emerge from the educational setting. The strategy is established at the same moment as the action takes place. It involves using the information produced during that action and integrating it to develop plans of action on the spot – "here and now" – in such a way that the person concerned is able to derive the maximum degree of certainty from something that is uncertain.

Alongside a constructive child and an adult more concerned with identifying possibilities than with reaching predefined targets, the context enters powerfully into the arena. This is the crucial placenta that generates, nourishes, contains and reflects the course of educational action, sustaining the child and adult protagonists and offering the support needed for the development of their constructive processes of reciprocal relationships and growth (Fortunati, 2016b).

No sooner has this perspective taken shape, than children immediately become the protagonists of their growth process, expressing their extraordinary natural aptitude and translating it into curiosity towards the world, showing their remarkable ability to have a constructive presence within the contexts of experiences in which they are involved.

Rather than being seen as a place for the uniform application of human technologies aimed at achieving standardized results, the ECEC service can – and must – be recognized as a context where children and educators share daily life as protagonists, create relationships and experiences and generate new understandings and therefore new knowledge.

The relationship between the educator and the child is resolved by exploring the respective strategic contributions within the interaction, not so much with the idea of making different viewpoints homogeneous and consistent, but with the aim of understanding how different points of view can develop reciprocally, at the same time remaining open to curiosity and change.

In the end, designing educative action based on organizing opportunities involves a shift for adults, a change from focusing on what children know how to do, to look at how children develop their experiences. This idea requires a very special kind of educator, a researcher, someone who can live with uncertainty, seeing it as a responsibility to make choices and as an indispensable condition for experimenting, discussing, reflecting and changing, concentrating on the processes of experience rather than on results, and enjoying the pleasure of astonishment and wonder.

And perhaps the notion that the pleasures of astonishment and wonder are experiences to be safeguarded in both children and adults is not such a bad idea when we talk of education, through which we contribute to designing and building the future (Fortunati, 2020).

We believe that this was a strongly held conviction of Malaguzzi: his pedagogy can serve as an incentive for developing open, participatory, discussed and renewed educational experiences, that are capable of provoking astonishment and wonder in that which sets us apart from certainty, but which perhaps brings us closer to the truth of life.

Children, girls and boys, around the world will certainly be delighted, along with their families, and not forgetting the many educators who every day dedicate themselves with passion to a demanding but also centrally valuable profession, leading, through the affirmation and practice of education as a child's right, to shape our present and our future through their gaze.

The evolution of San Miniato's experience demonstrates that the affirmation of children's rights is not a goal to be reached once and for all, but remains an "unfinished sketch" requiring constant pedagogical and political commitment. By weaving together the visionary legacy of Loris Malaguzzi and the Reggio Emilia experience with a solid local tradition of social responsibility, San Miniato has successfully transformed abstract principles into a unique and original educational identity. This relationship is not one of mere imitation, but a profound dialogue that has allowed San Miniato to reinterpret the Reggio philosophy into a new stable and shared community project.

The ongoing transition toward the National Integrated 0-6 System in Italy represents a crucial opportunity to overcome the historical fragmentation between welfare and education. However, as this chapter has explored, the quality of such a system does not depend solely on legislative decrees, but on the ability of local communities to recognize children as active citizens and true "protagonists" of their own growth and education.

In conclusion, the connection between the experiences of San Miniato and Reggio Emilia offers a valuable lesson for the international ECEC community: the "global challenge" of quality education is met when local identity remains open to research and innovation. By maintaining the "freshness" of that unfinished sketch shared with Malaguzzi, we can ensure that schools remain democratic spaces of listening and hope, where the rights of children are not merely protected, but vibrantly lived and continuously reinvented.

Ultimately, childhood is the opportunity that nature gives to humanity, and working for children's right to education means not only – as the Convention asks us to do – pursuing their best interests, but also finally understanding that children are the most important global challenge – and our best possible interest – in designing our future.

REFERENCES

Dahlberg, G., & Moss, P. (2005). *Ethics and politics in early childhood education.* Routledge.

Dahlberg, G., Moss, P., & Pence, A. (2013). *Beyond quality in early childhood education and care: languages of evaluation* (3rd ed.). Routledge. DOI: 10.4324/9780203371114

Edwards, C., Gandini, L., & Forman, G. (2011). *The hundred languages of children: The Reggio Emilia experience in transformation* (3rd ed.). Praeger. DOI: 10.5040/9798400667664

European Commission/EACEA/Eurydice. (2025). Key data on early childhood education and care in Europe 2025: Eurydice report. OECD, 2001.

Eurostat. (2025). *Eurostat Regional Yearbook: 2025 edition.* Publication Office of the European Union.

Fortunati, A. (1998). *Il mestiere dell'educare. Bambini, educatori e genitori nei nidi e nei nuovi servizi per l'infanzia e la famiglia*. Edizioni Junior.

Fortunati, A. (2006). *The education of young children as a community project. Children, teachers and parents in the infant-toddler centers and the new early childhood services.* Edizioni Junior.

Fortunati, A. (2010a). Children's identity and the quality of ECEC services. In: *Early Childhood Education and Care Services in the European Union Countries. Proceedings of the ChildONEurope Seminar and integrated review.* Istituto degli Innocenti.

Fortunati, A. (2010b). Italy. Public Policies. In: M. Cochran & R. S. New *(Eds.), Early childhood education. An international encyclopedia, vol. 4.* Praeger Publishers.

Fortunati, A. (2010c). Italy. Quality. In: M. Cochran & R. S. New (Eds.), *Early Childhood Education. An International Encyclopedia* (Vol. 4). Praeger Publishers.

Fortunati, A. (2014). *San Miniato's approach to the education of children. Children's protagonism, family participation and community responsibility toward a curriculum of possibilities*. ETS.

Fortunati, A. (Ed.). (2016a). *Towards a curriculum open to possibilities. Children's protagonism and education. Thoughts, actions, tools.* La Bottega di Geppetto.

Fortunati, A. (2016b). *Can design be sustainable? No, design must be sustainable.* Exchange Magazine.

Fortunati, A. (Ed.). (2020). *Trust, opportunity, time. Looking at, imagining, building the future with children's eyes*. La Bottega di Geppetto.

Fortunati, A., & Catarsi, E. (Eds.). (2012). *The Tuscan Approach to early childhood education*. Edizioni Junior.

Fortunati, A., & Pagni, B. (Eds.). (2018). *Children and the revolution of diversities*. La Bottega di Geppetto.

Fortunati, A., & Pucci, A. (Eds.). (2019). *Together, unique and different. New ideas from the Tuscan Approach to children's education*. Istituto degli Innocenti.

Fortunati, A., & Tognetti, G. (Eds.). (2017). *Towards a curriculum open to possibilities. Children's protagonism and education. MP4*. La Bottega di Geppetto.

Gardner, H. (1993). *Multiple intelligences: The theory in practice*. Basic Books.

Heckman, J. J. (2013). *Giving kids a fair chance*. MIT Press.

Legge (2016). n. 232. Bilancio di previsione dello Stato per l'anno finanziario 2017 e bilancio pluriennale per il triennio 2017-2019 [State budget for the 2017 financial year and multi-year budget for the 2017-2019 three-year period]. *Gazzetta Ufficiale*, No. 297. https://www.normattiva.it/uri-res/N2Ls?urn:nir:stato:legge:2016-12-11;232@originale

Legge (1971). n. 1044. Piano quinquennale per l'istituzione di asili-nido comunali con il concorso dello Stato [Five-year plan for the establishment of municipal nursery schools with State contribution]. *Gazzetta Ufficiale*, No. 316. https://www.normattiva.it/uri-res/N2Ls?urn:nir:stato:legge:1971-12-06;1044

Lgs, D. (2017). n. 65. Istituzione del sistema integrato di educazione e di istruzione dalla nascita sino a sei anni, a norma dell'articolo 1, commi 180 e 181, della legge 13 luglio 2015, n. 107 [Establishment of the integrated education and training system from birth up to six years, pursuant to article 1, paragraphs 180 and 181, of Law No. 107 of July 13, 2015]. *Gazzetta Ufficiale*, No. 112. https://www.normattiva.it/uri-res/N2Ls?urn:nir:stato:decreto.legislativo:2017;065

Lgs, D. (2022). n. 149. Attuazione della legge 26 novembre 2021, n. 206, recante delega al Governo per l'efficienza del processo civile e per la revisione della disciplina degli strumenti di risoluzione alternativa delle controversie e misure urgenti di razionalizzazione dei procedimenti in materia di diritti delle persone e delle famiglie nonché in materia di esecuzione forzata [Implementation of Law No. 206 of November 26, 2021, delegating the Government to improve the efficiency of civil proceedings and revise the discipline of alternative dispute resolution, and urgent measures to streamline proceedings concerning personal and family rights as well as enforcement proceedings]. *Gazzetta Ufficiale*, No. 243. https://www.normattiva.it/uri-res/N2Ls?urn:nir:stato:decreto.legislativo:2022-10-10;149!vig=2022-11-02

Malaguzzi, L. (2016). *Loris Malaguzzi and the schools of Reggio Emilia: A selection of his writings and speeches, 1945–1993* (P. Cagliari, M. Castagnetti, C. Giudici, C. Rinaldi, V. Vecchi, & P. Moss, Eds.). Routledge.

OECD. (2001). *Starting strong: Early childhood education and care*. OECD Publishing., DOI: 10.1787/9789264192829-

OECD. (2021). *Starting Strong VI: Supporting Meaningful Interactions in Early Childhood Education and Care*. OECD Publishing. https://doi.org/DOI: 10.1787/f47a06ae-en

Rinaldi, C. (2009). *Dialogue with Reggio Emilia: Listening, Researching and Learning*. Routledge.

Rinaldi, C. (2022). *Charter "Quality Education, a Global Challenge"*. Fondazione Reggio Children.

UN Committee on the Rights of the Child. (2019). *Concluding observations on the combined 5th and 6th periodic reports of Italy: Committee on the Rights of the Child (CRC/C/ITA/CO/5-6)*. United Nations. https://tbinternet.ohchr.org/_layouts/15/treatybodyexternal/Download.aspx?symbolno=CRC%2fC%2fITA%2fCO%2f5-6&Lang=en

UNICEF, & UNESCO. (2007). *A human rights-based approach to education for all: A framework for the realization of children's right to education and rights within education*. UNICEF; UNESCO.

United Nations. (1989). *Convention on the Rights of the Child*. United Nations. https://www.ohchr.org/en/instruments-mechanisms/instruments/convention-rights-child

ENDNOTES

1 San Miniato is a town of Lombard origin that had considerable importance during the Middle Ages serving as the seats of imperial vicars for nearly a century. An independent commune until 1370, it subsequently became part of the Florentine Republic, sharing its historical trajectory until the unification of Italy in 1861. The local economy is home to one of the most significant and richest production centers in Tuscany: the tanning and footwear industry. Within this socio-economic framework, the Municipal Administration has established robust community-oriented policies, long identifying early childhood education services as a defining feature of its local governance. The current coverage percentage for the Early Childhood Education and Care (ECEC) services for under threes is 65% (more than triple the Italian national average and double the regional average for Tuscany). In this framework, public funding covers most of the operating costs and guarantees general and equitable access to services.The consolidated pedagogical project, the strong roots within the local community and the widespread appreciation registered by national and international observers have led to the establishment of LA BOTTEGA DI GEPPETTO – International Research and Documentation Center on Childhood Gloria Tognetti, an Institution of the Municipality of San Miniato since 1999 aimed to: •promoting research and documentation activities related to the ECEC services;• developing the network (actually about 100 Institutions counted) of relationships with other organizations around the world;• supporting the evolution of the educational strategies within the ECEC services.

2 In the Concluding Observations addressed to Italy by the UN Committee in 2019, several recommendations were issued, including:• promoting the meaningful and strengthened participation of all children within families, communities, and schools, and establishing Children's Councils as permanent bodies, ensuring that they receive an effective mandate and adequate human, technical, and financial resources, in order to facilitate their effective involvement in national legislative processes;• developing tools for public consultation on national policy development to institutionalize such consultation at high levels of governance.

3 Convention on the Rights of the Child, adopted by the United Nations General Assembly on 20 November 20, 1989, ratified by Italy by Law No. 176 of May 27, 1991 – Art. 12: "*States Parties shall assure to the child who is capable of forming his or her own views the right to express those views freely in all matters affecting the child, with the views of the child being given due weight in accordance with the child's age and maturity.*"

4 Legislative Decree No. 149 (2022), aimed at improving the efficiency of civil proceedings, updated and reformulated the general provisions on the right of children to be heard in proceedings and matters concerning them, inserting Article 473-bis4 ("Hearing of the minor") and Article 473-bis5 ("Methods of hearing") into the Code of Civil Procedure. These provisions reiterate that *"A minor who has reached the age of twelve, and even a younger age if capable of discernment, is heard by the judge in proceedings in which provisions concerning him or her must be adopted. The minor's opinions must be taken into consideration taking into account his or her age and level of maturity."*

5 Convention on the Rights of the Child, approved by the United Nations General Assembly on November 20th 1989, ratified by Italy with Law No. 176 of May 27th, 1991 – Art. 28: "*States Parties recognize the right of the child to education and, with a view to achieving this right progressively and on the basis of equal opportunity, they shall, in particular: (a) Make primary education compulsory and available free to all.*"

6 The term ECEC was first used in academic and policy settings in the late 1990s, especially in European Union and OECD (2001) documents and policies. The report "Starting Strong: Early Childhood Education and Care" is one of the first international documents to systematically employ the term.

7 Legislative Decree No. 65 (2017) established the integrated system from birth to six years, implementing the provisions of Article 1 (paragraphs 180–181) of Law No. 107 (2015).

8 The "0-3 Bonus" was established by Law No. 232 (2016), specifically Article 1, paragraph 355, as part of the State Budget for the 2017–2019 period.

Chapter 3
Children's Right to Ecological Thinking:
The Reggio Emilia Approach in the Era of Environmental Crisis

Eloisa Di Rocco
http://orcid.org/0000-0003-4263-1647
Fondazione Reggio Children, Italy

ABSTRACT

The climate crisis is in children's speeches, and their concern is growing. As a science of relationships, ecology reminds us that on this planet humans are not a chosen species but intertwined with other species, in perpetual flux. Children have the right to perceive these other presences as possible encounters, rather than as dangers, and to feel part of a vibrant ecosystem that shapes them and that they can shape with responsibility. The pedagogy of listening, which the Reggio Emilia approach formulated in the 1990s, calls for a humble attitude towards the world. This chapter presents some research trajectories based on the pedagogical documentation of the Reggio Emilia schools and the Remida project, to prepare us, adults and children together, for a damaged world.

INTRODUCTION

The latest IPCC report, the Intergovernmental Panel on Climate Change, highlights that children born in 2020 will have a higher probability of experiencing extreme weather events during their lifetime than ever before in history (2023, p. 7). As Save the Children points out in a more recent report, "In this context, 'unprecedented' is defined as exposure to climate extremes you would only have a 1 in 10.000 chance

DOI: 10.4018/979-8-3373-3431-8.ch003

of experiencing during your lifetime in a world without human-induced climate change." (2025, p. 6). These extreme events include heat waves, floods, tropical cyclones, droughts, wildfires, and crop losses.

In addition to catastrophic events, there is also climate migration, political instability, loss of biodiversity, and pollution. A recent article by Philip J. Landrigan et al. (2025) published in *The Lancet* reports on the impact that plastics and microplastics are having on the health of children, infants, and even fetuses.

Children are not unaware of this reality. The environmental crisis, in its various forms, is a topic of conversation among them, as noted in *Sfere di influenza: Un'analisi dei fattori che condizionano il benessere dei bambini nei paesi ricchi* (Spheres of influence: An analysis of factors affecting child well-being in wealthy countries[1]), a UNICEF report that examined 41 countries in the industrialized world (2021, p. 52). Concern is growing among children and young people in many parts of the world (Sanson & Bellemo, 2021), and this is affecting their well-being and their ability to face the future with optimism. This analysis is not surprising, considering that they are growing up in the midst of an emergency that will impact the rest of their lives.

While it is crucial to work to mitigate the environmental effects of climate change, the field of education must also consider the necessary learning required to face the intellectual and cognitive challenges that await the younger generations.

As philosopher Félix Guattari writes in *The Three Ecologies* (2005), it is not only the ecology linked to the protection of our ecosystem—environmental ecology—that matters, nor is it only social ecology (which investigates how cultural and economic behaviors, capitalism in particular, affect this emergency). We must also take into account the third ecology, the psychological one, concerned with how human beings form their knowledge, how we *think* about the crisis.

It is important to consider how the first two ecologies intertwine and influence the third, namely, ecological thinking.

The UNICEF report shows that children's physical and psychological well-being comes mainly from family ties, but also from activities such as riding a bike and playing outdoors (2021, p. 23). However, engaging in these activities obviously depends on the nature of the territory, the available infrastructure (e.g., the presence of bike paths), and finally, on the ability of adults to see them as *possibilities*.

This chapter focuses on this third condition, arguing that ecological education is a child's right that schools, families, and communities are called upon to fulfill, not so that children learn how to save the planet in the future, but for the sake of their psycho-physical development in the present.

THE LACK OF AN ECOLOGICAL CULTURE

In Reggio Emilia, in the spring of 2025, the city administration launched an experimental project called "low-mowing green areas," which consists of allowing grass to grow in certain green areas of the city, such as flower beds, roadsides, some sections of bike paths, and parts of parks[2]. The choice was motivated by the awareness that tall grass allows for a much richer animal and plant life, increases biodiversity and therefore soil quality, as well as mitigating high summer temperatures. Lawns with tall grass have a greater variety of flowers and therefore a greater number of pollinating insects, as well as being more colorful and pleasing to the eye.

In addition to this, walking in uncultivated meadows, according to what agronomist Gilles Clément wrote in *Piccola Pedagogia dell'Erba* (A short pedagogy of grass), can be an excellent exercise in humility (Clément & Jones, 2015). Unlike a manicured garden where nature has been tamed, uncultivated land puts humans back in their place, within a complex ecosystem dominated by multiple forces. Clément writes that walking where human design has not prevailed over other forms of life is an experience of decentralization.

So, not just designed outdoor playgrounds but common meadows with tall grass can be educational contexts, natural classrooms, even more so if they are rich in biodiversity.

However, the citizens of Reggio Emilia did not appreciate the decision made by the local administration, complaining that it was impossible to walk easily to reach a bench and reporting the risk for children playing in tall grass of being bitten by ticks and other insects[3].

It is clear that ecological education does not mature solely through the implementation of certain policies, such as the creation of bicycle paths and the decision to keep the grass long in urban parks, but also through raising awareness of ecological thinking among families, teachers, and communities, who, instead of seeing danger, see the enrichment of an encounter with the world—natural and beyond.

To continue with the example, we need bike lanes, but we also need *a culture of biking*. It is not just by building bike lanes that we will increase bike use, but by working on the desire to bike, the need to bike, and the possibility of choosing eco-friendly behavior over anti-eco-friendly behavior.

Certainly, education plays a role in the collective construction of this eco-friendly culture.

To date, however, school staff and families lack the adequate training and skills necessary to help children and young people deal with the complexity of the environmental crisis (Spiteri, 2025) and, above all, to give legs to children's right to grow up in an ecological culture. This lack of expertise only increases safety concerns, as seen in the case in London where children were banned from touching snow[4], or the alarm raised in a school in Italy when a pine cone fell on a teacher's head[5], and the direction many schools are taking, where even practices such as the pedagogical use of materials are often hampered by safety regulations (Spencer et al., 2021).

Although literature has shown that manipulating materials and exploring the body are important in learning processes (Guerra & Zuccoli, 2012), some Italian infant-toddler centers and preschools prefer not to use informal materials because they are considered non-compliant with European safety regulations. The paradoxical result is that teachers end up buying stones, pinecones, shells, and branches just because they are certified for use in schools, rather than venturing outdoors with the children to explore.

As many educators point out, school should be a place of learning, including learning about danger, where children can "explore, walk and run, jump and climb, slide on wet grass to learn how to keep their balance and take calculated risks"[6]. Not offering these opportunities to children is "a theft of opportunities, experiences, skills, and occasions that are either experienced in the early years of life or risk being lost forever," as school principal and writer Gianfranco Zavalloni writes in *Manifesto dei Diritti Naturali dei Bambini* (Children's Natural Rights Manifesto)[7].

This chapter aims to propose the thesis that the right to quality education is upheld in the European Pillar of Social Rights, whereby "Every child in the European Union (EU) has the right to affordable and high-quality early childhood education and care"[8] should be understood as the right to an *ecological education.*

WHAT IS MEANT BY ECOLOGICAL EDUCATION

Articles 28 and 29 of the United Nations Committee on the Rights of the Child (2023) refer to the right to environmental education, which must be understandable to children, explain the connections *in* nature and *with* nature, and take place in a safe environment (p. 4).

According to philosopher Luigina Mortari, ecological education (1994; 2017; 2020) requires us to move away from the anthropocentric paradigm, to reject the exceptional nature of the human species in the name of which it feels entitled to exploit the planet's resources (as well as those forms of human species considered inferior).

The idea of humans no longer being at the center of the universe and the ecosystem, being the only thinking and acting beings but part of a larger design in which they play a small part, is the basis of many recent ecological philosophies, especially the posthumanist strand nourished by the work of Karen Barad, Donna Haraway, Rosi Braidotti, and, in part, Bruno Latour.

Today's world, posthumanists argue, is one that humans don't own, but rather share with other life forms and forces that govern our bodies, transform our flesh, make us sick, and heal us, shape our thoughts, and mold our experience of the environment (Barad, 2003). It is a world in which humans are no longer alone and unique. It is a world in which our species is intertwined, bodies within bodies, in perpetual becoming.

Education in ecological thinking supports children's right to inhabit this world. Children have the right to coexist with all other forms of life, to feel like one species among many, for a finite time and within what philosopher Haraway in *Staying with the trouble: Making kin in the Chthulucene* calls a cycle of lives and deaths (2016). They have the right to feel the presence of others as possible encounters and not necessarily as dangers; to feel part of a rich, complex, and vibrant ecosystem that shapes them and that they can shape, with harmonious responsibility: a practice that Haraway in *When species meet* describes as "becoming with" or "becoming worldly" (2008, p. 3).

Children have the right to feel their bodies and matter, responsive to the materials that make up the world around them. They have the right to feel, aesthetically, the materials that things are made of, to have direct, embodied, and bodily experiences.

In essence, they have the right to an ecological education. Not only because this leads to ecological knowledge, but because ecological knowledge leads to well-being.

This responsibility must be assumed by schools, even before families.

Italy is far from this. With Decree 35 of June 22, 2020, pursuant to Law 92/2019, so-called "sustainability education" has been included in the Guidelines for teaching civic education, and therefore in the learning objectives (DM 35/2020). The skills that the Ministry of Education and Merit, in the version updated to 2024 (DM 183/2024), has considered essential to achieve these learning objectives are contained in the new Guidelines (2024) and include: a general development of "responsible attitudes and behaviors aimed at protecting the environment, urban decorum, ecosystems, and natural resources for environmentally friendly economic growth" (p.13); an understanding of the causes of climate change but also to learn more about "the action of civil protection in the prevention of environmental risks" (p.14); finally, a series of skills for the protection of urban and artistic decorum (p.14) and recognition of the value of money, work, and savings (p.15).

The emphasis on economic growth, work, decorum, and a paternalistic respect for nature (which sees human beings as saviors, once again at the center of the world) does not lead to ecological education in the sense that is meant here. That is, the right to feel like a small part of a large and complex ecosystem of amazing relationships.

THE GAP FROM WHAT TO TEACH TO HOW TO LEARN ECOLOGICAL EDUCATION

The actions identified by the UN in 2015 with the 2030 Agenda[9] indicate the urgent need to establish a culture of sustainability to limit not only environmental damage but also social and economic damage. The 17 sustainable development goals included in the Agenda are not limited to protecting the environment and nature, as superficially indicated in the Italian Guidelines, but include the fight against poverty, hunger, war, gender inequality, pollution, educational poverty, salary injustice, and the inaccessibility of primary care.

The 2030 Agenda shows that everything is entangled. For a sustainable future, it is not enough to consume less meat, recycle properly, and convert to renewable energy, unless we also work for policies that guarantee quality education for every child on the planet, basic health care for every citizen of the world, and decent work that does not discriminate against anyone.

The complexity of the challenge would require "robust cultural literacy" (Mortari, 2020, p. 9), a concept that has been taken on by the Education for Sustainability field (EfS) in recent decades.

In 2017, with *Education for Sustainable Development Goals: Learning Objectives*, UNESCO defines education as both a goal in itself (number 5) and a strategy for working towards the other 16 goals of the Agenda (p. 7). Starting from that, the European Commission Joint Research Centre published *GreenComp, the European sustainability competence framework* (2022), with 12 specific competences to be cultivated in schools and society to educate for sustainability. The skills that are identified as crucial include cognitive, affective, intentional, and motivational elements, and comprise, first and foremost, systemic thinking (p. 16).

Education for Sustainability is defined as a frame of mind (Bonnett, 2002; Lang, 2007), a mental approach that requires a deep understanding of ourselves, other living beings, social and cultural processes, and the connections between all these things. It is distinguished by a more global and holistic attitude than the early theories on environmental education of the 1980s and 1990s.

In the philosophical sphere, this change would require a real paradigm shift, an epistemological revolution, as professor Stephen Sterling argues (Sterling, 2003).

Mortari attempted to describe this epistemological revolution in *Educazione Ecologica* (Ecological education) (2020). Starting from an analysis of the environmental crisis (Giovannini, 2018) not only as an ethical crisis but also as a noological crisis, i.e., a crisis of the tools of thought, Mortari advocates the need for a *philosophy of ecological education*, a new cultural literacy, which must start in schools and spread to society as a whole (2020, p. 10).

In attempting to put this theoretical philosophy into practice, the 2017 UNESCO document seeks to translate key competencies into concrete actions, but warns of the complexity of this educational challenge: "People must learn to understand the complexity of the world in which they live. They need to be able to collaborate, speak, and act for positive change" (p. 10). That is why any kind of education would not be sufficient (p. 7), but rather an approach that creates interactive, learner-centered learning environments that support participation, collaboration, problem solving, interdisciplinarity, and transdisciplinarity, and the connection between formal and informal learning (p. 10).

Education for Sustainability, understood in this way, seems to respond to the urgent need to educate human beings to decentralize themselves, to collaborate, and to respect diversity.

The skills gained through this kind of education would not only serve to educate us to respect the environment, but also to learn skills that allow us to better interpret reality, address it with different and more effective tools, and ultimately allow us to live a life closer to our deepest needs.

The transition from theory to practice is the area where part of the research on Education for Sustainability is focusing and questioning.

Once the key competencies for educating about sustainability had been identified, studies multiplied to theorize the most effective ways to apply them. Eco-schools have emerged, which support the need to keep children in contact with nature and involved in experiential activities to promote what physicist and environmentalist Fritjof Capra defines as *eco literacy* (2005; 2014). However, there is still no research proving the effectiveness of this type of sustainability education in terms of a paradigm shift.

It seems that there is a gap in current research: from what to teach, which is clear, to how to learn, which lacks scientific evidence (Davis, 2009; Bianchi, 2020).

Mortari identifies an a priori weakness in the pedagogical system and in the related educational proposal tasked with establishing reflective ecological thinking (or systemic thinking). It would not be a matter of providing normative guidelines, but rather "visions to be interpreted." (2020, p. 11).

Compared to a Western culture that struggles to break away from an anthropocentric (and even more adult-centric) ethic, it must be possible to outline ecocentric theories, otherwise known as bioethical theories. These have the merit of problematizing complex issues by focusing on the need to develop an awareness of the primacy of relationships.

Finally, Mortari refers to Capra's systemic thinking, but as a need to overcome the opposition between anthropocentrism and ecocentrism through the recognition of the value of relationships in a constantly changing reality.

Posthumanism theories, with Braidotti, Haraway, Barad, and Tsing among their leading exponents, argue for the need to abandon a dualistic view of the world and embrace the intertwining in which humans and non-humans live. Posthumanism no longer accepts the albeit noble intentions of reconciling man with nature, or harmonizing humans with nature, opting instead for what French sociologist Bruno Latour in *Politics of nature: How to bring the sciences into democracy* calls the "common world" (2004, p. 184), which transcends the human/nature dichotomy. The common world is not the encounter between a human subject who acts and a non-human subject who undergoes the action; it is a third place that begins to exist at the moment of their encounter. It is a world in which human beings shape things, but things also shape human beings. It is a world deeply founded on relationships, interdependence, and reciprocity.

From this perspective, educating children solely to respect nature or understand its laws—to reiterate what is required in the Italian Guidelines—perpetuates the dualism that sees human beings at the center, as the only active side, and nature as the passive side of the equation. Furthermore, it is a perspective that, in addition to nature, also betrays the child (and their right to have a voice), who is once again considered the purely receptive player in the educational process.

THE REGGIO EMILIA APPROACH AND THE PEDAGOGY OF LISTENING

What new knowledge is needed today to address the paradigm shift required by ecological education? What new epistemologies? And how does the Reggio Emilia Approach respond to children's right to develop ecological thinking?

At the time of the first Reggio Emilia schools, in the 1970s and 1980s, the environment was not yet a global emergency. Today, adults must ask these questions and take responsibility, especially as teachers, educators, and early childhood professionals, to reflect on these issues and educate ourselves *with* children, and with the common worlds we inhabit, to new postures (Pacini-Ketchabaw et al., 2016; Taylor, 2013; Taylor et al., 2012, 2021).

The Reggio Emilia Approach, and the pedagogy of listening (Rinaldi, 2012) in particular, originated as a political project that can contribute to building a sustainable future because, as professor Peter Moss argues in the introduction to *The Role of the Pedagogista in Reggio Emilia* (Giamminuti et al., 2024), it is an antidote to neoliberal excess, one of the main causes of ecological imbalance. But above all, the Reggio experience can function as a philosophy for decentralizing the human being, just as it once decentralized the adult to give centrality to the child.

The pedagogy of listening formulated by pedagogist Carla Rinaldi (1999; 2001; 2012; 2021), within the Reggio Emilia Approach speaks to us of a gentle and humble attitude towards the world.

Listening is not limited to the physical act of hearing children, but is a form of human knowledge involving all the senses. Human beings cannot live without meaning, argues Rinaldi in *The pedagogy of listening: The listening perspective from Reggio Emilia* (2021, p. 37), but the act of knowing must not take us back to the Cartesian idea of the human, who dominates with reasoning a nature considered the passive object of human knowledge.

Listening is a contrary practice to traditional and rational knowledge. It is not a movement from the center (or from above) to the outside (or below) but a coming and going, where there is no longer a privileged subject who learns and a helpless object that is learned, but there is a third place. What learns is also what is learned.

The practice of listening—Rinaldi suggests—makes it clear that the meanings humans give to things are only a small part of a larger picture that escapes total understanding, and "It demands that we have clearly in mind the value of the unknown and that we are able to overcome the sense of emptiness and precariousness that we experience whenever our certainties are questioned." (2021, p. 39).

Listening creates a context of respect and acceptance of different points of view. It is a delicate, intuitive form of knowledge that does not move towards the object of its knowledge to conquer its secrets but welcomes the environment and its unintelligible complexity; it feels part of the environment and its representation, aware of the countless and mysterious connections that bind all things together.

Since Rinaldi published the first text on the pedagogy of listening in 1999, Reggio Emilia schools have repeatedly referred to those concepts. In the statements of pedagogists, atelieristas, and teachers, we find several references to listening that point in the direction of ecological education as understood in this chapter. That is, as an (aesthetic) sensitivity to connections. Or, to quote anthropologist Gregory Bateson in *Mind and Nature*, "responsive to the pattern which connects" (1979, p. 8).

In *Il Pensiero Ecologico* (Ecological thinking), Reggio pedagogist Maddalena Tedeschi discusses the need for a curriculum that allows schools to offer children a context in which to make these connections, where they can practice—together with adults—systemic thinking, or ecological thinking (2016, p. 231). Tedeschi talks about the different actors that need to be brought into dialogue in school, not only human actors but also non-human ones, such as spaces and materials. She adds that listening—empathic listening—to different points of view is the true nature of ecological thinking (p. 232).

The pedagogy of listening, which at first and for some time was called the pedagogy of listening *and relationship*, would be a natural pedagogy for children. Tedeschi writes that "every child is born predisposed to building relationships" (p. 231).

This becomes clear, I might add, when observing 5-year-olds through the pedagogical documentation of the Reggio schools. For them the concept of "friendship" is a vital element of knowledge because it helps them distinguish things and phenomena through analogies and differences, or connections:

Hard things are friends with iron
Iron and wood are friends because they are dark
Stone is different, but it is a friend of iron
(Diana Municipal Preschool, 2001, p. 13)

In the school project on the creation of a Luna Park for birds[10], documented by atelierista Giovanni Piazza, we read that "knowledge is constructed as a system of relations, so that the simple association between two stimuli, or between a stimulus and a response, is insufficient for defining the knowledge-building process" (2001, p. 6). It is friendship and the building of relationships (not necessarily sympathetic relationships) that bring true knowledge, i.e., ecological knowledge, whereas non-ecological knowledge is simply information, as Vea Vecchi, an atelierista at the Reggio Emilia schools for many years, points out:

"Without an active imagination, without a tension that allows us to notice what we encounter and to renew ourselves through the wonder of supportive relationships, we take the risk of responding to the physical world with senses and minds numbed by a daily routine that often confuses information with knowledge". (Diana Municipal Preschool, 2001, p. 7)

At the heart of an ecological attitude, writes Reggio atelierista and botanist Stefano Sturloni in *Lasciate che vi parli di foglie* (Let me tell you about leaves), is a particular sensitivity in human beings, "developed in the early years of life, as a result of prolonged contact with nature in the company of adults who act as significant witnesses in the conduct of such experiences" (2022, p. 20).

Humans need to know how to observe, Sturloni continues, to forge strong bonds with those around us, putting ourselves "at the service of a supportive, ethically sustainable future" (p. 20). This is a task, he adds, "that inevitably entrusts children with a fundamental role" (p. 20).

Recognizing children's extraordinary ability to see relationships, bonds, and connections between things in the world is the Reggio Emilia Approach's response to children's right to develop ecological thinking. Furthermore, offering contexts, opportunities, and tools to express this ability, and possibly expand it, is how the Reggio experience puts it into practice.

THE PEDAGOGICAL DOCUMENTATION METHOD

The revolution that the Reggio philosophy has brought to Western pedagogy is to make adults aware of how children are born with the ability to listen empathically to the world around them.

This is the task of pedagogical documentation, the working methodology that the schools of Reggio Emilia have developed over the years to make the learning processes of the children and adults they observe visible and shareable. These include videos, audio recordings, photos, written comments, diagrams, and notes that accompany the educators' daily work with the children. This material is then re-read, re-interpreted, and revisited as a group (Giudici et al., 2011). Recognizing, documenting, and sharing children's ecological culture, their way of always thinking in terms of relationships, is another way in which the Reggio Emilia Approach supports the right to ecological thinking.

On the occasion of the children's Christmas greetings to the city, the infant-toddler centers and preschools of Reggio Emilia in 2014 created a video called *Messaggi Planetari* (Planetary messages). The video showed phrases, drawings, and photos of children aged 2 to 6, collected and selected from conversations throughout the school year.

The video was screened in one of the city's main squares, in the presence of hundreds of families and citizens. It opened with this dialogue between three 4-year-old children:

The thread of life starts from the heart
The thread has to stay in the body, it's like a fish that has to stay in the water
If the threads meet, what happens is that they weave together
You take a bit of other people's thread, give some to other people, and yours gets to be the perfect measure
(Reggio Children, 2014)

Pedagogical documentation is particularly effective for ecological education because, as Mortari argues, quoting philosopher Hannah Arendt, dialogue is the field in which ecological thinking is practiced, that is, the collective search for meaning (1994, p. 12). Dialogues, rather than simple conversations, allow different points of view to meet, forcing people to argue their cases and question themselves. Dialogue and the pedagogy of listening, therefore, go hand in hand.

Pedagogical documentation is also the tool that best responds to children's right to participation, enshrined in the *Charter of Children's Rights* (United Nations Committee on the Rights of the Child, 2023), i.e., their right to be heard, to be kept informed, and to count in public debate, as pedagogists Paola Cagliari and Claudia Giudici write in *The Role of the Pedagogista in Reggio Emilia* (Giamminuti et al., 2024). Children demand that their abilities to develop theories, construct knowledge, express themselves, and change their minds be recognized as rights, as stated in *A Journey into the Rights of Children* (Ferri, 1995), a collection of children's ideas on the subject of rights. The book is the result of several recorded conversations between 25 children aged between 5 and 6 from the Diana Municipal Preschool in Reggio, divided into groups of three, boys and girls separately:

> *Children have to know things. It's better to know things instead of things happening without knowing them, for example, war or death. (p. 22)*
>
> *If children know things, they are not afraid. They know about dangerous things too. (p. 22)*
>
> *If you know more things, you can decide more things. (p. 26)*
>
> *Everybody imagines that they don't know how to think. Me too! I told my mommy that I didn't know how to think, but it wasn't true. Really, everybody knows how to think. Thoughts can be told, and they change. (p. 48)*

Research conducted in schools thus becomes pedagogical documentation, exhibitions, and books. Children's culture, children's ecological culture, enters into adult debate. This includes difficult and complex issues (such as the climate emergency), as Loris Malaguzzi, director of the first municipal preschools in Reggio Emilia, has been quoted in *Rechild,* the Reggio Children magazine:

> *"We adults need first and foremost to be convinced that children are not only holders of rights, but that they are holders of their own culture, they are holders of a capacity for developing more culture, and they are capable of building their own culture and contaminating our culture." (2021, p. 10)*

Legitimizing children's points of view, supporting them, documenting them, and taking them seriously is also important because, as Rinaldi wrote, "we have to listen to children not only because we can help them but also because they can help us" (2001, p. 1).

This ability to observe/listen/create bonds is the empathy that underpins the concept of sustainability promoted not only by the schools of Reggio Emilia but also by Remida, the research project that, more than any other expression of Reggio's philosophy, deals with ecological thinking, studying the educational potential of materials through industrial waste (Gandini & Kamisky, 2005).

The following paragraph presents some research trajectories and educational practices based on experiences in Reggio Emilia schools and the Remida project.

Specifically, I will present some pedagogical documentation for the project *Le mani, la Mente, la Materia* (Hands, mind, matter); the research on metaphors; and the workshops on storytelling *Binomi Materici Fantastici* (Fantastic material binomials).

THE *HANDS, MIND, MATTER* PROJECT FOR A SENSITIVE LISTENING

Remida, the Creative Recycling Center, was founded in 1996, thanks to the director of the Reggio infant-toddler centers and preschools director, when Italy did not even have a national law on waste collection (the Ronchi Decree dates back to 1997). Remida is a research center where encounters between materials, children, and adults are designed, observed, and documented, applying the pedagogy of listening as a way to recognize the interconnection that underlies the common destiny of humans and non-humans. At Remida, sustainability is conceived as an expression of participation in life that includes not only living beings but also non-living matter (Di Rocco, 2024).

Remida's pedagogical documentation shows that both children and adults are capable of listening sensitively, seeking connections with objects and materials to create strong bonds with living and non-living entities.

In 2019, Remida launched a project entitled *Le Mani, la Mente, la Materia* (Hands, mind, matter) to promote the exploratory dimension of industrial waste materials that, being unusual, unknown, nameless, and without instructions for use, trains intelligence, creativity, and divergent thinking. Through the creation of metaphors, images, stories, and questions, Remida's atelieristas investigated the interdependent relationship that characterizes the presence of human beings on the planet.

The 2-hour-long activity took place with groups of about 15 adults at a time, of different nationalities and ages, men and women together. It initially consisted of observing and choosing a material from among many previously set up on a table in the center of the studio (Figure 1).

Figure 1. Workshop with a group of German teachers. (Reggio Emilia, 2019). Remida archive. © Comune di Reggio Emilia

The proposal did not consist of building something with the chosen material, but rather exploring it individually, intimately, and at length (about half an hour): a kind of listening that allowed participants to get to know it.

Each participant was asked to write or draw their reflections, memories, questions, and discoveries. One teacher wrote about a scrap of blue rubber (Figure 2):

It's soft, it's blue, you can put your fingers in the holes, it looks like an octopus's suction cup, or a jellyfish, folded, it looks like a peacock's fan, folded again, it looks like a face, it's translucent, it reminds me of rain, raindrops, and air bubbles.

Figure 2. Blue rubber scrap (Reggio Emilia, 2019). Remida archive. © Comune di Reggio Emilia

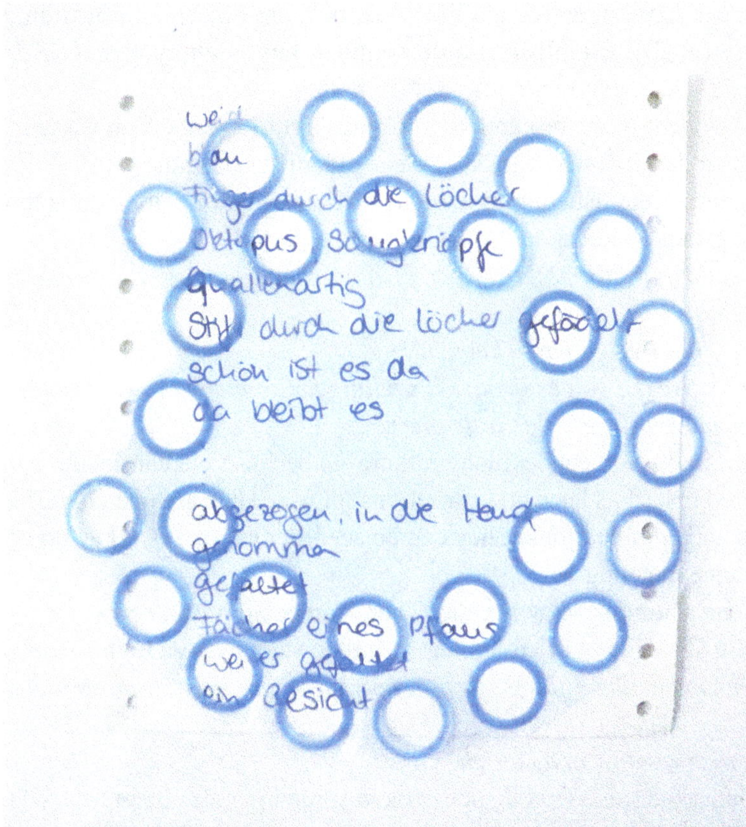

Another educator, on the other hand, reports on a piece of tree bark:

It is bare, rough, but fragile. It made me think of the woods, a landscape, barbecues, and summer. It looks strong, but it isn't. You have to treat it gently, like certain people.

It is interesting to note how the time people allow themselves to find a connection with the material often leads to affection. What was considered an insignificant remnant becomes something we grow fond of, like a friend:

I really liked this piece and couldn't wait to get it! I grabbed it before anyone else could! I folded it, made a fan, and liked how it could be manipulated. It takes the shape of a star, of a staircase. I wanted to have more.

The Remida project recognizes the agency of materials and conducts research into their ability to trigger memories, questions, and sensations (Ferrari & Giacopini, 2005). This is the effect whereby an object ceases to be anonymous, banal, identical to a thousand others, but acquires an aura, a surplus of meaning, which anthropologist Franco La Cecla in *Non è cosa. Vita affettiva degli oggetti* (Not a thing. The emotional life of objects) calls "objectivity" (2013, p. 39). Objects, writes La Cecla, can have an emotional life when they are objects of affection, vehicles of memory (p. 23). Establishing an emotional bond with an object saves it from homogeneity and anonymity.

This is evident in the research that Remida's staff conducts on waste materials. "Every object has its own soul," a 12-year-old girl once said.

At the end of the listening to the materials activity, one often empathizes with them, as a group of educators from Germany reported:

I can't let go of this material. I can't stop investigating it, it's wonderful. It's a part of
me, now that I've gotten to know it.
I want to give it a voice because it's telling me so many things. I wondered how I would move if I were this little piece.

Unlike familiar objects, which reassure us because we can identify their use, unstructured materials have no instructions for use. They are open to infinite interpretations and combinations. They can be seen in many ways. They do not have a single, unique meaning.

Everyone's point of view is valid. There can be no mistake.

Looking at a slice of dried lemon, an Italian student from high school said:

This lemon slice is different from a normal lemon slice. It looks like a bicycle wheel,
or the rose window of a church.

Days later, the same lemon slice evoked something else in an Irish educator:

I never noticed how interesting it is. It makes me think of gin, and it has wrinkled skin that my grandmother used to scrape off...

The bonds formed are emotional, as La Cecla says (2013), "correspondences," as Tim Ingold states (2021), "kinships," as Haraway argues (2008), "friendships," as children report.

From a linguistic perspective, they can be defined as metaphorical processes.

THE RESEARCH PROJECT ON METAPHORS

In 2016, Reggio Children and the Istituzione Scuole e Nidi d'infanzia of Reggio Emilia (which manages the city's educational services for children aged 0-6) launched a research project with the Department of Education and Human Sciences at the University of Modena and Reggio Emilia on children's metaphorical processes. Children, as stated in the introduction, are natural producers of metaphors (Corte et al., 2022, p. 10). The creation of metaphors helps us understand the world; it is not embellishment but a necessary cognitive process.

The research, which involved children, teachers, atelieristas, and pedagogists from two infant-toddler centers and two preschools, resulted in an exhibition and catalog entitled *Un Pensiero in Festa* (A festive thought) (Corte et al., 2022).

Looking back at these materials and the pedagogical documentation produced, the metaphorical processes implemented by the children are moving in the direction of an education in ecological thinking.

Metaphorical processes train the creation of bonds and relationships. As scholars Annamaria Contini and Alice Giuliani explain in the catalog, metaphor "implies the interaction between two semantic-conceptual domains, the possibility of putting them in precise correspondence and seeing one through the other" (p. 14). They say that "a metaphor is a tool of thought and language that connects distant elements of reality, constructing a new reality and a new meaning" (p. 9).

When a 2-year-old child says, "The kenzia plant is a shower" (p. 32), he demonstrates that he lacks the elements to view the plant from a scientific, poetic, or economic perspective, i.e., as a natural resource from which to obtain nutrients or profit. Instead, ecological thinking emerges, bringing something unknown (the kenzia) closer to the known (the shower), perhaps through a similarity in form or the involvement of the body. The metaphor brings distant elements into the same world. The kenzia, from a mysterious plant, an object of our knowledge, becomes a friend, something familiar, because it is re-known. Metaphorical processes create the kinships that Haraway mentions (2008), making alive what would otherwise be dead, helpless, other-than-us.

Even familiar objects can trigger metaphorical processes, reinventions, and new recognitions. A stapler becomes a shark, a cow, or a wolf (Corte et al., 2022, pp. 92–93). A feather becomes a sword that "makes you die laughing" (p. 81).

But even more interesting are the metaphors triggered by unfamiliar objects. A deconstructed material, such as corrugated white cardboard, becomes a cloud (p. 149) because the sound of fingers running along the vertical lines resembles the sound of rain.

Metaphor not only creates relationships but also makes the common world real, where distant elements can be friends or relatives. As Annamaria Contini says, "Once connections are perceived, they are then truly present" (p. 17).

Metaphor can be an excellent tool (including for teaching), not only for education but also for ecological re-education because "it changes our perspective on things we are used to looking at according to certain conventions" (p. 16). Metaphor is, therefore, a good practice for the regeneration and decolonization of thought.

STORYTELLING TO MAKE BONDS: THE *FANTASTIC MATERIAL BINOMIALS* WORKSHOPS

A great producer, scholar, and juggler of metaphors for all ages was the Italian writer Gianni Rodari, who, after visiting the schools of Reggio Emilia in the 1970s, became a close friend of pedagogist Loris Malaguzzi. His encounter with Reggio Emilia inspired Rodari to write *Grammatica della Fantasia* (The grammar of fantasy) (1973), which is dedicated to the city. In this essay, Rodari theorizes Fantastica, an imaginary discipline that opposes Logic and recognizes metaphor and creativity as vehicles for systemic and ecological thinking. Rodari states that imagination is not the opposite of rational thinking, but its expansion. Imagination becomes an epistemological tool capable of disrupting the rigid conceptual boundaries between the real and the unreal, the possible and the impossible, and opening up spaces for alternative ways of knowing. Fantastica also has a profoundly democratic nature. By legitimizing the imaginative capacity of every child, it resists the cultural elitism that relegates creativity to a select few. For Rodari, the creation of stories is a collective and dialogical process that allows students to question authority, reconfigure their experiences, and imagine social change. Therefore, Fantastica is not only an art of storytelling, but a pedagogy of possibility, a political practice aimed at imagining a different world.

Rodari's *fantastic binomials*, born from the combination of two apparently unrelated words or ideas, are not just linguistic exercises, but testify to a theory of knowledge rooted in surprise, relationality, and invention. To have *fantastic binomials*, Rodari writes, "distance between the two words is necessary. One must be sufficiently strange or different from the other, and their coupling must be fairly unusual, for the imagination to be compelled to set itself in motion to establish a relationship between them" (2023, p. 25). It is therefore Rodari himself who uses the term "relationship", as if to refer to an operation in which bringing together two different entities can create a family, if a fantastic – and therefore unusual – link is found to bridge the gap between them.

Whether they are words or objects makes no difference. For Rodari, words are things that can be shaped with creativity, and that shape us if we leave them.

In 2023, on the occasion of the fiftieth anniversary of the *Grammatica della Fantasia* book, a series of workshops entitled *Binomi Materici Fantastici* (Fantastic material binomials) took place at Remida. In this case, it was not two words that were put together, but two waste materials, which evoked an image, a character, or an interpretation.

The workshop consisted of randomly selecting two materials from two black fabric bags, each containing 25 different materials. It was therefore not possible to choose the pair of materials. The game consisted of putting the materials together to form a third imaginary subject: a "hearth with a pedal" (Figure 3), or "two flower friends" (Figure 4).

Figure 3. "A hearth with a pedal". (Reggio Emilia, 2023). Remida archive. © Comune di Reggio Emilia

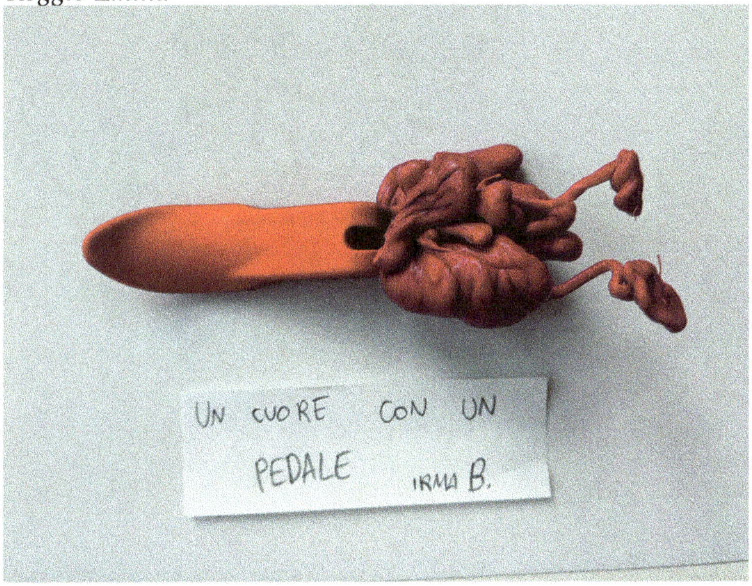

Figure 4. "Two flower friends". (Reggio Emilia, 2023). Remida archive. © Comune di Reggio Emilia

The *Fantastic Material Binomials* proposed by the Remida's staff are encounters between "subjects with strong but mysterious personalities. Alone, they may appear shy, but when paired together, they become friends."[11].

According to Rodari, the creativity underlying metaphorical processes and, more generally, children's research attitude, is "completely comfortable in fluid situations where others sense danger" (2023, p. 225).

This is another exercise that trains us in ecological education in this Anthropocene era.

Remida's long experience testifies to the intertwining between humans and things, and that it is possible and desirable to recognize the bonds with matter. Narrative intervenes to repair broken connections. In Reggio schools, Jerome Bruner's lesson on the importance of narrative is well established. Storytelling—Bruner writes in *Making Stories: Law, Literature, Life*—is a tool for learning, being in the world, and forming meaningful relationships (2003).

Storytelling means putting together pieces that are far apart, weaving a common thread, seeing links and connections between phenomena in the world where there would seem to be none.

The biographies of objects, materials, and things, whose stories are constructed and whose pieces are reassembled, are another form of ecological education that intervenes to find a dialogue with the materials of the world. These are not invented stories about materials or purely human games of imagination applied to inanimate and defenseless materials. Rather, they are encounters halfway between the two, in which materials play an important role, because, as Remida's teacher Alba Ferrari says, "they suggest something to those who encounter them" (Gandini & Kaminsky, 2005, p. 4).

By cultivating this form of material empathy, Remida and the Reggio Emilia Approach contribute to the development of the ecological culture they hope for: a transition from consumption to care, from utility to relationship, from shaping to being shaped. The experiences in schools, projects, and pedagogical documentation in Reggio Emilia aim to cultivate sensitivity to the invisible networks that sustain life, in which human and non-human presences participate. Learning thus becomes a process of re-cognizing connections, a discovery of correspondences that extend beyond the walls of the school to the social, material, and environmental fabric of the world.

TRAJECTORIES FOR FUTURE RESEARCH

The experience of Reggio schools and the Remida project illustrates that the ecological orientation of education cannot be achieved in isolation, but must emerge from ongoing collaboration between educators, policymakers, researchers, and citizens. The dialogue between pedagogical theory and community practice is the fertile ground on which ecological thinking can flourish.

At the global level, this dialogue must also include the voices of the Global South and indigenous pedagogies that have long embodied an ecological worldview. Many indigenous epistemologies conceive of knowledge as relational and co-constructed. They teach that learning occurs through reciprocity and gratitude towards the more-than-human world (Smith, 2021). Bringing these traditions into dialogue with Reggio Emilia's pedagogy of listening could enrich both perspectives and contribute to decolonizing the field of ecological education. As scholars such as Affrica Taylor (2013) and Veronica Pacini-Ketchabaw (2016) remind us, posthuman and multispecies pedagogies are not abstract theories, but invitations to decentralize Western human exceptionalism and learn from situated practices of coexistence.

Future research should therefore focus on how the principles of the Reggio framework—listening, documentation, political project, and relational ethics—can interact with different cultural contexts. How could the pedagogy of listening work in communities around the world most affected by capitalist exploitation, social injustice, and climate change? How can teachers and educators facilitate children's encounters with wounded but resilient landscapes? These questions point to a transdisciplinary field of inquiry that integrates education, political ecology, geography, and social justice.

CONCLUSIONS

The ecological crisis has revealed the limitations of anthropocentric epistemologies that have long dominated Western educational institutions. In a world structured around the logic of extraction, productivity, and control, children are often presented with the concept of ecology as if nature were an external reality; a set of objects to be studied, used, or be afraid of, rather than a network of relationships in which they are already embedded. Listening, as conceived in the Reggio Emilia thinking, is not only a communication technique but an epistemic act, a way of knowing that decentralizes the self and creates space for encounter with the other. In this sense, listening becomes a form of ecological thinking, which recognizes the interdependence and mutual transformation between humans and non-humans. It allows both educators and children to live with uncertainty and to value the unknown as a source of meaning (albeit temporary) rather than as a threat to be controlled (Rinaldi, 2021).

In the face of the current global crisis, the Reggio Emilia Approach offers itself not only as a pedagogical model, but also as a cultural and ethical posture capable of redefining the meaning of educating, living, and thinking *with* the world's matters. The environmental emergency—a combination of ecological degradation, social inequality, and epistemological blindness—of which children are aware, requires a transformation of the very foundations of education. The philosophy practiced in the Reggio Emilia educational system and in the Remida project offers a convincing response to this need, not by prescribing environmentalist actions, but by cultivating a sensitivity that allows the human species to perceive itself as part of a living network of relationships.

The future of ecological education depends on our collective ability to embrace uncertainty and complexity, resisting the discomfort of what we cannot control but which controls us. The pedagogy of listening teaches that knowledge does not come from mastery, but from dialogue, openness, and care. This lesson is particularly relevant in an unpredictable era, in which no single discipline, institution, or technical innovation can provide definitive solutions on its own. The practice of listening—to children, to other species, to materials, to the Earth itself—becomes a way of living in the Anthropocene era.

The Reggio Emilia Approach, therefore, reveals that ecological education cannot be separated from aesthetics, ethics, or politics. It is a form of cultural literacy that prepares both children and adults to think systemically and act responsibly.

At the political level, the right to ecological education should be recognized as a fundamental social right, along with the rights to health, work, and peace. The European Pillar of Social Rights already affirms every child's right to quality early childhood education; it is time to interpret this right through an ecological lens. To ensure that children can grow, learn, and thrive in sustainable environments, governments must invest not only in infrastructure but also in the professional development of educators capable of implementing a pedagogy of ecological thinking, or "third ecology" (Guattari, 2005).

The Reggio Emilia educational system does not offer a naive optimism that everything will be solved through education. Rather, it embodies what Haraway (2016) calls "staying with the trouble": a commitment to living and learning in damaged worlds, seeking forms of repair and respons-ability.

Such acts cultivate what philosopher Rosi Braidotti (2013) might call "affirmative ethics", an ethic that celebrates interdependence and potentiality rather than guilt, fear, or pessimism.

If we take seriously the idea that education shapes the way we think, feel, and act in the world, then education—as Rinaldi (2022) once argued—is one of the most powerful strategies for addressing the environmental crisis. However, this ecological culture cannot be imposed through top-down reforms, but must grow organically and collectively from local practices of listening, experimenting, and reflecting with children, adults, other cultures around the world, other species, and other presences. Creating bonds creates an ecological culture that can strengthen the policies and technologies put in place to address the environmental emergency. But more than anything else, it allows us to choose bicycles over cars, to venture into the woods rather than buy natural materials online, to accept the risk of facing what is different from us by implementing *fantastic binomials*. The history of the Reggio Emilia education system shows how a city, through sustained investment in education from early childhood, can become this living laboratory of planetary democracy.

REFERENCES

Barad, K. (2003). Posthumanist Performativity: Toward an Understanding of How Matter Comes to Matter. *Signs (Chicago, Ill.)*, *28*(3), 801–831. DOI: 10.1086/345321

Bateson, G. (1979). *Mind and Nature: A necessary unity*. Dutton.

Bianchi, G. (2020). *Sustainability competences: A systematic literature review*. https://op.europa.eu/publication/manifestation_identifier/PUB_KJNA30555ENN

Bonnett, M. (2002). Education for sustainability as a frame of mind. *Environmental Education Research*, *8*(1), 9–20. DOI: 10.1080/13504620120109619

Braidotti, R. (2013). *The Posthuman*. Polity Press.

Bruner, J. S. (2003). *Making Stories: Law, Literature, Life*. Harvard University Press.

Capra, F. (2005). *Ecoalfabeto. L'orto dei bambini*. Stampa Alternativa.

Capra, F., & Luisi, P. L. (2014). *The Systems View of Life: A Unifying Vision* (1st ed.). Cambridge University Press., DOI: 10.1017/CBO9780511895555

Clément, G., & Jones, L. (2015). *Piccola pedagogia dell'erba. Riflessioni sul giardino planetario*. DeriveApprodi.

Corte, E., Giudici, C., & De Poi, S. (A cura di). (2022). *Un pensiero in festa: le metafore visive nei processi di apprendimento dei bambini*. Reggio Children.

Davis, J. (2009). Revealing the research 'hole' of early childhood education for sustainability: A preliminary survey of the literature. *Environmental Education Research, 15*(2), 227–241. DM 35/2020 [Decreto Ministeriale n.35 del 22 giugno 2020]. *Linee guida per l'insegnamento dell'educazione civica, ai sensi dell'articolo 3 della legge 20 agosto 2019, n. 92*. Italian Ministry of Education and Merit.DOI: 10.1080/13504620802710607

Di Rocco, E. (2024). Sostenibilità è creare (buoni) legami. In Augelli, A. (Ed.), *Dello scarto e del recupero: Orientamenti di educazione alla sostenibilità* (pp. 120–124). Franco Angeli.

Diana Municipal Preschool. (2001). *Forme aformate*.

DM 183/2024 [Decreto Ministeriale n.183 del 7 settembre 2024]. *Adozione delle Linee guida per l'insegnamento dell'educazione civica*. Italian Ministry of Education and Merit.

European Commission. Joint Research Centre. (2022). *GreenComp, the European sustainability competence framework.* Publications Office of the European Union. https://data.europa.eu/doi/10.2760/13286

Ferrari, A., & Giacopini, E. (2005). *Remida day: Muta... menti* (1st ed., Engl. version). Reggio Children.

Ferri, G. (Ed.). (with Malaguzzi, L., Castagnetti, M., Rubizzi, L., & Vecchi, V.). (1995). *In viaggio coi diritti delle bambine e dei bambini: Autori i bambini stessi: bambine e bambini fra i 5 e i 6 anni della scuola "Diana" = A journey into the rights of children: as seen by children themselves: 5 and 6 year-old children of the "Diana" school* (L. Morrow, Trans.). Reggio Children.

Gandini, L., & Kaminsky, A. (2005). Remida, the creative recycling center in Reggio Emilia: An interview with Elena Giacopini, Graziella Brighenti, Arturo Bertoldi, and Alba Ferrari. *Innovations in Early Education: The International Reggio Exchange, 12*(3), 1–13.

Giamminuti, S., Cagliari, P., Giudici, C., & Strozzi, P. (2024). *The role of the pedagogista in Reggio Emilia: Voices and Ideas for a Dialectic Educational Experience.* Routledge., DOI: 10.4324/9781003181026

Giovannini, E. (2018). *L'utopia sostenibile.* Laterza.

Giudici, C., Barchi, P., & Rinaldi, C. (Eds.). (2011). *Making learning visible: Children as individual and group learners.* Reggio Children.

Guattari, F. (2005). The three ecologies. *Continuum.*

Guerra, M., & Zuccoli, F. (2012). Finished and Unfinished Objects: Supporting Children's Creativity Through Materials. *Procedia: Social and Behavioral Sciences, 51*, 721–727. DOI: 10.1016/j.sbspro.2012.08.231

Haraway, D. (2008). *When species meet.* University of Minnesota Press.

Haraway, D. (2016). *Staying with the trouble: Making kin in the Chthulucene.* Duke University Press.

Ingold, T. (2021). *Corrispondenze* (N. Perullo, Trans.). Cortina.

IPCC. (2023). IPCC 2023: Summary for Policymakers. In: *Climate Change 2023: Synthesis Report. Contribution of Working Groups I, II, and III to the Sixth Assessment Report of the Intergovernmental Panel on Climate Change* [Core Writing Team, H. Lee and J. Romero (eds.)]. IPCC, Geneva, Switzerland (pp. 1-34). DOI: 10.59327/IPCC/AR6-9789291691647

La Cecla, F., & Vitone, L. (2013). *Non è cosa. Vita affettiva degli oggetti - Non siamo mai stati soli. Oggetti e disegni*. Elèuthera.

Landrigan, P. J., Dunlop, S., Treskova, M., Raps, H., Symeonides, C., Muncke, J., Spring, M., Stegeman, J., Almroth, B. C., Chiles, T. C., Cropper, M., Deeney, M., Fuller, L., Geyer, R., Karasik, R., Mafira, T., Mangwiro, A., Matias, D. M., Mulders, Y., & Rocklöv, J. (2025). The Lancet Countdown on health and plastics. *Lancet, 406*(10507), 1044–1062. Advance online publication. DOI: 10.1016/S0140-6736(25)01447-3 PMID: 40769171

Lang, J. R. (2007). *How to succeed with education for sustainability*. Curriculum Corp.

Latour, B. (2004). *Politics of nature: How to bring the sciences into democracy*. Harvard University Press. DOI: 10.4159/9780674039964

Ministero dell'istruzione e del merito. (2024). *Linee guida per l'insegnamento dell'educazione civica.*

Mortari, L. (1994). Educating ourselves to think with a view to 'ecologically inhabiting the earth' in the light of the thought of Hannah Arendt. *Australian Journal of Environmental Education, 10*, 91–111. DOI: 10.1017/S0814062600003116

Mortari, L. (2017). La materia vivente e il pensare sensibile: Per una filosofia ecologica dell'educazione. *Mimesis.*

Mortari, L. (2020). Educazione ecologica (1st ed.). GLF editori Laterza.

new Charter of Values of the Reggio Children Foundation. https://www.youtube.com/watch?v=rfHdTlaf_8U

Pacini-Ketchabaw, V., Taylor, A., & Blaise, M. (2016). Decentering the Human in Multispecies Ethnographies. In *Posthuman Research Practices in Education* (pp. 149–167). Palgrave Macmillan UK.

Piazza, G. (A c. Di). (2001). *Le fontane: Da un progetto per la costruzione di un luna park degli uccellini = The fountains: from a project for the construction of an amusement park for birds* (L. Morrow, Trad.). Reggio Children.

Reggio Children. (2014). *Planetary Messages.* https://vimeo.com/394903249

Reggio Children (Ed.). (2021). Perché i bambini non siano invisibili. *Rechild, December 2021.*

Rinaldi, C. (1999). *L'ascolto visibile.* Comune di Reggio Emilia. https://books.google.it/books?id=HxQjjwEACAAJ

Rinaldi, C. (2001). The pedagogy of listening: The listening perspective from Reggio Emilia. *Innovations in Early Education: The International Reggio Exchange, 8*(4).

Rinaldi, C. (2012). The pedagogy of listening. The listening perspective of Reggio Emilia. In *The Hundred Languages of Children: The Reggio Emilia experience in transformation* (3rd ed., pp. 233–246). Praeger.

Rinaldi, C. (2021). *In dialogue with Reggio Emilia: Listening, researching and learning* (2nd ed.). Routledge. DOI: 10.4324/9780367854539

Rinaldi, C. (2022). *Quality education, a global challenge.* Video presentation of the

Rodari, G. (1973). *Grammatica della fantasia: introduzione all'arte di inventare storie*. Einaudi.

Rodari, G. (2023). *Grammatica della fantasia. Introduzione all'arte di inventare storie. 50 anni*. Einaudi Ragazzi.

Sanson A, Bellemo M. (2021). Children and youth in the climate crisis. *BJPsych Bull. Aug;45*(4), (pp. 205-209). DOI: 10.1192/bjb.2021.16

Save The Children. (2025). *Born into the Climate Crisis 2: An unprecedented life: Protecting children's rights in a changing climate.* https://resourcecentre.savethechildren.net/pdf/Born-into-the-Climate-Crisis-2.-An-Unprecedented-Life-Protecting-Childrens-Rights-in-A-Changing-Climate.pdf

Smith, L. T. (2021). *Decolonizing methodologies: Research and indigenous peoples*. Bloomsbury Publishing. DOI: 10.5040/9781350225282

Spencer, R. A., Joshi, N., Branje, K., Murray, N., Kirk, S. F., & Stone, M. R. (2021). Early childhood educator perceptions of risky play in an outdoor loose parts intervention. *AIMS Public Health, 8*(2), 213–228. DOI: 10.3934/publichealth.2021017 PMID: 34017887

Spiteri, J. (2025). Climate anxiety in early childhood: A state-of-the-art review. *Journal of Childhood. Education and Society*, *6*(2), 230–248.

Sterling, S. (2003). *Whole Systems Thinking as a Basis for Paradigm Change in Education: Explorations in the Context of Sustainability*. University of Bath.

Sturloni, S. (2022). *Lasciate che vi parli di foglie: Educatori e bambini alla scoperta di un mondo insospettabile*. Junior.

Taylor, A. (2013). *Reconfiguring the natures of childhood.* Routledge. DOI: 10.4324/9780203582046

Taylor, A., Pacini-Ketchabaw, V., & Blaise, M. (2012). Children's Relations to the More-Than-Human World. *Contemporary Issues in Early Childhood, 13*(2), 81–85. DOI: 10.2304/ciec.2012.13.2.81

Taylor, A., Zakharova, T., & Cullen, M. (2021). Common Worlding Pedagogies: Opening Up to Learning with Worlds. *Journal of Childhood Studies, 46*(4), 74–88. DOI: 10.18357/jcs464202120425

Tedeschi, M. (2016). Il pensiero ecologico nell'esperienza educativa del Comune di Reggio Emilia. In G. Bonini & R. Pazzagli, *Paesaggio nel piatto. Storia del paesaggio agrario italiano* (VII) (pp. 231-233). Istituto Alcide Cervi.

Tsing, A. L., Gan, E., Swanson, H. A., & Bubandt, N. (A c. Di). (2017). *Arts of living on a damaged planet*. University of Minnesota Press.

UNESCO. (2017). *Education for Sustainable Development Goals: Learning objectives*. UNESCO., DOI: 10.54675/CGBA9153

UNICEF. (2021). *Sfere di influenza: un'analisi dei fattori che condizionano il benessere dei bambini nei paesi ricchi*. United Nations.

United Nations Committee on the Rights of the Child. (2023). *General Comment No. 26 on Children's Rights and the Environment, with a special focus on climate change—Version for Children*. United Nations.

ENDNOTES

1 All translations from Italian are my own.

2 https://www.comune.reggioemilia.it/argomenti/ambiente/progetti/aree-verdi-a-sfalcio-ridotto

3 https://www.ilrestodelcarlino.it/reggio-emilia/cronaca/erba-troppo-alta-nei-parchi-5b1c55f6. https://www.facebook.com/watch/?v=747740991298098

4 https://www.independent.co.uk/news/uk/snow-ban-headteacher-good-morning-britain-ges-smith-jo-richardson-community-school-piers-morgan-a8231621.html

5 https://www.lastampa.it/imperia-sanremo/2016/10/08/news/pigna-cade-in-testa-a-un-insegnante-chiusi-i-giardini-della-scuola-materna-1.34784133/

6 https://quimamme.corriere.it/neonati/asilo-nido/nido-ai-raggi-x

7 https://www.scuolacreativa.it/web/diritti-naturali-dei-bambini/

8 https://education.ec.europa.eu/education-levels/early-childhood-education-and-care/about-early-childhood-education-and-care

9 https://sdgs.un.org/2030agenda

10 The Luna Park for birds project was conceived in the 5- and 6-year-old section of the "La Villetta" Municipal Preschool in Reggio Emilia, in early 90's. Like all projects in Reggio Emilia's 0-6 year old schools, this one also originated from the daily assemblies held with the children at school.This time, the children wanted to design and build a pond in the school garden that could provide drinking water for thirsty birds. All stages of the process were supervised by two teachers: one who recorded the children's conversations, the other who filmed with a video camera and took photographs (Piazza, 2001).

11 http://bit.ly/4q5pgoD

Chapter 4
Fostering Children's Rights to Literacy Through the Reggio Emilia Approach

Pamela Beach
http://orcid.org/0000-0002-4980-9447
Queen's University, Canada

ABSTRACT

This chapter draws on current research on language and early literacy development and instruction, offering a critical perspective on evidence-informed literacy practices within the Reggio Emilia classroom. It explores language and literacy development through the lens of social constructivist theory, emphasizing that children's development of language and literacy occurs through social interaction and collaborative knowledge-building activities. Practical examples from Reggio settings illustrate how educators can nurture early literacy in meaningful ways. By bridging theory and classroom practice, this chapter advocates for responsive literacy instruction that honours children's voices and experiences while at the same time fosters children's right to become literate members of our global community.

INTRODUCTION

Based on the fundamental principle that literacy is a human right, this chapter explores early literacy through a social constructivist lens, positioning children as active participants in the learning process (Gandini, 2012; Malaguzzi, 2012). Within this framework, literacy learning is not viewed as a passive endeavor, but one as

DOI: 10.4018/979-8-3373-3431-8.ch004

something that emerges through relationships, dialogue, and purposeful engagement with materials and the environment. The Reggio Emilia approach places children's ideas, questions, and interactions as the centre of the learning experience. Building on this theoretical notion, this chapter provides an overview of the research in early literacy development and highlights practical, play-based experiences where early literacy skills are fostered through exploration, inquiry, and the arts. These multimodal and integrated experiences offer rich contexts for children to engage with oral and written language in meaningful ways (Beach, 2025). Carefully designed, literacy-rich environments that support curiosity and communication enable children to experiment with symbols, storytelling, and mark making, all of which contribute to the development of foundational literacy skills. By aligning the principles of the Reggio Emilia approach with evidence-based literacy instruction, this chapter presents a model for early childhood educators committed to supporting the complex process of language and early literacy development across diverse and multilingual educational settings.

Before delving into the research on language and literacy development, this chapter will begin with a review of how the Reggio Emilia approach views children as active agents in their learning. This foundation will lead to a discussion on the essential role of play in early childhood education, followed by an overview of early literacy including the key components of literacy that should be embedded in every early learning program. This chapter will then explore how early literacy principles align with the Reggio Emilia philosophy, highlighting key elements of literacy learning within a Reggio environment. Finally, four classroom vignettes will be presented illustrating how developmentally appropriate practices in Reggio settings can foster growth in children's language and literacy skills.

CHILDREN AS ACTIVE AGENTS

The Reggio Emilia approach provides children with opportunities to be socially active in the construction and determination of their lives, and was developed based on the belief that all children are naturally curious, capable of constructing their own learning in an environment that invites them to collaborate with their peers and provides them with a sense of ownership and autonomy (Gandini, 2012; Malaguzzi, 2012). The idea that children are active citizens capable of constructing their own learning with their collaborative peers, stems from renowned researchers and philosophers in child development and learning: Lev Vygotsky, John Dewey, and Jean Piaget. A common thread of Vygotsky, Dewey, and Piaget is the shared belief that children actively construct knowledge through interactions with their peers, teachers, and their environment (Bruner, 1997; Glassman, 2001). Vygotsky's

Zone of Proximal Development (ZPD), for instance, highlights how the teacher is a co-constructor of knowledge as well as a collaborator. Children are provided with opportunities to explore real-life experiences and expand upon their ideas and theories through hands-on experiential learning. Dewey similarly argued for learning to occur through real-life experiences in which classroom environments resemble democratic communities where children are encouraged to voice their thoughts and learn through active participation. Piaget also believed that children should learn through these types of knowledge building activities in which their current understandings are extended through problem-solving. Together, these theories lay the foundation for viewing children as capable and curious individuals who engage with the world around them in meaningful ways.

Influenced by their work, Loris Malaguzzi, the early childhood educator who first proposed the Reggio Emilia approach, believed that children are guided by their curiosity and interest to communicate in and with the world in multiple ways (Malaguzzi, 2012). The term, "hundred languages" was first introduced by Malaguzzi in a poem he wrote (Malaguzzi, 2012) and has since become a key distinction of the Reggio approach, referring to the many ways children communicate and share their thinking about the world around them. Aligned with social constructivist theory, children are guided by their curiosity and interest, and through paint, puppetry, dance, music, drama, and collage, to name a few, children have numerous "languages" to express themselves and their ideas. Malaguzzi also emphasized the importance of following the lead of the child during inquiry projects rather than adhering to a fixed curriculum (Gandini, 2012). Reggio teachers "improvise" their programming; however, this improvisation is not left to chance. By offering children provocations, inquiry-based questions, and thoughtfully selected materials, teachers purposefully design learning environments that evolve alongside the child's exploration and engagement.

Another key component of the Reggio philosophy, particularly relevant to language and literacy development, is that of the third teacher. Through the Reggio approach, the learning environment itself acts as the third teacher, supporting children's language and literacy growth by offering rich opportunities for experimentation and exploration. Within this stimulating space, children are encouraged to question, discuss, hypothesize, and observe (Beach, 2025), taking a constructivist role in building knowledge about print and other types of media. They are guided to understand reading and writing as much more than the alphabet; literacy involves not only learning the code but also uncovering the rules by which the code functions (Rubizzi & Bonilauri, 2012). Through meaningful interactions with text and materials, peers, and teachers, children begin to see language as a tool for communication, expression, and interpretation. These authentic, play-based literacy experiences promote a deeper understanding of language, where meaning-making is central to the learning process.

LEARNING THROUGH PLAY

Play is an important avenue for children's development and learning (Rand & Marrow, 2021), as it provides a meaningful context in which children can demonstrate their agency. Within this context, research has shown that play also supports the development of language and literacy skills (Pyle et al., 2018). For example, Hadley et al. (2019) examined the role of play in vocabulary development, particularly its impact on increasing a child's depth of vocabulary. Vocabulary depth refers to how thoroughly someone knows and understands a word—its multiple meanings, usage in different contexts, and relationship to other words—and plays a key role in reading comprehension. In their study, children who participated in a "play intervention" showed significantly greater vocabulary depth than those in the control group (Hadley et al., 2019). The play intervention included a scaffolded interactive book reading followed by two teacher guided play sessions and two child directed play sessions (Hadley et al., 2019). Children in the play intervention group were better able to provide semantic and contextual information about targeted words than their same-age peers.

In another study that examined the role of play in language and literacy development, Maureen et al. (2020) investigated the effects of storytelling and play on print awareness, alphabet knowledge, and phonological awareness for a group of 4-6 year olds. The storytelling play-based sessions incorporated singing, visual arts, and dramatic role play and occurred over six unique units. Findings indicated that when compared to the control group, the children who experienced the storytelling approach demonstrated overall stronger literacy development suggesting that the playful activities positively impacted the children's early literacy skills.

Similarly, Cavanaugh et al. (2017) explored the effects of "literacy-rich sociodramatic guided play" on a variety of kindergarten children's early literacy skills, including phonemic awareness and alphabet knowledge (p. 831). The children in the experimental group received a supplemental 15-minute block of time designated for play-based literacy activities which incorporated miniature items, toys, and letter tiles. During this time, they were invited to invent a game with the given materials. When compared to the children in the control group who continued with their regular play schedule, the children in the experimental group scored higher on phonemic awareness, first-sound fluency, and oral reading fluency. While the game component was noted as a key reason for the higher scores, the children in the experimental group were observed in story-composing, sequencing ideas into complex cause and effect events, application of new vocabulary, and repeated practice of phonics and phonemic awareness skills. Combined with the higher scores, these observations suggest that when children are provided with opportunities to guide their play and use purposefully selected materials to compose and create, they can engage in literacy behaviours and, ultimately, increase their literacy skills.

Play is indeed a natural vehicle for children's learning and development and reflects the philosophy that all children, regardless of their geographical and linguistic contexts, have the right to reach their full literacy potential. Play creates rich, inclusive opportunities for linguistically diverse children and non-native speakers to communicate, collaborate, and participate meaningfully; it serves as a powerful platform for the "hundred languages" of expression. In multilingual environments, play also functions as a unifying language, enabling children to invent and negotiate ways of communicating that extend beyond spoken words.

When enriched through inquiry and the arts, play becomes an authentic context for the development of language and literacy skills. In play-based, inquiry-driven environments, children are positioned as active agents in their own learning, constructing meaning through exploration, dialogue, and creative expression. This perspective frames early childhood curriculum as emergent and continually evolving in response to children's experiences, questions, and interests. Adopting this approach enables educators to intentionally honor each child's unique voice while fostering motivation for literacy, a love of reading, and the capacity to critically engage with the world as literate individuals. Within play-based inquiry environments informed by the Reggio Emilia approach, intentional collaboration between children and educators strengthens oral language development and lays a strong foundation for early literacy skills. The following section provides an overview of early literacy and explores how play, inquiry, and the arts create avenues for literacy learning and enriched literacy experiences.

EARLY LITERACY: AN OVERVIEW

Literacy is a fundamental human right, a principle upheld by organizations like UNESCO and the International Literacy Association, which advocate for its promotion and protection worldwide. Regardless of linguistic background, literacy empowers individuals by helping them understand their rights and responsibilities and by enabling them to advocate for justice and equality. Becoming literate begins at home as well as in early childhood education settings, where children build their language and early literacy skills through play, exploration, and inquiry projects. Research has shown a direct link between early literacy and later academic achievement, suggesting that instructional approaches during a child's early years can have an enormous impact on their literacy achievements (Sparks et al., 2014; Stanley et al., 2018). Sparks et al. (2014), for instance, conducted a longitudinal study examining the relationship between children's early literacy skills and their reading comprehension scores in tenth grade. Findings clearly showed that first grade reading skills were a strong predictor of tenth grade outcomes confirming the long-term benefits of providing children with early literacy experiences. Similarly, findings from a longitudinal study spanning 15 years and including 58 children, showed specific language and literacy skills were generally strongly correlated over time (Suggate et al., 2018); reading comprehension at age 12 was predicted by vocabulary at 19 months of age (Suggate et al., 2018). Studies, such as these, suggest the critical importance of early literacy and its impact on later academic achievement.

In the English-language context, early literacy encompasses the foundational skills, understandings, and dispositions that children develop prior to achieving fluent reading and writing in English. These include oral language development, vocabulary growth, and phonological awareness, as well as print awareness, alphabet knowledge, and emerging skills in written composition (Lonigan & Shanahan, 2009; Rand & Morrow, 2021; Snow, 2017). Access to high-quality early learning experiences that intentionally support these competencies is essential to fulfilling children's right to become literate participants in a global society. The following section provides an overview of the core components of early literacy: oral language and vocabulary; phonological and phonemic awareness; print awareness and alphabet knowledge; and early written composition skills.

Oral Language and Vocabulary Development

Oral language, vocabulary development, and the process of acquiring new words develop through both implicit and explicit learning opportunities. Implicit learning occurs through everyday conversations and interactions with parents, caregivers, and other children, whereas explicit learning opportunities are prepared experiences often with a clear goal or outcome. Regardless of the route of acquisition, oral language and vocabulary development are foundational to becoming literate. A main goal of vocabulary instruction is to promote word consciousness or an enjoyment in learning about and using words in a variety of ways and contexts (Schwanenflugel & Knapp, 2015). Knowing a word contributes to our comprehension of information, whether through texts, conversations, or other modes of communication; provides us with opportunities to construct and remember ideas; and helps build connections between new information and our prior knowledge (Schwanenflugel & Knapp, 2015).

Phonological and Phonemic Awareness

Phonological awareness involves the ability to notice, think about, and manipulate sounds in spoken words (Torgesen & Mathes, 1998). Children who develop skills in phonological awareness have built a strong foundation for becoming literate, especially for word-level reading since understanding that speech sounds can be divided into smaller sounds helps children break the code of written language and acquire the alphabetic principle (Piasta, 2023). There are four levels of phonological awareness, including the word level, syllable level, onset and rime level, and phoneme level. The phoneme level is the most challenging level associated with phonological awareness and involves the ability to identify and manipulate the smallest speech sounds. Research-based activities that support a child's ability to develop phonemic awareness include identifying phonemes (e.g., the first sound in the word *dog* is /d/[1]), blending phonemes (e.g., combining or blending the phonemes /h/ /a/ /t/ makes the word *hat*), segmenting phonemes (e.g., the sounds you hear in the word *cat* are /c/ /a/ /t/) and deleting phonemes from words (e.g., without the /s/ the word *smile* is *mile*) (Armbruster et al., 2001).

Print Awareness and Alphabet Knowledge

Along with phonological and phonemic awareness skills, supporting children in developing an awareness of print and alphabet knowledge, including letter-sound correspondences, is an essential component of any early literacy program (Justice & Pullen, 2003; Piasta, 2023). Print awareness refers to children's understanding of how written language functions (Riley-Ayers, 2013). For example, recognizing that words are composed of letters and that sentences are composed of words, as well as acquiring behaviours related to book orientation, directionality (e.g., left-to-right in English and right-to-left in Arabic), and text positioning, are key aspects of print awareness.

Piasta (2023) describes knowledge about print and the alphabetic principle as "recognizing that printed words comprise letters and that these letters correspond to sounds heard when the word is read aloud" (p. 83). The main goal of instruction associated with alphabet knowledge, also known as phonics instruction, is to help children learn that there are visual symbols (letters or graphemes) that represent the sounds of spoken language; the alphabet is a code and breaking the code involves learning to read (Cheatham & Allor, 2012). Effective phonics instruction is explicit and systematic, and provides frequent opportunities for children to apply their knowledge of letters and sounds to the reading of words, sentences, and stories. These opportunities can occur through chants, rhymes, songs, and explicit activities (Armbruster et al., 2001).

Early Skills in Written Composition

The earliest skills in written composition are usually observed through a child's marks they make with a crayon or paint brush. Mark making is an early understanding that written language provides an avenue for expressing ideas. It also shows an understanding of cause and effect—if I do this, then that happens. Whether marks are lines formed across the entire area where the crayon has barely left the page or strong staccato-like dots resulting from a strike on the page with the tip of the crayon, these early behaviours set a foundation for developing skills in written composition (Peterson, 2023).

Learning to form the letters of the alphabet (and any sign, symbol, or mark) begins with holding a writing utensil with a full grasp and making randomly assorted marks. Although there is always a range of skills and abilities to consider with any developmental sequence, children do, for the most part, pass through predictable stages of handwriting. As a child's fine motor skills develop, they begin to use a stronger grasp to draw and form letters and begin to make words. A child might progress through the early stages of written composition, but, as with all stage-like models, a child might not progress in a linear way. Flexibility with respect to the way in which a child might progress in their letter formation and mark making is key. Following random marks or scribbling, children might begin to string letters together; capital letters are usually easier to form at this early stage, and spaces aren't always present. As a child begins to develop an understanding of letter-sound relationships (and as their fine motor skills[2] grow) they start to represent words with the correct sound(s), at least the initial sounds. These more complex writing tasks require a more integrated knowledge system including knowing the letter sounds and the symbols that represent them.

Taken together, developing early literacy skills is essential to the building blocks of literacy and reading comprehension (Adams, 1990; Snow, 2017). Indeed, reading comprehension is a product of both decoding, or print-related skills, and linguistic comprehension, or language-related skills (Hoover & Gough, 1990). Decoding skills are those that promote the ability to recognize and read words while language-related skills are those that support the ability to make meaning of text. According to the simple view of reading (Hoover & Gough, 1990), both sets of skills are equally important to reading comprehension. If someone can easily decode print but has weaknesses in vocabulary or background knowledge, or syntax and grammar (components of linguistic comprehension), they will have difficulty applying any meaning to the words they are reading. Likewise, if someone has trouble decoding words, even though they have strong language-related skills, they too will have difficulties comprehending text.

Providing children with access to high-quality early learning opportunities that support the development of early literacy skills through developmentally appropriate approaches, such as play and inquiry, is essential to upholding their right to become literate members of our global community. The Reggio Emilia approach honors children's early literacy learning by fostering curiosity, language-rich interactions, and meaningful engagement with texts and ideas. When early literacy experiences are responsive, inclusive, and engaging, they lay a strong foundation for lifelong learning, critical thinking, and equitable participation in society. The Reggio Emilia approach offers a unique context for fostering foundational literacy skills, one that respects each child's natural curiosity as they embark on their early literacy journey.

Language and Early Literacy in a Reggio Environment

Within the Reggio Emilia approach, literacy-rich play environments that incorporate adaptable materials and open-ended props support children's problem-solving abilities, creativity, and language and literacy development, while also upholding children's right to become literate participants in a global community. These thoughtfully designed environments, combined with educators' purposeful planning and responsiveness to children's interests and targeted needs, create meaningful contexts in which language is actively constructed. Through explorations and long-term projects, children question, discuss, hypothesize, and observe, thereby expanding their vocabulary and refining their oral language skills. In Reggio-inspired settings, reading and writing are understood as tools for communication and expression and as essential skills that develop through thoughtfully-directed support and instruction in oral language, phonological awareness, and letter–sound knowledge. Writing materials are intentionally distributed throughout the environment to invite children to write, draw, and make marks as part of their meaning-making processes (Logaridis et al., 2012). Alongside direct and systematic instruction, particularly in letter-sound knowledge, these experiences provide children with opportunities to deepen their understanding of print. Children also come to recognize the purpose of conveying ideas, identities, and perspectives through multiple modes, reinforcing their role as capable, literate contributors within a broader social and cultural context (Rubizzi & Bonilauri, 2012).

AVENUES FOR LITERACY LEARNING

In a scoping review examining early literacy in Reggio classrooms (Beach, 2025), findings indicated that play, inquiry, and the arts served as key avenues for literacy learning, enabling children to develop early literacy skills through purposefully integrated experiences. For instance, a study by Henningsen (2013) documented examples of children's literacy learning while engaging in inquiry projects. Henningsen (2013) found that skills in oral language and writing occurred in authentic ways. Play, exploration, and the children's self-initiated activities often acted as a vehicle for literacy development, particularly oral language development. These play-as-learning opportunities led to meaning-making processes and growth in language and literacy skills.

Along with inquiry projects, the arts are also found to be important *avenues for literacy learning*. For example, in their ethnographic observational study, Souto-Manning and James (2008) explored how a multi-arts approach can develop greater literacy skills and retention of more knowledge. Souto-Manning and James (2008) argue that "multi-arts pedagogy has the potential to make learning experiences more meaningful and longer lasting" and that through ownership and choice, the arts are not only a tool for learning but also a venue for growth in language and literacy skills (p. 84). Through teacher questionnaires, observations, field notes, and video data, Souto-Manning and James (2008) found that the arts supported a variety of early literacy skills. The interactions, dialogue, creative problem-solving, and collaborations with peers and teachers contributed to growth in oral language, vocabulary, knowledge building, and storytelling. These arts-integrated experiences provided children with multiple entry points into literacy, catering to diverse learning styles and interests.

Through a sociocultural lens, Magnusson (2024) also demonstrated how literacy, such as oral communication and writing, can be enriched through the use of visual arts and digital technology. In their ethnographic study, Magnusson (2024) video recorded and photographed "literacy events" of children aged two to four during blocks of time dedicated to the arts. Literacy events can be described as "occasions in which written language is integral to the nature of participants' interactions and their interpretative processes and strategies" (Heath, 1982, p. 50). The literacy events that Magnusson documented over the course of 18 months highlighted how the children's arts experiences, digital explorations, and interactions with literacy materials inspired them to engage in oral and written literacy behaviours. Magnusson's findings suggest that integrating the arts and technology into early childhood education can create meaningful avenues for literacy learning.

ENRICHED LITERACY ENVIRONMENTS

In addition to highlighting avenues for literacy learning, Reggio spaces have been described as *enriched literacy environments* (Beach, 2025). As noted earlier, the Reggio philosophy considers the physical learning space as a "third teacher"

(Gandini, 2012). This space is thoughtfully designed to include provocations, music and arts materials, books and storytelling supplies, props for dramatic play, and labels throughout the room, among other elements. A literacy-focused provocation, for example, might feature a table with inviting letter tiles, alphabet rubber stamps or stencils, wooden letters, or sandpaper letters. The teacher or educator serves as a facilitator during play, guiding children's learning primarily based on their interests. For instance, if a child shows interest in writing a word to represent an object, the teacher works alongside them, supporting their attention to the sounds within the word and the formation of letters. These experiences can then be brought into a more directed and systematically oriented lesson or activity.

Beltchenko (2016) specifically examined the role of the environment in fostering language and literacy development in Reggio classrooms by focusing on the how purposefully selected materials, such as picture books, can contribute to a language-rich environment. The children in Beltchenko's study (2016) were invited to interact with picture books including Eric Carle's *The Very Hungry Caterpillar* (1987) after a read aloud. Observations highlighted how the children were able to transfer elements of the story to their play and to working with the objects and materials around the room. This integration of storytelling into play provided authentic opportunities for language use in meaningful contexts. The stories along with their illustrations led the children in Beltchenko's study (2016) to communicate their thinking about story elements and build their narrative skills, listening comprehension, and vocabulary.

These types of provocations are meant to inspire children, spark discussion, and prompt interactions. Strong-Wilson and Ellis (2007) note that it is through aesthetically pleasing objects and materials or provocations placed around the environment that children's curiosity and imagination are piqued. When children become interested in or begin to interact with provocations, the teacher observes and reflects on the child's learning and then carefully guides the child's next steps. In the context of early literacy, materials are presented in such a way as to provoke language and support children in learning new words, identifying print, and learning letter names and letter sounds.

MULTIMODAL STRATEGIES AND PROJECTS FOR LITERACY LEARNING

The following four vignettes present narrative accounts that illustrate how specific language and literacy skills can be fostered through multimodal strategies and project-based learning within a Reggio Emilia inspired environment. Grounded in a rights-based perspective, these stories reflect Reggio Emilia's commitment to realizing children's rights in a global context by honoring children as capable communicators, thinkers, and co-constructors of knowledge. Through play, inquiry, and the arts, the vignettes demonstrate how language and literacy development emerge when children's ideas and ways of knowing are respected and valued.

The narratives follow three children from an early childhood classroom—Eli, Camryn, and Connor—as they engage with one another and with their teachers, Sonya and Trevor. Each vignette is accompanied by a brief reflection and analysis that highlights how children's curiosity, the physical environment, the selected materials, and responsive teaching practices collectively supported a language or literacy event. As described earlier, a *literacy event* is an occasion in which written language plays a central role in how children interact with and make sense of information (Heath, 1982). Language is intentionally foregrounded here in recognition that the Reggio Emilia concept of the "hundred languages of children" and the essential role of oral language, vocabulary, and background knowledge in understanding and producing written text.

FOSTERING ORAL LANGUAGE THROUGH DRAMATIC PLAY

Eli, a 4-year-old preschooler eagerly swung open the fridge door of the play kitchen and started pulling out wooden fruits and vegetables with both hands. He carefully placed them onto a tabletop tray. Upon observing this activity, Camryn, a nearby preschooler asked, "What are you making?" Eli didn't answer right away; he was too focused on making sure the pile of play food didn't tumble off the tray. Camryn took a step closer and repeated the question, "What are you making?" "Ice cream," Eli finally replied without looking up, still arranging the pretend produce like it was the most important job in the world. Camyrn continued to observe him shuffle the play food for a moment before opening one of the play kitchen cupboards where cutlery, bowls, and cups were stored. She stood up with her arms full and facing Eli she started directing, "Put the fruit in this bowl and we can sell the ice cream." Eli paused, looked up, and said, "Okay." With a shared purpose, the children began organizing their ice cream shop.

Sonya, a teacher who had been watching this early interaction and allowing time for the dialogue to unfold, pulled a second table over to the area and suggested that it could serve as the counter for their ice cream shop. Continuing to work side-by-side, an example of *associative play*, the children lined up the bowls and placed various fruits and vegetables into them, occasionally picking up a ladle or spoon to stir their concoction. Sonya prompted, "What kind of ice cream are you selling?" to which Eli immediately stated, "Chocolate," followed by a satisfied, "Yummy." "I think we'll also make strawberry and rainbow ice cream," Camryn added. Sonya continued prompting their dialogue by exclaiming, "I bet your ice cream tastes delicious!"

Both the children nodded in agreement, now demonstrating elements of emerging cooperative play. Sonya continued to expand upon the children's initial talk about making and selling ice cream by asking, "Have you ever had delicious ice cream?" Eli responded first with a simple, "Yes," as he continued setting up the supplies. Sonya paused to consider whether she should step back from the children's play, but decided to support Eli's thinking with one more open-ended question: "Are you just selling ice cream or do you have any more delicious foods?" "We might sell pizza too," Eli replied, his eyes widening.

Reflection and Analysis

This brief interaction at the sociodramatic play area was initiated by the children, unfolded into a co-constructed learning experience, and was based on the presence of a shared pretend theme (ice-cream selling). Sonya observed first before thoughtfully intervening to help deepen the experience. By repositioning the environment to support the emerging idea of an ice cream shop, she used the physical space as the third teacher. Her questions were not directives but invitations, extending the children's play by highlighting the vocabulary word *delicious* as well as helping Eli enrich his ideas by asking open-ended questions. She invited the children to elaborate on their ice cream selling process, valuing their voices as active participants in their own learning, allowing the children to communicate verbal negotiations. By intentionally building on their play, Sonya supported the co-construction of knowledge and encouraged deeper exploration through meaningful dialogue.

USING "WORD PAINTING" TO ENHANCE VOCABULARY[3]

Over the past few weeks, the children in the preschool room had been gathering together as a community to listen to a collection of books by Roald Dahl. As Trevor, a visual arts teacher or *atelierista*[4], opened *James and the Giant Peach* (1961), the novel currently on the go, he invited the children to listen for new or interesting words while he read aloud. Connor, one of the preschoolers listening to the story, raised his hand after a few minutes and said, "Whirl." Trevor paused and wrote this word down on a nearby whiteboard or *word collector* before continuing to read. As he read, the children continued to raise their hands and share words that they had heard from the story. By the end of the chapter a list of 12 words had been generated. Though the children were just beginning to associate letters with sounds, this collective exercise became a shared exploration. It honored the children's voices and their capacity to notice and wonder. It also provided an opportunity for the children to deepen their understanding of how written text and language communicate information.

After reading, Trevor invited the children over to a nearby table where large white canvases, jars of paints, and paint brushes were thoughtfully arranged as provocations. Each child found a stool, slipped on their smock, and joined the space with excitement. Trevor explained, "We're going to paint the words we heard from the story. Let's start with *whirl*." As he said the selected word, Trevor made a motion with his hand, swirling it in the air to resemble the action of the word. Connor quickly decided on the red paint before making swirling marks with his paintbrush. Around him, the other children selected colours and made various marks and lines across their canvases.

Reflection and Analysis

As the children created their word paintings, they were given the opportunity to connect the word to a visual and sonic representation directly related to the word's meaning (Beach & Bolden, 2019). The process of creating an action associated with the word provided the children with a chance to experiment and explore with visual arts while at the same time consider a visual way to illustrate how the word should sound. By integrating the visual arts with rhythm and literacy, the children were able to engage in "multimodal meaning making" (Beach & Bolden, 2019, p. 754). This type of process contributes to the development of vocabulary depth and also promotes word consciousness and an enjoyment for learning about and using new words. From a Reggio Emilia perspective, this approach upholds children's rights in a global context by honoring multiple languages of expression and positioning children as active meaning makers whose ideas and cultural ways of knowing are valued.

INCORPORATING MUSIC AND MATERIALS TO BOOST SKILLS IN PHONOLOGICAL AWARENESS AND LETTER-SOUND ASSOCIATIONS

Sonya had been noticing the preschool children's interest in the sounds of language during their informal conversations with each other and the adults in the room. She specifically noticed that several children were stretching out the sounds in some of the words that they were hearing, often exploring the associated rhythms and repetitions. One recent morning, Sonya had observed an exchange between Eli and Connor in which they stretched out the sounds in words while they co-constructed a castle using wooden blocks, colourful gems, and miniature characters. Eli had said, "I'm making a wall around the castle" to which Connor responded, "/c/ /c/ caaaaaaasssstle." This observation, along with other similar ones over the past week, inspired Sonya to build onto and extend the children's interest in playing with sounds in words by incorporating rhyming games, music, and other relevant materials into their play. She recognized this thread of inquiry and wanted to deepen the children's emerging interest in the sounds of language. This seemed especially timely given that many of the children were able to recognize the letter names and associate the names with the correct letter sounds and symbols.

The following day, Sonya introduced a variety of materials and provocations into the classroom environment, including rhyming picture cards, magnetic letters, wooden letters, light-box letters, instruments, and simple storybooks. These were not presented as lessons, but rather as open-ended possibilities designed to support the children's construction of meaning through sound and play. During an extended period of uninterrupted play, the children engaged with the provocations in a variety of ways. Eli, for instance, experimented with nonsense words by arranging the magnetic letters into both short and long strings. After forming the nonsense word *bokt*, Eli asked what it said. Sonya smiled as she read the word aloud, and Eli laughed. Other children invented rhymes for familiar objects in the room, and a few began creating rhythmic sound patterns using the instruments and picture rhyming cards.

Reflection and Analysis

Sonya's observations and reflections of the children engaged in their play led to meaningful and authentic avenues for them to deepen their phonological awareness and alphabet knowledge. Through their explorations of the sounds of language, the children expanded their understanding of the alphabet and letter-sound correspondences. This child-led inquiry stemmed from the children's interest in language, guiding both the curriculum and Sonya's planning. This experience can be described as a *play-as-learning* opportunity in which the children's self-initiated inquiry into language sounds acted as a vehicle for literacy development. While Sonya had also been using a letter-sound scope and sequence to ensure that the children were receiving direct and systematic instruction in letter-sound associations, in the play-as-learning context, her thoughtful planning and use of provocative materials also provided the children with multiple entry points from which new directions and lines of inquiry could be meaningfully created. By supporting children's agency and honoring their ideas, this Reggio Emilia inspired approach upholds children's rights in a global context, ensuring that all children are recognized as capable thinkers and valued contributors to their own learning.

SUPPORTING EARLY SKILLS IN WRITTEN COMPOSITION THROUGH SHADOW PLAY, DRAWINGS, AND LABELS

For several weeks, the preschool children had been exploring light through shadow play with their atelierista, Trevor. This line of inquiry began with projections of found objects and natural materials, like pinecones and leaves, onto a blank wall. The children's experimentations with these objects from around the room and outdoors led them to projecting illustrations from their collection of Eric Carle picture books. Camryn was the first to discover this when she splayed a page from *The Tiny Seed* by Eric Carle (2007), on top of the projector. Instantly, the page's illustration and accompanying text appeared on the wall canvas. The children were in awe of the page's magnification and began to collect other picture books and drawings to display.

At one point, Eli brought over his own drawing he had just finished illustrating and placed it on the projector. An image appeared on the wall; Eli stood proudly admiring his creation. Trevor stood nearby and tilted his head, "What have you drawn?" he asked Eli. "It's a monkey in a tree," Eli replied. With this response, Trevor moved closer and handed Eli a marker. "Would you like to write a label for your drawing?" Trevor asked. Eli took hold of the marker in a grip that closely resembled a standard tripod grip and waited. Recognizing this as a literacy event, Trevor prompted Eli to listen for the first sound in the word monkey; he stressed the beginning sound /m/. Eli responded with an excited "M!" and proceeded to write the capital letter, M. Trevor repeated the word several times as Eli attended to each sound before carefully writing, what he heard as, the corresponding letter. When the letters were formed and Eli put down the marker, Trevor and Eli looked up at the word "MUNKE" projected on the wall next to the image of the monkey in the tree that Eli had created.

Reflection and Analysis

When children listen for individual sounds in words and then proceed to write down corresponding letters, they are engaged in several literacy behaviours. They're demonstrating their phonemic awareness by isolating the individual sounds in the word, exhibiting their alphabet knowledge by connecting the sound to the corresponding letter, and practicing their letter formations and pencil grip by writing the letter on the provided surface. When combined, these behaviours can be described as *invented spelling*. Martins and Silva (2006) suggest that engaging in invented spelling can promote the capacity to analyze words at the phoneme level and can be used as a pedagogical practice for preschool children. This practice also follows the child's lead and positions the teacher as a facilitator co-constructing knowledge about print and language with the child. In the example above, *monkey* is not quite complete as the letter *y* is absent, and *u* is written in place of *o*. However, Eli has demonstrated knowledge of most of the letter-sound associations in the word, and it was the way in which the word was pronounced that led Eli to hear /u/ rather than /o/. Given Eli's proud response to writing this word, the teacher decides to wait before showing him the correct spelling of *monkey* or explaining the rule governing the *ey* spelling pattern. In doing so, Trevor supports Eli's right to explore and experiment with language, valuing his ideas and allowing him to take an active role in shaping his own literacy learning.

CONCLUSION

This chapter has emphasized the critical importance of fostering language and early literacy through high-quality early childhood education programs that respect and nurture children's natural curiosity about the world. The Reggio Emilia approach offers a distinctive context in which language and literacy can thrive through inquiry, play, and the arts. As educators, we must continually reflect on how our programs support children's learning, ensuring their right to literacy through rich, meaningful experiences while also creating environments that align with their needs and interests. Literacy learning is not solely about developing skills; it is also about cultivating a lifelong motivation for literacy. By helping children build this foundation, we can empower *all* children to explore the many functions of language and literacy, including understanding their rights and responsibilities, and advocating for justice and equality.

REFERENCES

Adams, M. J. (1990). *Beginning to read: Thinking and learning about print.* MIT Press.

Armbruster, B. B., Lehr, F., Osborn, J., O'Rourke, R., Beck, I., Carnine, D., & Simmons, D. (2001). *Put reading first.* National Institute for Literacy, National Institute of Child Health and Human Development, US Department of Education. https://www.nichd.nih.gov/publications/product/239

Beach, P. (2025). Research on early literacy in Reggio and Montessori classrooms: A scoping review. *Journal of Early Childhood Literacy, 25*(3), 694–722. DOI: 10.1177/14687984231186090

Beach, P., & Bolden, B. (2019). Word painting: Using a musical technique to enhance vocabulary. *The Reading Teacher, 72*(6), 750–754. https://www.jstor.org/stable/26801678. DOI: 10.1002/trtr.1780

Beltchenko, L. (2016). Intellectual pursuits of young children through picture book literacy, focusing on Italian preschools. *Gifted Child Today, 39*(3), 145–153. https://doi-org.proxy.queensu.ca/10.1177/1076217516644. DOI: 10.1177/1076217516644636

Bruner, J. (1997). Celebrating divergence: Piaget and Vygotsky. *Human Development, 40*(2), 63–73. DOI: 10.1159/000278705

Carle, E. (1987). *The very hungry caterpillar.* Philomel Books.

Carle, E. (2007). *The tiny seed.* Neugebauer Press.

Cavanaugh, D. M., Clemence, K. J., Teale, M. M., Rule, A. C., & Montgomery, S. E. (2017). Kindergarten scores, storytelling, executive function, and motivation improved through literacy-rich guided play. *Early Childhood Education Journal, 45*(6), 831–843. DOI: 10.1007/s10643-016-0832-8

Cheatham, J. P., & Allor, J. H. (2012). The influence of decodability in early reading text on reading achievement: A review of the evidence. *Reading and Writing, 25*(9), 2223–2246. DOI: 10.1007/s11145-011-9355-2

Dahl, R. (1961). *James and the giant peach.* Knopf.

Gandini, L. (2012). *The Hundred languages of children: The Reggio Emilia experience in transformation.* Praeger.

Glassman, M. (2001). Dewey and Vygotsky: Society, experience, and inquiry in educational practice. *Educational Researcher, 30*(4), 3–14. DOI: 10.3102/0013189X030004003

Hadley, E. B., Dickinson, D. K., Hirsh-Pasek, K., & Golinkoff, R. M. (2019). Building semantic networks: The impact of a vocabulary intervention on preschoolers' depth of word knowledge. *Reading Research Quarterly, 54*(1), 41–61. DOI: 10.1002/rrq.225

Heath, S. B. (1982). What no bedtime story means: Narrative skills at home and school. *Language in Society, 11*(1), 49–76. DOI: 10.1017/S0047404500009039

Henningsen, M. (2013). Making sense of experience in preschool: Children's encounters with numeracy and literacy through inquiry. *South African Journal of Childhood Education, 3*(2), 41–55. DOI: 10.4102/sajce.v3i2.39

Hoover, W. A., & Gough, P. B. (1990). The simple view of reading. *Reading and Writing, 2*(2), 127–160. DOI: 10.1007/BF00401799

Justice, L. M., & Pullen, P. C. (2003). Promoting the development of language and literacy in children at risk: A comparison of two early interventions. *Journal of Educational Psychology, 95*(2), 368–379.

Logaridis, L., Tranter, K., & Siegrist, L. (2012). Make it meaningful! Emergent literacy in the kindergarten years. *The Early Childhood Educator.* https://playfullyinspireddotcom1.wordpress.com/2014/04/13/make-it-meaningful/

Lonigan, C. J., & Shanahan, T. (2009). Developing early literacy: Report of the National Early Literacy Panel. Executive summary. A scientific synthesis of early literacy development and implications for intervention. *National Institute for Literacy.* https://files.eric.ed.gov/fulltext/ED508381.pdf

Magnusson, L. O. (2024). 'Look, my name! I can write'–Literacy events and digital technology in the preschool atelier. *Journal of Early Childhood Literacy, 24*(2), 253–275. DOI: 10.1177/14687984211058943

Malaguzzi, L. (2012). No Way. The hundred is there. In Edwards, C., Gandini, L., & Forman, G. (Eds.), *The Hundred Languages of Children: The Reggio Emilia Experience in Transformation* (p. 3). ABC-CLIO.

Martins, M. A., & Silva, C. (2006). The impact of invented spelling on phonemic awareness. *Learning and Instruction, 16*(1), 41–56. DOI: 10.1016/j.learninstruc.2005.12.005

Maureen, I. Y., van der Meij, H., & de Jong, T. (2020). Enhancing storytelling activities to support early (digital) literacy development in early childhood education. *International Journal of Early Childhood*, *52*(1), 55–76. DOI: 10.1007/s13158-020-00263-7

Peterson, H. (2023). Scribbling in early childhood: Why do young children make marks? *Exchange*, *270*, •••. https://hub.exchangepress.com/articles-on-demand/3182/

Piasta, S. B. (2023). The science of early alphabet instruction. In Cabell, S. Q., Neuman, S. B., & Terry, N. P. (Eds.), *Handbook on the science of early literacy* (pp. 83–94). Guilford Publications.

Pyle, A., Prioletta, J., & Poliszczuk, D. (2018). The play-literacy interface in full-day kindergarten classrooms. *Early Childhood Education Journal*, *46*(1), 117–127. DOI: 10.1007/s10643-017-0852-z

Rand, M., & Morrow, L. (2021). The contribution of play experiences in early literacy: Expanding the science of reading. *Reading Research Quarterly*, *56*(S1), S239–S248. DOI: 10.1002/rrq.383

Riley-Ayers, S. (2013). Supporting language and literacy development in quality preschools. In Barone, D. M., & Mallette, M. H. (Eds.), *Best practices in early literacy instruction* (pp. 58–78). The Guilford Press.

Rubizzi, L., & Bonilauri, S. (2012). From messages to writing: Experiences in literacy. In Edwards, C., Gandini, L., & Forman, G. (Eds.), *The Hundred languages of children: The Reggio Emilia experience in transformation* (pp. 213–231). ABC-CLIO.

Schwanenflugel, P. J., & Knapp, N. F. (2015). *The psychology of reading: Theory and applications*. Guilford Publications.

Snow, C. E. (2017). *Early literacy development and instruction: An overview*. The Routledge International Handbook of Early Literacy Education. DOI: 10.4324/9781315766027-2

Souto-Manning, M., & James, N. (2008). A multi-arts approach to early literacy and learning. *Journal of Research in Childhood Education*, *23*(1), 82–95. DOI: 10.1080/02568540809594647

Sparks, R. L., Patton, J., & Murdoch, A. (2014). Early reading success and its relationship to reading achievement and reading volume: Replication of 10 years later. *Reading and Writing*, *27*(1), 189–211. DOI: 10.1007/s11145-013-9439-2

Stanley, C. T., Petscher, Y., & Catts, H. (2018). A longitudinal investigation of direct and indirect links between reading skills in kindergarten and reading comprehension in tenth grade. *Reading and Writing, 31*(1), 133–153. DOI: 10.1007/s11145-017-9777-6

Strong-Wilson, T., & Ellis, J. (2007). Children and place: Reggio Emilia's environment as third teacher. *Theory into Practice, 46*(1), 40–47. DOI: 10.1080/00405840709336547

Suggate, S., Schaughency, E., McAnally, H., & Reese, E. (2018). From infancy to adolescence: The longitudinal links between vocabulary, early literacy skills, oral narrative, and reading comprehension. *Cognitive Development, 47*, 82–95. DOI: 10.1016/j.cogdev.2018.04.005

Torgesen, J. K., & Mathes, P. G. (1998). *What every teacher should know about phonological awareness*. Florida Department of Education, Division of Schools and Community Education, Bureau of Instructional Support and Community Services. https://www.fullertonsd.org/cms/lib/CA50010905/Centricity/Domain/1993/PA-_what_you_should_know_.pdf

KEY TERMS AND DEFINITIONS

Alphabet Knowledge: The understanding that printed words are made up of letters and that these letters are associated with sounds heard when the word is said aloud.

Associative Play: Instances of play in which children work independently alongside each other with similar materials; this form of play often leads to emerging cooperative play.

Oral Language Development: To acquire, understand, and use spoken language.

Phonemic Awareness: The ability to notice, think about, and manipulate the smallest speech sounds (phonemes) in words.

Phonological Awareness: The ability to notice, think about, and manipulate the sounds in spoken language.

Print Awareness: An understanding that print carries meaning and can be used to communicate ideas and information.

Vocabulary Development: To gain an understanding of words and their meanings through implicit and explicit interactions and instruction.

Word Consciousness: An enjoyment in learning about and using words in a variety of ways and contexts.

Word Painting: The process of sonically and visually representing a word and its meaning.

ENDNOTES

1 The back slashes surrounding a letter signify the letter sound rather than the letter name.

2 Fine motor skills are small hand muscle movements that require close hand-eye coordination and represent a skill set linked to handwriting, although fine motor movements are important for a range of activities (Bart, Hajami, & Bar-Haim, 2007).

3 This vignette is based on the article, Beach, P., & Bolden, B. (2019). Word painting: Using a musical technique to enhance vocabulary. *The Reading Teacher*, *72*(6), 750-754. https://www.jstor.org/stable/26801678

4 An atelierista is a teacher with a background in the visual arts who works closely with the other teachers and the children in a special workshop or studio known as the atelier (Gandini, 2012).

Chapter 5
An Absolute Possibility: The Reggio Emilia Approach in Diverse Settings in South Africa

Sarah Jane Browne
http://orcid.org/0009-0001-4718-5546
Africa Reggio Emilia Alliance (AREA), South Africa & Reddam House Waterfall Early Learning School, South Africa

ABSTRACT

This chapter is a comprehensive overview of the potential of the Reggio Emilia approach in diverse settings in South Africa. It traces aspects of the historical legacy of apartheid on education and the ongoing inequalities affecting early childhood education. It highlights ongoing challenges such as limited resources, formalised teaching methods, and disparities related to access. The chapter presents the Reggio Emilia approach as a philosophy of education that focuses on children's rights, agency, creativity, and the significance of learning environments while emphasising the culture of the atelier and the role of the atelierista. Through various case studies of South African schools and communities, it illustrates the transformative potential of this approach, even in under-resourced settings. The chapter underscores the resonance between the Reggio Emilia philosophy and South Africa's aspirations for social justice, advocating for educational reform, and professional development. It acts as a call to action to ensure every child's right to a quality, creative education.

DOI: 10.4018/979-8-3373-3431-8.ch005

INTRODUCTION

Background to the Education Landscape

South Africa, a land filled with promise, beauty, and numerous possibilities, also faces challenges that can be seen as creating rich learning opportunities in various settings. Education in South Africa has been influenced by many factors, both past and present. South African society consists of various cultures, economic backgrounds, with 12 official languages. While early childhood education is currently a hot topic of discussion, historically, little has been done to improve it or ensure children's rights and access to it.

Historical Context

Many of these challenges can be traced back to apartheid, a system of racial segregation resulting in unequal education. The Nationalist Party implemented apartheid, creating deep educational disparities reinforced by racist policies. The Bantu Education Act of 1952 further entrenched inequalities, with the black majority receiving education designed to limit their potential and maintain their position within the working class. This impacted the content, quality, and access to education for Black people, entrenching a divide and fostering racial segregation (Ocampo, 2004).

During apartheid, various Departments of Education were segregated by race, resulting in reduced funding and significant inequalities for Bantu Education. Schools affiliated with churches had their funding withdrawn, affecting the quality of teachers. The government justified this withdrawal of funding as a necessary separation between Church and State.

Current Challenges in Early Education

This history often affects early education today, with teachers' personal history of schooling frequently resulting in an inappropriate, formal approach. Historically too, early childhood teachers have not been highly regarded and even today receive minimal pay. This impacts their economic stability, their access to transportation and financial resources.

Early childhood education is much needed and many children in under-resourced contexts lack access to these services. Early childhood settings are often the only places where children receive daily meals, leading to overcrowding and limited resources. Additionally, the number of children living in dire need on the streets poses great challenges in terms of access to education, care and safety.

Furthermore, very many early childhood settings are unregistered and operate in small, cramped conditions. Registration with the Education Department is daunting and expensive, although the recent improvements and assistance have been encouraging.

Policy Changes

Until recently, Early Childhood Development (ECD) fell under the Department of Social Development in South Africa with many ECD centres receiving some supplies and assistance with meals. On the 1st of April 2022, ECD was migrated to the Department of Basic Education (DBE) in a bid to support ECD programmes. This caused some disruption and a gap that still needs to be urgently addressed in South Africa. (Department of Basic Education - Republic of South Africa, 2022)

In addition, the DBE has made Grade R or 0 (for 5 and 6-year-olds), compulsory as the entry point to Grade 1, the first year of formal education, and part of the Foundation Phase in the public schooling system. (Department of Basic Education - Republic of South Africa, 2025). An unintended consequence of this is that children younger than five are sometimes placed in these Grade R classrooms by parents since this is free or much cheaper than sending them to an ECD centre. This has a knock-on effect financially of reduced numbers in surrounding ECD centres.

Feedback From Teachers

At the Fondazione Reggio Children and Lego Foundation Play, Education and Research (P.E.R.) Conference in Johannesburg in October 2024, during a breakaway on policy development, led by Cristian Fabbi, Director General of the Fondazione Reggio Children, ECD teachers' feedback highlighted several challenges they face. Their key concerns included curriculum, assessment, reporting, funding, resources, and ongoing support with the government-mandated curriculum. Educators feel pressured by the DBE's 'blueprint,' which they perceive as restrictive, leading to a fragmented approach to curriculum, skills, and themes.

Figure 1. Africa Reggio Emilia Alliance at the Fondazione Reggio Children and Lego Foundation P.E.R (Play Explore Research) Conference in Johannesburg, Gauteng, South Africa, October 2024

CONSEQUENCES OF CHALLENGES

One of the challenges facing ECD, and education in general, in South Africa is that some universities seem to employ traditional teaching methods to train educators. This makes it difficult for students to adopt new approaches, often leading them to revert to more conventional methodologies when they get into a classroom. Consistent support and professional development in these settings are crucial.

There also appears to be misinterpretation among teachers whose home language is not English of aspects of the blueprint for Grade R as outlined in the national Curriculum and Assessment Policy (CAPS) curriculum. It would seem that they have understood the term "compulsory" to mean that Grade R must be taught formally, particularly as Grade R is now considered part of formal education. Consequently, this has stifled creativity among children, who are taught formally or in rote fashion as they sit behind desks. Instead, they should be experiencing an inquiry- and play-based approach allowing them freedom, agency, and autonomy to engage creatively and kinaesthetically, as they make sense of the world around them.

Furthermore, it appears as if teachers feel pressured by the CAPS grid assessment, which categorizes children's achievement according to various criteria. This stifles teachers' thinking and risks labelling children on the strength of superficial assessments.

Furthermore, the over-reliance on photocopied, colouring-in worksheets or DBE booklets, affects both teachers' and children's autonomy and creativity. Moreover, creativity has been relegated to the silo of Life Skills within the mandated CAPS curriculum, and not as a characteristic common to all disciplines and all children.

Numerous teacher-directed activities also fail to promote children's expression, critical thinking and reflection. Creativity is perceived as colouring in-between the lines, following instructions during collage-making, or completing craft-based, teacher directed tasks.

Another challenge for many schools is that they are held accountable for poor performance results, rather than the policymakers. This adds to the stress felt by teachers.

The need for urgent reforms in South Africa's early childhood education system remains critical.

RECENT RESEARCH

Several studies have been conducted in South Africa to examine the inequalities faced by individuals across various sectors of society. These studies highlight these disparities and the devastating consequences of apartheid, along with the ongoing racial segregation and division within society.

GINI Co-Efficient Study

The Gini coefficient, or index, is a statistical measure of inequality developed by Italian statistician Corrado Gini in 1912. The most recent data from 2023 highlight the significant inequality and the vast divide between the 'haves' and the 'have-nots,' which affects access to quality education.

South Africa's Gini coefficient is exceptionally high at 0.67, indicating the highest level of inequality in the world. The top 0.01% of the population owns approximately 15% of the country's wealth, while the top 1% holds 25%. In contrast, the bottom 50% of the population has a negative net worth, possessing more liabilities than assets. (Valodia, 2023).

This study highlights that race-based inequality continues to be a problem, which in turn affects access to quality education.

Progress in International Reading Literacy Study (PIRLS)

Another study conducted in 2021 is the Progress in International Reading Literacy Study (PIRLS), which assesses reading comprehension and monitors trends and indicators of growth in reading literacy every five years.

During this study, Africa was underrepresented, with South Africa being one of only three countries included. It was the only Sub-Saharan country to participate and ranked last among the 57 countries involved, scoring 288, which is significantly below the PIRLS centre point of 500. These alarming results can be attributed to several factors, including the COVID pandemic and the inaccessibility of quality education.

Thrive by Five Index

The Thrive by Five Index launched in April 2022, with a follow-up study in 2024, is the largest survey of preschool development in South Africa. The study aims to monitor enrolment in Early Learning Programmes and assess how many children are developmentally on track and ready for Grade 1. Areas of development evaluated include early learning, physical growth, and social and emotional functioning, all of which are predictors of performance in the Foundation Phase of schooling and beyond.

The key findings of the 2024 Index reveals that only 42% of enrolled children are developmentally on track, 7% are moderately or severely stunted, and 56% meet the standard for emotional readiness. (Department of Basic Education, 2024):

- Only 42% of enrolled children are developmentally on track in early learning, as measured by the Early Learning Measurement Tool (ELOM 4 & 5), with significant differences based on gender and socioeconomic circumstances.
- Girls outperform boys across all learning domains (except for gross motor development).
- Children in higher-fee early learning programs significantly outperform their peers in lower-fee programs.
- Across the domains, the strongest performance was in Emergent Literacy and Language, with 53% of children on track. This was followed by Gross Motor Development at 44%, Cognition and Executive Functioning at 40%, Emergent Numeracy and Mathematics at 33%, and Fine Motor Coordination and Visual-Motor Integration at 29%.
- Approximately 7% of enrolled children exhibit signs of moderate to severe stunting.
- Overall, 56% of children meet the standard for emotional readiness.

- 63% meet the standard for social relations with peers and adults.
- Girls are more likely than boys to meet the standards in both areas above.

The executive summary shows that most of the enrolled children are progressing well in early learning; however, a large portion of these children are experiencing moderate to severe stunting.

The results are concerning. Although the index shows improvement in the statistics of children thriving, a significant percentage are still not on track cognitively and/or physically. These children encounter numerous barriers that hinder their ability to reach their potential. South Africa will not achieve its developmental goals unless it addresses the substantial challenges faced by children in their earliest years. There is an urgent need for a collective effort to learn from past mistakes and to redefine a future that ensures quality education for every child in every context. (First National Bank (FNB) and Innovation Edge, 2022)

THE HOPE

In the dire situation facing education in South Africa, one must ask: "Where is the hope?"

On the flipside of the many challenges that early education faces in South Africa, it is a country filled with possibilities. There is a wonderful climate and a wide variety of ecosystems, wide open spaces, and landscapes, ranging from the mangrove swamps in KwaZulu Natal to the semi-desert in the Karoo. These rich possibilities are wonderful as children can explore and engage in these spaces.

Reflecting on the current state of early childhood education in South Africa, it is visibly apparent that the Reggio Emilia approach can bring hope to very bleak situations. Loris Malaguzzi, the founder of the Reggio Emilia approach, hoped for a childhood where children have many freedoms to investigate, to try, to make mistakes, and to correct them.

> *"Our experience once again confirms how children need lots of freedom. Freedom to investigate, to try things out, to make mistakes, and correct them. [Freedom] to choose where and with whom they will invest their curiosity, intelligence, and emotions; [freedom] to appreciate the infinite resources of hands, of sight and hearing, of shapes, of materials, of sounds and of colours; [freedom] to realise how rationality, thinking, and imagination, create constant weavings between things and how they move the world, they move it on." – Loris Malaguzzi (Reggio Children Srl, 2022)*

In the Reggio Emilia approach, children are placed at the centre and seen as competent, capable, resourceful, and curious individuals. Loris Malaguzzi wrote

"The 100 Languages," a poetic declaration that explores the many ways children can express themselves and how they make sense of the world around them. (Reggio Children Srl, 2022)

The beauty of the Reggio Emilia approach is that it places the rights of the child at the forefront of the approach. It is a philosophy of education that requires teachers to stand back and allow for meaningful learning.

A Description of the Reggio Emilia Approach

The Reggio Emilia approach was birthed in 1945 in Reggio Emilia, Italy. It is a rights-based, socio-constructivist educational philosophy centred on an image of children as strong, competent, and resourceful citizens from birth. Children construct their own knowledge, make meaning of experiences through relationships with others and the world around them, and communicate their understanding in various ways.

PEDAGOGICAL PRINCIPLES

There is a significant relationship between pedagogy and politics. In Reggio Emilia, children are recognized as subjects of law with their own rights. The city embraces the ideas of children, viewing itself as a large school dedicated to educating all children. The Municipal Preschools and Infant-Toddler Centres are regarded as public spaces that are interconnected with the city.

Loris Malaguzzi, founder of the approach, referred to children's ways of constructing their understanding as "languages" in his poem "The 100 Languages of Children." This poem serves as a poetic manifesto for the approach, articulating the rights, intentions, skills, and competencies of children while also highlighting the ineffective teaching methods often found in education.

Slow Pedagogy

The approach is a "slow pedagogy," allowing children time to engage in meaningful research and to express themselves through many symbolic "languages." It advocates for teachers to plan by design, considering children's interests and reactions in different contexts, recognizing that children need to engage autonomously in their own learning in relation to others and their environment. This demands a fully attuned teacher who walks alongside the children rather than leading from the front or directing from the back.

This philosophy of education offers hope and value to children's expressive potential and fosters a participatory love of lifelong learning. It presents a hopeful framework for improving early childhood education.

> *"The first pillar of this pedagogical approach is the centrality of the rights of children. Children are considered citizens of today and not just of tomorrow and, therefore, are the bearers of rights, including political rights, which must be respected and promoted." - Cristian Fabbi*
> (Fabbi, 2022)

Figure 2. Cristian Fabbi, Director General of the Fondazione Reggio Children at Bekezela Creche, Johannesburg, Gauteng, South Africa, October 2022

In the 1970s, Loris Malaguzzi introduced the role of an atelierista and the atelier to the Reggio Emilia approach to create a different lens on education in the schools of Reggio Emilia. This set the Reggio Emilia approach apart from all other educational theories or methodologies.

An atelierista is someone with an art background whose different perspective is a catalyst for thought, providing a scaffold for children, teachers, and parents. This person collaborates with children, documenting their learning processes and creating numerous opportunities for the expression of children's thinking and ideas. An atelierista is not an art teacher but a co-researcher and co-constructor of knowledge alongside the children.

The atelier, a laboratory of research, is like the engine room - a place of welcome where ideas are generated, expressed, and valued. It is more than just a physical space or concept but a mindset permeating throughout the school, so that the school becomes a large, widespread atelier. When setting up an atelier or a context for learning, we need to ensure that children have opportunities to use many of the expressive languages.

Figure 3. The Everywhere Atelier, a Reggio Emilia inspired laboratory of research at Reddam House Waterfall Early Learning School, Midrand, Gauteng, South Africa, April 2025

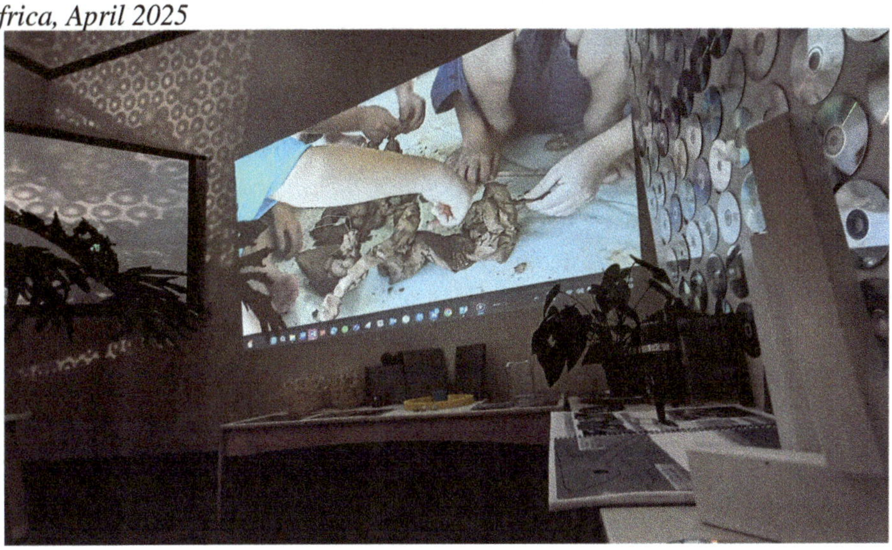

"The Reggio Emilia approach is not a recipe. It doesn't tell you what to do. Rather, it's an educational approach rooted in Reggio Emilia, one that asks you to be respectful and mindful of your context and community – to be aware of questions like where your children come from, where they live, what their days are like, what they miss or want, to be able to welcome the children and their culture. To think that it is a model to implement (that is, to do it in any other way) is to betray the approach." – Tiziana Filippini, Pedadgogista on the historical team with Loris Malaguzzi (Browne J., 2017)

It is important to remember education is a right, a right for everyone, for all children. It is the responsibility of the community to strengthen the educational dialogue in all contexts and to remember that each child has a unique identity, with his or her own relationship with the world and a personal story that takes place in a social setting.

Africa Reggio Emilia Alliance (AREA)

With this hope in mind, Tessa Browne, Co-Founder and Co-Ordinator of the Africa Reggio Emilia Alliance (AREA), began her journey in 2008 to research how to foster and ensure children's right to creativity.

Tessa Browne, Co-Founder and Co-Ordinator of the Africa Reggio Emilia Alliance, shares:

"South Africa has a proud history of activism for social justice and basic human rights of all the inhabitants of our country are enshrined in our constitution. Children's rights receive specific treatment ...in reality few people seem to question what protecting and advocating for children's rights means in the daily life of children, families, communities, societies, nations... Had I ever been asked (previously) for my opinion about children's rights and their citizenship, I would probably have said that children should be taught how to be citizens at home and at school - as if citizens are to be moulded and developed by others. I would not have given any thought to what it means to say that a new born or a young child has rights and that these need to be manifested in the contexts children inhabit - like my own classroom. (Browne T., 2025)

Tessa had long been interested in visiting the schools of Reggio Emilia and was thrilled when Desiree Hugo, the new Head of St Mary's Junior School, asked her whether she had heard about the Reggio approach.

With Desiree's support, Tessa applied for and was awarded an ISASA (Independent Schools Association of Southern Africa) overseas visitorship to participate in the Reggio Children International Study Group in April 2008 in Reggio Emilia, Italy. Desiree Hugo joined her and from the first presentation by Carla Rinaldi, they both recognised that the Reggio approach could significantly impact education in South Africa and felt compelled to share it with others. They invited Reggio Children from Reggio Emilia to hold a conference in South Africa, but it was decided this should be delayed untill more people knew about the approach.

Figure 4. Tessa Browne and Desiree Hugo, Co-Founder's of the Africa Reggio Emilia Alliance (AREA) arrive in Reggio Emilia, Italy, for the first time in April 2008 to attend Reggio Children's International Study Group

In an interview with Tessa, she shared these insights:

"My first visit to Reggio Emilia ... led me to believe that all children are born with rights and should be treated as citizens from birth. So what would this mean if as a society we really held this as a truth instead of only paying lip service to it? Children's rights to well-being – their nutrition, emotional and physical health, safety and education should be an imperative in society. Children's feeding schemes in marginalised communities and underserved ECD Centres, must be re-instituted, hazardous and unsanitary living conditions need to be prioritised for development and upgrades, pit latrines should be replaced immediately with safer and more hygienic toilets, children who are at risk (e.g. children in child-headed households) need to be identified and given the support they desperately need. This is something that we need to advocate for as South Africans." (Browne T., 2025)

Tessa and Desiree developed an organisation to promote the approach, settling on the name Africa Reggio Emilia Alliance (AREA). Tessa also attended the July 2010 Summer School in Reggio Emilia, and gained more experience of the approach and, as the Head of Little Saints, the Pre-Primary Department at St Mary's Waverley, helped grow the approach in practice. In June 2011 they were ecstatic when Reggio Children agreed to a conference being held at St Mary's. Desiree and Tessa invited others to help with the conference. Parents at the school, Maurizio Mariano and Franco and Katia Pisapia volunteered to help and arranged finances. Maurizio connected them with the HIP Alliance (Hellenic, Italian, and Portuguese Alliance of South Africa) and various Italian Embassy staff and Department of Education officials.

During the June 2011 conference, Reggio Children invited Tessa and Desiree to attend the next meeting of the Reggio Children International Network and to become national representatives. In September 2011, they attended the Reggio Children International Network meeting and were introduced as new members of the Network.

A Memorandum of Incorporation establishing AREA as a not-for-profit company, was signed on January 27, 2014. Board members included Revd Peter Lee, Maurizio Mariano, Thandi Chaane, Dr. Beverly Evangelides, Sifiso Thobakale, Desiree Hugo, and Tessa Browne. Desiree became the chairperson and Tessa Browne the coordinator and administrator of all activities. AREA's mission is to work towards a better future for children in South Africa by providing professional development for educators across Africa on the Reggio Emilia approach, with a specific focus on schools in underserved communities.

Figure 5. Africa Reggio Emilia Alliance (AREA) Board Members in January 2025 in Johannesburg, Gauteng, South Africa

"The transformation effected by the approach, on children, educators, parents, grandparents, school auxiliary staff is remarkable. It embodies a vision of a different, way of living in which one can dare to hope for peace in a more just, equitable society embracing a sustainable future for humankind." (Browne T., 2025)

Support and Connections Between Reggio Emilia and South Africa

The city of Reggio Emilia and the resistance movement in South Africa have enjoyed a long and significant relationship. In the 1970s, the city actively promoted the anti-apartheid movement abroad and supported struggle exiles like Oliver Tambo and Anthony Mongalo. The city signed a solidarity pact with the African National Congress (ANC) in 1977. Giuseppe Soncini, a driving force behind the Pact of Solidarity, became close friends with Oliver Tambo, the President of the ANC. In 1978, Reggio Emilia hosted the National Conference of Solidarity for the Independence and Sovereignty of the Peoples of Southern Africa against Colonialism, Racism, and Apartheid. (The Presidency of the Republic of South Africa, 2025)

In 1978, the Municipality of Reggio Emilia published *Sechaba*, the official newsletter of the ANC, in Italian. In 1982, they released the first Italian edition of *The Struggle is My Life*, a collection of Nelson Mandela's speeches and political writings. At the second national consultative conference of the ANC in Zambia in 1985, Reggio Emilia was declared "a constituted strength against the regime of apartheid," making it the only European city mentioned. (Africa Reggio Emilia Alliance (AREA))

During the apartheid years, aid was sent to South Africa, and Tambo frequently visited Reggio Emilia. (Africa Reggio Emilia Alliance (AREA))

Figure 6. 27 June 1977, Reggio Emilia: Oliver R. Tambo (ANC President), José Luis Cabaco (a minister of the People's Republic of Mozambique) and Giuseppe Soncini (a city councillor and the creator and promoter of popular internationalism in Reggio Emilia) arrive at the Tricolour Flag Hall to sign the solidarity pact between this town and the ANC (Istoreco Reggio Emilia - Reggio Africa Archives - Bruna Soncini Ganapini Archives - Comune di Reggio Emilia, 1997) (Comune di Reggio Emilia, 1977)

Figure 7. The Second Italian Solidarity Ship was set up by a national campaign managed by the city of Reggio Emilia (Istoreco Reggio Emilia - Reggio Africa Archives - Bruna Soncini Ganapini Archives - Comune di Reggio Emilia)

In a letter to the city of Reggio Emilia, Oliver Tambo expressed his deep gratitude for the incredible support that Giuseppe Soncini and the city provided to the ANC during the struggle against Apartheid. He wrote, "We always carry Reggio Emilia in our hearts; when we speak of Italy, we cannot help but think of Reggio Emilia. We are linked with profound attachment and immense gratitude that is hard to put into words." (The Presidency of the Republic of South Africa, 2025)

The poem "100 Languages" is like the starting point for research in an atelier and in the rest of the school. The poem serves as a reference to the many ways of teaching children. It is a poetic statement about the rights, intentions, skills, and competencies of children, and questions unsuitable ways of teaching that are often found in more traditional schools.

Loris Malaguzzi said that children have a hundred languages "but they (adults, schools, and culture) steal ninety-nine." This is from a metaphorical perspective. The main form of language is verbal, yet children use many other "languages" or ways to express themselves and make meaning. Since birth, humans possess the genetic capacity and skills to communicate in hundreds of ways. The more languages and possibilities we recognize in children, the greater their opportunities to develop and construct their own learning.

Figure 8. 6 year old engaging in the language of drawing in the Wetlands, an extension of the Everywhere Atelier at Reddam House Waterfall Early Learning School, Midrand, Gauteng, South Africa, 2025

Languages in the Reggio Emilia sense can be considered types of learning tools that both children and adults can use as competencies in their learning processes. In the Reggio Emilia approach, this refers specifically to expressive languages; the visual arts, drawing, painting, sculpting, theatre, dance, architecture, music, and poetry. It is important to reflect on and think about other creative concepts that relate to these, such as imagination, creativity, and expression, for example.

There is always a connection between children's languages and their learning processes. At times, alternative methods of communication are necessary beyond just spoken language. A broad, joyful, and playful approach to language is essential, encompassing not only verbal communication but also the language of sounds that helps children make sense of their experiences.

Figure 9. Two 6 year olds - The language of drawing in the Digital Landscapes and Light atelier at Reddam House Waterfall Early Learning School, Midrand, Gauteng, South Africa, 2025

Educators must create playful and joyful environments for children, allowing them the freedom to interpret the provided context. Integrating graphic arts into this approach acknowledges their tremendous value as tools for cognitive, linguistic, and social development.

> *"The atelier serves two functions. First, it provides a place for children to become masters of all kinds of techniques, such as painting, drawing, and working in clay – all the symbolic languages. Second, it assists the adults in understanding processes of how children learn... The atelier has an important, provocative, and disturbing effect on old-fashioned teaching ideas." – Vea Vecchi, Atelierista (Vea Vecchi, 1998)*

Atelieristas and teachers are not in the ateliers with children to solve problems; but to amplify problems, encouraging children to explore them more deeply. Whether their idea about a problem is effective or not, it becomes an invitation for others to engage in thought. If it doesn't work, it does not matter, as the process of thinking is beautiful in itself.

In Reggio Emilia, it is noteworthy that the various ateliers in schools are equipped with real instruments and tools typically used in professional settings; they are not plastic toys for children. There is a profound sense of trust, allowing children the agency to work with these resources, with an attuned adult coming alongside them in support.

Figure 10. The Digital Landscapes & Light Atelier, a Reggio Emilia inspired laboratory of research and extension of the Everywhere Atelier at Reddam House Waterfall Early Learning School, Midrand, Gauteng, South Africa, 2025

The atelier and the 100 Languages unlocks all children. Sarah Browne, resident atelierista in an Early Learning School shares some of her findings, *"The more time children with special rights spend in the Everywhere Atelier, a laboratory of research where many possibilities of the 100 Languages are offered, the more confident they become. I have noticed that they begin to experiment with media, often taking cues from other children in their small group. These children spontaneously find their way back to the atelier even when their class is not scheduled to be there, highlighting the children's sense of belonging in this space."*

The culture of the atelier, encompassing attitudes and mind-sets, needs to extend throughout all areas of a school. It should not be confined to the atelier and the atelierista but rather should be manifested and permeated throughout the entire school. This means that it is important for educators to spend time thinking through materials ahead of time when planning with intentionality. This preparation affects every aspect of the children's experience and engagement and significantly impacts their learning processes and right to a quality education.

Image of Child

In Reggio Emilia, the belief in children's rich potential, competence, creativity, curiosity and ability to construct their own understanding of the world around them, applies to all children. Children with special rights are prioritised for placement in the schools and an extra educator is allocated for each child with special rights. This educator serves as a liaison between the staff, the child with special rights and other children in the class. This creates a safe environment for children with special rights while benefitting all the children in the class.

Figure 11. 6 year olds in the Wetlands at Reddam House Waterfall Early Learning School, Midrand, Gauteng, South Africa, 2024

This inclusive strategy offers hope and significant implications for children with special rights in South Africa who are often kept at home or overlooked. By raising awareness of the special rights of these children, the Reggio Emilia approach acts as a catalyst for a crucial mindset shift among educators and the broader community.

A Relational, Listening, Participatory System

The Reggio Emilia approach is a participatory approach that invites all children, families, and educators to engage in an educational dialogue and collaborative projects. To foster this dialogue it is essential to create numerous opportunities for discussions between staff, children, parents and the wider community, strengthening these relationships.

Malaguzzi believed that fundamental concepts should be considered when engaging in educational dialogue. He emphasized the importance of providing children with spontaneous, rich experiences and contexts for learning, during which teachers can observe children's learning processes closely. Children require significant freedom - the freedom to discover and to explore new and meaningful spaces. They need to be able to build their own understanding of themselves, others, and their context in and through relationships with others – children, adults and the world they encounter around them.

Figure 12. 3 and 4 year olds engaging with light and shadow in the Everywhere Atelier at Reddam House Waterfall Early Learning School, Midrand, Gauteng, South Africa, 2025

Through this lens, South Africa can embrace the Reggio Emilia approach, listening closely to children. We are all born curious, and we must listen empathically to them by amplifying our senses, being fully immersed, and observing in a way that allows us to be amazed. When we, as adults, are curious, and pay close attention to children, we value the process of researching and constructing knowledge together with them.

Children learn best when they have strong relationships with teachers and community members, as these connections make them feel valued and foster a sense of belonging. Learning becomes visible when adults are present, fully attuned, and paying careful attention to the children's cognitive and learning processes. It is also important to remember that each child is unique and an unrepeatable subject with their own individual relationship with the world.

All children express themselves and interact with the world around them in different ways. Learning becomes visible when adults are present and pay careful attention to their cognitive processes. While the content is important, the process takes priority, and a teacher's empathetic listening is critical.

Figure 13. 3 and 4 year olds with the Atelierista, Sarah Browne, revisiting and reflecting on pedagogical documentation in the Everywhere Atelier at Reddam House Waterfall Early Learning School, Midrand, Gauteng, 2025

In the Municipal Preschools and Infant Toddler Centres in Reggio Emilia the word 'cura' is often used. This conveys not just the care for others and of the environment but a deep sense of respect and concern for ensuring that all spaces in the schools support the development of relationships. This emphasis highlights the depth of the Reggio Emilia approach in creating a sense of belonging for all members of the educational community - the children, the staff, and the parents. We need to reflect on the deep respect and 'cura' inherent in the approach, which can also be seen in children's thinking and empathy.

Environment, Spaces and Relations

Figure 14. 4 year old in the Wetlands, an extension of the Everywhere Atelier at Reddam House Waterfall Early Learning School, Midrand, Gauteng, South Africa, 2025

The Reggio Emilia approach can take place anywhere in Africa, in any setting, whether it be well-resourced or less so, even under a tree. It does not need to take place inside the four walls of a classroom or atelier; instead, it shifts thinking to practice the Reggio Emilia approach in an 'Everywhere Atelier' by seeing any environment as having the potential to support children's learning processes and research.

Figure 15. 4 year olds engaging in research in the Wetlands, an extension of the Everywhere Atelier at Reddam House Waterfall Early Learning School, Midrand, Gauteng, South Africa, 2025

Many of the Reggio-inspired schools in South Africa venture outdoors, as the climate and weather are optimal for doing so. The children have the opportunity to engage in an 'outdoor' atelier. This highlights the versatility of the Reggio Emilia approach, demonstrating that it can be practised in any context, in urban or in rural settings. Through this lens educators in Africa can fully embrace the approach anywhere, regardless of resources, buildings or dedicated spaces, respecting children's connections to their surroundings and fostering community involvement in education.

Figure 16. Children at Mimosa School engaging with light and shadow, Auckland Park, Johannesburg, Gauteng, South Africa, 2024

The potential of the environment as a teacher supports the Reggio idea of a "diffused atelier" in which ideas can spread. A place where the creative expression of children's research and theories about the world develops their thought processes, skills, and ability to communicate their ideas. The environment can be investigated by the children using all their five senses, not only through the teacher's words. This idea of it being the third teacher allows for different experiences and poses many questions. Children have a right to the environment which has different contexts provoking deeper engagement. The environment is open and speaks to children and seems to have its own linguistic code.

Figure 17. 3 year old seeing from a different perspective in the Everywhere Atelier at Reddam House Waterfall Early Learning School, Midrand, Gauteng, 2024

Environments that are rich in stimuli present possibilities and contexts for learning. It's almost as though the environment draws the children in and speaks to them as they make sense of the world around them. There are infinite ways in which children can interact with their environment and demonstrate their thinking and learning. This, in turn, creates an atmosphere that is welcoming and joyful.

To create an engaging learning environment, it is essential to ensure that it is secure and safe environment in which the children remain open to learning; that their voice is heard and valued, and that they all feel a sense of belonging in this environment. The African landscape is rich with possibilities for exploration and discovery and has its own language sparking children's curiosity and interest.

Combining the Reggio Emilia principles with an outdoor experience enhances the children's learning through meaningful encounters. This creates opportunities for evolving, interconnected learning experiences. Learning is generated by interconnectedness. To define learning as a natural process, one must find a space and a time during which one is in relation with others. Therefore, schools should enhance curiosity and wonder to ensure effective learning.

Organisation and Progetazzione (Design-Based Thinking)

Progettazione, or design-based thinking, is founded on the belief that children are curious, competent, relational, and valued citizens from birth. The school places a high value on this approach, which fosters curiosity, wonder, and joy both within the school and beyond.

The resources made available to the children need to be open-ended and should be introduced to them to assist in scaffolding their explorations and research. Nature can also be utilized to create connections and provide authentic learning experiences through the senses. As a teacher, facilitating these connections helps deepen children's knowledge while establishing respect and care.

> *"Prepare the environment so that it is rich in possibilities, for it to invite the children to explore and discover in meaningful ways. In setting up the environment, value needs to be placed on the aesthetics and ergonomics, organization, thoughtfulness, communication, interactions, and methods of engaging the children in active learning (provocations, invitations, intelligent materials)." – Marco Spaggiari (Spaggiari, 2024)*

Figure 18. 6 year old co-researcher in the Everywhere Atelier at Reddam House Waterfall Early Learning School, Midrand, Gauteng, South Africa, 2025

Educational Research

It is important to set up an atelier in a meaningful way, planning by design. The atelier is a place where you think with your hands. Every single instrument, every single material has its own intelligence, no matter which language you are engaging in. Every single person is so different in their own makeup and brings their own intelligence to this space too, which means that the thinking will never be the same.

Figure 19. 3 year old co-researchers in the Everywhere Atelier at Reddam House Waterfall Early Learning School, Midrand, Gauteng, South Africa 2025

It is important that the one station in an atelier is a place for drawing, as when one draws something, it gives an idea shape before one continues with the creation of a prototype. It is important to have an idea or shape before the creation; otherwise, you won't know what to choose or do. This really emphasizes the value of mark-making and drawing in the Reggio Emilia approach.

Teachers are facilitators of learning and should encourage children to explore, discover, inquire, experiment, and build understanding, knowledge, and skills. Children's thinking and experience of the world are diverse and interconnected. It is important to recognize that genuine knowledge arises from meaningful experiences, and continual observation and listening help identify learning opportunities and possibilities.

Educators in South Africa often rush through the curriculum, neglecting to plan with intention. They need to create a space for deeper research and exploration when setting up the learning environment, being mindful of the identity and potential of the resources and materials they place in the environment. This approach enhances the quality of children's thinking and research, fostering greater curiosity and engagement.

PEDAGOGICAL DOCUMENTATION

Pedagogical documentation is a key component of the Reggio Emilia approach, serving as a strategy to make the learning process visible. This practice involves visual listening, enabling both the child and the teacher to reflect on the learning experience and children's thought processes. Teachers observe children closely, either individually or in small groups. They take photos or videos, make notes about children's learning processes, documenting what children said or did, reflecting on and analysing this with colleagues and the children.

Figure 20. Teacher documenting the children's learning processes at Bekezela Creche, Johannesburg, Gauteng, South Africa, 2025

This documentation is critical in showcasing children's thinking and creating memories for the children, staff, and parents. It is important to be displayed and discussed, to make learning visible and help teachers design future projects during discussion on the process of learning.

It is fundamental for children to express themselves, reflect, and revisit their thinking, as well as to construct, reconstruct, and relaunch their ideas and thoughts. Through documentation, one can truly see the child in this ongoing process. True knowledge arises from meaningful experiences, and observation and active listening help us identify learning opportunities.

Figure 21. Documenting the 4 year old children's learning processes in the Wetlands at Reddam House Waterfall Early Learning School, Midrand, Gauteng, South Africa, 2025

Teachers are creative, innovative, and knowledgeable. Through documentation they are able to connect learning experiences to the curriculum in imaginative ways to meet the needs of the child. The term 'cura' also includes the teacher's deep care, attention, and respect for the children, their thinking, and learning processes. Documentation also reflects the way children work with materials and interact with the environment. In addition, it is evident in the time taken when documenting and archiving the documentation and the care spent in designing contexts for learning

Lauren Howden, Deputy Head - Academic in the Junior School at St. Mary's School for Girls shares her insight, *"With younger children, I am consistently struck by the sophistication of their observations and insights. When they revisit scripts, prior learning experiences, their own reflections, and pedagogical documentation, there is a clear progression in both linguistic complexity and conceptual depth. This process not only enhances their expressive language but also fosters increasingly nuanced and reflective thinking."* (Howden, 2025)

In South Africa we need to focus on exploring the crucial role of pedagogical documentation as educators dig deeper into the Reggio Emilia approach. It leaves a lasting impression of its potential to support children's thinking processes and metacognitive awareness. This highlights its value in planning for possibilities and in fostering children's research. Furthermore, it is directly connected to the development of literacy, numeracy, and other aspects of learning, as schools embrace reflective practices and advance the educational journey of every child.

LOCAL CASE STUDIES

Recently, the tide appears to be shifting as more South African teachers in underserved settings express openness to the approach's potential. A sense of community is also developing across diverse Reggio inspired contexts with requests for support in embracing the approach becoming more frequent.

Soul Action

At Soul Action School, a Reggio Emilia-inspired primary school in Durban, KwaZulu Natal, Principal Rachel Bowyer shares insights on how the approach has enriched their diverse educational community. By emphasizing respect, educational dialogue, and a sense of belonging, this school has fostered a culture that values children's voices and encourages learning driven by their curiosity and interests. Additionally, the school prioritizes strong partnerships with parents and caregivers by offering workshops designed to strengthen these connections. (Bowyer, 2025). Children are also encouraged to express their developing knowledge and understanding through a number of languages. The school has developed an Excel document to highlight particular languages introduced to the children.

Figure 22. Soul Action School in Durban, KwaZulu Natal, South Africa – Photo credit: Arnaud Rwasangabo

The school principal, Rachel Bowyer, explains, *"I think being a Reggio Emilia Inspired Primary School does mean we are quite unique... A child-led, inquiry-based approach ensures our students discover for themselves in authentic situations, constructing knowledge with others and expressing their developing understanding through many 'languages'."* (Bowyer, 2025)

Bekezela Creche

Bekezela Creche is a small creche founded by and located in an informal settlement of waste reclaimers which is situated under a motorway in downtown Johannesburg, South Africa.

It is involved in a collaborative research project with Mimosa School, a Reggio Emilia-inspired creche in Johannesburg and AREA, in which teachers at the creche receive mentorship embracing the principles of the Reggio Emilia approach.

Most community members in Bekezela struggle to find work and rely on recycling for survival, struggling to afford housing. Substance abuse is prevalent, and children are often exposed to very negative influences. Teachers at the creche are concerned about the impact these have on the younger generation.

Figure 23. Bekezela Creche in Johannesburg, Gauteng, South Africa, Oct 2022

The Bekezela teachers have no tertiary education but are nevertheless ensuring that the children at Bekezela receive quality early childhood education. With the support of Mimosa teachers and AREA, they are integrating the approach in practice under adverse conditions. This is a powerful testimony of belonging and mutual support under severe social risks. It is a place where education is framed as a hope-work, combining a vision and active involvement, amid precarious conditions and supported by an urgent rights agenda. Despite hardships, there is a sense of hope for improvement and opportunities, particularly for the children. Residents are grateful for the support and feel a strong sense of belonging, often helping one another during crises.

In an interview, Bekezela Creche teacher, Noluthando Zofika Ngema shares her insight, *"There is hope. The experience of being here. I think this place it gives hope."* The principal of Bekezela Creche, Melphy Silwana explained that this continues to be a "slow" process as the community members and children see that they need to respect the school. She says that the Reggio Emilia approach and the support they receive is a "big help" to them all.

Another Bekezela Creche teacher, Justin Ngozo, expresses his views about the community's perspectives, *"They're seeing the changes that is happening here and everything from the start. The kids, they are coming, they eat, they are doing everything, even their health now… Their bodies are changing because they are eating. They have normal time to eat. Other communities can learn that people must unite."* (Teachers, 2025)

Mimosa School

Mimosa School in Auckland Park, Johannesburg, emphasizes community participation by welcoming parents and interested members of the public in research involving the school and its children. The school strives to create an inclusive environment that respects diverse identities, fostering a curious and supportive community where collaboration is key and children are recognised as active citizens. Children, teachers, and community members engage in dialogue on social, ecological, and justice issues, as the school encourages participation and redefines what it means to be Reggio-inspired.

Figure 24. Mimosa School, Auckland Park, Johannesburg, Gauteng, South Africa, 2024

The current design-based project involves the outdoor alleyway that connects the Pre-School and the Foundation Phase. Here, children, teachers, and parents are collaboratively reimagining this space as they co-research together, creating a "Green Atelier."

Heather Barclay, Principal of Mimosa School and Fellow Researcher in PhD Reggio Childhood Studies explains, *"Provoked by the Mimosa Alleyway Project, the school is in the process of exploring what it means to organise around inquiries/*

projects rather than around a traditional school structure i.e. a teacher per class with atelierista and pedagogical support." (Barclay, 2025)

Figure 25. In the alleyway at Mimosa School, Auckland Park, Johannesburg, South Africa, 2024

Forest House School

Forest House School in Constantia, Cape Town, is a play-based preschool inspired by the Reggio Emilia approach and the forest school programme, integrating these into its approach to education.

Figure 26. Forest House School, Constantia, Cape Town, South Africa, 2025

Isabella Hulme, Co-founder and Pedagogista of the school explains her thoughts and experience of the Reggio Emilia approach in this setting, *"It brings value to the greater community in that the children spend much of their time learning and exploring in the Constantia Greenbelt, a public section of trails and forests that we can access directly from our school. Seeing groups of children move through these spaces with such agency, compassion, creativity and curiosity is a quiet gift for anyone who passes."* (Hulme)

Isabella continues *"The Reggio Emilia approach affirms and inspired my view of children as capable, competent and deeply relational, not just with other people, but also with places, materials, stories and ideas... Above all, it has shown me that childhood is not simple a preparation for the future, but a powerful meaningful time in itself. This perspective keeps me grounded in protecting children's right to wonder, to play, and to express themselves in a hundred different ways."* (Hulme)

Reddam House Waterfall Early Learning School

Reddam House Waterfall Early Learning School in Waterfall, Midrand, South Africa, is a Reggio Emilia-inspired learning environment with over 397 children ranging from 1 to 6 years old. In planning for rich possibilities of engagement, an

Everywhere Atelier, a Digital Landscapes & Light Atelier, and a Treasure Trove - a REMIDA-inspired creative recycling hub - have been curated by their resident Reggio-inspired atelierista, Sarah Browne. The Early Learning School's children's ideas, theories, and creations are appreciated and respected, as they are seen as curious, competent, and relational citizens.

Figure 27. 5 year old in the Wetlands at Reddam House Waterfall Early Learning School, Midrand, Gauteng, South Africa 2025

The children often venture out in small groups into the wetlands and school grounds together with the atelierista, Sarah Browne, co-atelierista, Rabelani Mudau, and the class teacher or teaching assistant to co-research and explore together while making sense of their world.

Sarah Browne, Atelierista shares *"In planning for possibilities for the children, the environment is intentionally set-up with research tools including and not limited to: magnifying glasses; mirrors; a stethoscope; clipboards; mark makers; paints and prisms as invitations to inquiry. What we have noticed is that making this visible to the parents when they drop their children off at school, is creating curiosity. These parents then stop and ask questions about what is happening. This leads to an educational dialogue about the Reggio Emilia approach and how Loris Malaguzzi took the school to the piazza to create visibility of the approach. Almost like a democratic piazza. As one of the five year olds says of the Everywhere Atelier, 'We connect our heart to the atelier so that there can be love. It's like a love connection'."*

St. Mary's School for Girls

At St Mary's School for Girls in Waverley, the Junior School community is comprised of approximately 507 pupils from Little Saints to Grade 7. The preschool section, Little Saints, is inspired by the Reggio Emilia approach. (St Mary's School, 2025)

Lauren Howden, Deputy Head: Academics in the Junior School explains, *"Over the last three years, we have increased both the visibility and the role of the atelierista. Our atelierista has become an active participant in the workshops and offerings of AREA, which has led to a deeper understanding of the role within the school and has positively influenced not only Little Saints but also the wider Junior School through her initiatives. These have included overarching inquiries, umbrella questions, and collaborative projects for our Arts Festival.*

The Little Saints Open Day, complete with learning provocations for prospective children, is followed by a hands-on, experiential workshop for parents introducing them to the approach. These sessions are always well received and do much to strengthen parents' relationships with the Little Saints teachers, as well as their understanding of the philosophy that underpins teaching and learning in this phase." (Howden, 2025)

Petra's Edu-Play

Petra's Eduplay, a small Reggio Emilia-inspired preschool in Bedfordview, Johannesburg, has recently created a main atelier that includes a small REMIDA, a creative recycling hub, for the children and teachers to work in. Petra Queiros, Head of the School and a music atelierista, reflects that this has allowed for a slower, more meaningful day for the children in the school and broadened the teachers' and parents' view of how children learn. This, in turn, has reflected a happier school with confident, independent children. (Queiros)

Figure 28. 1 year 5 month toddler engaging with the light at Petra's Eduplay, Bedfordview, Gauteng, South Africa, 2025

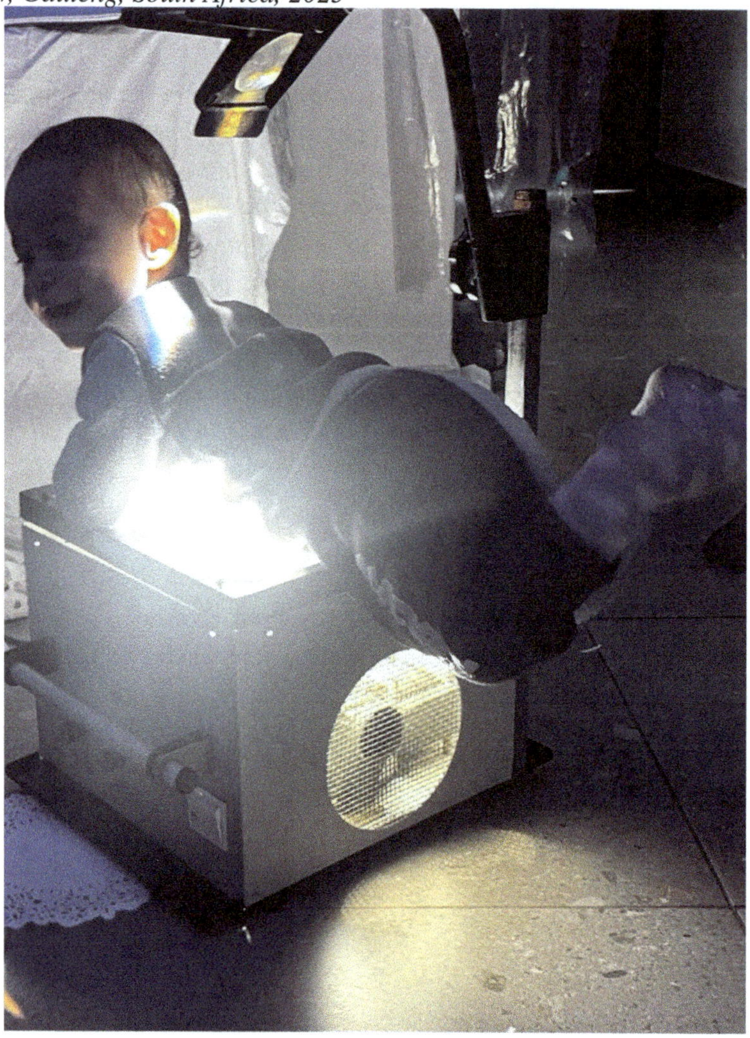

Capstone College

Figure 29. The language of materials at Capstone College, Gqeberha, Eastern Cape, South Africa, 2025

Farie Mubonderi, a Grade 00 (children who are 4 and 5 years old) teacher at Reggio Emilia inspired Capstone College in Gqeberha, Eastern Cape shares her insights about the children she teaches: *"I have noticed that children are not scared to explore, they are not scared to try new things, they are not scared to question and investigate anything."* (Mubonderi, 2025)

IMPLICATIONS FOR PRACTICE

The Reggio Emilia approach embodies a pedagogy of hope and reconstruction. By prioritizing respect for children's voices, fostering creativity, and building collaborative learning communities, it aligns with the hopes of post-apartheid South Africa. However, realising this vision necessitates critical reflection on policy and practice, especially in underserved and under-resourced environments. We must challenge the tendency to equate "compulsory" early learning with formal instruction, advocating instead for pedagogies allow for children's agency, curiosity and creativity. Creativity is vital for cognitive, emotional, and social development.

Revising the language and vocabulary in planning policy amendments is crucial to emphasize play-based and inquiry-driven learning. This revision should clarify that "compulsory" early childhood development does not necessitate formal instruction. By aligning these policies with the Reggio Emilia philosophy of education, we can safeguard children's right to quality education. Investing in professional development focused on the Reggio Emilia approach, along with ongoing support, workshops, and mentorship, will inspire teachers and encourage thoughtful engagement. This effort will promote educational dialogue and networking, support reflective practices, and provide opportunities for meaningful engagement with materials, even in under-resourced settings.

CONCLUSION: THE REGGIO EMILIA APPROACH, A PROMISE OF HOPE FOR SOUTH AFRICA

Reflecting on the hope the Reggio Emilia approach brings to South Africa, educators are often surprised not only by the depth of children's metacognition and their ideas but also by the transformation of their own mind-sets, heart-sets, and practices. They realise the need to examine their preconceived ideas of their image of child and how these beliefs have influenced their teaching. This process encourages them to hold an image of child as competent and strong. As a result, many Reggio-inspired educators have changed their perspectives on children significantly. This in turn, alters how they intentionally plan for possibilities for children's engagement and research.

Figure 30. Africa Reggio Emilia Alliance (AREA) In-Person Workshop, Nova Pioneer, Ormonde, Gauteng, South Africa, 2019

Lauren Howden, Deputy Head of Academics, Junior School at St Mary's School for Girls shares her reflections, *"What stands out for me is that the Reggio Emilia approach is not confined to the early years. Its principles – respecting children's voices, using provocations to stimulate inquiry, and making learning visible – remain powerful tools even in the older grades. The approach has given me a renewed appreciation for children's capacity to construct knowledge and has reminded me that their questions and insights often drive learning in more meaningful ways than predetermined teaching alone."* (Howden, 2025)

The Reggio Emilia approach offers South Africa a wonderful invitation to reimagine education. With its pedagogy of listening, celebration of 100 languages of expression, and belief in the competence and creativity of every child, the Reggio Emilia approach speaks directly to the heart of South Africa's democratic aspirations.

Figure 31. 4 year old in the Everywhere Atelier at Reddam House Waterfall Early Learning School, Midrand, Gauteng, South Africa 2025

This is the work of hope - quiet, deliberate, and transformative. It is the work of educators who listen before they teach, who wonder alongside children, and who make visible the traces of thinking that often go unseen. It is the work of communities that understand that education is not solely the responsibility of schools, but a shared commitment of society to justice and renewal.

As we look toward the future, the call to action is clear. We must cultivate schools that are truly democratic spaces - where the child's voice is heard, teachers' research is honoured, and families are welcomed as co-constructors of meaning.

Figure 32. 3 year old engaging in the language of paint in the Wetlands at Reddam House Waterfall Early Learning School, Midrand, Gauteng, South Africa, 2025

Reflecting back on Malaguzzi's vision of an "amiable school," built on relationships and filled with possibility. A school where children and teachers are co-researchers of wonder, and where every act of learning becomes an act of hope.

It is in this light that the Reggio Emilia approach does not merely inspire South Africa; it helps to heal it.

Figure 33. The language of clay – Old man – 5 years old, Reddam House Waterfall Early Learning School, Midrand, Gauteng, South Africa, 2023

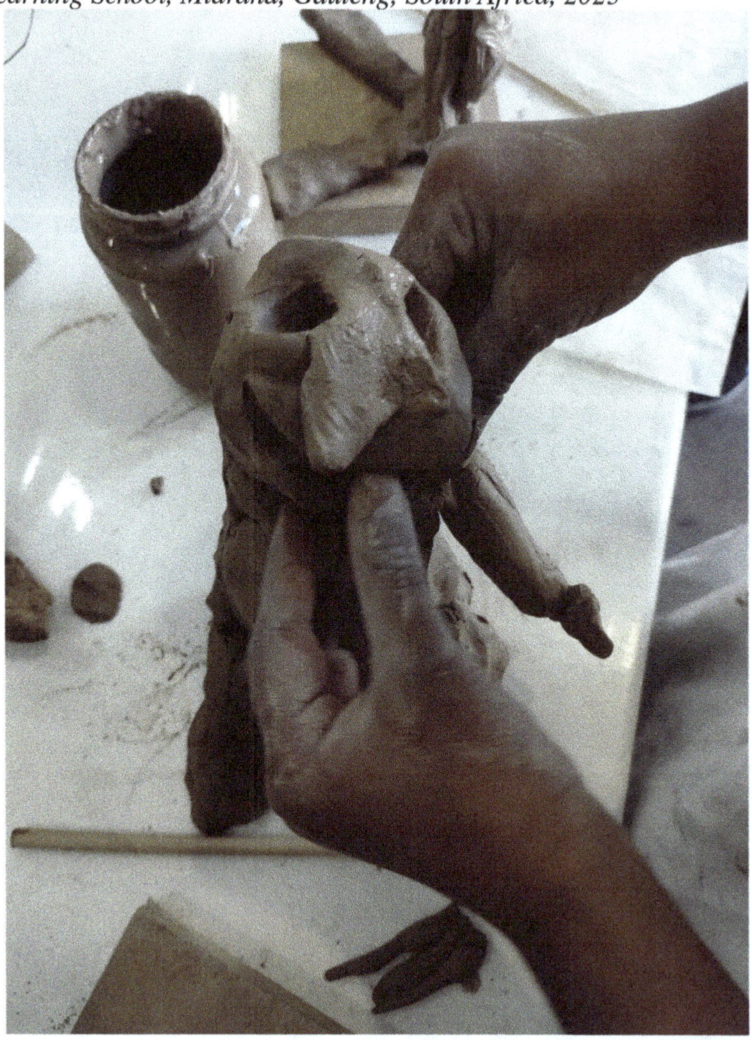

> *"Children have the right to be recognized as subjects of individual, legal, civil and social rights; as both source and constructors of their own experience, and thus active participants in the organization of their identities, abilities and autonomy, through relationships and interaction with their peers, with adults, with ideas, with objects, and with real and imaginary events of intercommunicating worlds.*

All this, while establishing the fundamental premises for creating better 'citizens of the world' and raising the quality of human interaction, also credits children, and each individual child, with an extraordinary wealth of inborn abilities and potential, strength and creativity. Irreversible suffering and impoverishment of the child is caused when this fact is not acknowledged. Starting from this point of reference, we recognize the right of children to realize and expand their potential, placing great value on their ability to socialize, receiving their affection and trust, and satisfying their needs and desires to learn. And this is so much truer when children are reassured by an effective alliance between the adults in their lives, adults who place higher value on the search for constructive strategies of thought and action than on the direct transmission of knowledge and skills. These constructive strategies contribute to the formation of creative intelligence, free thought, and individuality that is sensitive and aware, through an ongoing process of differentiation and integration with other people and other experiences. The fact that the rights of children are recognized as the rights of children is the sign of a more accomplished humanity." – Loris Malaguzzi (Malaguzzi, 1995)

Figure 34. Engaging with light in the Wetlands at Reddam House Waterfall Early Learning School, Midrand, Gauteng, South Africa, 2025

REFERENCES

Africa Reggio Emilia Alliance (AREA). (n.d.). *Reggio Emilia and SA's liberation struggle.* Retrieved from Africa Reggio Emilia Alliance - promoting inspired education from birth to 99: https://reggio.co.za/reggio-emilia-and-sas-liberation-struggle/

Barclay, H. (2025, October). Principal of Mimosa School and PhD Fellow Research Reggio Childhood Studies. (S. Browne, Interviewer)

Bowyer, R. (2025, August). Soul Action School Principal and Foundation Phase Teacher . (S. Browne, Interviewer)

Browne, J. (2017). Tizianna Filippini 2017 visit to SA insights answers advice. Johannesburg: Africa Reggio Emilia Alliance (AREA).

Browne, T. (2025, September). Co-Founder and Co-Ordinator of the Africa Reggio Emilia Alliance (AREA). (A. a. Sarah Browne, Interviewer)

Comune di Reggio Emilia . (1977, June 27). Foto storica Sudafrica. *Reggio Emilia, 27.06.1977 – Corteo cittadino contro il colonialismo e l'apartheid.* Reggio Emilia, Italy: Comune di Reggio Emilia .

Comune di Reggio Emilia . (n.d.). Foto storica Sudafrica. *Rea Silvia, la seconda nave della solidarietà italiana parte da Livorno l'16.03.1984 ed è diretta a Luanda, Maputo e Dar es Salam.* Comune Di Reggio Emilia.

Department of Basic Education. (2024). https://thrivebyfive.co.za/findings-enrolled-children/. Retrieved from Thrive by Five Index: https://thrivebyfive.co.za/wp-content/uploads/2025/09/TB5-Main-Report_FINAL.pdf

Department of Basic Education - Republic of South Africa. (2022). *Implications for ECD shift to Basic Education.* Retrieved from Basic Education - Department of Basic Education South Africa: https://www.education.gov.za/ECDFunctionShift2021.aspx

Department of Basic Education - Republic of South Africa. (2025, February 18). *DBE briefs Portfolio Committee on ECD and Grade R as the new compulsory grade.* Retrieved from Department of Basic Education - Republic of South Africa: https://www.education.gov.za/ArchivedDocuments/ArchivedArticles/ECDandGradeRasthenewcompulsorygradeR.aspx

Fabbi, C. (2022, October). The Reggio Emilia approach - quotation on the rights of the child. Johannesburg, Gauteng, South Africa.

First National Bank (FNB) and Innovation Edge, i. c. (2022). *Thrive By Five Index Report - Revised 2022.* First National Bank (FNB) and Innovation Edge, in collaboration with the DBE, and is supported by the United States Agency for International Development (USAID) and ECD Measure.

Howden, L. (2025, Septemeber). The Reggio Emilia approach at St Mary's School for Girls. (S. Browne, Interviewer)

Hulme, I. (n.d.). Co-Founder, Teacher and Pedagogista of Forest House School . (S. Browne, Interviewer)

Istoreco Reggio Emilia - Reggio Africa Archives - Bruna Soncini Ganapini Archives - Comune di Reggio Emilia. (1997, June 1997). Pact of Solidarity . Reggio Emilia, Emilia-Romangna, Italy: Istoreco Reggio Emilia - Reggio Africa Archives.

Istoreco Reggio Emilia - Reggio Africa Archives - Bruna Soncini Ganapini Archives - Comune di Reggio Emilia. (n.d.). *Second Solidarity Ship. Reggio Emilia.* Istoreco Reggio Emilia - Reggio Africa Archives - Bruna Soncini Ganapini Archives - Comune di Reggio Emilia.

Malaguzzi, L. (1995). A Charter of Rights. In Malaguzzi, L. (Ed.), *A Journey into the Rights of Children: As Seen by the Children Themselves* (pp. 67–69). Reggio Children Srl.

Mubonderi, F. (2025, July). Grade 00 Teacher at Capstone College. (S. Browne, Interviewer)

Ocampo, M. L. (2004, September 9). *Leland Standford Junior University.* Retrieved from Standford.edu: https://web.stanford.edu/~jbaugh/saw/Lizet_Education_Inequity .html

Queiros, P. (n.d.). Head of School and Music Atelierista - Petra's EduPlay. (S. Browne, Interviewer)

Reggio Children Srl P.IVA 01586410357. (2022). *Investigating natural phenomena - at home with the Reggio Emilia approach - school goes home.* Retrieved from Reggio Children S.r.l: https://www.reggiochildren.it/en/athomewiththereggioapproach/investigating-natural-phenomena/

Reggio Children Srl P.IVA 01586410357. (2022). *Reggio Emilia Approach - 100 Languages.* Retrieved from Reggio Children: https://www.reggiochildren.it/en/reggio-emilia-approach/100-linguaggi-en/

Spaggiari, M. (2024, April). Reggio Emilia approach quotation on the Environment. Reggio Emilia, Emilia-Romagna, Italy.

St Mary's School. (2025, October). *St Mary's School Waverley*. Retrieved from St Mary's School Waverley: https://www.stmarysschool.co.za/

Teachers, B. C. (2025, July). Bekezela Creche Interview - a Reggio Emilia inspired creche and research project. (S. Browne, Interviewer)

The Presidency of the Republic of South Africa. (2025, October). *Giuseppe Soncini (Posthumous)*. Retrieved from The Presidency Republic of South Africa: https://www.presidency.gov.za/giuseppe-soncini-posthumous

Valodia, I. (2023, September 14). *South Africa can't crack the inequality curse. Why, and what can be done*. Retrieved from The Conversation -: https://theconversation.com/south-africa-cant-crack-the-inequality-curse-why-and-what-can-be-done-213132?utm_medium=email&utm_campaign=Latest%20from%20The%20Conversation%20for%20September%2014%202023%20-%202736927673&utm_content=Latest%20from%20The%20Conv

Vea Vecchi, A.-T. (1998). "The Role of the Atelierista: An Interview with Lella Gandini.". In L. G. edited by Carolyn Edwards, *In The Hundred Languages of Children: The Reggio Emilia Approach – Advanced Reflections, 2nd edition* (pp. 139 - 147). Norwood, New Jersey, United States of America: Ablex Publishing.

Chapter 6
Children's Rights in Action at Acorn

Rosalba Bortolotti
http://orcid.org/0009-0004-1880-3255
Acorn Collaborative, Canada

ABSTRACT

This chapter explores the ethical and pedagogical dimensions of children's rights within early learning settings, emphasizing the image of the child as a capable, curious, and contributing citizen. Grounded in the principles of the Reggio Emilia philosophy and the United Nations Convention on the Rights of the Child, it examines how democratic participation, documentation, and inquiry-based learning cultivate environments where children's voices and ideas shape the work and projects. Drawing on examples from Acorn School in Toronto, Ontario, the chapter illustrates how everyday encounters with open-ended materials, community rituals, and shared projects become spaces for meaning-making, reflection, and co-construction of knowledge. Through these lived experiences, educators are invited to consider how pedagogy, ethics, and politics intertwine in fostering cultures of listening, belonging, and participation that honor children's rights as lived, relational, and transformative practices.

CHILDREN'S RIGHT IN ACTION AT ACORN SCHOOL

The Image of the Child as a Rights-Bearer

Truly realizing children's rights in education and society begins with a fundamental rethinking of childhood itself. For centuries, the concept of childhood has been far from static; it is a social and cultural construct, constantly evolving with

DOI: 10.4018/979-8-3373-3431-8.ch006

philosophical thought, economic shifts, and societal values. The 20th century saw the rise of developmental psychology with figures like Jean Piaget and Lev Vygotsky. Piaget's cognitive-developmental theory (Piaget, 1952) emphasized children as active constructors of knowledge, moving through distinct stages, interacting with their environment to build understanding. Vygotsky's sociocultural theory (Vygotsky, 1978), however, pushed this further, asserting that learning is fundamentally a social process, deeply embedded in cultural contexts and mediated by language and interaction with "more knowledgeable others" (adults or more skilled peers). Both theorists, in their own ways, challenged the notion of a passive child, laying groundwork for a more dynamic understanding of child intelligence. Drawing from the Reggio Emilia philosophy, the central belief for a genuine rights-based approach to education is the "image of the child as competent, capable, relational, and a full citizen." This is not just a teaching preference or a romantic ideal; it is a deep stance that redefines what it means to be a child. It asserts that from birth, children are active constructors of knowledge, meaning-makers, and participants in their world, not just passive recipients. They arrive with a rich array of potentials, curiosities, and a drive to connect and communicate. This intrinsic capacity is the very source from which their rights naturally emerge. In vivid contrast to older views, which often defined children by what they lacked compared to adults, the image of the competent child champions their inherent potential and agency. The powerful words of Janusz Korczak, an advocate for children's rights, perfectly capture this perspective: "Children are not the people of tomorrow, but are people of today. They are entitled to be taken seriously. They have a right to be treated with tenderness and respect and should be allowed to grow into whoever they were meant to be." (Korczak, 1967) His emphasis on children as "people of today" is a clear call for immediate recognition of their present worth and inherent dignity, challenging the instrumental view that sees children only as future adults or future economic contributors. This is a foundational statement for understanding children as rights-bearers, not merely future ones.

INTRODUCTION TO ACORN SCHOOL

Acorn School was founded in 2004, born from a desire to reconceptualize early childhood education and care. From its earliest days, Acorn was envisioned as a living community — a place where relationships stood at the heart of all learning. The school's philosophy was grounded in the belief that children are strong, capable, and full of potential, and that educators, too, are researchers and co-learners in this shared journey. These ideas were deeply inspired by my encounters and ongoing research with the infant-toddler centres and preschools of Reggio Emilia,

Italy, (Malaguzzi, 1993) where I first saw what it could mean to listen deeply to children's ideas and theories.

As one of the first schools in the city to embrace this perspective, Acorn invited families and educators to reimagine how a school might look, sound, and feel when children's voices truly guided the work. The school was built through the care and commitment of my family — with the help of my husband, parents, relatives, and children — whose presence made Acorn feel less like an institution and more like a home. We believed the school had to reflect community in its truest sense: a place of participation, shared responsibility, and joy.

There were challenges, of course, as we stepped into a new way of thinking about education. Our city was just to think of these new perspectives toward early learning. Yet it was within these moments — in dialogue with professors, educators, atelieristas, our cook, and families — that Acorn's identity began to take shape. Together we learned what it meant to live well together, to embrace uncertainty, and to see beauty in the everyday life of the school.

Over time, Acorn grew into more than a school. It became a study place — a hub for students, educators, administrators, and community members who gathered to think together about pedagogy, materials, and the image of the child. Workshops, study tours, and conferences filled the space with conversation, collaborative research, reflection, transforming the school into a living laboratory of learning.

The gardens soon became our gathering place — an open classroom where many inquiries were born. It was there that seeds of curiosity grew into projects that would come to define who we were as a community of learners. In the pages that follow, you will encounter traces of these projects and stories, each one offering a glimpse into Acorn's evolving pedagogical identity — one rooted in a profound and enduring relationship with the image of the child: as a thinker, a maker of meaning, and a contributor to the world.

Cultivating Our Pedagogical Identity at Acorn

At Acorn School (2005-2015), embracing this image of the child transforms the very nature of our educational environment. It moves beyond a curriculum driven solely by adult-imposed objectives or a rigid adherence to developmental milestones. Instead, it invites a pedagogy of inquiry, where:

- Children's questions are not dismissed or simplified: Rather than providing immediate, pre-packaged answers, adults take children's questions seriously as genuine intellectual provocations. For instance, a child's simple question like "Why does the sun follow us?" was not met with a quick scientific explanation, but with an invitation for shared investigation. We might provide materials like flashlights, or time for outdoor observation to allow the child and peers to explore their own theories.

Children's theories are not corrected, but explored: Children, in their efforts to make sense of the world, construct their own theories. A rights-based approach values these theories as evidence of active thinking and engagement. Educators become researchers alongside children, helping them test, refine, and articulate their ideas. For example, during a lengthy inquiry about light and shadow, children at Acorn hypothesized that the light was "following" or "chasing." They noticed how the shadow changed shape as they moved the light source and began to wonder if the shadow a life of its own, stretching, shrinking, hiding depending on where the sun or lamp was placed. The shadow was like a "magical monster with no eyes" and the children thought of it as a friendly monster that just wanted to play with them. Rather than correcting them, educators facilitated experiments with projectors and different light sources, allowing children to challenge and build upon their own understanding.

- Their interests are not diverted but cultivated: This approach prioritizes following and expanding upon children's emergent interests. This means weaving educational goals into authentic, child-initiated explorations, making learning more meaningful, and engaging. If a group of children becomes fascinated by insects, the educators might introduce magnify opportunities for outdoor observation, and provide materials for drawing, sculpting, or even writing "insect stories." This profound shift in the image of the child necessitates an equally significant transformation in the role of the adult. When children are viewed as capable protagonists, adults' roles evolve to become that of listeners, co-learners, researchers, and advocates. The implication here is critical: rights are not static entitlements "given" to children; they are dynamic, relational constructs that are lived with children, together. This means that the realization of children's rights is an ongoing process of negotiation, respect, and co-creation within daily interactions.

Our experience at Acorn School profoundly deepened this understanding. Alongside fellow educators and the broader community, we committed ourselves to ongoing study and dialogue, driven by a compelling interest in who the child is and what childhood truly means. Through group study tours and sessions with educators from across the province, we engaged in, learning, in deep dialogues and listened to different points of view. This was not a simplistic training; it was an immersive process of questioning our own ingrained assumptions. We developed questions, refined our thoughts, and explored theories about early education, delving into the works of Vygotsky, Dewey, Freire, and the extensive Reggio Children publications. It was in this rich environment that we began to think critically about the importance of relationships—not just with other people, but also with the more-than-human and non-human world. These relational perspectives guided our observations and listening, inviting us to see children's interactions with nature, objects, and ideas as part of a complex web of connections. In vivid contrast to older views, which often defined children by what they lacked compared to adults, the image of the competent child champions their inherent potential and agency.

STORIES OF INQUIRY

The following pages offer glimpses into some of the inquiries and projects that emerged from daily life at Acorn. Each began with a moment of curiosity — a question, a gesture, or an encounter that invited children and educators to think and work together. These examples reflect not only what the children discovered, but how relationships, environments, and materials shaped the learning process. They reveal a pedagogy rooted in dialogue, collaboration, and a deep respect for the child's way of constructing meaning in the world.

Living with Snails: Care and Coexistence

Everyday experiences often became openings for children to exercise their rights, engage in sustained inquiry, and collaborate meaningfully with peers and educators. The garden was a continual source of curiosity and ethical questioning.

In one ongoing project, a small group of children became concerned about the snails they observed outdoors. They noticed how easily the snails could be stepped on, pecked by birds, or displaced during play. Rather than dismissing these concerns as fleeting or sentimental, the educators treated them as intellectual and ethical provocations. The children's question—*How can we protect them?* This became the starting point of research.

Before acting, the children observed closely. They studied where the snails gathered, how they moved, what surfaces they preferred, and how they responded to light, moisture, and touch. Discussions unfolded:

Would bringing them inside make them safer?
Would they miss the garden?
Could they live with us?
What would "home" mean for a snail?

Some children proposed a traditional enclosed terrarium. Others questioned whether walls were necessary. "If they like it," one child suggested, "maybe they will stay." This shift in thinking reframed the project: protection would not come through containment, but through relationship and environmental responsibility.

Together, the children designed an indoor habitat that mimicked the outdoor conditions they had carefully documented layers of soil, small plants, stones, shallow trays of water, and natural light. Importantly, the space remained open. There were no enclosing walls. The snails were free to move beyond the designated area.

What followed became an extraordinary discovery.

The snails remained. They gathered closely within the environment the children had prepared, rarely venturing beyond it. The children interpreted this not as coincidence, but as communication: *We made it right for them.* Their observations deepened. They noticed how moisture levels influenced movement, how the snails clustered in areas, and how gentle handling affected their behavior.

This was not simply a science investigation about habitats. It was an inquiry into coexistence.

The children came to understand that safety does not always require confinement. Protection could emerge from attentiveness, from designing environments that respond to the needs of others. The snails were not objects of study; they were participants in a shared classroom ecology.

Through this project, children exercised agency and ethical responsibility. They negotiated decisions, listened to differing perspectives, revised their theories, and reflected on the consequences of their choices. Educators did not provide pre-packaged answers. Instead, they held the space for uncertainty, supporting observation, dialogue, and careful environmental redesign.

In living alongside the snails without walls, the children experienced trust as relational and reciprocal. The more-than-human world was not separate from classroom life; it was interwoven with it.

What began as a desire to "rescue" became an inquiry into how to live together.

Children's Theories of Fear

It began with the children's fascination for bats — how they flew, their shapes, and how they could see at night. During many meeting times with educators and the atelierista, we tried to trace and map the children's ideas, following their drawings, stories, and hypotheses. Yet, as we listened, there was always something beneath the surface — a quiet sense that their curiosity held a deeper question.

Together, we decided to visit the city's museum and explore the bat exhibit. Before going, the children shared what they already knew and what they hoped to discover. At the museum, the guide was impressed by their thoughtful questions about echolocation and how bats navigate the night. It was there, through their conversations, that we began to see more clearly: the children were not only wondering about bats, but about darkness itself. Their inquiry was connected to a shared unease — the fear of what cannot be seen or touched.

The bat became a symbol of courage and curiosity, helping the children reflect on how one might move confidently through the dark. When we returned to the school, stories, memories, and feelings poured out — moments of fear, comfort, and support for one another. What began as a scientific exploration evolved into a deeply emotional and human project, where empathy, kindness, and trust grew among the group. In learning about the bat, the children also discovered new ways of listening to one another — and of seeing themselves in relation to the unseen world around them.

The Living Table

Similarly, small, everyday gestures reinforced children's sense of belonging, responsibility, and collaboration. Setting the table for meals became an intentional act of participation and aesthetic expression. Different children took turns each day, adding flowers, fresh herbs, or a piece of their own artwork to enhance the space. At the table, conversations were lively and respectful, with children taking turns, listening, and occasionally disagreeing, yet always negotiating solutions collectively. Through this simple ritual, children experienced the intersection of community, responsibility, and aesthetic awareness, learning how to care for shared spaces and contribute to a group in meaningful ways. In all our classrooms, food is deeply integrated into everyday pedagogy.

The Transformation of the Tomato

From these natural explorations, we moved to human-made transformations, none more emblematic of Acorn School's identity than our annual tomato sauce project. Each year, the preparation of tomato sauce became more than a cooking activity—it was a multi-sensory, collaborative exploration that reflected our community, our traditions, and our pedagogical commitments. Returning children approached the project with pride and a sense of ownership, revisiting past documentation and sharing their insights with newcomers. Each year brought new questions, sometimes sparked by simple observations: the crushing machine that turned whole tomatoes into a smooth, runny sauce fascinated children. "Where did the whole tomato go?" they asked, peering into the mechanical transformation with wonder. The unfolding theories and hypotheses became a rich site for inquiry, discussion, and experimentation.

In Dialogue with an Artist

Another example that emerged from our daily life at Acorn School centered on the children's relationship with art and artists. We often introduced children to the work of different artists — some local and others from history — and visited museums and galleries, both in our community and at the Art Gallery of Ontario. These experiences were never about teaching art history, but rather about inviting children to enter a dialogue with the work — to see, wonder, and express what they felt and thought.

One day, the children were working with coloured glass stones on the light table, arranging, and layering them in ways that created shimmering, luminous patterns. Nearby, a small group was building with similar materials, and a conversation emerged about *The Starry Night* by Vincent van Gogh — a painting they had seen during one of our gallery visits. We had brought back a few books about Van Gogh to the classroom, and the children often revisited them. As they worked, their reflections began to flow:

"Sometimes colours at night are dark," Benjamin said thoughtfully.

"Maybe he liked night because no one can see him," Julian added.

The conversation lingered, full of pauses, questions, and new possibilities. The educator nearby listened carefully, noticing the emotion behind their words — the way they were trying to understand not only the artwork but the artist himself. Sensing their curiosity, she asked if they would like to learn more about Van Gogh's life. The children eagerly agreed. Together, they read and discovered some of the struggles and beauty that shaped his work.

We could have easily focused on creating beautiful paintings inspired by Van Gogh — and some children chose to do just that — but the story went deeper. It was the children who wanted to share *his* story with their families. Thus, our story of *Starry Night* came to life. They began presenting on Van Gogh's life, his work, and the sadness that seemed to echo through his art. We let the children lead with their ideas, supporting and facilitating their curiosity and wonder through further research and dialogue.

This project unfolded over several months, blending art, empathy, and storytelling. The children drew and painted their own interpretations of the night sky — not copies, but deeply personal expressions. Some used darker hues, while others filled their skies with light and movement. What stood out most was not the resemblance to the original painting, but the depth of feeling and dialogue that emerged around it.

Through this experience, we were reminded that children have the right to encounter art not as consumers of culture, but as participants in it. They have the right to interpret, to make meaning, and to be in relationship with beauty, complexity, and even tragedy. This right — the right to express, question, and feel — is a vital part of what it means to be a learner and a human being.

REFLECTIONS ON ACORN PROJECTS

As educators, our role was to honor these questions with patience and attentiveness. We asked ourselves: How do we enter this dialogue without imposing predetermined activities? How can we slow down to unpack what children say, do, and express, and respond in ways that deepen inquiry? Each question we posed was deliberate, designed to extend thinking, provoke curiosity, and invite reflection. Rather than rushing to complete tasks, we observed, documented, and revisited, allowing children to develop theories and ideas across multiple expressive "languages," from drawings and models to collaborative discussions and hands-on exploration.

The tomato sauce project exemplified the ways in which learning could be communal, sensory-rich, and iterative. Children engaged with the soil in the garden, cared for seedlings, and participated in harvesting, observing the life cycle of plants, and understanding the work involved in growing food. The transformation of tomatoes in the machine became an entry point into experimentation, reasoning, and imaginative thinking, just as the natural world provided spaces for observation, collaboration, and wonder. Each stage of the project—from garden to machine to sauce—was layered with questions, discoveries, and opportunities for dialogue, ensuring that children's ideas were honored and expanded.

The inquiry extended into more ambitious collaborative projects, such as creating a "bird city" in the garden. Birds visited the garden regularly but tended to fly away when children approached. Inspired by their observations, children came together indoors to discuss ideas for designing a space that could attract and accommodate the birds, allowing them to interact with the garden in safety. Drawing inspiration from a story I first heard in the early 1990s at the Reggio schools—*The Amusement Park for Birds*— (Reggio Children, 1997) the children brought their own unique perspectives to the project. A few used blocks and open-ended materials to construct the "bird city," negotiating spaces for the birds to perch, explore, and enjoy the vegetables from the garden. The project encouraged problem-solving, planning, and creative expression, while nurturing empathy and care for living beings.

These projects deepened our understanding of children as thoughtful and ethical participants in the natural and social world. Their questions and hypotheses were not random curiosities but reflections of their moral and relational awareness. Whether rescuing snails, building habitats, or setting the table, the children were enacting their right to participate, to express care, and to influence their environment—a vivid example of what it means to see children as citizens of today, not merely of tomorrow.

At Acorn School, classrooms, gardens, and shared spaces were alive with possibility. Nature was our constant source of learning — the gardens drawing joy, wonder, and countless inquiries. Open-ended materials invited children to explore, experiment, and express their ideas: clay and wire revealed the hundred languages of children, while paint, paper, and drawing opened paths for storytelling and meaning making. Together, these encounters wove a shared narrative of curiosity, creativity, and connection to the world around us.

IMAGE OF THE CHILD

As Loris Malaguzzi articulated, the child is not an empty vessel to be filled, but a subject who is "rich in potential, strong, powerful, competent, and most of all, connected to adults and other children" (Malaguzzi, 1998)This image of the child fundamentally disrupts deficit-based constructions that define children by what they lack in comparison to adults. Instead, it positions them as protagonists in the construction of knowledge—capable of forming theories, negotiating meaning, engaging in ethical reasoning, and participating in collective life. Malaguzzi's vision insists that education must be organized around listening, dialogue, and shared inquiry, where children's questions are treated not as naive curiosities but as serious intellectual and relational provocations. To view children as competent in this way is not to romanticize them; rather, it is to recognize their capacity to think with complexity, to co-construct their environments, and to participate responsibly in the social and ecological worlds they inhabit.

This core belief aligns directly with key articles of the UN Convention on the Rights of the Child (UNCRC), most notably Article 12, which states: "States Parties shall assure to the child who is capable of forming his or her own views the right to express those views freely in all matters affecting the child, the views of the child being given due weight in accordance with the age and maturity of the child."(United Nations General Assembly, 1989) This article is pivotal because it shifts from merely protecting children from harm to actively empowering them to participate. The image of the competent child makes Article 12 not just a legal obligation, but a practical imperative. If children are indeed capable of forming views, then their perspectives are valuable, worthy of consideration, and essential to decisions that impact them. This requires adults to adopt an attitude of deep respect and to create genuine opportunities for children's voices to be heard, recognizing that "capacity" is to be interpreted broadly, presuming children can form views from a very young age. In practice, embracing this image of the child transforms the very nature of educational environments. It moves beyond a curriculum driven solely by adult-imposed objectives or a rigid adherence to developmental milestones. Instead, it invites a pedagogy of inquiry.

THE ENVIRONMENT AS TEACHER

The environment is not only physical space. It is also the materials in the space and the broader community including the people in the community. In our gardens, hallways, and communal spaces, children's work was displayed with care and intention, honoring their ideas as meaningful contributions to the life of the school. These displays were never just decoration; they created spaces for conversation, inquiry, and reflection, where children's questions and theories were taken seriously. Educators, peers, and families engaged with the work thoughtfully, exploring, revisiting, and building on each child's thinking. Documentation was continuously referenced and revisited, allowing returning children to share prior knowledge with newcomers and to deepen ongoing explorations, emphasizing the value and respect we hold for children as citizens whose ideas spark collective curiosity and new understandings.

Through stories and inquires like the Living with Snails: Care and Coexistence, and the Transformation of a Tomato, the environment itself became a teacher. Spaces were intentionally arranged to support curiosity, collaboration, and reflection. Quiet corners invited contemplation and intimate dialogue, while open tables encouraged group problem-solving. Materials were carefully selected for their evocative power, offering open-ended possibilities for expression, transformation, and experimentation. Light tables, clay, paper, and natural materials communicated respect for children's capacities, inviting exploration that was meaningful and connected to their lived experiences.

The atelierista played a crucial role in this ecosystem of learning. Far from a traditional art teacher, the atelierista acted as a provocateur and researcher, attentive to children's symbolic development and skilled in guiding interdisciplinary inquiry. Collaborating with classroom educators, the atelierista suggested new materials, techniques, and approaches, supporting children as they translated ideas from one form of expression to another. Whether drawing a snail, building a bird city, or theorizing about the tomato machine, children were encouraged to explore, hypothesize, and represent their understanding across multiple modes, enriching both the process and the product of their learning.

Each project also contributed to the broader sense of school identity and community. Returning children saw themselves as custodians of knowledge, mentors, and co-investigators, while newcomers were welcomed into a culture of curiosity, care, and collaboration. This continuity reinforced the idea that learning is ongoing, iterative, and collective. Documentation was not a static record; it was a living conversation that connected past, present, and future, bridging individual and group understanding.

The integration of natural and found, upcycled, materials, the thoughtful orchestration of spaces, and the responsive guidance of educators together cultivated a profound respect for children as active participants in knowledge construction. It affirmed their capacity to inquire, theorize, and create, and nurtured their growing awareness of the interconnectedness of living systems, human creativity, and community life. From observing snails to designing bird habitats to investigating mechanical transformations, children were empowered to pose questions, seek answers, and express their understanding in rich, multidimensional ways.

The Acorn experiences, with their emphasis on continuity, responsiveness, and community engagement, exemplify the ways in which open-ended materials, thoughtful environments, and reflective pedagogy can support children's rights to explore, create, and engage with the world. They demonstrate that inquiry is not limited to discrete activities but emerges from sustained engagement, attentive listening, and the willingness to follow children's ideas wherever they lead. In this way, the tomato sauce project, and the other projects and stories becomes more than a task—it is a lens through which children, educators, and families co-construct knowledge, hold tensions, construct relationships, and celebrate the richness of learning together.

THE ATELIER AND THE HUNDRED LANGUAGES AS CULTURAL RIGHTS

Loris Malaguzzi's vision of the atelier extends far beyond a traditional art room. It is a space—or a way of being—that nurtures children's hundred languages, their many modes of expression, thought, and communication. Children's cultural rights, as outlined in Article 31 of the UNCRC, include play, recreation, and artistic participation. The atelier embodies these rights, providing children with opportunities to experiment, take risks, and communicate in diverse modalities.

Vea Vecchi described the atelier as *"a place for listening, for experimentation, for the practice of thinking in different languages."* (Vecchi, 2010) Here, thinking occurs through hands, bodies, materials, and movement. Clay, wire, paint, light, and found objects each foster unique cognitive processes. Children learn to problem-solve, create, and make meaning through these expressive languages.

At Acorn School, we embraced the concept of ateliers and atelieristas from Reggio Emilia because we believed that true educational partnership involves many contributors, each bringing unique perspectives. An atelierista, with a background in the arts and an eye for inquiry, helped us see the world through children's eyes and uncover deeper connections to their questions. We recognized that educators alone were not the only partners—chefs, artists, and other specialists enriched children's explorations.

The atelier was never just a room; it existed throughout classrooms, gardens, and shared spaces, bringing materials and tools that expanded possibilities for thinking and expression. Even after Acorn closed, the Acorn Collaborative continued as a studio where educators, students, and visiting collaborators could study, experiment, and engage in workshops. Collaborating with artist and art therapist Roberta Pucci reinforced the idea that the atelier could exist anywhere. Observing and exploring materials in studios, classrooms, or outdoors became a practice of slowing down, noticing, and valuing children's processes over predetermined outcomes. This "Everywhere Atelier" emphasized that the hundred languages are central to children's thinking, expression, and learning, and that collaboration with diverse partners enriches the life of the school.

Every space was alive with possibilities. Every space was thought out with care, intention, provoking and inviting exploration and encounters. The atelierista played a crucial role in guiding these experiences. Not simply an art teacher, they were a researcher, provocateur, and collaborator, skilled in multiple expressive media and attuned to children's symbolic thinking. Working alongside classroom teachers, the atelierista extended ideas, introduced new materials, and suggested ways of translating thought from one form to another—from clay to drawing, from drawing to dramatic play—allowing children to explore multiple perspectives and deepen their understanding of the natural and human world.

Every choice of space, material, and time was intentional. Materials were selected for their open-ended potential and the opportunities they offered for creative, ecological, and ethical thinking. Spaces were arranged to encourage collaboration, dialogue, reflection, and movement, while time was structured to respect children's rhythms and allow deep engagement. The aesthetic qualities of the environment communicated care and respect, demonstrating that beauty and order invite curiosity, focus, and ethical engagement.

Through these experiences, children practiced multiple "languages" of expression while learning to care for themselves, each other, and the world around them. They discovered that their actions mattered, that materials could be reused and transformed, and that life—whether a snail, a bird, or a tomato plant—deserves attention, respect, and care. Documentation became a vital tool for observing these processes, reflecting on growth, and sharing insights with peers, families, and educators.

The atelier, whether in a studio, classroom, or garden, became a space where we could truly listen to children, honoring their questions, ideas, and perspectives. Grounded in respect for the rights of children and the belief in their competence, these spaces affirmed the image of the child as an active, capable participant in shaping their own learning.

Even as the Reggio Emilia approach offered inspiration, we adapted these principles thoughtfully, considering our local context, culture, and resources. We aimed for authenticity over imitation, ensuring that every project, material, and space resonated with our children and community. Despite being a small school, our commitment to profound, meaningful learning allowed us to cultivate experiences that were rich, ethical, and deeply connected to both human and natural worlds.

The Acorn School experience reimagined children's rights as living, daily realities. By honoring children's curiosity, agency, and capacity for care, and by fostering environments that were thoughtful, sustainable, and reflective of ecological and social values, we created a community where every child's voice mattered and every potential could grow. Education, at its best, became an ethical, joyful, and imaginative practice, rooted in care for the child, the community, and the planet.

THE RIGHTS OF THE CHILD – FOLLOWING CURIOSITY

A rights-based approach values these theories as evidence of active thinking and engagement. Educators become researchers alongside children, helping them test, refine, and articulate their ideas. For example, during a lengthy project on light and shadow, children at Acorn hypothesized that shadows were "holes in the light" or "trapped darkness." Rather than correcting them, educators facilitated experiments with projectors, different light sources, and opaque objects, allowing children to challenge and build upon their own understanding. This iterative process fosters critical thinking, problem-solving, and a profound sense of intellectual agency.

Their interests are not diverted but cultivated. While structured learning has its place, a competent-child image prioritizes following and expanding upon children's emergent interests. This does not mean abandoning educational goals but rather weaving them into authentic, child-initiated explorations, making learning more meaningful, and engaging. If a group of children becomes fascinated by insects, the educators might introduce relevant books, magnify opportunities for outdoor observation, invite an entomologist to visit, and provide materials for drawing, sculpting, or even writing "insect stories." This respects the child's right to pursue their own pathways to knowledge and discovery, fostering deep engagement and sustained concentration. This profound shift in the image of the child necessitates an equally significant transformation in the role of the adult. When children are viewed as capable protagonists, adults can no longer remain mere instructors, disseminators of information, or even benevolent supervisors. Their role evolves to become that of:

Deep, active listening becomes paramount. This involves not just hearing words, but observing body language, interpreting non-verbal cues, and tuning into the implicit messages children convey through their play and interactions. As Carlina

Rinaldi emphasizes, listening is an "attitude of the mind," (Rindaldi, 2006) a sensitive receptivity to the child's communication in all its forms. This form of listening is an act of profound respect and an acknowledgement of the child's right to be understood, creating a sense of psychological safety and validation.

Educators position themselves as learners alongside children, open to new perspectives and unexpected discoveries. This shared journey dismantles traditional power hierarchies and fosters a collaborative learning environment where knowledge is co-constructed. Educators model curiosity and intellectual humility, demonstrating that learning is a lifelong process for everyone. This reciprocal learning enriches both child and adult.

From Wonder to Research

When a child's interest begins to surface, the work is not to immediately design a project. The work is to slow down. To listen. To notice. To step back and then listen again.

As Loris Malaguzzi reminded us, "Step aside awhile and leave room for learning, observe carefully what children do, and then, if you have understood well, perhaps teaching will be different from before." (Malaguzzi, 1994)

teaching is not the transmission of answers, but a relationship built through listening and research. Before educators can guide inquiry, they must be willing to question their own assumptions, to reconsider their habits, and sometimes to shift their way of teaching altogether.

Not every curiosity becomes a long-term project. Sometimes it opens new questions. Sometimes it asks us to pause longer. The real task is to ask ourselves:

Are we following the children, or leading them away from their thinking?

Have we truly understood what they are wondering?

What might change in us if we take their questions seriously?

DEMOCRACY, PARTICIPATION, AND COLLECTIVE RESPONSIBILITY

Crucially, a vision of democracy in early childhood education extends beyond children's participation to encompass the collective responsibility of adults. A democratic environment is co-constructed by everyone present—children, educators, parents, and community members. It requires educators to engage in shared listening: not only to children, but also to each other, to families, and to the broader environment. This multi-directional listening fosters a culture of mutual respect, transparency, and continuous learning. It involves:

Slowing down: Democratic processes require time for reflection, deliberation, and thoughtful exchange. Rushing can stifle genuine participation and the deep processing needed for complex learning. Educators must resist pressures to cover content quickly.

Suspending judgment: Listening with an open mind allows innovative ideas to emerge, empathy to grow, and unexpected solutions to arise. Educators must be willing to embrace vulnerability and consider perspectives different from their own.

Being open to transformation: Genuine dialogue requires willingness to adjust practices based on collective insights. Knowledge is fluid and co-constructed; pedagogical approaches are refined through shared inquiry and reflection.

Building trust: Democracy thrives on relationships of trust. Educators cultivate safety, consistency, and authenticity, enabling open communication, risk-taking, and vulnerability.

When adults embody these practices, children see that their voice matters, that disagreement can be productive, and that collective decision-making strengthens community life. They learn the value of compromise, the power of diverse perspectives, and the importance of collaborative action—skills that extend far beyond the classroom into engaged citizenship.

Fostering democratic participation in early childhood education has broader societal implications. Children who learn to negotiate differences, voice their ideas respectfully, and engage in critical thinking are more likely to become adults who participate constructively in society. They understand the consequences of their actions and the potential of collective action to effect change. In this way, democratic pedagogy cultivates dispositions necessary for informed, empathetic, and engaged citizens, fulfilling the vision of Articles 12 and 13 of the UN Convention on the Rights of the Child—the rights to be heard and to freely express ideas.

DOCUMENTATION AS A TOOL FOR VISIBILITY, RESEARCH, AND ADVOCACY

In progressive education, documentation is one of the most transformative practices. Far from being bureaucratic, it is a sophisticated pedagogical tool, a research methodology, and a powerful form of advocacy. Documentation makes visible the often-ephemeral processes of learning, thinking, and relating, affirming children's rights and presence in the world. Its purpose is not merely to evaluate what children know but to understand how they know, why they ask questions, and who they are in relation to others and their environment.

Our work with Lella Gandini, a pivotal figure in bringing Reggio-inspired approaches to North America, deeply influenced this understanding. Lella's visits to Acorn School involved not only observation but rich conversation and reflection. Her guidance emphasized that documentation should make visible "the traces of thought, the process of becoming, and the relationships that form the context of every idea." These encounters encouraged us to slow down, ask better questions, and focus on the process of learning rather than the final product.

For instance, our Tomato Sauce project became an exemplar of documentation's depth. We captured children's hypotheses, their conversations, the challenges they encountered, and their breakthroughs. Through photographs, notes, and transcriptions, the project revealed not only children's intellectual engagement but also their evolving relationships with peers, educators, and the natural environment. Meals and shared food became extensions of this pedagogy, fostering dialogue, reflection, and community participation.

Documentation serves multiple, intertwined roles:

Making learning visible: Capturing children's processes through photos, transcripts, drawings, and constructions allows educators, peers, and families to see the evolution of ideas, strategies, and problem-solving.

Supporting pedagogical research: Educators engage in continuous reflection, questioning assumptions, exploring emergent interests, and refining approaches. Documentation enables a cycle of observation, reflection, dialogue, and adjustment, embracing complexity rather than seeking simplistic answers.

Enhancing communication and connection: Thoughtful documentation communicates children's learning to families, colleagues, and the wider community, engaging them as co-participants and advocates.

Constructing memory and identity: Children revisit past projects, reflect on their growth, and see the progression of their thinking. The learning community gains a shared sense of history, identity, and belonging.

Advocacy for children's rights: Documentation provides tangible evidence of children's creativity, intelligence, and collaborative capacities. It affirms their rights to expression, cultural participation, and active citizenship, challenging societal assumptions that underestimate children's agency.

As **Reggio Children** emphasizes, *"Documentation is not a technique but an attitude. It is a tool for research, for listening, for making hypotheses, and for constructing memory."* It is a deeply ethical practice, requiring consent, careful representation, and attention to power dynamics.

CONCLUSION

At Acorn School, our journey has always been about more than curriculum; it has been about honoring the child as a competent, capable, and curious rights-bearer. Each moment—whether in the classroom, the studio, the garden, or the hallway—was an opportunity to listen, observe, and engage deeply with children's theories and ideas. Simple wooden blocks became intricate architectural explorations, prompting investigations into balance, stability, and imagination. Open-ended materials—shells, buttons, fabrics, natural objects—invited children to tell stories, create patterns, and express symbolic ideas, giving form to their thinking. In shared spaces, displays of children's work sparked dialogue, reflection, and further inquiry among peers, educators, and families, creating living documentation that continually provoked new ideas.

The tomato sauce project remains one of our most vivid illustrations of this approach. Each year, children revisited the previous year's documentation, building on the knowledge of those who had been at the school longer while welcoming new peers into the process. For returning children, there was a profound sense of pride in sharing and revisiting their contributions, anchoring the school's identity around this communal, multisensory endeavor. Inevitably, the project sparked new questions. One year, some children became fascinated by the machine used to crush the tomatoes. They watched intently as whole tomatoes transformed into a smooth, soupy texture, their eyes widening as they tried to trace where the tomato "went" and how the machine worked. The unfolding theories, hypotheses, and experiments were never about arriving at definitive answers. They were part of an ongoing process of thinking about thinking — questioning, revisiting, and deepening understanding. Rather than scripted activities, they became shared investigations, shaped by the children's evolving ideas. Each theory opened another possibility; each experiment generated new questions. What emerged was not a search for conclusions, but a sustained commitment to inquiry, guided by curiosity and a willingness to stay with complexity. As educators, we learned that understanding the image of the child at this time means honoring their drive to make sense of the world. This required slowing down, paying close attention to each question, action, and expression, and considering carefully how and when to engage, what to ask, and what new provocations might invite deeper thinking. It was not about rushing through predetermined lessons, but about entering dialogue with children, letting their ideas lead us into further investigations, and reflecting continuously on our own role in supporting their thinking.

Other stories from Acorn illustrate this philosophy in action. In the snail inquiry, children observed the slow movements, textures, and patterns of garden snails, generating questions about how they lived, what they ate, and how they interacted with their environment. This curiosity led to a rich, emergent exploration of biology, observation, and documentation, driven entirely by the children's hypotheses. In the Bird City project, children built elaborate nests and habitats, exploring relationships between living things and their environments. They collaborated, shared discoveries, and negotiated solutions, developing an embodied understanding of interdependence, care, and ecological responsibility. Each inquiry, each project, underscored our commitment to seeing children as active participants in knowledge-making, rather than passive recipients of information.

The environment—carefully designed spaces, thoughtfully chosen materials, and the relationships woven among children and adults—served as a third teacher. Every element, from the layout of the classroom to the natural materials in the garden, communicated respect for children's capacities and an invitation to exploration. The atelier, guided by the studio teacher, or atelierista, offered additional layers of provocation, introducing new materials, techniques, and ideas, fostering connections across artistic, scientific, and social domains. In these spaces, children were free to translate their ideas across multiple "languages": from spoken theories to drawings, from drawings to clay sculptures, from sculptures to dramatic play. Each translation deepened understanding, offered new perspectives, and honored the complexity of children's thinking.

Today, more than ten years after Acorn School closed its doors, we continue to honor and reflect upon its legacy through carefully curated mini books. These volumes capture glimpses of the school's practices—the thoughtful selection of materials, the open-ended tools, the design of environments that provoke curiosity, and the rich relationships that connected children, adults, and the natural world. They serve as living reflections of the school's pedagogy, allowing educators, families, and communities to engage with the processes that once animated Acorn. Revisiting these materials not only inspires but also illuminates how the principles of inquiry, collaboration, and rights-affirming practice can continue to guide educational experiences today.

Through these stories, we see that children's rights are not abstract ideals—they are lived realities. The right to create, to explore, to express identity, and to engage meaningfully with the natural world is enacted daily in spaces designed to provoke curiosity, foster collaboration, and respect each child's unique rhythms and interests. By valuing children's ideas, honoring their investigations, and entering dialogue with them, we affirm their intellectual, emotional, and social rights. Each inquiry, each carefully observed interaction, is an act of recognition: a declaration that children are capable, that their voices matter, and that their perspectives are central to our shared understanding of the world.

The projects and inquiries described throughout this chapter—from the snail inquiry and Bird City to the annual tomato sauce tradition—demonstrate that children are not passive recipients of education but active contributors to knowledge, theory, and shared understanding. Each inquiry reflects their curiosity, persistence, and unique ways of making sense of the world. At Acorn School, children's questions and ideas shaped the trajectory of investigations, guiding educators to listen carefully, respond thoughtfully, and enter genuine dialogues. For example, in the tomato sauce project, children returning from previous years took pride in revisiting earlier documentation, while new children brought fresh questions that sparked further exploration. Their fascination with the tomato-crushing machine led to unfolding theories, hypotheses, and collaborative problem-solving, highlighting the dynamic and reciprocal nature of learning.

Honoring the child as a contributor aligns closely with the principles articulated in the UN Convention on the Rights of the Child (1989), which asserts children's right to participate in decisions affecting their lives, to express themselves, and to have their ideas valued. Recognizing children as co-researchers also embodies Carla Rinaldi's pedagogy of listening, emphasizing that the role of the adult is to understand, document, and extend children's thinking rather than impose pre-determined activities. Each inquiry becomes a shared journey in which questions are raised not to fit an external curriculum, but to explore what is meaningful to the children, their peers, and the learning community.

As we reflect on the Acorn School journey, even nearly a decade after the school's closure, the lessons remain vivid. The carefully curated mini books capturing projects, materials, and relationships stand as a testament to the children's contributions and the enduring significance of environments, tools, and adults who listened deeply. These narratives continue to inspire educators to design spaces that honor children's agency, celebrate their ideas, and commit to their rights as central to every educational encounter. By acknowledging children as contributors, we embrace a pedagogy that is not only ethically responsible but deeply transformative—one that recognizes that the child's voice, curiosity, and intellect are not supplementary, but essential, to the creation of meaningful, rights-affirming learning communities.

This chapter calls educators, policymakers, and communities to embrace children's rights as living, ethical imperatives. By fostering environments that are democratic, participatory, and attentive to the multitude of "languages" through which children express themselves, we contribute to a more just and humane society. At Acorn, small in scale but mighty in conviction, we witnessed the powerful potential of a community that believed in children's knowledge, honored their curiosity, and committed to co-constructing learning together. Each child, like a small acorn, held within them the potential for remarkable growth—growth that flourishes when nurtured with respect, curiosity, and trust. They are not simply ideals to aspire to—they are the foundation of a vibrant, ethical, and imaginative approach to education that remains as urgent and inspiring today as it was in the classrooms, gardens, and studios of Acorn School.

REFERENCES

Korczak, J. (1967). *Selected works of Janusz Korczak* (Lewin, A., Trans.). Foreign Languages Publishing House. (Original work published in Polish)

Malaguzzi, L. (1993). History, ideas, and basic philosophy: An interview with Lella Gandini. In C. Edwards, L. Gandini, & G. Forman (Eds.), *The hundred languages of children: The Reggio Emilia approach to early childhood education* (pp. 9–16). Ablex Publishing.

Malaguzzi, L. (1994). Your image of the child: Where teaching begins. In C. Edwards, L. Gandini, & G. Forman (Eds.), *The hundred languages of children: The Reggio Emilia approach—Advanced reflections* (pp. 1–10). Ablex Publishing.

Malaguzzi, L. (1998). History, ideas, and basic philosophy: An interview with Lella Gandini. In C. Edwards, L. Gandini, & G. Forman (Eds.), *The hundred languages of children: The Reggio Emilia approach—Advanced reflections* (2nd ed., pp. 49–97). Ablex Publishing.

Piaget, J. (1952). *The origins of intelligence in children* (Cook, M., Trans.). International Universities Press. (Original work published 1936) DOI: 10.1037/11494-000

Reggio Children. (1997). *The amusement park for birds: A project from the infant-toddler centers and preschools of Reggio Emilia*. Reggio Children.

Rinaldi, C. (2006). *In dialogue with Reggio Emilia: Listening, researching and learning*. Routledge.

United Nations General Assembly. (1989). *Convention on the Rights of the Child.* United Nations, Treaty Series, vol. 1577, p. 3. https://www.ohchr.org/en/instruments-mechanisms/instruments/convention-rights-child

Vecchi, V. (2010). *Art and creativity in Reggio Emilia: Exploring the role and potential of ateliers in early childhood education*. Routledge. DOI: 10.4324/9780203854679

Vygotsky, L. S. (1978). *Mind in society: The development of higher psychological processes* (Cole, M., John-Steiner, V., Scribner, S., & Souberman, E., Eds. & Trans.). Harvard University Press.

Chapter 7

Moving Beyond Reggio Emilia's "Special Rights" to a Rights-Based Response for All Children in the Irish Context:

Learning From the Reggio Emilia Experience

Emer Ring
http://orcid.org/0000-0001-8459-8625
Mary Immaculate College, Ireland

Lisha O'Sullivan
http://orcid.org/0009-0007-5713-9387
Mary Immaculate College, Ireland

ABSTRACT

In Reggio Emilia, children typically referred to as 'children with disabilities or 'children with special needs' are described as 'children with special rights'. Propelled by a rights-based agenda, governments globally are grappling with the policy and practice demands of building inclusive education systems that each child can access, participate in and benefit from. The Leadership for INClusion in the Early Years (LINC) Programme in Ireland adopts the Reggio Emilia focus on the image of the child; the hundred languages of children; a pedagogy of listening and the environment as the third were among the key principles embedded in the programme.

DOI: 10.4018/979-8-3373-3431-8.ch007

Drawing on an extensive evaluations of the programme, the authors will consider how the Reggio Emilia foci of the programme have been instrumental to the success and overall impact of the programme on the lives of children, teachers and families.

INTRODUCTION

A key principle of the Reggio Emilia approach is that children typically referred to as 'children with disabilities or 'children with special needs' are described as "children with special rights" (Soncini, 2012, p.189). This is an important distinction and invokes the rights-based foundation on which the inclusive educational approach proposed by the infant-toddler centres (asili nido) and preschools (scuole dell'infanzia) of Reggio Emilia is built. Propelled by a rights-based agenda, governments globally are grappling with the policy and practice demands of building inclusive education systems that each child can access, participate in, benefit from and experience a sense of belonging (Ring, 2024). While each education system has unique social, political, economic, historical and cultural influences, the critical importance of prevention, early identification, assessment and stimulation of the young child together with teacher competency have been identified as intricately linked to effective inclusive education systems (European Agency for Special Needs and Inclusive Education [EASNIE], 2025; United Nations Educational, Scientific and Cultural Organisation [UNESCO)], 1994; Organisation for Economic Co-operation and Development [OECD], 2023).

In Ireland, the compulsory school-starting age is six, however, historically children can commence primary school at four years of age. Notably school-starting age has been increasing steadily over the past number of years with the overall proportion of four-year olds starting school reduced from 46.3% in 2002 to 16.9% in 2022 (Department of Education [DoE], 2023). One of the key factors contributing to this development is the introduction in 2010 of a universal free preschool year and its subsequent expansion in 2016 to two years (O'Sullivan & Ring, 2023). Cognisant of the contribution of prevention, early intervention and teacher professional learning to a competent early childhood system, in 2015, the Irish government launched a new programme of supports aimed at providing for the inclusion of children with 'special rights' (Ring & Breen, 2017). This initiative included a programme of teacher professional learning to support existing early childhood teachers in leading inclusive culture, practice and pedagogy for children in early childhood settings prior to the commencement of formal primary or elementary schooling.

The development of this programme, the Leadership for INClusion in the Early Years [LINC] Programme is located in research on prevention, early intervention and inclusion (LINC Consortium, 2019; 2024: 2025a). All early childhood teachers working with babies (birth-18 months), toddlers (12 months-3 years)and young children (2.5 years-6 years) in settings contracted to deliver the universal free preschool are eligible to participate in the programme which is free for participants. Once applicants fulfil this eligibility criterion, places are allocated on a first come, first served basis. Between 527 and 875 early childhood teachers per year have participated in the programme since its establishment in 2016. A total of 6,217 graduates have completed the programme to date with ongoing evaluations confirming its positive impact on teacher competency to provide for the diversity of learners in early childhood settings (LINC Consortium 2019; 2024; 2025a). The LINC programme is firmly located within the Irish curriculum and quality frameworks for early childhood education (Centre for Early Childhood Development and Education [CECDE], 2006; National Council for Curriculum and Assessment [NCCA], 2009; 2025; Government of Ireland [GoI] 2018; 2024a; 2024b). Focused on equipping learners with the requisite knowledge(s), practices and values to lead inclusive culture, practice and pedagogy in their settings, the LINC Programme prepares early childhood teachers to adopt the role of INclusion CO-ordinator [INCO] in their early childhood settings (LINC Consortium, 2019; 2022; 2024: 2025a). As INCOs, early childhood teachers continue to function in their role as a teacher, while also leading best practice through modelling and coaching for other colleagues in the setting.

We have been involved as researchers in the significant corpus of research that has been generated in relation to the LINC programme from its inception (LINC Consortium, 2019; 2024; 2025a). In this chapter, we will draw specifically on the research, Leading from Within: Developing a Professional Portfolio for Inclusion in the Early Years (LINC Consortium, 2025a). This research identifies the extent to which the professional portfolios compiled by the LINC Programme graduates reflect the competencies associated with providing high-quality early childhood education for babies, toddlers and young children. These competencies are discussed further below and comprise the Competency Framework underpinning the programme. In developing the programme, together with the Irish curriculum and quality frameworks, the Reggio Emilia principles at Figure 1. below relating to the image of the child; the hundred languages of children; a pedagogy of listening and the environment as the third teacher were among the key principles embedded in the Competency Framework underpinning the programme (Breen et al., 2018; Edwards et al., 2012).

Figure 1. Reggio Emilia principles embedded in the LINC programme.

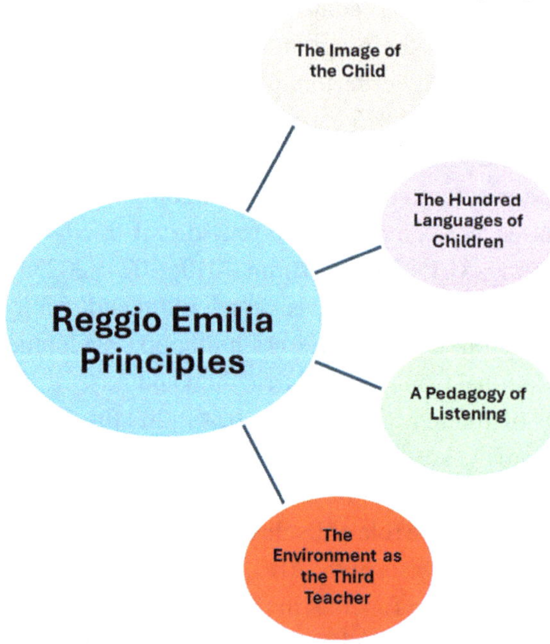

Note: The principles in the image are among the key principles underpinning the pedagogical approach that has evolved in the infant-toddler centres (asili nido) and preschools (scuole dell'infanzia) of Reggio Emilia as referenced by C. Edwards, L. Gandini, & G. Forman, (Eds), 2012, The hundred languages of children: The Reggio Emilia experience in transformation (3rd ed.).

Following a probing of the concept of 'Special Rights' and an examination of its alignment with the vision of the United Nations Convention on the Rights of the Child [UNCRC] (1989) and the United Nations Convention on the Rights of Persons with Disabilities [UNCRPD] (2006), a detailed overview of the content and foci of the LINC programme is presented (United Nations [UN] 1989; 2006). Each of the Reggio Emilia principles in Figure 1 is then interrogated in the context of their specific application to the Competency Framework underpinning the programme and the extent to which they are visible in graduates' professional portfolios identified. In concluding and taking into consideration developments in Irish curriculum frameworks, we will consider the potential of these principles to contribute to the next iteration of the LINC programme due to commence in 2026.

'SPECIAL RIGHTS': A RIGHTS-BASED IMAGE OF CHILDHOOD

Based on a range of cultural and historical influences, the lens through which human difference is viewed varies across societies and continues to shift as knowledge and understanding of human difference evolves. For much of the last century in western societies, difference was viewed through the lens of a medical model that differentiated typical from atypical development and equated difference with an impairment residing in the person that required curing, fixing or tolerating (Andrews et al., 2000). In the 1970s, a social lens propelled a shift from a medical model in identifying environments, attitudes and legislation as constraints generated by society that in effect disabled people (Broderick, 2015). The social lens has been critiqued for overlooking the experience of the individual, leading to more holistic lenses emerging based on Urie Bronfenbrenner's bio-ecological model (Bronfenbrenner, 1979; Morris, 1991). A bio-ecological lens prioritises the child's experience and underscores the need to focus on all of the relationships in the child's environment together with the uniqueness of each child's abilities and differences in order to foster each child's sense of belonging, wellbeing, learning and development (Ring 2021). Across education contexts this translates to an expectation that difference is a key defining feature, which must be appropriately responded to in order to ensure that each child thrives and achieves their potential from early childhood through their experience in the school system more broadly.

Together with a more holistic concept of children's learning and development afforded by a bio-ecological lens, the articulation and embedding of a rights-based approach across western democracies is increasingly influencing societal responses to children and childhood (Wyness, 2019; O'Sullivan & Ring. 2026). In a post-world-war (1939-1945) context, the Universal Declaration of Human Rights (UDHR) identified the universal freedoms and human rights that required safeguarding (UN, 1948). The UDHR's influence is apparent in the provisions of the Declaration of the Rights of the Child in 1959, the UNCRC in 1989 and the UNCRPD in 2006 (UN,1959; 1989; 2006). Marking a watershed moment for achieving children's social, cultural, civil, economic, political and educational rights, the UNCRC in its fifty-four articles positions the child as a protagonist in their own lives (Višnjić-Jevtić et al., 2021). Through the UNCRC reporting mechanisms required by the UN, countries who ratify the Treaty have an obligation to submit reports regularly, notifying the progress they have made in implementing the Treaty's provisions (UN Committee on the Rights of the Child, 2023). Annual Report Cards are also published by the Children's Rights Alliance [CRA] in the Irish context detailing how the government is fulfilling its obligations vis-à-vis the UNCRC (CRA, 2025). A key focus of the UN's monitoring process has been an assessment of how the State party is integrating a rights-based approach in the planning, implementation and monitoring of measures to achieve the Sustainable Development Goals [SDGs] (UN, 2015; 2025). While international law does not have the binding force of national law unless it is legally incorporated in legislation, in the Irish experience, a commitment to rights has exerted a compelling influence on children's experiences in early childhood contexts as evidenced in quality, curriculum and inspection frameworks that acknowledge children's agency (CECDE, 2006; GoI, 2024a; 2024b; DoE, 2025). Reflecting the quality, curriculum and inspection frameworks foci on realising the rights of all the children, the LINC programme is underpinned by a rights-based approach, which rather than advocating for 'special rights' for some children, advocates for the application of a rights-based approach for each child. It is envisaged that realising a rights-based approach for each child will ensure that the individual abilities of each child are understood and the needs of each child are met appropriately.

LEADERSHIP FOR INCLUSION IN THE EARLY YEARS PROGRAMME: AN OVERVIEW

In 1994, Ireland had been one of twenty-five international organisations and ninety-two governments subscribing to the principles adopted by the World Conference on Special Needs Education: Access and Quality in Salamanca, Spain in 1994 (UNESCO. 1994). Among these principles were a commitment to the early identification, assessment and stimulation of young children together with an associated acknowledgement of the need for systemic reform of teacher education. It was specifically noted that the success of the inclusive school was dependent on the effectiveness of early identification and intervention in early childhood education (Ring & O'Sullivan, 2019). For largely historical reasons, until relatively recently in Ireland, investment had focused primarily on elementary education to the detriment of early childhood education (Ring, 2024). The introduction of a universal free preschool year for all children from age three in January 2010, with a second year subsequently added in 2016 (O'Sullivan & Ring, 2023), signalled a recognition at policy-level that investment in early childhood education was becoming a government imperative, requiring both a universal and targeted approach.

In 2015, following an extensive inter-governmental consultation process that included parents of neurodivergent children and representative bodies and agencies for early childhood education in Ireland, a seven -level model was developed aimed at supporting the early identification and intervention for children with diverse needs and abilities in early childhood settings (Inter-Departmental Group [IDG], 2015; Ring & O'Sullivan, 2019). The seven-level Better Start Access and Inclusion Model [AIM] is located in national and international evidence and chimes with a rights-based image of childhood discussed above previously and referenced throughout this publication. The AIM at Figure 2 below mirrors the bio-ecological lens that acknowledges all of the relationships in the child's environment together with the uniqueness of each child's abilities and differences (Ring, 2021).

Figure 2. Better Start access and inclusion model

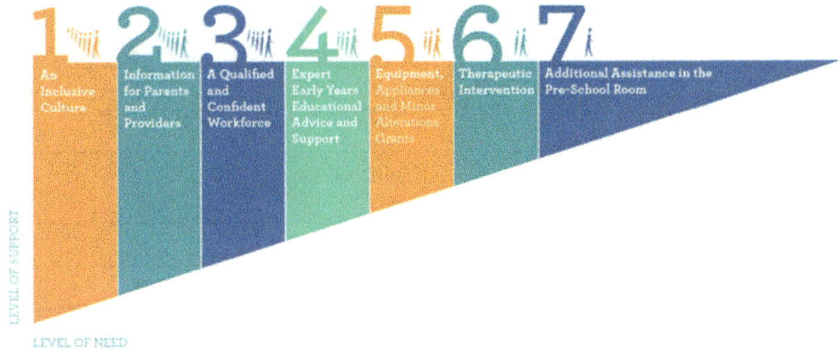

Note: Reprinted from "Supporting access to the early childhood care and education (ecce) programme for children with a disability" by the Inter-departmental Group 2015, p.6. Copyright 2026 by the Department of Children, Disability and Equality. Used with permission.

The access and inclusion model (AIM) was developed to provide both universal and targeted support in identifying, assessing and responding to each child's differences in early childhood settings in Ireland.

Eschewing an exclusive reliance on formal diagnostic processes, the AIM maintains a child-centred focus that recognises the professionalism of the early childhood teacher as key in identifying, assessing and responding to each child's differences (Ring & O'Sullivan 2019). It is envisaged that each level of the model is inextricably linked, with Levels 1-3 of the AIM focusing on universal supports and Levels 4-7 constituting a set of targeted supports. Together with free Equality, Diversity and Inclusion [EDI] professional learning, inclusive play resources and materials for early childhood settings, the LINC Programme is located at Level 1 of the AIM and is regarded as key to the policy vision of the development of an Inclusive Culture (Robinson et al., 2022). Following the completion of a government procurement process, the tender for the development of the LINC Programme was awarded to a Consortium led by Mary Immaculate College [MIC], Limerick and including Early Childhood Ireland [ECI] and Maynooth University Froebel Department of Primary and Early Childhood Education [MU-Froebel Dept.]. As the leader of the Consortium, MIC is responsible for the delivery and accreditation of the programme. Positioned as a 60 credit special purpose award at Level 6 on the Irish National Framework of Qualifications [NFQ] (Quality and Qualifications Ireland [QQI], 2021), the LINC programme encompasses the six modules at Table 1 below and includes asynchronous and synchronous delivery.

Table 1. Content and delivery of the leadership for INClusion in the early years (LINC) programme

Module	Credits	Semester
Inclusion in Early Years Settings: Concepts and Strategies	12	Autumn
Child Development*	6	Autumn
Promoting Collaborative Practice for Inclusion in Early Childhood Care and Education	12	Autum/Spring
Curriculum for Inclusion	6	Spring
Leadership for Inclusion	12	Spring
Professional Portfolio	12	Autumn/Spring

Note: Module titles, credits and semesters in which these modules are developed in the Leadership for INClusion in the Early Years (LINC) Programme. See *Interim evaluation of the leadership for inclusion in the early years (LINC) programme, LINC Consortium:* E. Ring, S. Kelleher, T. Heeney, M. McLoughlin, A. Kearns, P. Stafford, S. Skehill, K. Campion, K., D. Comerford, & L. O'Sullivan, 2019, pp.24-26.

The programme integrates online and in-person learning experiences, and adopts a flexible approach that aims to optimise learning through employing key principles of instructional and universal design together with recognised learning theories in supporting learners to translate the theoretical basis for inclusion into practice (Breen et al., 2018). Learners' existing experience in working with babies, toddlers and young children is built on and a differentiated approach adopted based on individual learners' contexts. A mentoring visit is also provided for each learner and is linked explicitly to the Professional Portfolio module. On completion of the programme, graduates may be appointed as INCOs in an early childhood setting and key aspects of the role of an INCO include leading inclusive practice, pedagogy and culture in the setting; cascading learning in the setting; supporting colleagues; sharing learning and good practice, engaging with local and national developments relevant to inclusion and engaging in ongoing professional learning (Better Start National Early Years Quality Development Service, n.d.). An INCO also has a role in relation to supporting the effective implementation of the AIM across both universal and targeted dimensions; promoting the Diversity, Equality and Inclusion Charter and Guidelines; advocating on behalf of, and for children and supporting families (Department of Children and Youth Affairs [DCYA], 2016; Better Start National Early Years Quality Development Service, n.d.). While the focus of this chapter is on the LINC Programme, it is noteworthy that, following graduates' articulation of their positive experiences on the programme and the need to extend their learning further, that a LINC+ programme commenced in 2021, to provide further professional learning for graduates of the LINC programme (LINC Consortium, 2025b). To date, 6,210 early childhood teachers have successfully completed the LINC Programme. Reflecting the universal and targeted approach of the AIM, the LINC Programme is built on developing the key inter-connected competencies at Table 2 that research indicates are essential to cultivating inclusive culture, practices and pedagogy for all children (EASNIE, 2017a; 2017b; 2025; UNESCO, 1994; OECD, 2023).

Table 2. Competencies Associated With Providing Early Childhood Education for all Children

A. An Inclusive Culture	
1	All children are welcome.
2	All children are valued.
3	A focus is placed on promoting respectful interactions.
4	There are high expectations for all children.
5	Partnership with parents/carers is actively promoted.
6	Difference is acknowledged and celebrated.
7	The environment accommodates the needs of all children.
8	All policies are inclusive policies.
B. Inclusive Practice	
1	Transitioning to and from the setting is a positive experience for children, families and staff.
2	Support for children with additional needs is co-ordinated.
3	Staff members are encouraged to avail of continuing professional development opportunities.
4	All staff are aware of their roles and responsibilities in relation to the promotion of inclusive practice.
5	The expertise of staff is acknowledged and utilised.
C. An Inclusive Pedagogy	
1	Children's experiences are planned with the needs of all children in mind.
2	Strategies are in place to promote the participation of all children in learning.
3	A range of appropriate pedagogical approaches is used to support the holistic development of all children.
4	Play and playful learning are key features of practice for all children.
5	All children's communication and interaction are promoted.
6	All children's views are valued and responded to.
7	Early identification of children who require additional support is central to practice.
8	A variety of approaches to observation, recording and assessment is in place.
9	Early years educators plan, implement and evaluate children's learning in partnership with children, parents/carers and relevant others.
10	Positive relationships are understood and nurtured.
11	Children's specific assessed needs are understood as 'signposts' that support children's learning and development.
12	External assistance is elicited where required to support the setting in meeting children's additional needs.

Note: These competences underpin the Leadership for INClusion in the Early Years (LINC) Programme. See *Interim evaluation of the leadership for inclusion in the early years (LINC) programme, LINC Consortium:*

E. Ring, S. Kelleher, T. Heeney, M. McLoughlin, A. Kearns, P. Stafford, S. Skehill, K. Campion, K., D. Comerford, & L. O'Sullivan, 2019, p.40.

Ongoing evaluation of the programme from its establishment indicates that the programme continues to be effective in contributing to the professionalisation of the early childhood sector through developing the key competencies identified in Table 2 above (Breen et al., 2018; LINC Consortium, 2019; 2024; 2025a; Ring & O'Sullivan, 2019; Robinson et al. 2022). Graduates consistently report a positive impact on their practice following completion of the programme, as encapsulated by Sally Harnett, a graduate of the programme:

> *My further studies through the LINC Programme and my role as INclusion CO-ordinator have shaped my approach to early childhood education. I critically reflect on how effectively I include children with additional needs, engage their families, and involve the wider community. I consider the way we set up our environments and learning experiences and question how we can work in a way that benefits all the children and families attending our early years' service. (LINC Consortium, 2025a, p. 24).*

Graduates of the programme, current students and personnel involved in the delivery of the programme variously contribute to the LINC Programme Blog Platform, which provides a further rich repository of insights into the experience and impact of the programme at individual and setting levels (LINC Consortium, 2016-2025). Learners' Professional Portfolios are a key source of data in assessing the impact of the programme at both individual and setting levels.

LEARNERS' PROFESSIONAL PORTFOLIOS

From the commencement of the LINC Programme in 2016, it has been a mandatory requirement for all participants to complete a Professional Portfolio with the specific aim of providing a mechanism for learners to probe and understand their individual journey of professional development, growth and change during their engagement with the programme (LINC Consortium 2025a). These portfolios reflect learners' experiences with babies, toddlers and young children. It is well acknowledged in the literature that the process of creating a portfolio can be a catalyst to generate new professional learning and insights; deepen the connections for the learner between theory and their own practice and effectively support competency assessment (Byrne et al. 2009; Jones & Shelton 2011; Bonfield & Horgan 2016: Gül Hazar & Yilmaz, 2025).

In this module, learners have an opportunity to demonstrate their learning throughout the programme and indicate how they have bridged the theoretical basis of the programme with their own practice in early childhood settings (LINC Consortium, 2025a). The compilation of a portfolio supports learners in documenting and reflecting on their attitudes, values, beliefs, and assumptions in relation to working with, and on behalf of babies, toddlers and young children. This module creates a space for each learner to reflect on, and document their own pedagogical practice; consider how their reflective practice has developed their own professional practice and that of the team in their setting to achieve a welcoming, inclusive space for all children. This module is framed within the competencies associated with providing early childhood education for all children detailed at Table 2, above and is expected to be linked to all of the other modules on the programme in addition to the mentoring visit each learner receives while engaging in the programme. According to Ann McDonagh, a graduate of the LINC Programme "The experience of completing my Portfolio and studying the LINC Programme has given me much more than a recognised professional standing. It has given me pride, a sense of accomplishment and confidence" (LINC Consortium, 2025a, p. 20).

In positioning the Reggio Emilia principles of the image of the child; the hundred languages of children; a pedagogy of listening and the environment as the third teacher across the LINC Programme Competency Framework (Edwards et al., 2012), it was envisaged that these principles would be prominent in learners' portfolios. With reference to the recent publication, *Leading from Within: Developing a Professional Portfolio for Inclusion in the Early Years* (LINC Consortium, 2025a), we will firstly summarise how these principles are envisioned in the LINC programme and interrogate the data to assess whether they are evident in the professional portfolios developed by students.

THE IMAGE OF THE CHILD: AS ENVISAGED IN THE LEADERSHIP FOR INCLUSION IN THE EARLY YEARS PROGRAMME COMPETENCY FRAMEWORK

The image of the child in the LINC Programme is understood through an interrogation of the dominant constructs of childhood that have influenced how the image of the child and childhood has been understood and accordingly responded to throughout history (Ariès,1962; Sorin, 2005; Lally, 2006; Lancy, 2015; O'Sullivan & Ring, 2026). A summary of these constructs is provided in Figure 3 below.

Figure 3. Dominant constructs of childhood

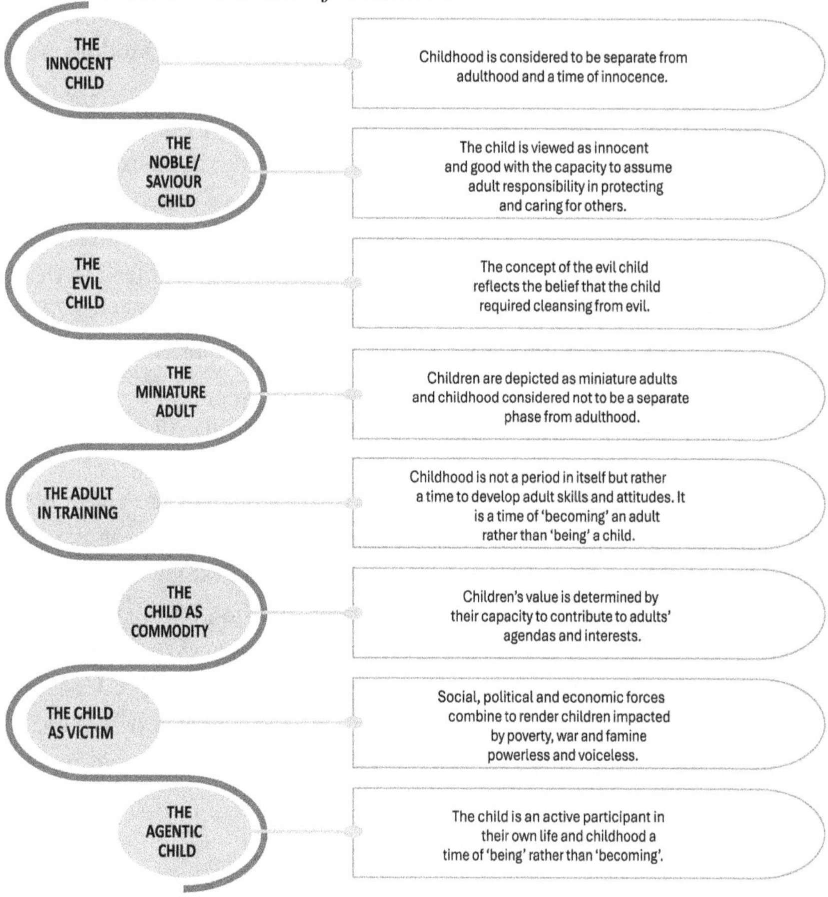

Note: This figure was designed by the authors based on the work of P. Ariès, 1962, Centuries of childhood; D.F. Lancy, 2015; The anthropology of childhood. Cherubs, chattels, changelings (3rd ed.); L.O'Sullivan & E. Ring, 2025, Play from the inside out: Theory, research and practice and R. Sorin, 2005, "Changing images of childhood: Reconceptualising early childhood practice" in International Journal of Transitions in Childhood, 1(1), pp. 12-21.

We further suggest that these constructs are not incompatible or confined to specific historical periods and can overtly or implicitly impact on how childhood is understood and experienced by children in the 21st century. For example, children can be perceived as: dependent on adults; fittingly assigned adult responsibilities; requiring adult direction; miniature adults with associated expectations in terms of how they should behave; deficient in not having achieved adult-identified developmental goals; commodities under adult control and powerless as victims of social, political and economic forces that contribute to child-poverty, famine, wars, homelessness and climate change (O'Sullivan & Ring, 2026). Other than the construct of the child as agentic therefore, all of these constructs are inconsistent with the image of the child as a rights-bearer envisaged in the terms of the UNCRC and the UNCRPD (UN, 1989; 2006). Malaguzzi, writing in 1993a, compiled a Charter of Rights for children, teachers and parents. He noted that:

> *Children have the right to be recognized as subjects of individual, legal, civil and social rights; as both source and constructors of their own experience, and thus active participants in the organization of their identities, abilities, and autonomy, through relationships and interaction with their peers, with adults, with ideas, with objects, and with the real and imaginary events of intercommunicating worlds. All this, while establishing the fundamental premises for creating better "citizens of the world" and raising the quality of human interaction, also credits children, and each individual child, with an extraordinary wealth of inborn abilities and potential, strength and creativity. Irreversible suffering and impoverishment of the child is caused when this fact is not acknowledged (Malaguzzi, 1993a, p. 5).*

The image of the agentic child is therefore rooted in the Reggio Emilia approach and was selected specifically in developing the LINC programme to provide opportunities for learners to probe the impact of their image of the child on their practice as early childhood educators and to ensure its alignment with the construct of the child as a rights-bearer.

The concept of the agentic child is rooted in what Carlina Rinaldi identifies as "the socialist ideas that took hold in our area of Italy in the late nineteenth century and early twentieth century" (2021, p.134), which she suggests were in effect a manifestation of the values of Liberty, Equality and Fraternity articulated during the French Revolution. As the radical ideas of socialism took hold in this area of Italy, Rinaldi notes their influence on women demanding their own rights outside the family leading them to demand quality public services as a right, including quality early childhood education. In a context where citizens were becoming attuned to their rights, children's rights also came into focus propelled by an image of the agentic child as "rich in potential, strong, powerful, competent, and most of all connected to adults and other children" (Malaguzzi, 1993b, p10). Agency is viewed as embedded in relationships involving children, adults, and an environment, which displays respect for children's interests, curiosity, questions and diversity (Manera 2022; Rinaldi 2021).

THE IMAGE OF THE CHILD: VISIBILITY IN LINC PROGRAMME GRADUATES' PORTFOLIOS

In the LINC Programme Portfolios, learners communicated an image of the child as agentic, competent and confident and reflect an understanding of childhood as a time of 'being' rather than 'becoming'. In articulating the value placed on each child, early childhood teacher, Amy D'Alton notes that:

In our setting we created a birthday wall to ensure each child feels special and valued. It shows their photo, name, and birthday, so everyone can celebrate together. Children enjoy comparing ages and begin to understand the passing of time as they see birthdays change throughout the year. It is a simple way to support children's self-esteem and sense of belonging. (LINC Consortium, 2025a, p. 37).

Early Childhood Teachers conveyed a deep understanding and appreciation of the uniqueness of each child and displayed a commitment in their work to celebrating each child's identity and connection with each other and with the early childhood setting as encapsulated in Zurane Foure's words:

We created personalised booklets with each child's photos, handprints, and interests, celebrating their identity and belonging. Children decorated their covers and enjoyed sharing them with each other. This values each child's uniqueness, voice, and sense of belonging, fostering pride and connection within our setting. (LINC Consortium, 2025a, p. 38).

An image of the child as a rights-bearer as envisioned in the provisions of the UNCRC and the UNCRPD (UN 1989; 2006) is clearly identifiable. The UNCRC in its fifty-four articles identifies the social, cultural, civic, political and economic rights to which all children are entitled and affirms children's position as rights' bearers and protagonists (O'Sullivan & Ring, 2026). Across the LINC graduates' professional portfolios, the influence of children's rights on practice in the early childhood setting was patently discernible. In particular, a concern to realise children's rights related to non-discrimination (Article 2); the best interests of the child (Article 3); the realization of children's rights (Article 4); family guidance as children develop (Article 5); name and nationality (Article 7); identity (Article 8); respect for children's views (Article 12); sharing thoughts freely (Article 13); freedom of thought and religion (Article 14); protection of privacy (Article 16); responsibility of parents (Article 18); children and young people with disabilities (Article 23); access to education (Article 28); aims of education (Article 29); minority culture, language and religion (Article 30) and rest, play, culture, arts (Article 31) was discernible in graduates' outcomes. Mireille Connolly, captures this concern in her statement that:

At Sunflowers Montessori School all children are valued and cherished equally and are respected as capable individuals who are central in their own learning and development. We scaffold and support the children in their journey as confident and competent learners to reach their full potential. The children create this family tree display in September to share a little about themselves with their friends.(LINC Consortium, 2025a, p. 39).

Underpinning the LINC Programme Competency Framework with the Reggio Emilia principle of the image of the child therefore has contributed to an approach that creates a lens with the potential to translate children's rights as envisaged in the UNCRC and UNCRPD to tangible outcomes.

THE HUNDRED LANGUAGES OF CHILDREN: AS ENVISAGED IN THE LEADERSHIP FOR INCLUSION IN THE EARLY YEARS PROGRAMME COMPETENCY FRAMEWORK

Children's agency is particularly visible in the extended interpretation of 'language' as acknowledging the multiple symbolic ways children communicate and represent their thinking through Malaguzzi's theory of the hundred languages of children developed in the 1970s (Manera 2022). In his poem, No Way, The Hundred is There, (Malaguzzi, 2012, p. 3), Loris Malaguzzi captures the commitment of the Reggio Emilia approach to enlarging our understanding of the palette of languages children communicate with and our responsibility to actively adopt a pedagogy of listening.

As human beings we display a desire to communicate before we are born and in inclusive early childhood settings, this desire is honoured and nurtured through ongoing observation of how children choose to engage with the environment, with each other and with adults in the environment. The principle of the hundred languages challenges us as early childhood teachers to nurture children's multiple means of expressive and receptive communication (Edwards & Gandini, 2020). The inclusion of an atelier in each setting in Reggio Emilia, together with a teacher who has an art background (an atelierista) embodied for Malaguzzi " "a strong and tangible statement of the importance attributed to imagination, creativity, expressiveness, and aesthetics in the educational processes of development and knowledge building" (Vecchi 2012, as cited in Gandini 2012, p.303). 'Atelier' translates from the French as a workshop or studio where designers/artists work together and 'atelierista' is an Italianised format of 'atelier' used to refer to the teacher who works in the atelier.

Drawing on Malaguzzi's principle of the hundred languages, the LINC Programme envisages inclusive early childhood settings as prioritising the availability of a variety of means of expression for children to include activities that support construction play; drawing; gesture; sign-language; music; dance; drama; information and communication technology [ICT]; music; dance and/or drama. In this context, the adults' responsivity is visible in how they demonstrate that an equal value is placed on each of the languages children choose to communicate with.

THE HUNDRED LANGUAGES OF CHILDREN: VISIBILITY IN LINC PROGRAMME GRADUATES' PORTFOLIOS

A wide range of means of expression for children was provided for children across the early childhood settings referenced in the portfolios. Jeannine Sheey referred to the play provocations that were specifically provided based on children's identified interests:

In our setting, we create a welcoming, calm, and familiar space by setting up Engaging play provocations that reflect the emergent interests of all children, such as
sand and dinosaurs. This helps every child feel included, supported, and excited to explore as they begin their day in our setting. (LINC Consortium, 2025a, p. 36).

Through the provision of thoughtfully designed open-ended materials, children were provided with a myriad of opportunities to communicate their thinking and endless creativity and in the words of Mary O'Brien "transform spaces into trains, boats, beds, pirate ships- even happy robots" (LINC Consortium, 2025a, p. 90). Reflective of the atelier in Reggio Emilia, Amy D'Alton emphasised the role of small group art activities "to encourage meaningful interactions between children and their key person", concluding that "these fun activities support communication, participation, and help ensure every child feels included and valued" (LINC Consortium, 2025a, p. 66).

Across the portfolios, activities were described that demonstrated an awareness of the importance of acknowledging children's individuality and how this was communicated by children as illustrated by the self-portrait activities in Emma McCann's setting:

Through self-portrait activities, children explore and express their unique features, helping them notice and appreciate differences in themselves and others. This learning experience encourages conversations about individuality, and it supports self-esteem, inclusion, and respect. It shows that every child is unique, and differences are something to celebrate and value. (LINC Consortium, 2025a, p. 48).

In describing the approach adopted to encouraging a child's communication, Margaret O'Sullivan encapsulates the considered understanding of the hundred languages of children engendered through participating in the LINC Programme:

All children's communication and interactions are actively supported in our setting. Inspired by knowledge gained on the LINC Programme, we created a puppet stage to help a shy child engage with peers. Using puppets to act out their own stories, all children are encouraged to express themselves confidently and creatively through play. (LINC Consortium, 2025a, p. 92).

Children's preferred means of expression were consistently accommodated through the planning of experiences based on the abilities and needs of each child. Sensory play activities were identified by Mandy O'Reilly as a vehicle for children "to express their feelings and take part in learning in their own way" (LINC Consortium, 2025a, p. 81). Anne-Claire Gordon noted that alternative and augmentative communication [AAC] methods were adopted through the use of lanyards and a sensory communication board to "promote inclusion by offering visual support, encouraging children to express needs, to make choices, and to engage with their peers and adults, building confidence and independence (LINC Consortium, 2025a, p. 94). Reference was made by Laura Leyden to providing individual children with choice boards to support communication through "giving all children the opportunity to select activities they want to engage in" (LINC Consortium, 2025a, p. 82). Margaret O'Sullivan referenced creating a tactile communication board for a preverbal child "by matching coloured buttons to corresponding photos, the child can communicate choices and intentions" (LINC Consortium, 2025a, p. 82). The role of assistive technology in supporting a child experience hearing loss was affirmed by Zurane Foure through "using assistive technologies such as hearing aids, sound amplification devices, and microphones" (LINC Consortium, 2025a, p. 83). Providing children with multiple means of expression is an acknowledgement that each child is unique and linked to a concern across graduates' portfolios to "celebrate what makes each child special" which in Jackie Durkan's view "helps them to understand and value differences and build caring friendships in our diverse community" (LINC Consortium, 2025a, p. 4).

A PEDAGOGY OF LISTENING: AS ENVISAGED IN THE LINC PROGRAMME COMPETENCY FRAMEWORK

While pedagogy can be equated with how we teach, it "emerges as a multi-faceted ever-changing concept that is inextricably entwined with the educator's beliefs about education; the child's interests and experiences, the prescribed curriculum framework, including the image of the child and the teacher in that framework, which in turn links to the broader cultural context" (O'Sullivan & Ring, 2026, p.113). Aistear: the Early Childhood Curriculum Framework in Ireland describes 'pedagogy' as "all the educator's actions or work in supporting babies, toddlers and young children's learning and development", which "infers a negotiated, respectful and reflective learning experience for all involved" (GoI 2024a, p.32). Listening to children is at the heart of this concept of pedagogy.

According to Article 12 of the UNCRPD, children have the right to express their views, and those views given due weight in matters that affect them (UN, 1989). In realising Article 12 of the UNCRPD therefore, adults have the associated responsibility of listening and responding respectfully and appropriately to the child. The Lundy Model of Participation at Figure 4 below developed by Prof Laura Lundy at the School of Education, Queen's University, Belfast is a useful scaffold within which to frame how Article 12 can be realised for children and crucially underscores the responsibility of the adult in realising this right (DCYA, 2015, p. 21).

Figure 4. The Lundy model of participation

Note: Reprinted from the "national strategy on children and young people's participation in decision-making 2015 – 2020" by Department of Children and Youth Affairs, 2015, p. 21.

The model identifies four necessary components in the achievement of the provisions of Article 12. Children should be given space to express their voice, understand that their voice is valued, will influence decisions and that there is an audience interested in listening.

A pedagogy of listening is at the heart of the Reggio Emilia approach, which is attained through the early childhood teacher constantly refining the spiral interwoven competencies of observation, documentation and interpretation of children's communication. According to Carlina Rinaldi "For us in Reggio, making listening visible means to be open to the theories of children. The elements of observation, interpretation, and documentation are strongly connected" (2012, p. 243). The complexity of transforming early childhood settings into 'listening contexts' is not to be underestimated and similar to our need to communicate as human beings we also have a need to be listened to. Rinaldi cautions that "real listening requires the suspension of judgements and prejudices" (2012,p. 236). Documentation is perceived as an act of love, care and relationship rooted in an authenticity that enables connection with the children, thus enabling the early childhood teacher to move from occupying a space on the periphery of children's experiences to becoming a participant-observer in their learning processes. Documentation becomes a language of learning that generates artifacts (e.g narratives; graphic representations; photographs; videos) for which early childhood teachers become one of many translators that make sense and meaning of children's processes. Translating documentation that emerges from observation is a co-constructed process between the early childhood teacher, colleagues in the setting and potentially community, parents, and most importantly the child. A pedagogy of listening as envisaged in the LINC Programme is imagined as a democratic process that involves the child, other educators in the setting and/or community, parents/carers and the early childhood teacher.

A PEDAGOGY OF LISTENING: VISIBILITY IN LINC PROGRAMME GRADUATES' PORTFOLIOS

A commitment to a pedagogy of listening and a belief in its power to promote children's learning, well-being and development is threaded through graduates' portfolios. Linda Madden captures this commitment in her description of the weekly planning session in the early childhood setting:

> *As part of our weekly planning, each Monday morning we sit with the children to hear their ideas for the week ahead. They share their thoughts using marks, drawings, or words. This approach values every child's voice, encourages creativity and choice, and ensures planning reflects their interests and supports inclusive, child-led learning. (LINC Consortium, 2025a, p. 95).*

An awareness of the importance of the visibility of children's voices in the acoustic of the early childhood setting was illustrated in the approach adopted in Orghialla Daly Holland's setting:

> *All children's views are valued, respected, and thoughtfully responded to. They are offered rich opportunities for messy and creative play, encouraging self-expression and exploration. Children are invited to display their artwork on the messy area notice board, celebrating their individuality. (LINC Consortium, 2025a, p. 96).*

The four components of space, voice, influence and audience identified in the Lundy Model of Participation to support the achievement of Article 12 of the UNCRC were evident in how children's views were valued and responded to as summarised by Sabrina O'Brien:

> *We actively value and respond to every child by listening to their views and involving them in decisions. All children are respected and included. For example, children collaborated to create a river in the sandpit using loose parts and natu-*

ral materials, demonstrating their voices are heard, encouraged, and supported through playful experiences. (LINC Consortium, 2025a, p. 96).

Graduates reported using a variety of approaches to observation and documentation, which they variously interpreted with the children, other educators in the setting, external specialist personnel and parents/carers to support children's experiences in the early childhood setting. Siobhán Browne described the approach her setting as:

We use a variety of methods to observe, record, and assess children's learning, including the Child Paths app (see https://childpaths.ie/), photographs, and written notes. Sticky notes are placed around the rooms for quick, on the-spot documentation, allowing us to capture important moments without interrupting the children's play. (LINC Consortium, 2025a, p. 100).

Claire Walsh affirmed the value of working with the Early Years' Specialist and the family to identify each child's sensory needs and use relevant resources "to promote regulation, engagement and inclusion across the setting and the home environment" (LINC Consortium, 2025a, p. 62). Reference was made to using an 'Observation Station' by Soirse Doheny, which allowed children's interests to be documented by early childhood teachers through daily observation. According to Soirse "Using these anecdotal notes helps identify children's emerging interests and plan fun and meaningful activities that reflect what children enjoy. This supports all children to participate in play" (LINC Consortium, 2025a, p. 101).

An approach to involving children in the process of assessment was documented by Eleanor Hawkins:

We use a range of observation, recording, and assessment methods to support each child's learning. From September to June, children compile personal journals, choosing what to include. These journals, regularly shared with parents, feature learning stories that assess and extend individual interests through small group activities and guided support. (LINC Consortium, 2025a, p. 101).

Documentation was shared with parents who were encouraged to share their own observations with the setting. Emma McCann refers to sharing "My Achievements at Home" page with parents to encourage them "to share their child's news and achievement" and this is then used "to plan learning experiences with children and parents, helping to shape our emergent curriculum" (LINC Consortium, 2025a, p. 102). Laura Cajal Goméz observed that sharing children's artwork with parents encourages parents involvement and "helps early childhood teachers plan, implement, and evaluate children's learning, strengthening connections between home and the setting" (LINC Consortium, 2025a, p. 103).

THE ENVIRONMENT AS THE THIRD TEACHER: AS ENVISAGED IN THE LEADERSHIP FOR INCLUSION IN THE EARLY YEARS PROGRAMME COMPETENCY FRAMEWORK

As a key pedagogical principle of the Reggio Emilia approach, the environment is regarded as the third teacher alongside the two teachers working with groups of children in the infant-toddler (4 months – 3 years) and preschool settings (3-6 years) (Edwards et al., 2012). The environment is expected to communicate the message that attention is consistently directed by adults to both the quality and instructive potential of the space, endorsing the pedagogical principle that a relationship exists between the quality of spaces children occupy and the learning and teaching they experience (Gandini 2008). Children and the environment interact with each other in a reciprocal way and how a child experiences visual, auditory, olfactory and tactile stimuli in the early childhood setting therefore has the potential to support or hinder the child's participation and sense of belonging in the setting.

Based on the principle of the environment as the third teacher, the LINC Programme places on emphasis on the central role of the environment in promoting a playful approach to learning in early years' curricula. Stemming from a literature review conducted to inform the development of the *Universal Design Guidelines for Early Learning and Care Settings,* learners on the programme are supported to engage with the role of the environment in facilitating diverse play opportunities; the possibilities in the indoor and outdoor environment; providing a wide range of play materials and collaborating with children in designing their play environment (Ring et al., 2019). Learners are also encouraged to consider the construction and organisation of spaces in the early childhood setting that enable children: to express their curiosity, abilities and potential; to become researchers on their own, with others and with adults in the setting; to collaborate and communicate with others and to reinforce their identities and culture (Rinaldi, 1998). For early childhood teachers, the organisation of the early childhood space should enable them to feel supported in their professional learning journey and contribute to the possibilities for deepening their connection with children, with each other and with parents (Rinaldi, 2018). Spaces should also ensure that parents have a sense of belonging in the space (Rinaldi, 2018). Envisaging the environment as the third teachers is essentially "process-oriented architecture, which fosters communication and is itself communication" (Rinaldi, 2018, p. 120).

THE ENVIRONMENT AS THE THIRD TEACHER: VISIBILITY IN LINC PROGRAMME GRADUATES' PORTFOLIOS

The role of the environment in supporting children's learning, wellbeing and development was a prominent theme across the LINC Programme graduates' portfolios as summarised by Amy D'Alton, who noted that: "Children learn best in a comfortable, secure and stimulating environment" (LINC Consortium, 2025a, p. 29) and Fiona Campbell's belief that "Creating a positive, creative space for exploration and learning is essential" (LINC Consortium, 2025a, p. 74). The cultivation of the playful approach to learning in Aistear: the Early Childhood Curriculum (GoI 2024a) was visible in early childhood teachers' portfolio narratives and artefacts. Orghialla Daly Holland shared the success of introducing a story box with hand puppets on promoting children's collaboration, social connection and creative expression:

We introduced a Story Box with hand puppets to encourage shared narrative play and foster peer interaction. Children eagerly created stories together building communication and confidence. This imaginative activity promoted collaboration, enhancing both social connection and creative expression in a fun learning environment. (LINC Consortium, 2025a, p. 37).

Multiple references were made in the portfolios to the value the early childhood setting placed on prominently displaying children's work, which was considered to contribute to building a positive inclusive environment where all children's identities were affirmed and valued as described by Zurane Foure:

In our setting, we show children that they are important by displaying their artwork. This helps them feel proud, happy, and confident about what they create. It also shows that their ideas matter and are respected. Displaying their work helps build a positive, inclusive environment where every child feels valued and supported. (LINC Consortium, 2025a, p. 39).

Attention was consistently directed to the potential impact of both the indoor and outdoor environment on how children might require support in sensory regulation. Fiona O'Sullivan explained how a Dark Den Cube that was provided to all early childhood settings for the AIM was utilised indoors and a wooden wigwam was provided outdoors so that there were no barriers to outdoor activities for children experiencing sensory regulation challenges:

We introduced the AIM "Dark Den Cube5" indoors as part of our inclusive learning environment, offering all children a safe, calming space when feeling overwhelmed. Outdoors, we provide a cosy wigwam with soft textures for similar support. One child needing help with self-regulation uses both regularly, showing improved emotional well-being. (LINC Consortium, 2025a, p. 52).

The role of early childhood teacher in creating an environment that connects children to the natural world and begins to develop their sense of environmental awareness was frequently referenced as described by Teresa Callanan:

Through hands-on nature play, children explore and connect with the natural world. Planting seedlings into the ground offers rich sensory experiences while nurturing responsibility and curiosity. By caring for their pumpkin plants daily, children develop a sense of ownership, environmental awareness, and a deeper appreciation for nature. (LINC Consortium, 2025a, p. 50).

The importance of the environment for fostering early childhood teachers' own sense of belonging in the environment was understood as noted by Laura Firth:

Displaying the INclusion COordinator (INCO) poster reminds our team of the importance of an inclusive culture, practice, and pedagogy. It highlights our shared responsibility to promote inclusion and create an inclusive environment. The poster supports consistent practice, encourages reflection, and strengthens our commitment to respecting and valuing each child. (LINC Consortium, 2025a, p. 65).

The environment as a space to deepen early childhood teachers' connections with each other was highlighted by Tanwa Allinson's approach to sharing insights from the LINC programme with colleagues, which "supports our daily practice and strengthens our collective ability to create a genuinely inclusive environment where each child feels valued, supported and included" (LINC Consortium, 2025a, p. 65). Cathy Boyle noted that "Staff are valued and supported through regular supervision and ongoing opportunities to build knowledge and skills" (LINC Consortium, 2025a, p. 63). Displaying children's and teachers' photographs in a creative attractive manner "reinforces our inclusion policy which is, that everyone belongs and everyone is welcome in our playschool" – Katie Dee (LINC Consortium, 2025a, p. 35).

An appreciation that "Families are at the heart of the setting and parents play a vital role in a child's learning" (LINC Consortium, 2025a, p. 29) was evident, and further reflected in an understanding of the importance of creating an environment where families experienced a sense of belonging as recounted by Racheal Govan:

We work closely with families by inviting them into our setting to take part in activities with the children. This helps build trust and strong relationships. When families join in, children feel happy, proud, and supported. It also helps everyone feel part of a team, working together to help children learn and grow. (LINC Consortium, 2025a, p. 44).

Through inviting family members "to share their professions, cultures and interests such as cooking, music or yoga" – Ciara Donohoe), (LINC Consortium, 2025a, p. 29) parents' sense of belonging in their children's experiences was strengthened. In Maxine Ryan's setting, parents are introduced to a wishing wheel suspended from the ceiling and invited to share their hopes for the child's year ahead, the wheel is then revisited throughout the year to encourage open conversation, deepen the shared understand of the child and support children's holistic development (LINC Consortium, 2025a, p.44).

CONCLUSION

We remain mindful of Tiziana Filippini's advice that "the Reggio Approach is not a recipe. It doesn't tell you what to do. Rather it's an educational approach rooted in Reggio Emilia, one that asks you to be respectful and mindful of your context and community" (Africa Reggio Emilia Alliance, 2017,p. 1.). We drew on the four specific Reggio Emilia principles, not as a model to replicate, but rather as principles for us to reflect on theory and practice in the context of our own curriculum framework and cultural context (Gandini, 2008). Evidence from learners' professional portfolios confirms that these principles are clearly discernible in how learners have self-assessed and interpreted their achievement of the key competencies associated with the programme and in their work with babies, toddlers and young children. While all self-reported data has inevitable limitations, the LINC Programme Professional Portfolios required that artefacts were submitted to illustrate learners' narratives on how they had achieved the specified competencies. These artefacts greatly strengthen the authenticity of the data and confirm the power of the Reggio Emila principles of the image of the child; the hundred languages of children; a pedagogy of listening and the environment as the third teacher as lenses that enable the strengthening of theory to practice and the realisation of a rights-based response for all children. The narratives in the portfolios demonstrate the applicability of these principles to achieving a welcoming inclusive space for neurodivergent learners; children at risk of, or experiencing socio-economic disadvantage; children who have experienced trauma; children from diverse and minority communities and so-called 'neurotypical children'. In essence, the alignment of the Reggio Emilia foci of the LINC Programme with the Irish curriculum and quality frameworks for early childhood education provides us with an impetus to question the necessity of the need for 'special rights' and articulate instead a vision for the realisation of rights for each child (CECDE, 2006; NCCA, 2009; 2025; GoI, 2024a; 2024b).

REFERENCES

Africa Reggio Emilia Alliance. (2017). Tiziana's 2017 visit. Insights, answers and advice. Au-thor. https://reggio.co.za/wp-content/uploads/2017/12/tiziana-filippini-2017-visit-to-sa-insights-answers-advice.pdf

Andrews, J. E., Carnine, D. W., Coutinho, M. J., Edgar, E. B., Forness, S. R., Fuchs, L. S., Jordan, D., Kauffman, J. M., Patton, J. M., Paul, J., Rosell, J., Rueda, R., Schiller, E., Skrtic, T. M., & Wong, J. (2000). Bridging the Special Education Divide. *Remedial and Special Education, 21*(5), 258–267. DOI: 10.1177/074193250002100501

Aries, P. (1962). Centuries of. *Childhood,* •••, 71.

Better Start National Early Years Quality Development Service. (n.d.). What is the role of the inclusion co-ordinator? Author. https://aim.gov.ie/app/uploads/2021/05/AIM-role-of-the-inclusion-co-ordinator.pdf

Bonfield, T., & Horgan, K. (2016). *Learning to teach: Teaching to learn.* Gill Education.

Breen, F., Ring, E., Stapleton, S., & Kelleher, S. (2018). LINC programme: Enabling leadership for inclusion through an innovative competency-based blended adult continuing professional learning programme. The Adult Learner 2018, 99-115. https://www.aontas.com/assets/resources/Adult-Learner-Journal/AONTAS-Adult-Learner-Journal-2018.pdf

Broderick, A. (2015). *The long and winding road to equality and inclusion for persons with disabilities. The united nations convention on the rights of persons with disabilities.* Intersentia.

Bronfenbrenner, U. (1979). *The ecology of human development: Experiments by nature and design.* Harvard University Press.

Byrne, M., Schroeter, K., Carter, S., & Mower, J. (2009). The professional portfolio: An evi-dence-based assessment method. *Journal of Continuing Education in Nursing, 40*(12), 542–552. https://journals.healio.com/doi/10.3928/00220124-20091119-07

Centre for Early Childhood Development and Education. (2006). Síolta: The national quality framework for early childhood education. Author. Síolta

Children's Rights Alliance. (2025). Report card 2025. Author. https://childrensrights.ie/wp-content/uploads/2025/02/FINAL-Report-Card-2025.pdf

Department of Children and Youth Affairs. (2015). National strategy on children and young people's participation in decision-making, 2015 – 2020. Author. https://assets.gov.ie/24462/48a6f98a921446ad85829585389e57de.pdf

Department of Children and Youth Affairs. (2019) An end of year one review of the access and inclusion model (AIM). Author. https://aim.gov.ie/app/uploads/2021/05/AIM-end-of-year-one-review.pdf

Department of Children and Youth Affairs. (2016). Diversity, equality and inclusion charter and guidelines for early childhood care and education. Author. diversity-equality-and-inclusion-charter-and-guidelines-for-early-childhood-care-and-e.pdf

Department of Education. (2023). Statistical bulletin – July 2023. Author. https://www.gov.ie/pdf/?file=https://assets.gov.ie/263000/f2932136-6191-4e56-9af0-5b315e85702f.pdf#page=null

Department of Education. (2025). A guide to early years education inspection. Author. https://assets.gov.ie/static/documents/a-guide-to-early-years-education-inspection-eyei-updated-january-2025.pdf

Edwards, C., & Gandini, L. (2020). The Reggio Emilia approach to early childhood education. In Roopnarine, J. L., Johnson, J. E., Flannery Quinn, S., & Patte, M. M. (Eds.), *Handbook of interna-tional perspectives on early childhood education* (pp. 365–378). Routledge.

Edwards, C., Gandini, L., & Forman, G. (Eds.). (2012). *The hundred languages of children: The Reggio Emilia experience in transformation* (3rd ed.). Praeger.

European Agency for Special Needs and Inclusive Education. (2017a). *Inclusive early child-hood education: New insights and tools – Contributions from a European study. (M, Kyri-azopoulou, P. Bartolo, E. Björck-Åkesson* (Giné, C., & Bellour, F., Eds.). Author., https://www.european-agency.org/sites/default/files/IECE_Synthesis_Report_2017.pdf

European Agency for Special Needs and Inclusive Education. (2017b) Inclusive early child-hood education self-reflection tool. (E. Björck-Åkesson, M, Kyriazopoulou, C. Giné & P. Barto-lo, (Eds)). Author. https://www.european-agency.org/sites/default/files/IECE%20Environment%20Self-Reflection%20Tool.pdf

European Agency for Special Needs and Inclusive Education. (2025). *Teacher professional learning in Finland and Ireland: Findings report* (Symeonidou, S., Topalli, P. Z., Bilgeri, M., Svarinskaite, R., & Kefallinou, A., Eds.). Author., https://www.european-agency.org/sites/default/files/Findings_Report_on_Teacher_Professional_Learning.pdf

Gandini, L. (2008). Introduction to the fundamental values of the education of young children in Reggio Emilia. Northern American Reggio Emilia Alliance. https://www.reggioalliance.org/wp-content/uploads/2021/08/INTRODUCTION-EDITED-FOR-BOOK-rev-LG-10-20-08.pdf

Gandini, L. (2012). The atelier: A conversation with Vea Vecchi. In C. Edwards, L. Gandini & G. Foreman (Eds.), The hundred languages of children: The Reggio Emilia experience trans-formation (3rd ed.) (pp. 303-316). Prager.

Government of Ireland. (2018). First 5: A whole of government strategy for babies, young chil-dren and their families. Government Publications Office. https://assets.gov.ie/31184/62acc54f4bdf4405b74e53a4afb8e71b.pdf

Government of Ireland. (2024a). Aistear: the early childhood curriculum framework. Author. https://curriculumonline.ie/getmedia/1e9e4eff-5d44-4950-bfa6-a28f43895d3f/Aistear-FW-ENG.pdf

Government of Ireland. (2024b). Aistear – Guidance for good practice. Author. https://curriculumonline.ie/getmedia/f2932ad8-326d-4cb7-9d6c-09bc138f9a8a/Aistear-G-ENG.pdf

Gül Hazar, R., & Yilmaz, A. (2025). Using a teacher portfolio as a professional development tool for Turkish early childhood teachers. *Journal of Early Childhood Teacher Education*, •••, 1–22. DOI: 10.1080/10901027.2025.2581790

Inter-departmental Group. (2015). Supporting access to the early childhood care and education (ecce) programme for children with a disability. Author. https://aim.gov.ie/app/uploads/2021/05/Inter-Departmental-Group-Report-launched-Nov-2015.pdf

Jones, M., & Shelton, M. (2011). *Developing your portfolio. Enhancing your learning and showing your stuff: A guide for the early childhood student or professional* (2nd ed.). Routledge.

Lally, J. R. (2006). Metatheories of childrearing. In J.R. Lally, P.L. Mangione and D. Greenwald (Eds.), 20 essays on infant/toddler development and learning (pp. 7–14). WestEd.

Lancy, D. F. (2015). *The anthropology of childhood. Cherubs, chattels, changelings* (3rd ed.). Cambridge University Press.

Leadership for INClusion in the Early Years Consortium. (2016-2025). Blogs. Author. https://lincprogramme.ie/linc-programme-blogs/

Leadership for INClusion in the Early Years Consortium. (2019). Interim evaluation of the leadership for inclusion in the early years (LINC) programme (Ring, E., Kelleher, S., Kelleher, S., Heeney, T., McLoughlin, M., Kearns, A., Stafford, S., Skehill, S., Campion, K., Comerford, D., & O'Sullivan, L.). Mary Immaculate College, Limerick, Ireland. https://acrobat.adobe.com/link/track?uri=urn%3Aaaid%3Ascds%3AUS%3Ad8c95d7d-2d75-40a8-9f65-b6582908c08d

Leadership for INClusion in the Early Years Consortium. (2022). The Role of INclusion Coordi-nator (INCO). Mary Immaculate College, Limerick, Ireland. https://aim.gov.ie/app/uploads/2022/08/Role-of-the-INclusion-COordinator-2022.pdf

Leadership for INClusion in the Early Years Consortium. (2024). Final evaluation of phase one of the leadership for inclusion in the early years (LINC) programme 2016-2020 (Kelly, L., Ring, E., Heaney, S., O'Sullivan, L., Fortune, N., Heeney, T., Kerrins, L., Stafford, P., & Thompson, H). Mary Immaculate College, Limerick, Ireland. Web-version-of-LINC-Evaluation-Report-2-page-view-1.pdf

Leadership for INClusion in the Early Years Consortium. (2025a). Leading from within: Devel-oping a professional portfolio for inclusion in the early years. A celebration of the leadership for inclusion in the early years (LINC) Programme graduates and their inspiring contributions to the lives of children and families (Heaney, S., Butterly, C., Horgan, K., Ring, E., O'Byrne, A., Donnellan, A., Harte, P., Madden, L., Joyce, M. &Thompson, H.). Mary Immaculate College, Limerick, Ireland. https://lincprogramme.ie/linc-programme-research/

Leadership for INClusion in the Early Years Consortium. (2025b). An interim evaluation of the leadership for inclusion in the early years continuing professional development (LINC + CPD) programme 2021-2023 (Kelly, L., Kerrins, L., Stafford, P., Heaney, S., Butterly, C., Heeney, T., Ring, E., O'Sullivan, L., Fortune, N., Kearns, A. & Thompson, H.), Mary Immaculate College, Limerick, Ireland. https://lincprogramme.ie/wp-content/uploads/2025/04/Interim-Evaluation-of-the-LINC-CPD-Programme-2021-2023.pdf

Malaguzzi, L. (1993a). A charter of rights. Reggio Children. https://www.reggiochildren.it/assets/Uploads/RC-100LM-CartaDiritti-3.pdf

Malaguzzi, L. (1993b). For an education based on relationships (translated by Lella Gandini). *Young Children*, *49*(1), 9–12.

Malaguzzi, L. (2012) No way. The hundred is there. In In C. Edwards, L. Gandini, & G. Forman (Eds.), The hundred languages of children: The Reggio Emilia experience in transformation (3rd ed.) (pp. 2-3). Praeger.

Manera, L. (2022). Art and aesthetic education in the Reggio Emilia Approach. Education 3- 13, 50(4), 483-493. https://doi.org/DOI: 10.1080/03004279.2022.2052230

Morris, J. (1991). *Pride against prejudice: Transforming attitudes to disability: A personal poli-tics of disability*. Women's Press.

National Council for Curriculum and Assessment. (2009). Aistear: the early childhood curricu-lum framework. Author. Aistear (2009) | Curriculum Online

National Council for Curriculum and Assessment. (2025). Aistear (2024) as a rights-based ear-ly childhood curriculum framework. Author. aistear-as-a-rights-based-early-childhood-curriculum-framework.pdf

O'Sullivan, L., & Ring, E. (2023). On the path to developing a high-quality inclusive preschool system in the Irish context: Outcomes from a systemic focus on structural and process quality dimensions. In H. Şenol, H. (Ed.), Recent perspectives on preschool education and care (pp.1-22). IntechOpen. https://www.intechopen.com/chapters/88601

O'Sullivan, L., & Ring, E. (2026). *Play from the inside out: Theory, research and practice per-spectives*. Peter Lang.

Organisation for Economic Co-operation and Development. (2023). Equity and inclusion in ed-ucation. Finding strength through diversity. Author. https://www.oecd.org/en/publications/2023/01/equity-and-inclusion-in-education_e8cfc768.html

Quality and Qualifications Ireland. (2021) National framework of qualifications. Author. https://www.qqi.ie/Articles/Pages/National-Framework-of-Qualifications-(NFQ).aspx

Rinaldi, C. (2018). The space of childhood. In Ceppi, G., & Zini, M. (Eds.), *Children, spaces, re-lations. Metaproject for an environment for young children* (pp. 114–120). Reggio Children.

Rinaldi, C. (2021). *In dialogue with Regio Emilia. Listening, researching and learning* (2nd ed.). Routledge.

Ring, E., & O'Sullivan, L. (2025). Play, learning and teaching in a redeveloped primary curricu-lum. National Council for Curriculum and Assessment. https://ncca.ie/en/resources/play-learning-and-teaching-in-a-redeveloped-primary-curriculum/

Ring, E., & O'Sullivan, L. (2019). Creating spaces where diversity is the norm. *Childhood Education*, *95*(2), 29–39. DOI: 10.1080/00094056.2019.1593758

Ring, E. (2021). Introduction: Looking towards a new era of leading education for all from the inside out: The potential of a bioecological lens in creating early childhood experiences where diversity becomes the norm. In E. Ring, L. O'Sullivan, L., M. Ryan, & P. Daly (Eds.), Leading inclusion from the inside out: A handbook for parents and early childhood teachers in early learning and care, primary and special school settings (pp. 3-27). Peter Lang.

Ring, E. (2024). *Special education in an independent Ireland 1922-2022. Insights from a jour-ney through the century*. National Council for Special Education., ncse.ie/wp-content/uploads/2024/09/Emer_Ring_Special_Education_Independent_Ireland_NCSE2024.pdf

Ring, E., & Breen, F. (2017). *Changing lives: The transformative possibilities of blended learn-ing: Initial findings from a national programme in Ireland. In the Future of Education Confer-ence Proceedings* (7th ed.). Libreria Universitaria.

Ring, E., Grey, T., O'Sullivan, L., Corbett, M., Sheerin, J., & Heeney, T. (2019). Universal de-sign guidelines for early learning and care settings: Literature review. The Government Publica-tions Office. https://aim.gov.ie/app/uploads/2021/05/universal-design-guidelines-for-elc-settings-literature-review-2.pdf

Robinson, D., Gowers, S., Codina, G., Artess, J., Delgado Fuenes, M.A., Mycock, K., Qyreshi, S., Shepherd, R., IFF Research., & Ní Luanaigh, A. (2022). End-of-year three evaluation of the access and inclusion model: Full technical and research Report. University of Derby, Institute of Education. https://assets.gov.ie/281416/efef74fb-04d6-4f8b-ba80-f7af48c6d8b1.pdf

Soncini, I. (2012). The inclusive community. In C. Edwards, L. Gandini, & G. Forman (Eds.), The hundred languages of children: The Reggio Emilia experience in transformation (3rd ed.) (pp.187-211). Praeger.

Sorin, R. (2005). Changing images of childhood: Reconceptualising early childhood practice. *International Journal of Transitions in Childhood, 1*(1), 12–21. https://citeseerx.ist.psu.edu/document?repid=rep1&type=pdf&doi=9594881ae4f396a654957f719b1bb4e3589d0819

United Nations Committee on the Rights of the Child. (2023). Concluding observations on the combined fifth and sixth periodic reports of Ireland. Author. https://tbinternet.ohchr.org/_layouts/15/treatybodyexternal/SessionDetails1.aspx?SessionID=2600&Lang=en

United Nations Educational. Scientific & Cultural Organisation. (1994). The Salamanca state-ment and framework for action on special needs education. Adopted by the World Conference on Special Needs Education: Access and Quality, Salamanca, Spain, 7-10 June 1994. Author. https://unesdoc.unesco.org/ark:/48223/pf0000098427

United Nations. (1948). Universal declaration of human rights. Author. https://www.un.org/en/about-us/universal-declaration-of-human-rights

United Nations. (1959). Declaration of the rights of the child. Author. https://digitallibrary.un.org/record/195831?ln=en&v=pdf

United Nations. (1989). Convention on the rights of the child. Author. https://www.ohchr.org/sites/default/files/crc.pdf

United Nations. (2006). Convention on the rights of persons with disabilities. Author. https://treaties.un.org/doc/Publication/CTC/Ch_IV_15.pdf

United Nations. (2015). Transforming Our world: The 2030 agenda for sustainable develop-ment. UN Doc A/RES/70/1. Author. Document Viewer

United Nations. (2025). The sustainable development agenda. Author. https://www.un.org/sustainabledevelopment/development-agenda/

Višnjić-Jevtić, A., Sadownik, A. R., & Engdahl, I. (2021). Introducing human rights for children. In Višnjić-Jevtić, A., Sadownik, A. R., & Engdahl, I. (Eds.), *Young children in the world and their rights* (pp. 1–16). Springer Nature Switzerland AG.

Wyness, M. (2019). *Childhood and society* (3rd ed.). RedGlobe Press.

Chapter 8
Reimagining Education Through Participation, Dialogue, and Listening:
Local Communities, Global Perspectives

Benedetta Melloni
http://orcid.org/0009-0003-6797-4467
Fondazione Reggio Children, Italy

Elisa Ferrari
http://orcid.org/0009-0008-6834-8878
Fondazione Reggio Children, Italy

Mara Davoli
Fondazione Reggio Children, Italy

Alfonso Trillicoso
Istituto Comprensivo "A. Manzoni", Italy

ABSTRACT

Rooted in a local context yet carrying global significance, the chapter examines how the integration of formal and non-formal education can benefit children, families, and the community as a whole by transforming children's rights into everyday learning experiences. The chapter is based on Peace Between Cultures, an action research project that tackled cultural diversity and religious illiteracy, involving children, teachers, families, and local institutions in a peripheral area of Reggio Emilia. The chapter draws on the pedagogical framework of the Reggio Emilia Approach (REA)

DOI: 10.4018/979-8-3373-3431-8.ch008

and uses the project as a case study to explore how education can function as a democratic and relational process. It specifically examines how the school tackles significant challenges that hinder participation and foster isolation, and can establish itself as an 'educating community'—a shared space where children, educators, families, and community members engage in a collaborative learning process.

THEORETICAL FOUNDATIONS

Tensions and conflicts between majority and minority populations, as well as among minority groups themselves, have troubled pluralistic societies for centuries, with policies serving as the main tool to address discrimination. Early examples date back to the Renaissance: the Peace of Augsburg (1555), which protected religious minorities in Germany; the Edict of Nantes (1598), which safeguarded Calvinists in France; and the Treaty of Westphalia (1648), which put an end to the Thirty Years' War and established peace among states and their minorities. Later, the Vienna Treaty (1815) granted civil rights and religious freedoms to minorities in the Netherlands, Belgium, the German Confederation, Switzerland, and Poland. In the last century, the 1919 post-World War I peace treaties required both old and new states to protect all citizens regardless of birth, nationality, language, race, or religion. After World War II, the newly founded United Nations [UN] adopted the Universal Declaration of Human Rights [UDHR] in 1948. Recognizing that peaceful and lasting coexistence cannot rely solely on political or economic arrangements, the UDHR (UN, 1948) promoted the "full development of the human personality" and "respect for human rights and fundamental freedoms" (Article 26), linking rights and responsibilities between institutions and individuals to promote peaceful societies.

Declarations and recommendations have a non-binding nature; however, they represent a shared international consensus and a call for action (UNESCO, 2006). Indeed, many other instruments have been developed based on this principle of education and peaceful societies, such as the UN Declaration on the Promotion among Youth of the Ideals of Peace, Mutual Respect and Understanding between Peoples (1965), the International Convention on the Elimination of All Forms of Racial Discrimination (1965), the International Covenant on Economic, Social, and Cultural Rights (1966), and the Declaration on the Elimination of All Forms of Intolerance and of Discrimination Based on Religion or Belief (1981) (UNESCO, 2006). Among these, the Convention on the Rights of the Child [CRC] (UN, 1989) is particularly significant, as it prompted policymakers to view children not only as objects of protection but as subjects with rights.

The CRC states that children, who are capable of forming their own views, have "the right to express those views freely" in accordance with their age and maturity, and "shall in particular be provided the opportunity to be heard" (Article 12). It also decrees that the education of the child shall be directed to the "development of the child's personality, talents and mental and physical abilities to their fullest potential (...) in the spirit of understanding, peace, tolerance, equality of sexes, and friendship among all peoples, ethnic, national and religious groups and persons of indigenous origin" (Article 29). Furthermore, it recognizes "the right of the child to rest and leisure, to engage in play and recreational activities appropriate to the age of the child and to participate freely in cultural life and the arts" (Article 31).

Similar to the international scenario, education and democracy are closely intertwined in the European policy discourse, in light of the fact that the European project cannot be reduced to a mere technical endeavor (Bekemans, 2013). Education, indeed, plays a central role in fostering long-standing, prosperous democratic societies (Bayer & Bárd, 2020) and in enabling individuals to develop the attitudes, skills, and knowledge necessary for living together in a democratic society (Bekemans, 2013). Since the first decade of the 21st century, the European Union has adopted the discourse on interculturalism, positioning it as an alternative paradigm to multiculturalism, in order to foster peaceful societies by promoting intercultural skills and attitudes.

The European discourse stems from the initiative of the Council of Europe, which launched a six-month consultation resulting in the publication of the White Paper on Intercultural Dialogue in 2008. This perspective proposes a dialogue grounded in the equal dignity of all individuals (Barrett, 2013) and supported by intercultural skills. However, skills alone are insufficient to ensure meaningful participation (Council of Europe, 2016). The emphasis then is on the need of active contact among individuals under conditions of equality for reducing prejudice (Zapata-Barrero, 2017). Therefore, contact acts not as a result of coexistence but as a necessary precondition for inclusion, aligning closely with Allport's (2004) contact theory.

The discourse on diversity management and its impact on the educational system has been a point of focus at the national level in Italy. This shift is further driven by the fact that, historically, Italy, a country with a long history of emigration, has in recent decades become a destination for migration flows (Azzolini et al., 2019), with approximately 1.3 million minors with migrant backgrounds in 2025 and about 600,000 students with migrant backgrounds enrolled in the school system in the 2022/2023 school year (Organismo Nazionale di Coordinamento delle Politiche di Integrazione degli Stranieri, 2024). The demographic shift demanded a reevaluation of educational strategies to accommodate a growing number of students from migrant backgrounds (Azzolini et al., 2019).

The first significant policy of the Italian Ministry of Education[1] came with the Ministerial Document 73/1994 entitled Intercultural Dialogue and Democratic Coexistence (MPI, 1994), which positioned a comprehensive, intercultural approach not limited to the presence of students with a migrant background in schools but extended to the complexity of the dialogue between cultures in the European and global dimensions. However, its impact remained limited. Many schools struggled to integrate respect for diversity into their programs, resulting in inconsistent application of intercultural education (Wallace et al., 2021).

In 2004, the Ministry of Education set up a Unit for the Integration of Foreign Students. Yet this initiative lacked a clear multicultural focus and coincided with budget cuts that impacted, among other things, the presence of cultural mediators in schools (Wallace et al., 2021). A few years later, a new attempt reiterated the importance of intercultural education in a plural society. This commitment was most shown in the Ministerial Guidelines for the First Reception and Integration of Foreign Students (MIUR, 2006), which were followed by the guidelines The Italian Way for an Intercultural School and the Integration of Foreign Students (MPI, 2007), aiming to support integration and intercultural activities for all students (Santagati & Bertozzi, 2022). In 2014, the 2006 guidelines were updated, emphasizing intercultural education against assimilation and communitarianism (Rondanini, 2024).

In 2022, the Intercultural Orientations (MI) encouraged teaching that includes different cultures and openness to non-European civilizations, connects with citizenship education, focuses on teamwork, participation, conflict resolution, and pays attention to the classroom environment, while also highlighting the importance of working together with local institutions, organizations, and volunteer groups.

Despite these efforts, intercultural dialogue remains a complex and underdeveloped field. These documents aimed to integrate students with migrant backgrounds while respecting their cultural differences, but their practical application varied widely across schools (Wallace et al., 2021). Schools have significant leeway in how they address cultural diversity, resulting in a patchwork of practices with varying effectiveness. While some schools have made significant progress in promoting inclusion, the system still lacks a consistent and structured framework for implementation.

In this context, both the CRC and the White Paper on Intercultural Dialogue offer guiding principles that can inspire schools, emphasizing the importance of respecting children's right to be heard and fostering dialogue through individual interactions within an institutional support framework. These principles can still inform educational practices, particularly when viewed through the theoretical lens of the REA, which adds depth to the theoretical framework by proposing an ecosystem of relationships among children, teachers, families, and community members (Edwards et al., 1998). As Rinaldi wrote:

> *It is only when this accreditation and this recognition are given that listening, dialogue and the exchange of ideas are activated, and that there is negotiation to construct projects and proposals that are the result of the contribution of all and in which all can, albeit in different ways, identify themselves. And therefore,*

the processes of participation and democracy that we consider to be fundamental elements of the educational project itself can be activated. This is the deepest meaning of participation. (Rinaldi, 2021, p. 177)

This framework serves as the theoretical foundation for understanding learning processes that encourage relationships and meaningful interactions among children, adults, and the larger community (Bruner, 1997), helping to tackle the challenges of diverse societies and fostering inclusive and participatory educational settings.

METHODS

The Study

This study adopts a qualitative case study design (Mertens, 2020) to examine how high-quality education can be achieved through the active participation of children, families, teachers, and the wider community in developing an inclusive, cohesive "educating community" (Rinaldi, 2021, p. 174), grounded in the values of participation, dialogue, and listening. The study focuses on the *Peace Between Cultures* project, an action research initiative aimed at innovating teaching methods and fostering teacher training with a focus on intercultural education and peace. The project took place at the Manzoni Comprehensive School, which includes one kindergarten, three elementary schools, and one middle school, all located in the suburban area of Reggio Emilia.

The National and Local Context

The project was developed in a local context characterized by significant demographic diversity compared to the Italian national and regional levels. In 2021, individuals of migrant origin accounted for 10.3% of Italy's population and 12.1% at the regional level in Emilia-Romagna (MI, 2022), whereas in the city of Reggio Emilia the rate reached 17.3% (Bonacini & Girardi, 2021).

The city of Reggio Emilia has consistently shown a strong commitment to families with migratory backgrounds. The municipality and local associations, including the Italian Federation of Migrant Workers and Families, the municipal Intercultural Center, and trade unions, have consistently maintained close contact with the world of migration, serving as an important point of reference for families arriving in the city. Within this context, schools developed a collaborative familiarity with these organizations, which became fertile ground for further initiatives.

This scenario brings us to 2021, when the Manzoni Comprehensive School had 307 students with non-Italian citizenship out of a total of 889, with a significant internal variability among its schools (Passarelli, 2022). The Comprehensive School actively responded to challenges and opportunities associated with diverse populations by implementing a strategic choice to ensure every student's right to quality education. In the 2019/2020 school year, the teachers' board voted to allocate three specific roles, rather than two, to oversee areas of interest. As a result, the Comprehensive School established a committee on intercultural education tasked with identifying needs, proposing initiatives, and monitoring actions.

Beyond the demographic features, the *Peace Between Cultures* project unfolded within a historical and institutional context that contributed to shaping its design and implementation. During the COVID-19 pandemic, the Municipality and the schools of Reggio Emilia worked together to ensure the right to education while safeguarding public health through social distancing measures. In this context, the Manzoni Comprehensive School chose to decentralize its activities to public buildings, such as a museum or disused spaces, with the support of the city's municipal educational service, Officina Educativa. This initiative evolved into an Educating Community Pact between the local authority, the school, the third sector, and local associations. This Pact, whose underlying idea is rooted in the REA, reaffirmed the centrality of the relationship between school and territory, enabling the creation of new alliances within the framework of school autonomy, as outlined in the Italian Presidential Decree 275/1999 (Landini, 2022).

The *Peace Between Cultures* project operated within this historical and institutional context from August 2021 to December 2022. Activities were led by an interdisciplinary working group composed of atelieristas and one pedagogista from the Reggio Children Foundation, teaching staff from the Manzoni Comprehensive School, experts from the public Intercultural Center Mondinsieme, and researchers in educational and historical studies from the University of Modena and Reggio Emilia and the Foundation for Religious Studies.

At the beginning of the project, the partners established a steering committee that analyzed the local context, organized and participated in training events, and co-designed educational activities to be conducted in eight classes. The University of Modena and Reggio Emilia hosted a full-day conference to conclude the project.

Participant Population

The case study analyzes the *Peace Between Cultures* project and, in accordance with the scope of this volume, focuses on elementary and middle school classes. The case study utilizes three complementary data sets, comprising a sample of 129 children from elementary and middle schools, 10 teachers, and 335 parents.

Children's learning experiences took concrete form through drawings, dialogues, photographs, and notes. Teachers and atelieristas gathered these traces and worked on the documentation through cycles of shared reflection. Indeed, documentation is much more than a collection of images or words: it is a way of giving visible form to children's thoughts and inquiries and a tool for designing future educational interventions. Acting as a vital form of teacher research, this process allows the staff to read and reread the materials as a basis for planning the next steps and for the continuous modification and adjustment of teaching strategies (Edward et al., 1998).

Teachers' voices were explored through transcripts of steering committee meetings involving ten teachers over the course of the project. Participants were selected partly voluntarily and partly through selection by the School Principal. In addition, an ex-post focus group was conducted in 2025 with four teachers and two atelieristas to explore the project's longer-term transformative impact on professional practices and school–family relationships. Transcriptions were coded using MAXQDA (Verbi Software Gmbh, n.d.), and the analysis followed three main steps. First, transcripts from the steering committee and the 2025 focus group were collected and organized with contextual notes. Second, an initial reading applied three coding methods: (a) attribute coding to record contextual and descriptive information; (b) descriptive coding to identify the main topics addressed within each excerpt; and (c) versus coding to highlight tensions and contrasts emerging in teachers' reflections, such as trust versus mistrust (Saldaña, 2013). Lastly, the resulting codes were reorganized according to the three analytical themes: participation, dialogue, and listening, thus aligning empirical findings with the project's conceptual framework. This analytical structure ensured that the findings remained grounded in teachers' daily experiences while maintaining coherence with the project's broader theoretical and ethical framework.

Families' views were collected through a questionnaire administered during the project to 335 parents to investigate their perspectives on intercultural education and their perceptions of the project's outcomes. The Foundation for Religious Studies created and analyzed the questionnaire, which had both multiple-choice and open-ended questions; the analysis presented in this chapter draws on the report published by researcher Passarelli (2022). Family perspectives were further enriched during the steering committee meetings, in which teachers shared families' concerns as they emerged in daily interactions. This reflective practice provided important context for the findings from the questionnaire.

These datasets allow for an in-depth exploration of the following research question: How can the principles of the REA inspire and sustain inclusive educational activities focused on cultural diversity, enhance teacher development, and encourage meaningful participation from families and the community in elementary and middle schools?

This study analyzes three data sets and presents the findings individually for children, teachers, and families. The discussion section will concurrently analyze these perspectives, preserving a strong interconnectedness despite their individual examination.

Results

The Children's Perspective on Peace and Culture

This section highlights and values the reflections and viewpoints of children on the different meanings of "peace" and "culture," developed through dialogue and interaction with all participants in the *Peace Between Cultures* project.

Within the REA, listening and dialogue are not merely seen as pedagogical supports but as value-based, ethical, and political choices that redefine education as a collective process of meaning-making, occurring within a context and culture where children are active participants in the educational process. Listening, relationships, and dialogue also redefine the idea of school as a living ecosystem, capable of respecting the intelligence, potential, and sensitivities of every child, each of whom has the right to be seen and recognized in their uniqueness.

Thus, the school has a relational architecture that places children at the heart of the educational project, offering a broad and differentiated range of learning contexts, conceived as both physical and mental spaces, where children and teachers experience and, above all, share meanings to access new knowledge.

It is a school where cultural reciprocity is practiced, entailing a greater awareness of what children do, how they do it, and why they do it. Learning, in all its complexity, involves the creation and negotiation of meanings (Bruner, 1997).

Within this vision of education, the concept of space is fundamental: a space conceived as "the relational qualities between the individual and his/her habitat are reciprocal, so that both the person and the environment are active and modify each other in turn" (Rinaldi, 2021, p. 53). As Malaguzzi (1987, p. 30) noted: "Education must come to be recognized as the product of a set of complex interactions, many if which can be realized only when the environment is a fully participating element in education."

Finally, a core assumption of the REA is the idea of children as interpreters of the world they live in, genetically predisposed to relationships and constructors of their own learning processes and culture. From this perspective, the right to quality education is inseparable from their right to express themselves freely, to be seen, heard, and recognized as subjects who carry and build their own culture. This idea aligns with Article 12 of the CRC, which plays a pivotal role in recognizing children's right to express their opinions in situations that concern them (UN, 1989; Lücker-Babel, 2008).

With this in mind, it should not be surprising that the depth and beauty of children's thoughts on complex concepts such as peace and culture, as proposed by the project, are conveyed through a poetic, light, yet powerful language, making use of metaphor to break free from both formal and substantive stereotypes.

Peace and culture are the two key concepts of the *Peace Between Cultures* project, which became both a context and an opportunity for dialogue, reflection, cognitive conflict, and exchange of ideas among children aged 9 to 11 from elementary and middle schools. The words of the children are shared in this section. Above all, peace and culture became the living substance of experiences shared in an intense, and at times, chaotic and joyful dialogue between the children themselves, with the teachers, and with the wider community.

The choice and use of various languages, visual, material, analogical, and digital, gave substance and visibility to children's points of view, presenting a kind of manifesto of their desires and rights, carrying an invitation to listen and an implicit call to responsibility. One example is a nine-year-old girl's simple statement: "Promoting peace means giving priority to peace."

PEACE AS A DESIRE AND A NATURAL RIGHT

In the hands and thoughts of the children, particularly those from elementary school, the concept of peace expands its semantic boundaries to embrace the concreteness of their feelings, their daily lives, and their existence in the world, becoming an indispensable and natural condition of being human. Peace, in their words, takes the form and meaning of "home, refuge, welcome, comfort, security, care, and kindness" because, as one child explained, "you have to be kind to have peace."

Peace is the desire and the right to feel welcomed in one's uniqueness, a generative concept that respects and embraces the qualities and passions of each individual, opening the way to relationships with others, as expressed by (M) "I think you can feel at home anywhere in the world, because home is the people around me" and by (A) "For me, feeling at home anywhere means being with people I know I can say everything to without the fear of being judged."

Peace is a place of citizenship, capable of tightly intertwining the "here" and the "there" that these new young citizens experience daily in their evolving sense of belonging: "There, I like the food more. There are my cousins, many of my friends, my grandparents, uncles... and then I go with my dad to watch the games. Here, I don't feel totally from Reggio. I feel Nigeria" (D).

The children involved in the *Peace Between Cultures* project carry with them a delicate and precious baggage of worlds: they are global children who strongly claim not only the right to be welcomed in their uniqueness but also their equal right to citizenship within their shared belonging to the human species, because "we are all unique, but we are all people" (E).

CULTURE AS A SHARED SPACE AND A KEY TO PEACE

In the context of a first-year secondary school class, culture was introduced as a polysemic term, one to explore, question, and discuss within a school setting restructured to encourage and support free expression, critical thinking, and the circulation and contagion of ideas. The result was a rich and engaging conversation that, once transcribed and reread, became fertile ground for the development of the experience.

Culture emerged as knowledge, understanding, and an antibody against stereotypes, ignorance, and fear of others: "Culture means many things: different traditions, different religions, and different ways of living" (B); "Knowing certain cultures and understanding them means fighting the stereotype that can turn into racism" (A) and "Culture is also a concept, because with different ethnicities and with different cultures, a multiethnic society is created" M).

Culture also emerged as a space for knowing and imagining where past, present, and future coexist: "Culture is knowing from history, so we don't repeat mistakes... the mistakes of the past" (J). Culture is a process of active and elaborative learning, different from acculturation, which concerns both the individual and society as a whole: "Culture is something you don't learn but that represents you and is a part of you" (M); "For me, culture is something you learn over time. You can learn it at school but also in life through experiences and traveling" (L): "I think culture and "being cultured" are two very different things. Being cultured means knowing things. Culture is a way of living, it's a shared space" (A).

The students' different definitions of culture, though seemingly simple, go directly to the heart of the subject. They speak to us about their lives, aspirations, and their capacity to reason, imagine, and formulate hypotheses through dialogue and listening to their own and others' points of view. This dialogue, based in their reflections, dares to cross the thresholds of the school and expand to the city: the students become reporters for a day, equipped with notebooks, pencils, and cameras, to interview Reggio residents in the square on a market day, described by one girl as "a shopping center of different ethnicities".

They meet men and women, young couples, and mothers with children, exploring places in the city that they believe represent ideas of culture. They interview, photograph, document, and collect thoughts and traces of the experiences they are living: impressions of thoughts, words, and images that will later return to the school to be reinterpreted, put back into circulation, and become shareable documentation open to new readings.

It is impossible to convey the richness and variety of the materials collected and produced. In summary, the collection of definitions of culture, a combination of the students and the men and women they met in the city, includes:

Culture is a concept / knowledge and imagination / traditions, religions, habits / an intimate part of you / the opposite of ignorance / learning from history to avoid repeating past mistakes / reading books and newspapers / being informed about the world we live in / sharing / what distinguishes us from animals / the environment that surrounds us / essential for living well / open-mindedness / progress / a fire always burning / a lifestyle / respect / a way of thinking / a way to bring people together / a value, a good way to preserve / a way of living, a shared space / culture is the key to peace.

Finally, the image of a large tree with its strong trunk and wide-reaching branches photographed by a boy in a city park, becomes an emblem and metaphor for an idea of culture: "The trees and branches are like the branches of different cultures".

CULTURE, PEACE, AND THE RIGHT TO QUALITY EDUCATION

Through these reflections, the *Peace Between Cultures* project has reinforced the idea of school as an educating community, a public meeting space where knowledge circulates among children, teachers, families, and citizens. The project affirmed the right to education as the right to participate in city life and to reimagine it as a space for co-existence and dialogue. The children's reflections reveal the transformative potential of education when listening and dialogue become the organizing principles of school life. Their interpretations of peace and culture demonstrate children have the ability to think in ethical, symbolic, and relational ways. Recognizing children as cultural researchers and active citizens means reaffirming that realizing the right to education involves ensuring the right to expression, participation, and belonging.

Furthermore, the project affirmed the right to quality education, understood as the shared construction of knowledge and meaning. The children understood peace not merely as the absence of conflict but as a natural right linked to safety and belonging, emphasizing emotional and relational aspects of human life. As shared by a teacher: "For the children, it was essential to give space to their emotional experiences, which were particularly important for fostering self-awareness and understanding others" (Teacher 7, Focus Group 2025).

Their reflections on culture deepened the shared understanding of participation in culturally diverse societies. Their words: culture is openness, a way of life, a shared space, express an understanding of citizenship not as a status, but as a practice: a continuous effort to recognize, include, and connect.

THE TEACHERS' PERSPECTIVES

The voices of teachers in *Peace Between Cultures* offer a window into how the project translated the right to quality education into pedagogical practice. The thematic analysis of the conversations held during the steering committee meetings and the ex-post focus group shows how participation, dialogue, and listening contributed to sustaining teachers' professional development through reflective praxis and the enactment of the "work of teachers as researchers" (Edwards et al., 1998, p. 340).

Across their trajectories, nearly half of the teachers encountered cultural diversity before entering the teaching profession, via civic engagement, volunteering in multicultural environments, or specializing in language and pedagogy, experiences that fostered both civic and teaching awareness. The others engaged with interculturality for the first time in the school context, as teachers. They were first concerned with the linguistic aspect, driven by a commitment to help newcomers learn Italian; however, their perspective soon aimed to extend beyond the emergency approach: "How can we build good practices of welcome? Welcome in the full sense of the word, of the children, the families, and their migration project" (Teacher 9, steering committee June 2021).

Such a question exemplifies how, for these teachers, the effort to build structured and meaningful practices of welcome, emphasizing the reception of the whole family and the understanding of each migration story, embodies a specific vision of the school as an educational community in which participation plays a key role.

Participation as Alliance with the Local Context

Teachers' narratives indicate that collaboration with various community stakeholders, public institutions, cultural centers, non-profit organizations, and families, was perceived as both an essential prerequisite and a professional asset for facilitating inclusion. Indeed, teachers' discussions revealed numerous prior collaborations with municipal educational services, local public health authorities, social cooperatives, public non-profit cultural institutions, and philanthropic foundations, from which teachers declared having learned "a lot." Working in collaboration with others emerged as a shared commitment, intended to avert isolation and gather support from external organizations to enhance teaching practices in the complex field of intercultural education: "The institution, the third sector, and the administration must work together so that teachers do not feel abandoned" (Teacher 10, steering committee March 2021). This understanding of participation resonates with the

REA, where "participatory democracy and civic community are fundamental to the (...) educational vision and mission" (Edwards et al., 1998, p. 8).

Additionally, several teachers expressed how the project fostered professional growth, allowing them to borrow and adapt strategies and ideas developed through interinstitutional projects: "What stayed with me most as a teacher is co-design, this reciprocal desire to work with different figures and the possibility to "borrow" ideas and strategies ... I later reused some of them, adapting them for new classes" (Teacher 5, Focus Group 2025). From this perspective, cooperation among teachers and other actors became a tool for professional growth and didactic innovation, but not only. Partnerships with local services and associations have enabled the participation of families, particularly foreign mothers involved in literacy programs held within the school premises. This is an example of how collaboration can generate reciprocal empowerment between schools and their communities: "Some foreign mothers took part in first-literacy courses in elementary school, with very positive outcomes for the group. It wasn't a large group, but the impact was significant" (Teacher 7, Focus Group 2025).

Literacy courses for families represent a concrete example of how to support the mutual understanding between school and families. Communication barriers specifically impacted relationships with mothers, who often had more difficulties with the language and, therefore, with school communications, despite frequently serving as the primary liaison with the school in daily interactions. The literacy courses were therefore a strategy to build bridges with the families, who represent one of the three holders of rights in the REA and should be given the right to participate in the educational path of their children (Malaguzzi, 1993).

DIALOGUE AS A PROCESS OF MUTUAL UNDERSTANDING

Dialogue with Families

Even when linguistic barriers are addressed, the school-family relationship can still be hindered by other challenges, such as differing educational perspectives, values, or habits. Dialogue emerged as a central theme in the teachers' reflections, with many recognizing it as both a complex and essential part of their work. This was evident during an initial steering committee meeting focused on the biggest challenges of school life, when seven out of nine teachers identified dialogue with families as a critical priority. Teachers emphasized how communication with families requires constant support and stated the need to establish simple and clear communication capable of guiding families step by step, reminding them of appointments and deadlines. The school system can appear as a bureaucratic apparatus that is difficult to decipher. Indeed, circulars and other school communications are often hard to understand for those who are unfamiliar with the Italian language or school system. However, teachers aspired to make communication welcoming and inclusive, delving into meanings and values: "Families with a migrant background need to be supported even if they have been in Italy for many years. (...) Therefore, this means supporting them during meetings, reminding them of various deadlines and meetings, and sharing their meaning and their importance" (Teacher 9, steering committee February 2021).

The encounter between the school and the family has a cultural dimension, with a double facet. On one hand, the school represents an institution worthy of respect and trust, a form of social mobility and an expression of a successful migration project. On the other hand, teachers also perceived elements of mistrust, which could be attributed to negative lived experiences, either personal or within their circle of acquaintances, or could be fueled by informal networks. In a similar way, teachers can be seen as: "mythical figures that should not be touched, but who can also be judged" (Teacher 5, steering committee March 2021).

Over the course of the project, teachers continued to actively involve the families. Specifically, they invited parents to create multilingual podcasts aimed at future and newly enrolled families at the Manzoni Comprehensive School. This initiative served as a meaningful strategy to foster closer relationships: "The project allowed for a much greater mutual understanding between families and the school, even on a more personal level, getting to know the person more than just the parent" (Teacher 5, Focus Group 2025).

Dialogue with and between Children

When addressing dialogue "with" and "between" children, teachers reported an inclusive classroom environment. Children appeared to experience their childhood with little concern for cultural differences. Teachers noted that conversations about different nationalities occasionally emerged without hindering socialization. While children sometimes encountered challenges typical of group dynamics, these were not associated with diversity nor perceived as obstacles to their daily interactions.

Children's feelings regarding their origins were highly varied and cannot be generalized. Some were proud of their culture and were not afraid to share it. For instance, a child who offered his knowledge of his mother's native language. Others, however, felt ashamed and hid their language and culture. Some children felt more rooted in the context in which they lived rather than in their parents' country of origin, while others experienced a stark conflict between the desire to keep their culture alive and the need to integrate into the new environment. The daily pedagogical choice for teachers was to foster openness and respect toward others, regardless of migratory background, recognizing that school can support children as they construct both their individual identities and their role as part of a group, aware that:

If this feeling is not created, if this loneliness, which belongs not only to immigrants but to all of us, is not addressed in the right way, we end up thinking that "my identity is my language, my identity is my religion, my identity is my culture". Instead, we should think that my identity is all of these things, as well as the language and culture of the country in which I live or have chosen to live. (Teacher 1, steering committee March 2021)

Within this framework, the steering committee collaboratively designed educational activities that integrated cultural connections and individual identities, such as the discourse on "peace" and "culture" initiated by the elementary school class, which encompassed peer-led discussions transitioning from personal experiences to collective knowledge. The co-design process and the educational activities with children were thoroughly valued by the teachers and, in certain instances, persisted beyond the project's end date.

The school is trying to characterize itself as a museum-oriented school, but we also did education outside the classroom with the Institute for the Blind. (...) We would like to try the same model with the Postal Police. When you start to hybridize, you feel like going more and more beyond classroom walls. (Teacher 5, Focus Group 2025)

LISTENING AS TRANSFORMATIVE PRACTICE

Listening is an essential practice for teachers. From the early phase of the project, listening was prioritized as a fundamental step in establishing relationships with families, aimed at comprehending their context and fostering connections without being overly explicit or intrusive. To support this encounter, the steering committee organized several seminars on the cultures and religions represented within the schools' population. This choice allowed them to better recognize certain dynamics previously gone unnoticed, for instance, understanding why some children missed school during specific periods of the year, insights that could have gone unnoticed. Similarly, a teacher shared how conversations in the classroom about culture and religion had uncovered cultural layers that were hidden, transforming them into shared topics of discussion with and among the children.

The extended and intensive lapse of time dedicated to reflection within the steering committee played a pivotal role and sustained the co-design of educational activities that appeared to be in line with teachers' daily work and well-integrated into the specific contexts and habits of each classroom. Teachers expressed a clear sense of satisfaction with the work done, particularly in terms of the exchange and reciprocity:

There is a satisfaction (…) of realizing that, perhaps, over these five years we've done a good job in the classroom and achieved something beyond it as well. We've engaged the children in the right way, not in a purely academic or instructional sense, but with a genuine outlook toward others (…). And that's exactly why, in my opinion, it's an important project, because it gives value to values. (Teacher 3, steering committee April 2022)

In addition, teachers described how reflective practices within the steering committee and collaborative work with other adults in the classroom enabled a shift in their professional stance. They reported having the opportunity to adopt a more decentered role allowing them to better grasp children's ideas and ways of understanding the world:

So, what do I take home? (…) I take home a new perspective, in a sense it's a play on words, but it's true. I had the opportunity to see my students in a different context, engaged in activities led by others, under a new light. This allowed me to position myself, at times, as an observer. A valuable perspective, but one that in elementary school is extremely difficult to achieve due to the limited time for co-teaching. (Teacher 2, steering committee April 2022)

These reflections on the teacher's role illustrate a shift in perspective that was also confirmed in the ex-post focus group, revealing a positive gain in professional development:

"I believe it was a very meaningful, mutual enrichment for the people involved, something you can't go back from. I've said this before, but it opens you up a bit, gives you a 360-degree perspective. It's a positive exchange, with everyone bringing their own specificities" (Teacher 5, Focus Group 2025). Furthermore, teachers reported being more empowered to engage more deeply with the lives of children outside of school, guided by the belief that school can be "the space, the moment, where they are truly listened to" (Teacher 7, Focus Group 2025).

Despite these results, the 2025 ex-post focus group also indicated a change in the school-family relationship: "These are different families from those we met during the Peace project. They really struggle. They find it very, very difficult to participate, even when we try to accommodate them with schedules or proposals" (Teacher 5, Focus Group 2025). Teachers shared renewed difficulties in specific situations, namely where a high concentration of students from the same national background was present within the same class, complicating communication and relationships with families:

The most extreme difficulties came when, last year, for example, one community was dominant. (…) We struggled a lot to establish relationships, it wasn't simple at all. Despite having completed a cycle after the Peace project with parents from completely different cultures who were very engaged, I found myself in a completely different situation. (Teacher 2, Focus Group 2025)

Teachers tended to associate this change with a marked deterioration in the socio-economic status of newly arriving families, coupled with a substantial rise in illiteracy rates, especially among mothers who serve as the primary liaison in the family-school dynamic.

FAMILIES

At first glance, the space dedicated to families within this project may appear more limited than that devoted to teachers and students. However, families' perspectives did not emerge solely through direct project activities, such as the questionnaire, the recording of video podcasts, or participation in literacy courses, but also through an indirect, yet well-documented dimension: the daily experience of teachers in school. Together, these sources provide insight into families' engagement and participation during the 2021–2022 period.

The Voice of Families

Within the project, and in an effort to gain a deeper understanding of the Manzoni Comprehensive School's intercultural landscape, the most evident form of participation took shape through an invitation addressed to families to complete a questionnaire between April and May 2021. A total of 335 families participated, covering 50% of the enrolled children, compared to 17% of children directly involved in the project, thus portraying an engaged and participatory community. Among respondents, there was a clear female majority (81%), mostly within the 31–40 age group (43%), followed by those aged 41–50 (40%).

The following data represents a selection of the 46 questions included in the questionnaire, with only a portion of the responses considered here. Overall, parents' participation in institutional activities proved to be very high, for example, in meetings with teachers, where over 90% reported taking part "always" (83%) or "often" (10%). Parents viewed these encounters as valuable opportunities for exchange and dialogue with the teaching staff, as well as occasions to "learn about their children's academic and personal growth" and to receive guidance for anticipating possible difficulties. This behavior aligns with the belief, shared by one parent, in the communal nature of the school, an institution that should not be limited to the student-teacher relationship but should also involve families. This aspect is further confirmed by parents' feedback on participation in collective moments, such as class assemblies, where engagement levels remain high, although somewhat lower than in individual meetings. It is particularly interesting to note that among the main motivations for participation, the desire for mutual understanding and relationships within the parent group clearly emerges.

However, some barriers to participation appeared. Parents indicated the difficulty of reconciling work schedules with school meetings and the lack of childcare services during meetings. Among the reasons for non-participation, only a small number of parents mentioned language barriers. Yet this contrasts with the expressed interest in receiving school documentation in multiple languages and in having a more frequent presence of cultural mediators—requests made by 30% and 25% of parents, respectively.

Focusing on the dimension of dialogue, operationalized through school-family communication, the questionnaire reveals a particularly high level of satisfaction with the relationship between parents and teachers, described as "very satisfactory" by 57% of respondents. Communication with the school office, while still positive, was mostly rated as "satisfactory" (52.5%). Among the suggested areas for improvement, parents noted the need for a simplification of bureaucratic language used in school office communications, more direct contact with teachers and the principal, and the presence of a cultural mediator. Finally, among the suggestions, one parent also expressed an invitation to listen more closely to the children.

Converging Perspectives Between Families and Teachers

It is particularly interesting to observe how, over the two years of the *Peace Between Cultures* project, a sustained dialogue occurred between teachers and families. This dialogue becomes visible through the comparison of two different data sources: the families' questionnaire responses and the teachers' reflections that emerged during the steering committee. The steering committee, small in number yet highly qualified, given its experience and daily direct contact with school life, devoted considerable attention to families with a migratory background, especially during the first three sessions. Alongside the gaps often identified as an area requiring specific training, the teachers' testimonies made it possible to explore in greater depth some aspects of the questionnaire.

The questionnaire data and the steering committee discussions confirmed the central role of female figures, who often acted as cultural mediators between the school and families' cultures of origin. At the same time, women frequently faced challenges related to more limited language proficiency, hindering their participation in institutional settings. To overcome this communication barrier, teachers relied on individual listening practices, which became the primary means of effective communication, focusing not only on factual understanding but also on the construction of shared meaning:

The individual meeting is still a way to reach them, maybe for 5 or 10 minutes outside the school or at the end of the morning or afternoon and stop them one by one to explain that there will be a meeting or assembly the next day, what an assembly is, and invite them to come to it. We can also explain why the meeting will take place. In short, we try to get them involved. (Teacher 9, steering committee March 2021)

This type of one-to-one communication also could compensate for families' difficulties in understanding and managing administrative aspects, issues that emerged from the parents' questionnaire and of which teachers were equally aware: "The school is also a bureaucratic system, so it's not always easy for them to read circulars, understand notices, and make sense of everything, especially if it's their first experience, their first child attending" (Teacher 9, steering committee March 2021). Along similar lines, teachers repeatedly emphasized the need for a more consistent presence of cultural mediators within the school, a request that mirrors the needs expressed by parents in the questionnaire.

Perspectives on Families' Engagement over Time

The ex-post focus group conducted in 2025 offered additional insights into how family engagement evolved over time. Although not directly reporting families' voices, the reflections of the steering committee provide insight into the school-family relationship through teachers' interpretations of daily interactions.

While the *Peace Between Cultures* project was described by teachers as fostering lasting professional growth and relational awareness, participants also reported perceiving changes in families' modes of participation compared to earlier phases of the project. In particular, some teachers described families with a migrant background as appearing more reserved and less inclined to engage in school life, despite the implementation of multiple strategies aimed at fostering participation:

What has changed compared to today? I see a context of families with a migrant background that is more closed off, as my colleagues mentioned earlier, and less inclined to participate. Many strategies are put in place in an attempt to involve them in school life, but it is really a struggle. (Teacher 5, Focus Group 2025)

The lack of essential documents, such as the tax code for certain children, exacerbated the integration challenges, both within the educational system and across public services. This situation has engendered progressively precarious conditions that threaten to result in social exclusion. Families may become increasingly insular and less willing to interact with others, including in the educational setting. The outcome is an increasing sense of mistrust and division, which, for the first time, a teacher observed, has begun to affect the children, who are starting to emulate these exclusionary behaviors.

DISCUSSION

This case study illustrates how the *Peace Between Cultures* project sustained the quality of education through the engagement of children, teachers, families, and the community. The project occurred within a distinct historical and geographical context where the connection between school and community was already acknowledged as a strategic asset. The initiatives organized by the project concretized rights established in international policies, ranging from children's right to be heard and to participate in cultural life (UN, 1989) to the concept of dialogue that integrates individual and institutional dimensions, as advocated in the White Paper on Intercultural Dialogue (Council of Europe, 2008). By prioritizing participation, dialogue, and active listening, the project concretized the rights to quality education as a collaborative process, engaging all educational stakeholders, children, teachers, families, and the community.

PARTICIPATION

The first strand of the analysis focuses on the concept of participation, which involves the idea of a school extending beyond its physical boundaries to build relationships with the community, and vice versa. The steering committee collaboratively designed educational activities that provided children with a calm and extended period of peer interaction. During this time, children shared their individual experiences and engaged with the perspectives of their peers, free from the pressure of right or wrong answers. Their interactions with citizens they encountered in the city center further enriched these connections.

Teachers found an opportunity for enhanced collaboration with local educational agencies. Together, they assessed the specific context and needs, designed implementation actions, and created spaces for reflective practice. Furthermore, atelieristas actively participated in school life by joining teachers in the classroom, which allowed teachers to take on an observer's role within their own classrooms.

The significance of family participation is evident in the high attendance at institutional activities, with over 90% of families attending individual meetings. However, this level of engagement was not without challenges, including the need for more accessible communication tools and facilitated dialogue.

DIALOGUE

Dialogue, understood as a continuous process of negotiating meanings, emerged as a complex yet decisive dimension. It characterized both peer discussions among children and the relationship with teachers and families.

The children developed deep reflections on peace and culture in the exchange with one another, their teachers, and the city. Becoming reporters for a day and interviewing citizens in the town center allowed the children to enrich their hypotheses. This process gave them time to exchange ideas and perspectives, sharing their stories and lived experiences with the classroom. Through this work, they came to define culture as a set of religions, languages, and ways of living that must be understood to avoid falling into prejudice or racism. As one of the children said, "For me, feeling at home anywhere means being with people I know. I can say everything to without the fear of being judged". This opened possibilities for dialogue in which individual uniqueness met the collective, moving from the "I" to the "we."

The dialogue between teachers and families emerged as a fundamental activity for addressing cultural diversity, but a complex one. On the one hand, teachers showed sensitiveness in welcoming families, especially guiding the ones with migrant backgrounds in decoding the school system and co-building shared values. Yet, the linguistic barriers represented a concrete obstacle for families' participation in school life, especially for mothers. Over the course of the project, teachers enacted strategies to reach out to parents with the aim of benefiting the wider community, specifically, they created podcasts in various languages for newly enrolled families. This combination allowed the teachers to "get to know the person more than just the parent" (Teacher 5, Focus Group 5). However, these measures proved partially sufficient. The questionnaires administered to families also called for the systematic presence of cultural mediators to support relationships and communication, particularly in discussions concerning children's school progress. This is a sensitive issue, given the high expectations families place on academic success as a means of fulfilling their migratory project and achieving upward social mobility, expectations that place significant power in the hands of teachers and may, in turn, give rise to feelings of mistrust or fear. The contrast between trust and fear highlights the complex dynamics in school-family relationships due to the connection between academic success and social and personal aspirations.

LISTENING

Finally, listening emerged as a transformative dimension of the project. Thanks to training and co-design of educational activities, teachers reported having acquired a "new, 360-degree perspective" that allowed them to see themselves and their students in a different light. The project enabled teachers to position themselves as observers, a valuable and rare vantage point in schools, where co-teaching opportunities are limited. Teachers also noted an increased sense of self-efficacy, confirmed by their observations of the children, with whom they felt they had worked "in the right way, not in a purely academic or instructional sense, but with a genuine outlook toward others" (Teacher 3, Focus Group 5).

KEY INSIGHTS, TENSIONS, AND FUTURE DIRECTIONS

This project exemplifies how collaboration between schools, children, families, and communities, grounded in shared values, can achieve inclusion. The experiences gained during the *Peace Between Cultures* project have demonstrated core principles that could and should become programmatic. Mainly, the collective work of teachers within a vertically integrated curriculum, enriched by the collaboration of diverse professional skills focused on creating innovative and inclusive projects. Another key element is recognizing each child's potential and embracing the uniqueness of every individual in a group dimension, a perspective that emphasizes the need to give each child time and space for reflective practice in a group setting. Furthermore, the convergence of school and parents towards a collaborative culture contributes to a climate of trust, with particular sensitivity to families with a migratory background, a process that must be approached with full awareness of the potential temporality of the choices and solutions identified collectively.

Indeed, transformative achievement does not represent a permanent attainment. The work initiated by the Manzoni Comprehensive School has set a solid foundation, yet it calls for the integration of its innovations into a coherent and sustainable system. The ex-post focus group revealed how teachers, who felt empowered during the project, reported increased difficulties in 2025. Among the reasons are the variability of migratory flows and the instability of their composition, which increased the complexity in managing the engagement of families, particularly in classes characterized by a single ethnic group, parents' low levels of literacy, and tensions among families that might affect children.

Deeply rooted in the local context, the *Peace Between Cultures* project also carries global significance. The project initiated a research process focused on the implementation of children's universal rights, with a deliberate emphasis on rights over needs, and specifically, the right to quality education for all and the right of children to be heard as rights-holders. From this locally grounded project, the role of the school as a catalyst for change was linked to three interconnected dimensions of the educational process: participation, dialogue, and listening, other educational settings engaging in a similar research process may identify additional underlying principles.

A key area for further research is how to update both initial and ongoing teacher training to better support the reciprocal exchange between teaching and learning, particularly the concept that "teaching can strengthen learning how to learn" (Malaguzzi, 1998, p. 83), thereby providing children and teachers with multiple options, suggestive ideas, and sources of support.

REFERENCES

Allport, G. W. (2004). *The nature of prejudice*. Basic Books.

Azzolini, D., Mantovani, D., & Santagati, M. (2019). Italy: Four emerging traditions in immigrant education studies. In P. A. J. Stevens & A. G. Dworkin (Eds.), *The Palgrave handbook of race and ethnic inequalities in education*. Palgrave Macmillan. DOI: 10.1007/978-3-319-94724-2_17

Barrett, M. (Ed.). (2013). *Interculturalism and multiculturalism: similarities and differences*. Council of Europe Publishing.

Bayer, J., & Bárd, P. (2020). *Hate speech and hate crime in the EU and the evaluation of online content regulation approaches*. European Parliament.

Bekemans, L. (2013). Educational challenges and perspectives in multiculturalism vs. interculturalism: Citizenship education for intercultural realities? In Barrett, M. (Ed.), *Interculturalism and multiculturalism: Similarities and differences* (pp. 169–187). Council of Europe.

Bonacini, L., & Girardi, R. (Eds.). (2021). *Annuario della scuola reggiana. Anno scolastico 2021-2022*. Provincia di Reggio Emilia.

Bruner, J. (1997). *The culture of education*. Harvard University Press. DOI: 10.2307/j.ctv136c601

Council of Europe. (2008). *The White Paper on intercultural dialogue – Living together as equals with dignity*. Council of Europe.

Council of Europe. (2016). *Competences for a democratic culture. Living together as equals in culturally diverse and democratic societies*. Council of Europe Publishing.

Edwards, C., Gandini, L., & Foreman, G. (Eds.). (1998). *The hundred languages of children*. The Reggio Emilia Approach. Advanced Reflections. Ablex Publishing Corporation.

Landini, A. (2022). La scuola che abita al museo: Dall'emergenza all'immersione nella cultura, per innovare spazi e contesti dell'apprendimento. *IUL Research, 3*(6), 206–219. DOI: 10.57568/iulres.v3i6.349

Lücker-Babel, M. F. (2008). Il diritto ad esprimere opinioni e ad essere ascoltato. In Belotti, V., & Ruggiero, R. (Eds.), *Vent'anni d'infanzia: Retorica e diritti dei bambini dopo la Convenzione dell'ottantanove* (pp. 157–172). Guerini e Associati.

Malaguzzi, L. (1987). *The hundred languages of children exhibition catalogue.* Reggio Children.

Malaguzzi, L. (1993). *Una carta per tre diritti.*

Passarelli, A. (2022). Report relativo alla raccolta e all'analisi dei dati sulle famiglie frequentanti l'Istituto Comprensivo "Alessandro Manzoni": Anagrafica, relazioni, soddisfazione e bisogni. In Ferrari, E., Landini, A., & Righi, L. (Eds.), *Pace fra le culture. Ricerche e azioni per il dialogo interreligioso e interculturale tra famiglie, studenti e insegnanti dell'I.C. "A. Manzoni" di Reggio Emilia* (pp. 63–89). Fscire Press.

Rinaldi, C. (2021). *In dialogue with Reggio Emilia.* Routledge. DOI: 10.4324/9780367854539

Robinson, K., & Robinson, K. (2021). *IMMAGINA CHE... Come creare un futuro migliore per tutti.* Erickson.

Saldaña, J. (2013). *The coding manual for qualitative researchers.* Sage Publications.

UNESCO. (2006). *Guidelines on intercultural education.* UNESCO.

United Nations. (1948). *Universal declaration of human rights.* https://www.un.org/en/about-us/universal-declaration-of-human-rights

United Nations. (1989). *Convention on the rights of the child.* Adopted and opened for signature and ratification by General Assembly resolution 44/25, 20 November 1989. https://www.ohchr.org/en/instruments-mechanisms/instruments/convention-rights-child

Wallace, R., Tolley, E., & Vonk, M. (2021). *Immigrant minorities index.* School of Policy Studies, Queen's University.

Zapata-Barrero, R. (2017). Interculturalism in the post-multicultural debate: A defence. *Comparative Migration Studies, 5*(14). [1] The Italian Ministry of Education is referred to by different names depending on the period: *Ministero della Pubblica Istruzione* (MPI) in 1994 and in 2007, *Ministero dell'Istruzione, dell'Università e della Ricerca* (MIUR) in 2006, and *Ministero dell'Istruzione* (MI) in 2022. This section will use these acronyms to refer to the Ministry.

Chapter 9
Children's Right to Early Education:
Bridging Reggio Emilia Philosophy With Global Educational Practices

Ashraf Alam
http://orcid.org/0000-0001-6178-1187
Alliance University, Bengaluru, India

ABSTRACT

This chapter explores the Reggio Emilia philosophy as a compelling global model for realizing the child's right to early education, grounded in the UNCRC's principles of access, participation, and benefit. Tracing its post-World War II origins and theoretical lineage through constructivist, sociocultural, and critical pedagogical frameworks, the chapter demonstrates how Reggio operationalises rights in early childhood through democratic learning environments, inclusive practices, and child-led curricula. It critically examines global inequities in access, the participatory mechanisms embedded in Reggio pedagogy, and the multidimensional benefits, i.e., cognitive, social, and emotional, derived from such a rights-based approach. Drawing on comparative international implementations and innovations, it analyses the institutional challenges of embedding Reggio principles in diverse contexts. Finally, the chapter offers policy recommendations and envisions future directions for integrating Reggio-inspired practices into digital, cross-sectoral, and post-pandemic educational landscapes.

DOI: 10.4018/979-8-3373-3431-8.ch009

INTRODUCTION

Early childhood education is increasingly recognized as a fundamental human right. The United Nations Convention on the Rights of the Child affirms in Article 28 every child's right to education, and in Article 29 that education should develop the child's personality, talents and abilities to their fullest potential. It also guarantees in Article 12 the child's right to express views in matters affecting them and have those views respected. Together, these principles establish even the youngest learners as active subjects of rights, not passive objects, within education. Yet worldwide, the right to early education is far from realized. Severe inequities in access to early childhood care and education persist, due to poverty, conflict, disability, gender discrimination, and policy neglect. Globally, only about half of children aged 3 to 6 attend any form of pre-primary program, and in low-income countries the rate is barely 20% (versus around 80% in high-income countries). This amounts to roughly 350 million young children, i.e., about 40% of under-fives, having no access to organized early learning. The most excluded are often children with disabilities, girls in certain societies, and those in conflict zones or remote areas, who face compounding barriers to early education. Such disparities between the promise of universal rights and the reality on the ground highlight the need for models of early education that can bridge this gap.

Against this global backdrop, the Reggio Emilia approach has emerged as a compelling model for enacting the child's right to quality early education. Originating in the city of Reggio Emilia in Italy, this philosophy is distinctive in viewing the young child as a capable, rights-bearing person and the protagonist of their own learning experience (Hočevar, Šebart, & Štefanc, 2013). In Reggio-inspired schools, classrooms function as democratic communities where children's ideas drive long-term project work, teachers act as collaborators and researchers alongside children, and even the physical environment is designed to invite exploration and dialogue (Arseven, 2014; Soler & Miller, 2003). The Reggio Emilia approach demonstrates how access, participation, and meaningful learning outcomes can be realized together. It operationalises children's rights by ensuring not only access to schooling but also active participation in learning and holistic developmental benefits.

This chapter argues that the Reggio Emilia philosophy gives practical form to the child's right to early education as defined by international frameworks, offering a globally relevant pedagogical model that aligns with the rights to access, participation, and development. The discussion will first situate Reggio Emilia in its historical context. It will then examine how Reggio practices address inequities in access and elevate participation as a pedagogical right,Next, it will explore the outcomes and benefits associated with Reggio's holistic approach to early learning. The translation of Reggio principles into different contexts will then be considered and the discuss policy implications of adopting a Reggio-inspired, rights-based approach considered. Finally, the chapter concludes with reflections on future directions, suggesting that Reggio Emilia's example points the way toward a paradigm shift from education *for* children to education *with* children.

THE REGGIO EMILIA PHILOSOPHY IN CONTEXT

Historical Emergence

The Reggio Emilia approach was born in Italy just after World War II, as local communities strove to create a new kind of school for young children. In 1945, parents in Villa Cella (a village near Reggio Emilia) used rubble and salvaged materials to build a preschool for their children. Loris Malaguzzi, a young teacher, joined this grassroots initiative and became the driving force behind what grew into a grassroots educational movement (Chicken, 2023; Fernández Santín & Feliu Torruella, 2017). Throughout the late 1940s and 1950s, dozens of similar parent-run preschools opened in the area, a women-led movement to nurture democracy, cooperation, and hope through early education. In 1963 the municipality of Reggio Emilia began supporting these schools as a public system, with Malaguzzi as pedagogical director. By the 1970s, the city's network of infant-toddler centers and preschools was renowned for its innovative, child-centered practices. This unique origin, literally built by citizens after the war, gave Reggio's schools a strong communal ethos. Education was seen not as top-down instruction but as a collaborative, community project focused on inclusion, social renewal, and respect for children.

Theoretical Roots

Although not derived from one doctrine, Reggio Emilia's philosophy aligns with several progressive theories. It reflects Jean Piaget's constructivism (children as active learners who construct knowledge) and Lev Vygotsky's sociocultural theory (learning as a social, collaborative process). One can see Piaget's influence in the emphasis on hands-on discovery and Vygotsky's in the rich group dialogue and adult-child interaction. The approach also echoes John Dewey's idea of experiential learning and democracy in education, where classrooms encourage learning by doing and treat the classroom as a community. Additionally, Reggio embraces Paulo Freire's vision of education as liberating and participatory, i.e., even at preschool age, children in Reggio are treated as thinkers whose voices matter. Scholars have noted that Reggio's practice rejects the *universal child* model and instead honours multiple perspectives and cultural contexts, aligning with postmodern critiques of one-size-fits-all education. In essence, Reggio Emilia is rooted in an image of the child as capable and full of potential, but it is ultimately defined by a willingness to learn from children themselves rather than apply theory rigidly.

Key Principles of the Reggio Approach

Several core principles characterize the Reggio Emilia approach in action. One is the notion of the *hundred languages of children*. Malaguzzi used this metaphor to describe the myriad ways children express themselves and understand the world, not only through speech and writing, but through art, play, construction, movement, music, and more. Reggio classrooms therefore provide diverse materials and opportunities for children to communicate in different languagesAll forms of expression are valued equally as cognitive tools (İnan, 2021). This approach ties into the Reggio image of the child as competent and creative. Every child is seen as rich with potential, curiosity, and the desire to relate to others (Fernández-Santín & Feliu-Torruella, 2020; Wood et al., 2015). Rather than a fixed curriculum, learning projects in Reggio emerge from children's own ideas and questions, which teachers respect and help to develop. The result is a curriculum that is highly responsive and engaging, because it is co-constructed with the children themselves (Edwards & Gandini, 2018).

Another core principle is documentation of learning. Reggio teachers carefully document classroom experiences by taking photographs, recording children's words, saving drawings and creations, and then use this documentation to reflect on what the children are thinking and how they are progressing (Edwards et al., 2011; New, 2007). Documentation is displayed in the school (e.g. panels showing a project's evolution) so that children can revisit their experiences and parents can follow the learning journey (McNally & Slutsky, 2017; Rigney & Kelly, 2023). It serves as an assessment method that captures the depth of children's inquiries and growth, in contrast to simplistic testing. Alongside documentation, the physical environment is treated as a third teacher. Classrooms and common spaces are thoughtfully arranged to be inviting and stimulating, e.g., there are nature corners, art studios (*atelier*), ample natural light, and open-ended materials neatly organized at children's height (Giamminuti & Merewether, 2023; Inan, Trundle, & Kantor, 2010). The space encourages exploration, communication, and autonomy. For instance, a group table with intriguing loose materials might prompt a collaborative building experiment, and a mirror placed at a child's level might spark self-awareness or artistic symmetry play. The environment is continually adapted in response to ongoing projects, provoking new interactions (Abdelfattah, 2015). This principle reflects Reggio's belief that setting and atmosphere significantly shape learning. A beautiful, well-organized space teaches children to value beauty, to take care of materials, and to feel respected and calm, thereby enhancing their ability to engage deeply with activities (Cutcher, 2013).

Pedagogical Roles and the Child as Citizen

The collaborative roles of adults in Reggio Emilia schools are another defining feature. Teaching is a team effort where each classroom typically has two co-teachers who plan together, observe and document together, and reflect on the children's learning as a team. In addition, a pedagogical coordinator (*pedagogista*) supports multiple classrooms, helping teachers connect practice with theory and ensuring that the values of the approach are maintained (Aljabreen, 2020; Barbour & Shalilee, 1998). An *atelierista* (art specialist) works across classes to integrate artistic media and project work, bringing expertise in visual arts or music and working with children and teachers in the atelier. This multi-disciplinary teamwork means that curriculum ideas are enriched by many viewpoints, and teachers receive continual professional development through dialogue with colleagues (Feliu-Torruella et al., 2021; Lindsay, 2015).

Parents are considered essential partners as well. From Reggio's inception, parents have had an active voice, i.e., parents serve on advisory councils, volunteer in classroom activities, and join events and discussions about the children's learning (Elliott, 2005; Foerch & Iuspa, 2016). The schools thus become an extension of the community, blurring the line between home and school. This close partnership builds trust and reinforces for the child that their education is a shared, meaningful endeavor (Senent et al., 2022; Westerberg & Vandermaas-Peeler, 2022). Underlying these roles is a profound respect for the child as a citizen. Reggio Emilia's founders and practitioners explicitly see children as citizens of their community from birth, i.e., with rights to be heard, to be respected, and to participate in community life (Hong, et al., 2017). This view revolutionizes the traditional notion that young children are merely *citizens in the making*. In practical terms, it means children in Reggio schools are given authentic opportunities to influence their environment and the activities they engage in (Lino & Parente, 2018). Teachers facilitate class discussions where children's opinions are solicited, for example, deciding on a theme for a project or shaping the layout of a new play area. Children learn that their voices matter and that with rights come responsibilities. They practice listening to peers, voting or reaching consensus on group matters, and taking care of their shared space, all in developmentally appropriate ways. This nurtures in children a sense of agency and belonging to society (Dodd-Nufrio, 2011; Rinaldi, 2021). They see the school as a micro-society where their ideas carry weight, an experience that lays the groundwork for active, responsible citizenship in later life.

Child's Right to Access and Reggio's Response

Access to early education encompasses multiple dimensions, i.e., physical (proximity and infrastructure, including disability access), economic (affordability and support for families), cultural (linguistic and religious inclusion), and pedagogical (relevance and adaptability of the curriculum). Around the world, these factors often intersect to deny certain groups of children their right to access education. Geographic and physical barriers can be stark. In rural or conflict-affected regions, preschools may simply not exist nearby, or be unsafe to attend. Children with disabilities frequently confront a lack of accommodations or even explicit exclusion from early education. Economic barriers are also significant, where preschool is privatized or costly, low-income families struggle to enroll their children, especially in the absence of public funding or childcare subsidies. Cultural and linguistic factors play a role as well, where minority-language speakers or children from indigenous and nomadic communities might find no programs in their mother tongue or aligned with their traditions, leading to alienation or low enrollment. Gender bias can further compound access issues in some societies (for instance, if families prioritize boys' education over girls' at this age). Additionally, policy fragmentation often undermines access when early childhood falls between health, education, and social services, it can result in patchy provision or lack of clear entitlements.

These inequities are reflected in global data. In many low-income countries, fewer than one in three children attends any form of early childhood program. Even within wealthier nations, enrollment disparities persist. Children from the poorest households, from rural areas, or from marginalized ethnic groups tend to have significantly lower preschool attendance rates than their more advantaged peers. Fulfilling the right to education requires tackling these disparities head-on. The policy challenge is not only to expand the number of preschool places but to ensure those places are accessible and welcoming to all children, including girls, children with special needs, and those from culturally diverse backgrounds.

Reggio Emilia's approach offers strategies that help overcome various access barriers. One key aspect is its community-governed, inclusive model. Reggio schools in Italy are municipally managed and closely tied to local neighborhoods, with decisions made by councils that include parents, teachers, and administrators (Cagliari et al., 2016). This local autonomy allows resources and curricula to be tailored to community needs, for example, adjusting operating hours to suit working families, or incorporating the home languages of immigrant children into school activities (Schneider et al., 2014; Zhang et al., 2025). The Reggio philosophy holds that a school should be a welcoming *piazza* of the community, meaning it is open to everyone and responsive to the local context. In practice, Reggio-inspired centers strive to remove gatekeeping and segregation. There are no entrance tests or *readiness* hurdles that would gatekeep children with special needs; on the contrary, inclusion is a foundational value. Children with disabilities are actively welcomed, and supports (such as learning support educators or adapted materials) are provided so they can participate fully in the daily life of the school. The physical environment is designed to be accessible where classrooms are on ground floors with ramps or elevators available, learning materials are arranged so that children using wheelchairs or with mobility challenges can reach them, and visual/tactile cues (like picture schedules) help children with different abilities navigate the day (MacDonald, 2011).

Economically, Reggio Emilia's system demonstrates how public investment can promote equitable access. The city of Reggio Emilia historically commits a significant portion of its municipal budget to early childhood services, enabling fees for families to be kept affordable and scaled to income (and providing exemptions or subsidies for low-income families). Essentially, early education is treated as a public good, much like primary schooling, so that no child is excluded for financial reasons (Emerson & Linder, 2021; Harris, 2021; Vecchi, 2010). In Reggio's case, this has led to very high enrollment rates across social classes in its preschools. For global contexts, the lesson is that rights-based access often requires public or collective funding solutions. Some Reggio-inspired programs outside Italy have used public-private partnerships, for instance, a community might secure government funding to cover basic teacher salaries and facility costs, while a foundation provides grants for the atelier and special projects, allowing the school to operate without pricing out families. The aim is always to avoid exclusivity, if Reggio approaches were confined to elite private schools, they would fail the equity aspect of the right to education. Encouragingly, several countries (such as Sweden and New Zealand) have universally accessible early childhood systems that share philosophical ground with Reggio, illustrating that scale and inclusion are possible alongside child-centered quality.

Cultural inclusion is another arena where Reggio's methods shine. Because Reggio educators start by listening to children and families, a Reggio-inspired school tends to adapt to the cultural identities of its community rather than expecting children to assimilate to a rigid school norm. Parents and extended family are invited into the educational process through workshops, storytelling sessions, and collaborative events, which validates the cultures and languages children bring (Rouse, 2023). For example, a Reggio school in a diverse urban area might hold an *international snack* day where families contribute a food from their culture and story behind it, integrating those into a class project about food and community. Or, if a number of children speak a minority language at home, teachers will incorporate key words from that language in songs or labels around the classroom, signaling to children that their home language is valued, not forbidden (Swann, 2008). In Italy, there have been instances of Reggio centers developing special outreach to marginalized groups, one notable case was a project working with Roma (Gypsy) families on the outskirts of Reggio Emilia, where an itinerant atelier (art workshop) traveled to Roma camps and engaged young children and parents in play and creative activities. This built trust and eventually encouraged many Roma families to enroll their children in the municipal preschools, bridging a gap that had long existed due to discrimination and mutual mistrust (Johnson, 2000; Manera, 2022). Such examples show how flexible, community-driven approaches can draw in families who might otherwise remain outside the formal system.

Reggio's pedagogy itself, with its flexibility and project-based, child-centered orientation also improves access in a subtler way, i.e., it adapts to each child, rather than expecting each child to fit one mold. In a rigid, highly academic preschool, a child who is different (whether due to disability, behavior, or learning style) may struggle or be asked to leave, effectively losing access despite being nominally enrolled (Theodotou & Aden, 2019). In a Reggio-style setting, that same child's unique qualities are more likely to be seen as strengths or opportunities for inquiry. For example, if a child has hearing impairment, a Reggio teacher might initiate a class project on communication without sound, exploring sign language, gesture, and art as languages, thus turning what could be a barrier into a shared learning experience (Eckhoff & Spearman, 2009; Moss, 2016). The inclusive, adaptive curriculum thus keeps children engaged and present; access is not only getting through the door but accessing the learning itself on one's own terms (Freeman, 2011; Manera, 2022). By rejecting a one-size-fits-all curriculum, Reggio ensures that children with different needs or backgrounds are not left behind or informally excluded.

In terms of policy influence, Reggio Emilia has shown how local practices can eventually shape broader systems. Italian early education policy since the 1970s has embraced concepts pioneered in Reggio and similar municipalities, for instance, the national guidelines emphasize the importance of community participation, continuity between infant-toddler centers and preschools, and the image of the child as an active subject. Internationally, Reggio's success has been cited in policy dialogues about universal preschool. It provides evidence that if you invest in quality and empower educators and communities, you can achieve both high access and high quality together, countering a fear that expansion might dilute quality (Balfour, 2016; Becker, 2016). In the rights discourse, Reggio offers a concrete model to argue that *how* we provide early education (democratically, inclusively) is just as important as *how many* children we reach (Kinney & Wharton, 2015).

Achieving the child's right of access to education is a multi-faceted endeavor. The Reggio Emilia approach contributes valuable lessons, make preschools locally grounded and culturally open, ensure public funding to eliminate financial barriers, design environments and curricula that welcome diverse abilities and backgrounds, and treat every child as worthy of full participation. These measures help transform access from a mere enrollment number to a living reality where each child, whatever their circumstances, can physically enter, feel at home, and learn meaningfully in early education (İnan & Kayır, 2015; Turner & Wilson, 2009). That, ultimately, is what honoring the right to education in early childhood looks like, an open door and an inclusive space beyond the door.

Participation as a Pedagogical Right

If access is about entering the door of education, participation is about having a voice and agency once inside. Children's right to participate in their education is articulated in Article 12 of the UNCRC, which says that children capable of forming their own views have the right to express those views freely and to have them given due weight in accordance with their age and maturity (UN, 1989). In early childhood settings, this means even very young children should be listened to regarding matters that affect them, including the daily activities, rules, and environment of their preschool. Educational theorists have developed frameworks to interpret genuine participation for children. Roger Hart's *Ladder of Participation* (adapted for early childhood) illustrates levels from tokenism (where adults include children in superficial ways) up to true child-initiated, shared decisions. Similarly, Laura Lundy's model emphasizes providing children with space, voice, audience, and influence, that are concrete elements needed to realize participation rights. These ideas set a high bar, where participation is not simply children doing assigned tasks or speaking when prompted, but children actively shaping their learning experience.

Reggio Emilia's philosophy and practice meet this high bar and indeed were ahead of their time in making participation a pedagogical cornerstone. In Reggio classrooms, children's opinions, questions, and ideas fundamentally drive the curriculum (Maynard & Chicken, 2010). The day often begins with a group discussion (a morning assembly or circle time) where children and teachers talk about ongoing projects or new interests. Teachers are trained to be skilled listeners, practicing what pedagogista Carlina Rinaldi calls the *pedagogy of listening*. Rather than planning every detail in advance, teachers observe and pick up on the threads children themselves introduce. For example, if a group of children become fascinated by shadows on the playground, the teacher will recognize this interest and help transform it into a full-fledged project on light and shadow by setting up an overhead projector and screens in the atelier, providing black paper for children to trace silhouettes, encouraging the group to ask questions about how shadows change. The initial spark comes from the children, and the teacher's role is to nourish and extend it into a rich inquiry (Kaynak-Ekici et al., 2021). This approach exemplifies what Hart's ladder would consider a high level of participation, adults and children co-constructing the learning process.

Daily life in a Reggio school provides myriad opportunities for child participation. Children make choices throughout the day, selecting which activity center to work in, which materials to use for a creation, or how to spend time during free play (Giamminuti, et al., 2023). They are given real responsibilities, i.e., they help set up and tidy the classroom, they assist in preparing snacks, they take care of class plants and pets (Balfour, 2022). Such duties are not merely chores; they instill a sense of ownership of the space and encourage the children to exercise autonomy in a safe way (Tijnagel-Schoenaker, 2018). Class meetings are convened whenever needed. If two children are in conflict over a toy, a teacher may invite them and a couple of peers to a short meeting to discuss what happened, with the teacher moderating in a neutral way and encouraging the children to propose solutions or rules to prevent future conflict. This models democratic problem-solving. Because children's words and proposals are taken seriously, over time Reggio children become adept at communication and negotiation. They learn to listen to peers, articulate their own thoughts, and collectively decide on actions, i.e., experiences that build their confidence and moral reasoning (Wexler, 2004).

The atelier (art studio) in Reggio is another arena of deep participation. In the atelier, children often work on group art projects where their collective creative decisions steer the outcome. An atelierista (art teacher) may introduce an intriguing new medium, say, a large block of ice with salt and watercolor for children to explore melting and color blending, but then follows the children's lead as they experiment and decide how to use it. The final artwork or installation that emerges (perhaps a sculptural piece combining melted patterns the children created) is a product of the children's ideas and collaboration. This process not only yields a beautiful result but teaches children that their ideas, combined with peers', can materialize into something real and valued by others. Documentation plays a special role in reinforcing participation. When teachers document children's conversations and work, and then display those documents at children's eye level, it creates a feedback loop, i.e., children see that their ideas are literally on the walls and become objects of reflection. Often teachers will review documentation with the children, for instance, showing them photos from an ongoing project and asking, *What do you notice? What should we do next?*, thereby involving them in assessing and guiding their own learning. In this way, documentation becomes a mirror that shows children their influence on the learning process, further empowering them to contribute new ideas. It also invites them to critique and adjust their thinking, essentially, young children in Reggio learn to think about their own thinking (a metacognitive skill) precisely because adults take their thinking seriously.

Teachers in Reggio identify not as instructors delivering knowledge, but as co-learners or researchers alongside children. This relational view shifts the power dynamic to a more equitable one (Lanphear & Vandermaas-Peeler, 2017). It is common to observe a Reggio teacher kneeling or sitting at the children's level, genuinely pondering a question the children raised rather than immediately answering it. The teacher might say, *Hmm, I'm not sure, how could we find out?* and thereby validate the children's role in the process of discovery. This stance encourages children to take initiative and pursue their curiosity, seeing that even the adult is curious and learning (Thornton & Brunton, 2015). Over time, it cultivates a classroom culture where asking good questions is as valued as knowing *correct* answers.

The impact of this participatory pedagogy on children is significant. Reggio educators and outside observers alike note that children develop notable self-confidence and autonomy. They become aware that their ideas matter and thus are motivated to express themselves (Avetisyan & Konjoyan, 2023; Firlik, 1994; McCormick et al., 2018). They also internalize a sense of justice and respect, having been listened to by adults, they learn to listen to others and expect a culture of mutual respect. Through constant collaboration, they build advanced social skills, i.e., by age five, many Reggio children work through disagreements or plan a group project with minimal adult intervention (You, 2014). Teachers frequently remark that older preschoolers in Reggio act as considerate mentors to younger ones, for example, spontaneously organizing a game and ensuring everyone, even the shy child, has a role, which reflects the empathy and leadership developed and nurtured by participatory practice. Treating participation as a right in early education transforms the learning environment. Reggio Emilia's example shows that when children are given real responsibility and voice in choosing topics, in negotiating rules, in creating together, they rise to the occasion. They become more engaged learners and more caring, capable young citizens. This participatory approach not only aligns with children's rights but also yields immediate educational benefits (higher motivation, better communication skills) as well as laying the groundwork for democratic dispositions in later life (Gouzouasis & Yanko, 2018).

Benefiting from Early Childhood Education

Beyond access and participation, the true fulfillment of the right to education lies in children actually benefiting from their educational experience. In early childhood, *benefit* cannot be measured only by immediate academic skills; it includes well-being, identity, socio-emotional development, creativity, and democratic values, which are the foundations for lifelong learning and citizenship. The Reggio Emilia approach is deliberately structured to yield rich benefits across all these dimensions, and research on Reggio and similar child-centered programs provides evidence of its positive outcomes (Bond, 2013; Hunsburger, 2015; Strong-Wilson & Ellis, 2007). First, children in Reggio-inspired preschools show high levels of engagement and curiosity (İnan, 2022). Observers note that Reggio children are deeply absorbed in activities, sustain attention for long periods on self-chosen projects, and ask complex questions about how things work. They approach problem-solving creatively, for example, trying multiple ways to build a taller block tower or mixing paints to get a precise shade of green, reflecting cognitive flexibility nurtured by an open-ended curriculum. Their language skills flourish in the dialogue-rich environment; even at four or five years old, many Reggio children can articulate their ideas and describe their reasoning with confidence, because they are continually invited to discuss, narrate, and negotiate meaning with peers and adults (Bond, 2015).

Socially and emotionally, the benefits are equally pronounced. Reggio children learn cooperation and empathy by working in groups from an early age. They practice listening to each other and considering different points of view during class meetings and joint projects (Baker, 2015; Nxumalo, Gagliardi, & Won, 2020). Teachers report fewer behavioral problems or aggressive incidents compared to more authoritarian settings, likely because the school climate emphasizes respect and responsive attention to each child's emotional needs. When conflicts do arise, children in Reggio classrooms are accustomed to resolving them through conversation or finding creative compromises (with gentle adult guidance), which over time internalizes strong conflict-resolution skills (Kołodziejski & Butvilas, 2021; Vallberg Roth & Månsson, 2011). Moreover, being valued as active participants appears to boost children's self-esteem and sense of belonging (Alaçam, 2025; Samuelsson, Sheridan, & Williams, 2006). They see themselves reflected in documentation panels and class decisions, which communicates that they are important members of the community, which is a powerful affirmation for a developing child's identity (Murris & Reynolds, 2018).

Importantly, these early benefits set the stage for long-term gains. Longitudinal research is beginning to confirm what Reggio educators intuitively believed, i.e., a high-quality early childhood experience can have lasting positive impacts. A notable evaluation by a team of economists and education researchers (including Nobel laureate James Heckman) examined adults who had attended Reggio Emilia preschools decades ago versus those who had not attended any preschool. The findings were striking, i.e., those who experienced the Reggio approach had higher rates of high school graduation, better employment outcomes in young adulthood, greater civic participation (measured by voting rates), and even healthier behaviors (such as lower incidence of obesity) compared to peers who had no formal preschool. The researchers concluded that the Reggio approach *significantly boosts* outcomes related to employment, socio-emotional skills, high school graduation, participation in civic life, and even long-term health. While many factors influence life outcomes, this study, controlling for background variables, strongly suggests that the Reggio early education experience yields measurable advantages well into adulthood. These long-term effects mirror findings from other renowned early childhood interventions (like the HighScope/Perry Preschool study in the US), but it is noteworthy that Reggio Emilia achieved them through a very different, non-directive pedagogy focused on creativity and relationships, as opposed to a didactic, skills-driven curriculum.

The emphasis on well-being and democracy in Reggio may also yield intangible long-term benefits. Children leave Reggio preschools not only ready for primary school (in terms of cognitive and social skills) but with a disposition to love learning and a positive view of school as a place where their ideas matter. Primary school teachers often note that alumni of Reggio-inspired preschools adapt quickly to classroom routines and show leadership in group work, likely because they are used to being proactive and collaborative. Additionally, Reggio's stress on *readiness for life*, i.e., resilience, creativity, and adaptability, may prove especially valuable in a fast-changing world. Anecdotally, during difficult times (for instance, economic downturns or the recent COVID-19 disruptions), educators observed that children who had been through Reggio Emilia's program, and their families, exhibited strong creativity and solidarity in coping, arguably reflecting the resilience and problem-solving orientation developed and nurtured in their early years.

Equity is another aspect of *benefit*. A truly beneficial educational model should not just advance children who are already advantaged; it should uplift those who might otherwise be left behind. Reggio Emilia's experience includes working with many children from disadvantaged backgrounds (including immigrant, refugee, and low-income families, as well as children with special needs) (Gilman, 2007). The narratives from these contexts are encouraging. In Reggio's Diana preschool, for example, a documented project involved refugee children from a war-torn country who initially were withdrawn and anxious. Through patient engagement in a long-term class project about *building our dream house*, these children gradually began to draw, build models, and tell stories about homes, expressing feelings and hopes in a supportive environment. Teachers observed that over weeks the refugee children became more relaxed, started to form friendships, and used Italian words learned from peers, an indication that the participatory, play-based approach helped them heal and integrate far more effectively than rote language drills would have. Similarly, in a Reggio-inspired inclusive preschool in Stockholm, educators noted that children on the autism spectrum often thrived when allowed to follow their deep interests and lead projects. One autistic child's fascination with subway maps, for instance, turned into a class exploration of maps and journeys, giving that child a source of pride and enabling peers to appreciate his expertise. These examples illustrate that the Reggio approach's flexibility and respectful attitude allow each child to benefit in their own way. Rather than forcing children into a single metric of success, Reggio's individualized approach ensures that a wide range of children, i.e., shy or exuberant, neurotypical or neurodivergent, fluent in the school language or just learning it, all find a way to participate and learn meaningfully (Omidvar, Wright, Beazley, & Seguin, 2019).

It is instructive to contrast the depth of benefits from a Reggio-like education with the outcomes from more standardized early education models. Many conventional programs fixate on short-term academic goals (e.g. letter recognition, counting to 20) as the main indicators of success. While such skills are important, an overemphasis on drilling academics in the early years can sometimes dampen children's natural curiosity and creativity, and gains in testable skills may prove temporary. Reggio Emilia, by focusing on play, inquiry, and social collaboration, arguably equips children with more robust *learning how to learn* abilities (Rigney & Rinaldi, 2023; Smidt, 2012). These abilities, such as, curiosity, persistence, communication, and problem-solving form a strong foundation that underpins later academic and life success (Sani, Mahmudah, & Muhammad, 2022). Indeed, longitudinal comparisons often find that by the end of primary school, children from play-based, child-centered preschools perform as well or better on academic measures than peers from didactic preschools, and significantly better on measures of creativity, self-regulation, and social skills. In essence, Reggio's emphasis on holistic growth and a love of learning does not come at the expense of academic preparation; rather, it enhances it by producing well-rounded, motivated learners.

The Reggio Emilia approach shows that when early education is approached holistically, i.e., nurturing the many languages of children, their social hearts and creative minds, the benefits are multifaceted and enduring (Guo & Rouse, 2025; Hesterman, 2011). Children not only gain cognitive and linguistic skills but also learn *how* to learn, how to collaborate, and how to see themselves as competent, valued individuals (Kinney & Wharton, 2007). These outcomes fulfill the spirit of the right to education, i.e., it is not merely a right to attend a school, but to develop one's fullest potential through education (Bond, 2015). The children of Reggio Emilia, in benefiting so broadly, are living proof of what is possible when early education is conducted with deep respect for the child's capacities and rights (Mages, 2016; Stone, 2012).

Implementation in Global Contexts

The Reggio Emilia philosophy, while developed in a specific Italian community, has proven remarkably adaptable across diverse global contexts. Implementing Reggio principles abroad requires thoughtful adaptation rather than literal replication. Educators often speak of *fidelity versus adaptation*, i.e., maintaining the core values of Reggio's approach (such as respect for children's ideas, documentation, and the environment as *third teacher*) while adjusting practices to fit local culture, resources, and constraints (Edwards, 2005). Around the world, many schools call themselves

Reggio-inspired rather than claiming to be exact copies of Reggio Emilia. This is intentional. Malaguzzi himself encouraged others not to import the schools of Reggio wholesale, but to reinterpret the approach within their own contexts. For example, in Japan some progressive preschools have embraced Reggio-style documentation, where teachers regularly photograph and journal about children's project work, because it aligns with Japanese reflective teaching practices, even though other aspects of Japanese early education (like larger class sizes or uniform routines) differ from Reggio. In South Africa, a country with limited preschool resources in many areas, educators have adapted Reggio by using plentiful local materials (sticks, clay, recycled bottles) as provocations for play and by training community volunteers to assist as co-teachers. The spirit of Reggio, i.e., innovation, listening, and creativity, is thus kept alive even if the material conditions differ.

One key challenge in global implementation is resource intensity. Reggio Emilia's success is partly due to well-trained staff, low child-teacher ratios, and generous time for collaborative planning, i.e., the conditions not easily met in under-resourced settings. To address this, some countries have formed professional learning communities and networks so that teachers can collectively adopt Reggio techniques step by step. For instance, in the United States, where public funding for preschool is uneven, many Reggio-inspired initiatives are in private or charter schools. However, a few public school districts (in cities like Chicago, New York, and Seattle) have started pilot classrooms that use Reggio Emilia practices, often by transforming one pre-K classroom at a public school with Reggio materials, giving those teachers special training, and documenting the children's progress to build a case for broader adoption. These American adaptations highlight both successes (children thrive under the approach, even in different cultural settings) and tensions (teachers sometimes struggle to reconcile Reggio's emergent curriculum with state-mandated early learning standards). Generally, educators find it is possible to meet required standards through Reggio methods, but it takes dialogue with administrators and creative planning, for example, showing that a child-led project on *bridges* naturally covers math (shapes, measurement), language (new vocabulary), and science concepts, thus fulfilling curriculum goals in an integrated way.

Cultural expectations can also pose challenges. In societies where education has traditionally been very teacher-directed, expecting young children to sit quietly and follow adult instructions, the Reggio approach's emphasis on child agency may initially raise eyebrows among parents or officials. Bridging this gap often involves gradual change and clear communication. Reggio implementers frequently start by introducing visible elements like art ateliers or more play-based learning, which tend to be well-received, and concurrently educate parents about the value of child-initiated activities. Often, seeing children excited and engaged convinces skeptics. Moreover, many cultures have practices that resonate with Reggio if framed appropriately. For instance, Indigenous educators in Canada and Australia have noted that Reggio's respect for multiple *languages* of expression and learning through nature aligns with First Nations and Aboriginal traditions of storytelling, art, and learning from the land. By highlighting these resonances, saying, in effect, that Reggio's approach will help revitalize *their* ways of learning, and educators can build community support for adaptation.

A powerful tool for bridging contexts is action research and reflective practice. Many teachers implementing Reggio outside Italy engage in cycles of experimentation, i.e., trying out Reggio-inspired strategies, observing children's responses, reflecting with colleagues, and then adjusting methods. This mirrors how Reggio itself evolved through continuous teacher research. For example, a kindergarten in Mexico City might introduce an atelier corner in a cramped classroom and see how children use it, then refine the setup based on their interactions. Through such iterative adjustments, even a very different physical or cultural environment can gradually *grow* a Reggio-like culture. Reggio Children (the international organization) also facilitates study groups and exchanges, allowing practitioners from different countries to visit Reggio Emilia or connect with each other. These exchanges plant seeds. A teacher from India might return home inspired to involve parents more, or an educator from China might start documenting conversations, and over time these seeds adapt to local soil.

Another innovation aiding global implementation is the use of digital technology for documentation and connection. While Reggio's roots are analogue (pens, clay, light tables), modern educators have incorporated digital cameras, tablets, and even simple projectors to enhance children's explorations (for example, projecting children's drawings large on a wall for them to re-interpret). In situations where resources are scarce or mobility is high (like refugee settings), digital documentation can help sustain Reggio-like continuity. For instance, in a Syrian refugee camp preschool on the Turkish border, teachers used a tablet to record children's artwork and stories, creating digital portfolios that could travel with families if they moved and be shared with the next teacher, thus preserving the child's learning journey. Digital platforms also connect Reggio-inspired educators worldwide, who share documentation and advice on blogs and social media, creating a virtual community of practice.

Not all aspects of Reggio transfer easily. Some national education systems impose strict curricula or high-stakes assessments even in early years, which conflict with Reggio's emergent, individualized pedagogy (Saracho & Evans, 2022; Vakil, Freeman, & Swim, 2003). In these contexts, teachers navigate a delicate balance, i.e., they might use the Reggio approach *under the radar* in their classrooms, while still checking the boxes for required content. Encouragingly, there is a global trend (supported by organizations like UNESCO and OECD) toward play-based and competency-based early childhood frameworks, which gives cover for Reggio-like methods. Policymakers in many countries are now talking about socio-emotional learning, creativity, and child participation as key goals, which is the language that legitimizes what Reggio teachers have done for decades. For example, Australia's national Early Years Learning Framework emphasizes *belonging, being, and becoming* and encourages learning through play and inquiry, which has made it easier for Australian educators to justify Reggio-inspired approaches within the official system.

To support global practitioners, networks and organizations have emerged. The North American Reggio Emilia Alliance (NAREA), the Reggio Emilia International Network, and various Reggio study groups across Asia, Europe, and Latin America all provide resources, workshops, and conferences. These networks consistently stress that there is no one Reggio recipe. Rather than exporting Italian school designs or Italian topics of study, they urge educators to embrace the *processes* of Reggio, i.e., observing children closely, talking with them, collaborating with colleagues, documenting and reflecting, and then to design contextually appropriate curricula. The measure of success is not how closely a classroom in Jakarta or Johannesburg resembles one in Reggio Emilia, but whether it upholds the image of the child as competent and creates a vibrant environment for exploration and dialogue.

Success stories from around the world demonstrate that Reggio's core ideas *can* take root in different soils. In a rural village in Laos, a volunteer-led preschool took inspiration from Reggio by involving grandparents in teaching local crafts, turning an initially rote learning setting into an interactive cultural project space. In a bustling city in the United States, a public elementary school reworked its kindergarten classes to be Reggio-inspired, leading to noticeable gains in student engagement and parent satisfaction, so much so that the district expanded the approach to other schools. Each adaptation is unique, but all share a common thread, i.e., deep respect for children's voices and creativity, and a conviction (borne out by experience) that children everywhere, when given the chance, respond with inventiveness and insight. Implementing Reggio Emilia globally is less about copying Italian classrooms and more about adopting a mindset, i.e., viewing children as competent co-constructors of knowledge and valuing creativity and relationships in learning (Inan, 2021; Rogers, 2010). With that mindset and a willingness to innovate around local challenges, educators across continents have shown that Reggio's principles can indeed flourish in vastly different environments (Smith-Gilman, 2015). The result, when done well, is not a carbon copy of Reggio Emilia, but a vibrant new manifestation that retains the Reggio essence, i.e., an early education where children's rights to participate, express, and thrive are truly realized.

Policy and Institutional Implications

The lessons from Reggio Emilia carry significant implications for early childhood policy and institutions. One major implication is aligning early education policy with a rights-based perspective, notably Sustainable Development Goal 4.2, which aims for all girls and boys to have access to quality early childhood development, care and pre-primary education. Reggio Emilia shows that *quality* in ECE is not just about structural inputs (teacher ratios, materials) but about upholding the child's rights to participation, identity, and agency. Policymakers can draw on Reggio principles when designing national curriculum frameworks. Rather than overly prescriptive curricula, they can formulate guidelines that emphasize child-initiated exploration, socio-emotional learning, and partnerships with families. Indeed, some countries have done so, e.g., New Zealand's *Te Whāriki* curriculum, for example, treats the child as an active weaver of their learning story, and Sweden's preschool curriculum highlights democracy and environment, where both clearly influenced by progressive approaches like Reggio. By embedding such concepts in official policy, governments signal that the purpose of early education is not drilling academic skills but nurturing well-rounded growth and rights fulfilment.

At the institutional level, one of the clearest implications is the need to reform teacher education and professional development. To implement approaches like Reggio, teachers must be prepared not as instructors of a fixed syllabus but as researchers and collaborators. This means training in observational skills, documentation techniques, designing open-ended projects, and facilitating group learning rather than lecturing. Some teacher training institutes have introduced modules on the Reggio Emilia approach and on emergent curriculum, giving student-teachers exposure to these methods. Additionally, existing preschool teachers benefit from study tours and workshops, where Reggio Emilia itself has hosted thousands of educators from around the globe, and many return home to become change agents in their schools. Education ministries might institutionalize regular learning circles or learning communities for early educators. For instance, in the Italian municipal schools, teachers meet weekly to reflect together; a ministry could mandate or support a similar structure, ensuring teachers have paid time for joint reflection and planning. This moves the system toward the Reggio model of a *learning* institution, where teachers are continually learning and improving, just as children are (Chiwamba, 2016).

Infrastructure and space design are also key institutional considerations. Governments or school boards investing in new early childhood centers can incorporate the idea of the environment as a third teacher. While not every school can have an architecturally stunning design, basic principles can be followed, i.e., provide natural light, access to an outdoor garden or play yard, flexible indoor spaces that can be configured for different projects, child-sized furnishings and plenty of accessible, open shelving for materials. Even small renovations can transform existing preschools, for example, knocking out a non-structural wall to create a central piazza area where children from different classes mingle (a hallmark of Reggio schools), or converting an unused storage room into a mini-atelier for art exploration. In resource-poor settings, policy can encourage low-cost improvisations, i.e., using local arts and crafts as classroom materials, painting walls in inviting colors, displaying children's work prominently (which costs nothing yet values children's creations). The underlying principle is that the physical environment should stimulate interaction, independence, and a sense of belonging, not just be a container for children (Waks, 2015). Some policy frameworks now include environment quality in their rating systems; incorporating Reggio-based environment criteria (such as aesthetic and intellectual richness of the space) could elevate what is expected from ECE facilities.

Funding and governance models may need to shift to support a Reggio-like approach at scale. Because Reggio emphasizes comprehensive services and low ratios, it can be perceived as expensive. However, proponents can point to the long-term cost-benefit evidence of quality ECE. Policymakers could explore dedicated funding streams, for instance, earmarking a portion of education budgets specifically for early childhood innovation or using public-private partnerships to fund teacher training in Reggio methods. The Italian example of municipal financing is instructive. Reggio Emilia's city government decided that early childhood centers were as crucial as roads or hospitals, and funded them accordingly through local tax revenue. Other cities could emulate this by enshrining early education funding in law (as some German cities have with a *right to a kindergarten place* from age 3, ensuring funding flows). Public-private models are also possible, e.g., a government funds core teacher salaries while a partner NGO funds special atelier projects or materials. What's vital is to avoid inequity, i.e., quality approaches like Reggio should not be available only to affluent communities. Thus, any partnership or fee system must include subsidies for low-income families, or else it undermines the rights approach.

Another policy aspect concerns assessment and evaluation. Traditional monitoring of preschools often relies on checklists of whether children can recite certain facts or perform tasks. But in a Reggio-inspired system, assessment is qualitative and continuous (Alaçam & Olgan, 2025; Murris, 2017). Policymakers might need to broaden accountability measures to include portfolios of children's work, documentation records, and parent and child feedback, rather than simplistic tests. Some countries have started to move in this direction, for instance, England's early years foundation stage profile relies largely on teacher observations of children's activity. A rights-respecting evaluation might also look at process indicators, i.e., *How much do children talk in class versus teachers? Do children have choice in activities daily?*

Are parents involved in decision-making? These are all evaluative questions one can derive from Reggio Emilia's philosophy, and they could be incorporated into inspection frameworks or quality rating systems to incentivize participatory practice.

Finally, embracing Reggio Emilia's philosophy has broader institutional implications, i.e., it calls for a culture shift in how we view young children within our society. Institutions that adopt it often have to do substantial advocacy and consensus-building among staff and parents. School principals and administrators should be prepared to educate stakeholders about why, for example, children might spend three weeks studying *rainbows* instead of following a set workbook, explaining the depth of learning that occurs in such projects. When institutions internalize the values of Reggio, they may also adjust policies on discipline (moving from punitive rules to community agreements), on scheduling (allowing longer uninterrupted play/project periods instead of chopping the day into many small segments), and on family engagement (treating parents as partners who have insight into the curriculum). These changes, while sometimes challenging initially, have been found to create more harmonious and effective schools. Policy can support this at a higher level by providing guidelines that encourage positive discipline, flexible scheduling, and family inclusion.

Translating Reggio Emilia into policy and institutions means reimagining many aspects of early education systems through a rights lens. It means committing resources and trust to the notion that children's self-directed exploration is as important as alphabet lessons, that teachers need time to reflect not just to administer, and that preschools are spaces of culture and democracy, not mere service-delivery points (Wien & Dudley-Marling, 1998). The payoff for such alignment is substantial, leading not only more joyful and meaningful educational experiences for children, but also potentially stronger communities and future citizens. Reggio Emilia's success has already influenced policies toward these ends; the continued advocacy of its principles can help ensure that early childhood institutions worldwide evolve to truly honor children's rights and potential.

CONCLUSION AND FUTURE DIRECTIONS

In reflecting on the Reggio Emilia approach, we return to the core thesis, i.e., early education can truly realize children's rights when it is conceived as an ethical, aesthetic, and democratic pedagogy. Reggio Emilia's experience shows that treating children as strong, active protagonists in their learning is not only a moral ideal but a practical model yielding excellent educational outcomes and vibrant school communities. By operationalizing the principles of access, participation, and benefit, Reggio Emilia stands as evidence that the child's right to education can be fulfilled in its fullest sense, even with young learners. This chapter has highlighted how aligning early childhood practices with children's rights, i.e., the right to inclusive access, to be heard and to influence, to develop one's full potential, transforms educational settings. It calls on educators and policymakers globally to view young children not as passive recipients of instruction but as people with voices and agency. As countries strive to expand early childhood provision (spurred by global goals like SDG 4.2), Reggio Emilia offers both inspiration and a challenge, where quality must be defined not only by structural standards or narrow academic gains, but by the presence of child agency, joy in learning, and meaningful relationships in the classroom. In other words, fulfilling the right to education is about qualitative richness as much as quantitative reach.

Looking ahead, new opportunities and questions are emerging for Reggio-inspired practice. One future direction is integrating digital technology in ways that amplify rather than diminish Reggio's relational ethos. Educators are experimenting with digital documentation tools that allow children to revisit their project photos or recordings on tablets, and to share their learning with families in real time. The COVID-19 pandemic unexpectedly pushed Reggio educators to innovate with virtual interactions, for instance, teachers maintained dialogue with children through video calls and digital project work when schools were closed. They discovered that while screens can never replace hands-on interaction, principles like listening and co-construction can be adapted to virtual formats to some extent (e.g., children at home sending photos of their *findings* to the teacher, who then creates a slideshow that all children discuss together online). In the future, finding the right blend of digital tools, perhaps child-friendly cameras, interactive projectors, or online portfolios accessible to parents, could enhance documentation and connection without undermining the sensory, social nature of Reggio learning. The goal will be to use technology to support children's *hundred languages* (for example, enabling a child to animate their clay figures with a simple app) while preventing technology from narrowing those languages or isolating children.

Another vital future direction is strengthening cross-sector collaboration around early childhood. Reggio Emilia has always viewed early education in a broad context, intertwined with family support, community life, art and culture, and even health and social services. Future efforts to realize children's rights will benefit from similarly holistic strategies. We may see more preschools that double as family resource centers, offering parenting workshops or health screenings, thus addressing rights to health and nurturing care alongside education. The concept of *children's hubs* is gaining traction in some regions, e.g., one-stop centers that include preschool classrooms, pediatric advice, libraries, and safe play spaces, often inspired by the idea that supporting the whole child and family yields the best outcomes. This reflects Reggio's legacy of integration (for example, Malaguzzi worked closely with psychologists and pediatricians in the early days to ensure schools met children's emotional and physical needs). As governments and NGOs plan post-pandemic recovery in early years, integrating education with nutrition, mental health, and social protection, essentially, cross-sector teamwork, will be crucial, and Reggio provides a philosophical blueprint for how to keep the child at the center of such integrated practice.

The upheavals of the COVID-19 era also emphasized the importance of resilience in education systems. Approaches grounded in relationships and creativity, like Reggio's, proved relatively adaptable amid crisis, where teachers could shift emphasis to home life projects and emotional well-being, because they were not bound to a strict academic script. Going forward, building resilience means maintaining the capacity for flexibility, innovation, and trust at the school level, which are exactly the capacities that Reggio-style decentralization and teacher empowerment nurture. In a sense, one can view Reggio Emilia's approach as *future-proof* not because it uses cutting-edge technology or content (it does not), but because it cultivates human and community strengths that can weather change, e.g., relationships, creativity, critical thinking, and solidarity. These strengths will be needed to tackle whatever future challenges may come, from climate change to social upheaval, today's children may face as adults.

Reggio Emilia invites us to embrace a fundamental paradigm shift in how we conceive education, i.e., from seeing it as *for* children to seeing it *with* children. This shift in preposition captures a move from doing things to passive recipients, to collaborating with active participants. It implies that education is not something adults deliver to children, but a mutual journey that adults and children undertake together. This is a powerful idea with implications beyond preschool, i.e., it speaks to how we might re-imagine schooling at all levels, parenting, and children's role in society. If the next generation grows up experiencing education as a partnership, they are more likely to become adults who engage constructively in democratic processes and community life, having been respected from their earliest memories. The Reggio Emilia approach is far more than a local pedagogical experiment, rather it is a globally relevant demonstration that children's rights in education can be realized in practice. It shows that when given a nurturing environment, the freedom to explore, and a voice in their learning, children everywhere thrive and exceed our expectations. Future pathways for early education will likely draw increasingly from approaches like Reggio as the world recognizes that the early years set the tone for lifelong learning and citizenship. As we carry Malaguzzi's legacy forward, continuing to innovate and adapt his principles for new contexts, we take a step closer to a world where every child's right to a stimulating, empowering, and caring education is not just promised, but delivered, i.e., where education is truly *with* children, in partnership with them, from the start.

REFERENCES

Abdelfattah, M. (2015). Realizing a progressive pedagogy: A comparative case study of two Reggio Emilia preschools in San Francisco. *Universal Journal of Educational Research, 3*(12), 1074–1086. DOI: 10.13189/ujer.2015.031217

Alaçam, N. (2025). The role of pedagogical documentation in child and parent participation: An investigation of educator and parent perspectives in a Reggio Emilia-inspired preschool. *European Early Childhood Education Research Journal*, •••, 1–18. DOI: 10.1080/1350293X.2025.2508319

Alaçam, N., & Olgan, R. (2025). How do child portfolios enable assessment? Content analysis of portfolios from a Reggio Emilia-inspired preschool and a university preschool in Türkiye and the United States. *Education 3-13, 53*(5), 756-767. DOI: 10.1080/03004279.2023.2220339

Aljabreen, H. (2020). Montessori, Waldorf, and Reggio Emilia: A comparative analysis of alternative models of early childhood education. *International Journal of Early Childhood, 52*(3), 337–353. DOI: 10.1007/s13158-020-00277-1

Arseven, A. (2014). The Reggio Emilia approach and curriculum development process. *International Journal of Academic Research, 6*(1), 166–171. Advance online publication. DOI: 10.7813/2075-4124.2014/6-1/B.23

Avetisyan, M., & Konjoyan, H. (2023). A Comparative Analysis Between Traditional and Alternative Early Childhood Education, such as the Maria Montessori Method, Reggio Emilia Pedagogical Approach. *Armenian Journal of Special Education, 7*(2), 65–77. DOI: 10.24234/se.v7i2.8

Baker, F. S. (2015). Reflections on the Reggio Emilia approach as inspiration for early childhood teacher education in Abu Dhabi, UAE. *Early Child Development and Care, 185*(6), 982–995. DOI: 10.1080/03004430.2014.974036

Balfour, B. (2022). Early childhood education, politics, and memory: Tracing social imaginaries in Reggio Emilia schools' diaries of the 1970s. *Paedagogica Historica, 58*(1), 19–31. DOI: 10.1080/00309230.2020.1769143

Balfour, B. J. V. (2016). Feminist tales of teaching and resistance: Reimagining gender in early childhood education (Reggio Emilia, Italy). *Gender and Education, 28*(3), 445–457. DOI: 10.1080/09540253.2016.1167176

Barbour, N. E., & Shalilee, B. D. (1998). Gifted education meets Reggio Emilia: Visions for curriculum in gifted education for young children. *Gifted Child Quarterly, 42*(4), 228–237. DOI: 10.1177/001698629804200406

Becker, S. (2016). Developing pedagogy for the creation of a school makerspace: Building on constructionism, design thinking, and the Reggio Emilia approach. *The Journal of Educational Thought (JET). Revue de la Pensée Éducative, 49*(2), 192–209. DOI: 10.55016/ojs/jet.v49i2.46293

Bond, V. L. (2013). Follow and facilitate: What music educators can learn from the Reggio Emilia approach. *General Music Today, 27*(1), 24–28. DOI: 10.1177/1048371313480798

Bond, V. L. (2015). Created in context: A comparative case study of the use of music in two Reggio Emilia-inspired schools. *Early Childhood Education Journal, 43*(2), 119–126. DOI: 10.1007/s10643-014-0639-4

Bond, V. L. (2015). Sounds to share: The state of music education in three Reggio Emilia–inspired North American preschools. *Journal of Research in Music Education, 62*(4), 462–484. DOI: 10.1177/0022429414555017

Cagliari, P., Castagnetti, M., Giudici, C., Rinaldi, C., Vecchi, V., & Moss, P. (2016). *Loris Malaguzzi and the schools of Reggio Emilia: A selection of his writings and speeches, 1945-1993.* Routledge., DOI: 10.4324/9781315778631

Chicken, S. (2023). 'Doing Reggio?' Exploring the complexity of 'curriculum' migration through a comparison of Reggio Emilia, Italy and the EYFS, England. *Global Studies of Childhood, 13*(4), 322–340. DOI: 10.1177/20436106211068041

Chiwamba, S. V. (2016). Investigation on the applicability of Reggio Emilia Approach in teaching early childhood education: An intensive comparison between China and Tanzania. DOI: 10.5539/jedp.v6n2p29

Cutcher, A. (2013). Art spoken here: Reggio Emilia for the big kids. *International Journal of Art & Design Education, 32*(3), 318–330. DOI: 10.1111/j.1476-8070.2013.12028.x

Dodd-Nufrio, A. T. (2011). Reggio Emilia, Maria Montessori, and John Dewey: Dispelling teachers' misconceptions and understanding theoretical foundations. *Early Childhood Education Journal, 39*(4), 235–237. DOI: 10.1007/s10643-011-0451-3

Eckhoff, A., & Spearman, M. (2009). Rethink, reimagine, reinvent: The Reggio Emilia approach to incorporating reclaimed materials in children's artworks. *Art Education, 62*(2), 10–16. DOI: 10.1080/00043125.2009.11519007

Edwards, C., Gandini, L., & Forman, G. (Eds.). (2011). *The hundred languages of children: The Reggio Emilia experience in transformation* (3rd ed.). Bloomsbury Publishing USA., DOI: 10.5040/9798400667664

Edwards, C. P., & Gandini, L. (2018). The Reggio Emilia approach to early childhood education. In Roopnarine, J. P., Johnson, J. E., Flannery Quinn, S., & Patte, M. M. (Eds.), *Handbook of international perspectives on early childhood education* (pp. 365–378). Routledge., DOI: 10.4324/9781315562193-26

Edwards, S. (2005). Children's learning and developmental potential: Examining the theoretical informants of early childhood curricula from the educator's perspective. *Early Years Journal of International Research and Development, 25*(1), 67–80. DOI: 10.1080/09575140500043161

Elliott, E. M. (2005). Changing perspectives in early childhood education: Recasting the Reggio Emilia approach. *Journal of Early Childhood Teacher Education, 25*(2), 153–163. DOI: 10.1080/1090102050250208

Emerson, A. M., & Linder, S. M. (2021). A review of research of the Reggio Inspired approach: An integrative re-framing. *Early Years Journal of International Research and Development, 41*(4), 428–442. DOI: 10.1080/09575146.2019.1591350

Feliu-Torruella, M., Fernández-Santín, M., & Atenas, J. (2021). Building relationships between museums and schools: Reggio Emilia as a bridge to educate children about heritage. *Sustainability (Basel), 13*(7), 3713. DOI: 10.3390/su13073713

Fernández Santín, M., & Feliu Torruella, M. (2017). Reggio Emilia: An essential tool to develop critical thinking in early childhood. *Journal of New Approaches in Educational Research, 6*(1), 50–56. DOI: 10.7821/naer.2017.1.207

Fernández-Santín, M., & Feliu-Torruella, M. (2020). Developing critical thinking in early childhood through the philosophy of Reggio Emilia. *Thinking Skills and Creativity, 37*, 100686. DOI: 10.1016/j.tsc.2020.100686

Firlik, R. J. (1994). Reggio Emilia, Italy Preschools: The Synergies of Theory and Practice.

Foerch, D. F., & Iuspa, F. (2016). The internationalization of the Reggio Emilia philosophy. *Contrapontos, 16*(2), 321–350. DOI: 10.14210/contrapontos.v16n2.p321-350

Freeman, R. (2011). Reggio Emilia, Vygotsky, and family childcare: Four American providers describe their pedagogical practice. *Child Care in Practice, 17*(3), 227–246. DOI: 10.1080/13575279.2011.571236

Giamminuti, S., & Merewether, J. (2023). The Reggio Emilia atelier as a place of disruption: Remaking pedagogical alliances through aesthetics and experimentation. *Pedagogies, 18*(4), 746–766. DOI: 10.1080/1554480X.2022.2106233

Giamminuti, S., Merewether, J., & Blaise, M. (2023). Aesthetic-ethical-political movements in professional learning: Encounters with feminist new materialisms and Reggio Emilia in early childhood research. In *Non-Linear Perspectives on Teacher Development* (pp. 240–252). Routledge., DOI: 10.4324/9781003372097-16

Gilman, S. (2007). Including the child with special needs: Learning from Reggio Emilia. *Theory into Practice*, *46*(1), 23–31. DOI: 10.1080/00405840709336545

Gouzouasis, P., & Yanko, M. (2018). Learning stories and Reggio Emilia-inspired pedagogical documentation: Formative methods of assessment for the elementary school music classroom. In *Handbook of cultural studies and education* (pp. 486–502). Routledge., DOI: 10.4324/9781351202398-30

Guo, K., & Rouse, E. (2025). Searching for evidence-based practice: A qualitative meta-synthesis of the research on Reggio Emilia practices in Australian early years settings. *Australian Journal of Education*, *69*(1), 58–78. DOI: 10.1177/00049441241302831

Harris, H. A. (2021). Parental choice and perceived benefits of Reggio Emilia inspired programs. *Early Child Development and Care*, *191*(1), 123–135. DOI: 10.1080/03004430.2019.1608194

Hesterman, S. (2011). Extending Reggio Emilia principles in the middle school context: A western Australian case study. *Educational Practice and Theory*, *33*(1), 73–91. DOI: 10.7459/ept/33.1.05

Hočevar, A., Šebart, M. K., & Štefanc, D. (2013). Curriculum planning and the concept of participation in the Reggio Emilia pedagogical approach. *European Early Childhood Education Research Journal*, *21*(4), 476–488. DOI: 10.1080/1350293X.2013.845437

Hong, S. B., Shaffer, L., & Han, J. (2017). Reggio Emilia inspired learning groups: Relationships, communication, cognition, and play. *Early Childhood Education Journal*, *45*(5), 629–639. DOI: 10.1007/s10643-016-0811-0

Hunsburger, W. (2015). A Reggio Emilia-Inspired Pedagogy of Listening. *Listening to Teach: Beyond Didactic Pedagogy*, *15*, 15–23. Advance online publication. DOI: 10.1515/9781438458335-002

İnan, H. (2022). Sustainability of early childhood education inspired by the Reggio Emilia Approach during the emergency times: A phenomenographic research. *International Journal on Lifelong Education and Leadership*, *8*(1), 36–48. DOI: 10.25233/ijlel.1094854

Inan, H. Z. (2021). Challenges of Distance/Online and Face-to-Face Education in the New Normal: Experiences of Reggio Emilia-Inspired Early Childhood Educators in Turkey. *Pedagogical Research, 6*(1), em0086. Advance online publication. DOI: 10.29333/pr/9304

İnan, H. Z., & Kayir, G. (2015). Reggio Emilia Inspired Projects Conducted in a Preschool: An Action Research. *Journal of International Social Research, 8*(38), 733. Advance online publication. DOI: 10.17719/jisr.20153813682

Inan, H. Z., Trundle, K. C., & Kantor, R. (2010). Understanding natural sciences education in a Reggio Emilia-inspired preschool. *Journal of Research in Science Teaching, 47*(10), 1186–1208. DOI: 10.1002/tea.20375

Johnson, R. (2000). Colonialism and cargo cults in early childhood education: Does Reggio Emilia really exist? *Contemporary Issues in Early Childhood, 1*(1), 61–78. DOI: 10.2304/ciec.2000.1.1.8

Kaynak-Ekici, K. B., İmir, H. M., & Temel, Z. F. (2021). Learning invitations in Reggio Emilia approach: A case study. *Education 3-13, 49*(6), 703-715. DOI: 10.1080/03004279.2020.1775272

Kinney, L., & Wharton, P. (2007). *An encounter with Reggio Emilia: Children's early learning made visible.* Routledge., DOI: 10.4324/9780203937143

Kinney, L., & Wharton, P. (2015). *An encounter with Reggio Emilia: Children and adults in transformation.* Routledge., DOI: 10.4324/9781315750309

Kołodziejski, M., & Butvilas, T. (2021). Creativity and parental involvement in early childhood education in the Reggio Emilia approach and philosophy. *Edukacja Elementarna w Teorii i Praktyce, 16*(3 (61), 103-112. DOI: 10.35765/eetp.2021.1661.07

Lanphear, J., & Vandermaas-Peeler, M. (2017). Inquiry and intersubjectivity in a Reggio Emilia–inspired preschool. *Journal of Research in Childhood Education, 31*(4), 597–614. DOI: 10.1080/02568543.2017.1348412

Lindsay, G. (2015). Reflections in the mirror of Reggio Emilia's soul: John Dewey's foundational influence on pedagogy in the Italian educational project. *Early Childhood Education Journal, 43*(6), 447–457. DOI: 10.1007/s10643-015-0692-7

Lino, D. M., & Parente, C. (2018). Play and learning in early childhood education: The contribution of High Scope, Reggio Emilia, and Montessori Pedagogical approaches. In *Early childhood education from an intercultural and bilingual perspective* (pp. 147-163). IGI Global. DOI: 10.4018/978-1-5225-5167-6.ch010

MacDonald, M. (2011). Review of Kathy Hall et al. loris malaguzzi and the Reggio Emilia experience. *Studies in Philosophy and Education, 2010*(6), 631–639. Advance online publication. DOI: 10.1007/s11217-011-9224-0

Mages, W. K. (2016). Taking inspiration from Reggio Emilia: An analysis of a professional development workshop on fostering authentic art in the early childhood classroom. *Journal of Early Childhood Teacher Education, 37*(2), 175–185. DOI: 10.1080/10901027.2016.1165763

Manera, L. (2022). Art and aesthetic education in the Reggio Emilia Approach. *Education 3-13, 50*(4), 483-493. DOI: 10.1080/03004279.2022.2052230

Manera, L. (2022). The Reggio Emilia Approach to Early Childhood Education. An Analysis to Its Inclusive Perspectives and Their Relationships to Aesthetic Aspects. In *Fostering Inclusion in Education: Alternative Approaches to Progressive Educational Practices* (pp. 145–153). Springer International Publishing., DOI: 10.1007/978-3-031-07492-9_7

Maynard, T., & Chicken, S. (2010). Through a different lens: Exploring Reggio Emilia in a Welsh context. *Early Years Journal of International Research and Development, 30*(1), 29–39. DOI: 10.1080/09575140903443000

McCormick Smith, M., & Chao, T. (2018). Critical science and mathematics early childhood education: Theorizing Reggio, play, and critical pedagogy into an actionable cycle. *Education Sciences, 8*(4), 162. DOI: 10.3390/educsci8040162

McNally, S. A., & Slutsky, R. (2017). Key elements of the Reggio Emilia approach and how they are interconnected to create the highly regarded system of early childhood education. *Early Child Development and Care, 187*(12), 1925–1937. DOI: 10.1080/03004430.2016.1197920

Moss, P. (2016). Loris Malaguzzi and the schools of Reggio Emilia: Provocation and hope for a renewed public education. *Improving Schools, 19*(2), 167–176. DOI: 10.1177/1365480216651521

Murris, K. (2017). Reading two rhizomatic pedagogies diffractively through one another: A Reggio inspired philosophy with children for the postdevelopmental child. *Pedagogy, Culture & Society, 25*(4), 531–550. DOI: 10.1080/14681366.2017.1286681

Murris, K., & Reynolds, R. A. (2018). Reggio Emilia inspired philosophical teacher education in the Anthropocene: Posthuman child and the family (tree). DOI: 10.18357/jcs.v43i1.18262

New, R. S. (2007). Reggio Emilia as cultural activity theory in practice. *Theory into Practice, 46*(1), 5–13. DOI: 10.1080/00405840709336543

Nxumalo, F., Gagliardi, L. M., & Won, H. R. (2020). Inquiry-based curriculum in early childhood education. In *Oxford research encyclopedia of education.* DOI: 10.1093/acrefore/9780190264093.013.1064

Omidvar, N., Wright, T., Beazley, K., & Seguin, D. (2019). Examining children's indoor and outdoor nature exposures and nature-related pedagogic approaches of teachers at two Reggio-Emilia preschools in Halifax, Canada. *Journal of Education for Sustainable Development, 13*(2), 215–241. DOI: 10.1177/0973408219872066

Rigney, L. I., & Kelly, S. (2023). Reterritorialising pedagogies of listening: Bringing into dialogue culturally responsive pedagogies with Reggio Emilia principles. *Discourse (Abingdon), 44*(1), 147–161. DOI: 10.1080/01596306.2021.1961688

Rigney, L. I., & Rinaldi, C. (2023). Teaching in cultural and linguistic super-diverse Australian classrooms: A north–south exploration of Reggio Emilia. In *Affirming the Rights of Emergent Bilingual and Multilingual Children and Families* (pp. 209–225). Routledge., DOI: 10.4324/9781003294405-19

Rinaldi, C. (2021). *In dialogue with Reggio Emilia: Listening, researching and learning*. Routledge., DOI: 10.4324/9780367854539

Rogers, S. (2010). Play and pedagogy: A conflict of interests? In *Rethinking play and pedagogy in early childhood education* (pp. 13–26). Routledge., DOI: 10.4324/9780203839478

Rouse, E. (2023). 'If you don't feel respect then morally, it just takes a lot out of everything you're doing": Learning in a pedagogical approach inspired by Reggio Emilia middle years school settings. *Australian Educational Researcher, 50*(4), 1089–1104. DOI: 10.1007/s13384-022-00538-z

Samuelsson, I. P., Sheridan, S., & Williams, P. (2006). Five preschool curricula—Comparative perspective. *International Journal of Early Childhood, 38*(1), 11–30. DOI: 10.1007/BF03165975

Sani, A. N. H., Mahmudah, S., & Muhammad, A. A. (2022). The Concept of Merdeka Belajar in Early Childhood: Comparative Study of Reggio Emilia and Ki Hajar Dewantara's Thoughts. *JOYCED: Journal of Early Childhood Education*, 2(2), 156–175. DOI: 10.14421/joyced.2022.22-06

Saracho, O. N., & Evans, R. (2022). Early childhood education pioneers and their curriculum programs. In *The Influence of Theorists and Pioneers on Early Childhood Education* (pp. 159–166). Routledge., DOI: 10.4324/9781003120216-14

Schneider, B. H., Manetti, M., Frattini, L., Rania, N., Santo, J. B., Coplan, R. J., & Cwinn, E. (2014). Successful transition to elementary school and the implementation of facilitative practices specified in the Reggio-Emilia philosophy. *School Psychology International, 35*(5), 447–462. DOI: 10.1177/0143034313511003

Senent, I. G., Kelley, K., & Abo-Zena, M. M. (2022). Sustaining curiosity: Reggio-Emilia inspired learning. In *The Influence of Theorists and Pioneers on Early Childhood Education* (pp. 262–273). Routledge., DOI: 10.4324/9781003120216-23

Smidt, S. (2012). *Introducing Malaguzzi: Exploring the life and work of Reggio Emilia's founding father*. Routledge., DOI: 10.4324/9780203111857

Smith-Gilman, S. (2015). Culture matters: The arts, the classroom environment, and a pedagogy of EntewateNikonri: Sake: A study in a first nations pre-school. *Canadian Review of Art Education, 42*(2), 53–68. DOI: 10.26443/crae.v42i2.1

Soler, J., & Miller, L. (2003). The struggle for early childhood curricula: A comparison of the English Foundation Stage Curriculum, Te Wha riki and Reggio Emilia. *International Journal of Early Years Education, 11*(1), 57–68. DOI: 10.1080/0966976032000066091

Stone, J. E. (2012). A Vygotskian commentary on the Reggio Emilia approach. *Contemporary Issues in Early Childhood, 13*(4), 276–289. DOI: 10.2304/ciec.2012.13.4.276

Strong-Wilson, T., & Ellis, J. (2007). Children and place: Reggio Emilia's environment as third teacher. *Theory into Practice, 46*(1), 40–47. DOI: 10.1080/00405840709336547

Swann, A. C. (2008). Children, objects, and relations: Constructivist foundations in the Reggio Emilia approach. *Studies in Art Education, 50*(1), 36–50. DOI: 10.1080/00393541.2008.11518754

Theodotou, E., & Aden, F. (2019). Reggio Emilia and the arts approach: Two exceptional examples of multimodal learning in early years. *Journal of Global Education and Research, 3*(2), 158–167. DOI: 10.5038/2577-509X.3.2.1050

Thornton, L., & Brunton, P. (2015). *Understanding the Reggio approach: Early years education in practice*. Routledge., DOI: 10.4324/9781315744018

Tijnagel-Schoenaker, B. (2018). The Reggio Emilia Approach… The Hundred Languages. *Prima Educatione, 1*, 139. DOI: 10.17951/pe.2017.1.139

Turner, T., & Wilson, D. G. (2009). Reflections on documentation: A discussion with thought leaders from Reggio Emilia. *Theory into Practice*, *49*(1), 5–13. DOI: 10.1080/00405840903435493

Vakil, S., Freeman, R., & Swim, T. J. (2003). The reggio Emilia approach and inclusive early childhood programs. *Early Childhood Education Journal*, *30*(3), 187–192. Advance online publication. DOI: 10.1023/A:1022022107610

Vallberg Roth, A. C., & Månsson, A. (2011). Individual development plans from a critical didactic perspective: Focusing on Montessori-and Reggio Emilia-profiled preschools in Sweden. *Journal of Early Childhood Research*, *9*(3), 247–261. DOI: 10.1177/1476718X10389148

Vecchi, V. (2010). *Art and creativity in Reggio Emilia: Exploring the role and potential of ateliers in early childhood education*. Routledge., DOI: 10.4324/9780203854679

Waks, L. J. (Ed.). (2015). *Listening to teach: Beyond didactic pedagogy*. Suny Press., DOI: 10.1515/9781438458335

Westerberg, L., & Vandermaas-Peeler, M. (2022). How teachers, peers, and classroom materials support children's inquiry in a Reggio Emilia-inspired preschool. In *The Influence of Theorists and Pioneers on Early Childhood Education* (pp. 274–291). Routledge., DOI: 10.4324/9781003120216-24

Wexler, A. (2004). A theory for living: Walking with Reggio Emilia. *Art Education*, *57*(6), 13–19. DOI: 10.1080/00043125.2004.11653571

Wien, C. A., & Dudley-Marling, C. (1998). Limited vision: The Ontario curriculum and outcomes-based learning. *Canadian Journal of Education/Revue canadienne de l'education*, 405-420. DOI: 10.2307/1585755

Wood, J., Thall, T., & Parnell, E. C. (2015). The move: Reggio Emilia-inspired teaching. *Complicity: An International Journal of Complexity and Education*, *12*(1). Advance online publication. DOI: 10.29173/cmplct24241

You, H. (2014). Learning from Learning Environments: The Effects of the Reggio Emilia Approach in Early Childhood Education Centers. *Creativity in Educational Research and Practice*, 95-109. DOI: 10.1163/9781848883086_010

Zhang, Q., Yin, J., & Jiang, K. (2025). Glocalization of early childhood curriculum: An ethnographic study on the integration of the Reggio Emilia approach into the Chinese kindergarten curriculum. *Asia Pacific Education Review*, *26*(March), 49–60. DOI: 10.1007/s12564-023-09851-3

Chapter 10
Other Worlds and Other Possibilities:
Re-Envisioning Early Childhood and Children's Rights Through Collaboration of a Child's Global World of Community, School, and Family

Judith N. Levin
Independent Researcher, USA

Angela Vatalaro
http://orcid.org/0009-0004-1156-8571
Independent Researcher, USA

Suzette Turner
University of Central Florida, USA

Kelcie Burke
University of Nebraska-Lincoln, USA

Marisa Galliano Macy
University of Wyoming, USA

ABSTRACT

This chapter explores how the Reggio Emilia Approach can be re-envisioned through global collaboration among children's key systems of community, school, and family. Grounded in Bronfenbrenner's ecological systems theory and the United

DOI: 10.4018/979-8-3373-3431-8.ch010

Nations Convention on the Rights of the Child, it emphasizes children's rights to participation, voice, and agency. Drawing from a decade of Reggio-inspired study abroad experiences with pre-service and in-service early childhood professionals, the authors propose a new educational partnership that unites parents and teachers through shared experiential learning in Reggio Emilia, Italy. This model seeks to bridge theory and practice, reduce power imbalances between home and school, and strengthen the child's global world by fostering collaborative, rights-based education that values the hundred languages of children.

INTRODUCTION

This chapter explores the Reggio Emilia Approach (afterwards referred to as "the Approach") through a global lens, considering how its principles intersect with the systems that shape a child's life within their community, school, and family. Guided by Bronfenbrenner's ecological systems theory (1977; 1979; 1986) and the United Nations Convention on the Rights of the Child [UNCRC] (United Nations [UN], 1989), we examine how collaborative partnerships within these systems can advance children's rights and foster their development as capable, creative global citizens. We reflect on how study abroad programs for pre-service teachers and study trips for parents and in-service professionals can be used as a mechanism to ensure children's rights are met while increasing the impact of Reggio-inspired programs in the United States.

In this chapter, we use the word *parent* to be inclusive of biological parents, legal guardians, and others who have primary, consistent contact with the child in their home life. We define *pre-service teachers* as university students enrolled in a teacher preparation program designed for early childhood and elementary educators. *In-service professionals* refers to practitioners serving children and families in community settings, including but not limited to practicing teachers, administrators, and early interventionists.

ECOLOGICAL SYSTEMS AND THE CHILD'S GLOBAL WORLD

Urie Bronfenbrenner was born in Moscow in 1917. As a child he experienced turmoil in his home country, immigrating to the U.S. at 6 years old. Bronfenbrenner actively witnessed the upheaval faced by children during the unrest and social change in Russia, which shaped his ideas about how a child's environment can influence child development (Guy-Evans, 2025). The ecological systems theory highlights the complexity of relationships that impact a child's life and development. The "set of nested structures, each inside the next" (Bronfenbrenner, 1979, p. 3) is made up of concentric circles surrounding the child. Each circle encompasses a system: micro-, meso-, exo-, macro-, and chronosystem. These interconnected structures shape each human being (Sadownik & Jevtić, 2023). The microsystem is the most significant level, which includes the child's immediate environment such as family and school (Guy-Evans, 2025).

There are modern realities affecting young children that extend beyond traditional interpretations of the ecological systems theory. Bronfenbrenner's ecological systems theory evolved over time as he continued his research. The revised theory expanded into the bioecological model. Its focus is on the interactions between an individual and their environment. These interactions are the "true engines of development" (Guy-Evans, 2025).

Modern challenges such as the high cost of quality child care; the influence of technology; unpredictable events such as the global COVID-19 pandemic; non-stop news reports of shootings; and climate change leading to extreme weather situations are issues which cut across all systems. These unhealthy influences impact both daily experiences and long-term development. With this understanding, we should be asking what actions we can take to protect the rights of children to live in a healthy environment (Fisher & Lombardi, 2025).

THE RIGHTS OF THE YOUNG CHILD

Bronfenbrenner's (1977; 1979; 1986) ecological systems theory provided a helpful context in which the UNCRC (UN, 1989) can be situated. As part of the systems that interact with children in the microsystem, parents, schools, and communities are ideally positioned to facilitate the rights of the young child. If children have rights from birth, then parents are a primary source for ensuring their rights are met.

Since the UN first began meeting to discuss rights of children, tensions have existed between supporting the rights of children and the rights of parents, which stem from viewing the child as having individual civil and political rights versus the civil rights parents have to make choices for their children (Quennerstedt, 2009). After much negotiation and refinement, Article 5 of the UNCRC specifically states that parents have a right to provide "appropriate direction and guidance" in ensuring the rights of children are met (UN, 1989). Thus, parents have some leeway to consider their personal ideals as they strive to fulfill the rights of their child.

The rights of the child cannot be honored unless parents receive the assistance they need to facilitate those rights (Bruyere & Garbarino, 2010; UN, 1989). Children's rights in the UNCRC are often categorized in the context of three P's: provision rights (access to basic needs); protection rights (safety from harm such as abuse and neglect); and participation rights (children are listened to, heard, and respected) (Mayall, 2000). In most developed nations, there are resources parents can access to ensure provision and protection rights are addressed, as well as mechanisms in place for governments to intervene if parents are not able to fulfill those rights. When attention is limited to provision and protection rights, the child may be viewed primarily as vulnerable and reliant on caregivers to support their well-being (Dillen, 2006).

When including participation rights, which are explicitly outlined in Articles 12 and 13 of the UNCRC (UN, 1989), the role of the adult might be that of a "child liberator" (Dillen, 2006) who views the child as a "citizen of the present" (Rinaldi, 2020, p. 12). From this perspective, the child has agency over issues that directly impact them. In viewing provision, protection, and participation rights as rights that coexist, adults can be both caretaker and liberator, protecting the child while also incorporating their ideas and viewpoints (Dillen, 2006). However, facilitating children's participation can be much harder to accomplish than ensuring they are protected and have their basic needs met.

Hart (1992) defined participation in the context of children's rights as "...the process of sharing decisions which affect one's life and the life of the community in which one lives" (p. 5). Lundy (2007) further developed the concept of participation into a model that includes four interrelated dimensions for fostering children's participation: a *safe* space to discuss views; adequate information and support to use their *voice;* their views are respected and validated so they have *influence* over decisions which directly impact them; and they are given access to the right *audience* to include them in decision making processes. To be citizens who fully participate in society, children must have meaningful participatory interactions with adults, including parents and teachers.

Research outcomes indicate that while social and economic factors, including parent education level, may contribute to knowledge of children's rights, they do not influence the application of children's rights within the home (Voicu et al., 2015). Even when familiar with the UNCRC (UN, 1989), many parents find it challenging to recognize the significance of involving children in decisions that affect their lives. Children who do not have access to their participation rights can struggle to make large decisions, such as choosing a profession, as they enter adulthood (Tomanović-Mihajlović, 2000). Children who believe they can fully participate in family decisions are more likely to have fewer behavior issues in adolescence (Pećnik et al., 2016). Thus, promoting participation in the home produces short and long-term benefits.

Parenting style can have a direct impact on children's participation. For example, an authoritarian parenting style (Sanvictores & Mendez, 2022) stifles participation because it does not allow for children to be listened to or heard. From the viewpoint of ensuring children's participation rights are met, ideally parents should adopt a democratic style (Sanvictores & Mendez, 2022; Tiwari, 2022), where parent-child interactions focus on "cooperation, fairness, equality, and mutual respect" (American Psychological Association [APA], 2018, para. 1). Democratic parenting aligns with Lundy's (2007) model of providing safe spaces for the child to use their voice to influence decisions in which they are impacted.

A democratic parenting style can produce positive child outcomes academically, socially, and emotionally (Ali et al., 2023; Estrella Acencio & Cordero, 2023; Lavrič & Naterer, 2020; Tiwari, 2022; Tripon, 2024). In a study focusing on well-being through life satisfaction with participants in 10 countries across Southeast Europe (Lavrič & Naterer, 2020), researchers found that those who were not exposed to any form of democratic parenting had lower life satisfaction. In addition to democratic parenting contributing to the UNCRC (UN, 1989) through promoting children's participation, it also contributes to the UN's Sustainable Development Goals (SDGs) which are designed, in part, to improve health and education globally (UN, 2015). Democratic parenting promotes good health and well-being (SDG 3), quality education (SDG 4), and a more peaceful and just society (SDG 16) (Tripon, 2024). Therefore, a democratic parenting style supports children's participation as well as produces sustainable benefits for the child, family, and larger society.

In examining the relationship between the SDGs and parenting style, Tripon (2024) found that collaborative partnerships between families and teachers are needed to capitalize on positive child outcomes. To meet the rights of the young child, parents from all backgrounds need concrete professional development that increases understanding of democratic parenting and also provides them with tools for the application of meaningful parent-child interactions that promote children's participation (Voicu et al., 2015). Although difficult and not often implemented, this can be achieved by purposefully allowing parents to contribute in school and community activities to learn more about meaningful ways to include children in child-initiated, shared decisions with adults (Hart, 1992).

ACADEMIC CONFLICTS

While schools are a mechanism for children to explore their participation rights, an extreme focus on academic content limits them to a provisional right of a basic need of education, which too often is equated to passing a standardized test (Bagnato & Ho, 2006). Early childhood education in the United States often trends towards a more teacher-directed, academic approach that emphasizes skills and knowledge acquisition while leaving out the social and global development called for by the UN (Barblett et al., 2016; Harmon & Viruru, 2018). Over the past two decades, an awareness has developed among in-service professionals and researchers that preschool and kindergarten classrooms have rapidly become more academically oriented and less focused on exploration, social skills development, and play (Bassok et al., 2016). The emergence of the Common Core State Standards, with specific content standards for kindergarten in literacy and math, has led to discussion about what is appropriate instruction in the early grades (Carlsson-Paige et al., 2015).

The intense focus on drilling content knowledge is not producing positive educational outcomes. An examination of a state-funded preschool program (Lipsey et al., 2018) indicated that any short-term gains in literacy, language, and math skills at the end of the preschool year disappeared by the end of the kindergarten year when compared to a control group of children who did not attend preschool. By third grade, the control group of children performed better on achievement tests than the preschool group. The phrase "high quality preschool" in the United States does not necessarily consider the essential elements that adequately serve the development and learning of young children (Lipsey et al., 2018) and is not the best environment to foster children's participation.

THE HUNDRED LANGUAGES OF CHILDREN

With participation rights often overlooked or underdeveloped and academic learning being pushed in ways that are developmentally inappropriate, it is necessary to have a framework for assisting parents, teachers, and community members in understanding how to encourage children's voice in family, school, and social situations (Hart, 1992; Lundy, 2007). The Reggio Emilia Approach can provide that framework. The spirit of the Approach is emphasized in the poem written by its founder Loris Malaguzzi, titled "No Way. The Hundred is There" (translated in Edwards et al., 2012, p. 3). The poem describes the "hundred languages" children possess to express themselves using all of their senses and their unique approaches to participation. Yet too often parents, schools, and the larger community stifle those languages and reduce the child to one overly structured, adult-controlled "language" (Hart, 1992). When considering the ways in which we should view children's participation in their ecological systems (Bronfenbrenner, 1977; 1979; 1986), the philosophy of the Approach rests in "...an ethics of coexistence, which is respect, tolerance, care, dialogue, participation, reciprocity and solidarity among all stakeholders, each with their own culture" (Rinaldi, 2020, p. 15).

There is a direct connection between fostering children's hundred languages and the Rights of the Young Child (UN, 1989). Both view the child "...not only as an age of life, but as a quality of life..." (Rinaldi, 2020, p. 15). When we consider participation rights in particular, the child should be afforded the opportunity to use their hundred languages to participate in family, school, and community decisions in which they are directly impacted. From the viewpoint of Bronfenbrenner's ecological systems theory, an agentic educator fosters learning and development, viewing children as capable and competent learners (Ruscoe, 2018). They are informed by their relationship with the child, the family, and knowledge of the elements of the different environments in which the child interacts. The agentic educator supports the child to become an active participant in their own learning and in society, reinforcing how relationships within the micro and mesosystems impact human development, including how the child views themself (National Council for Curriculum and Assessment [NCCA], 2025). With this framework in mind, we have explored paths in which the Approach can be brought to the United States to break through some of the barriers we see in our education system with the goal of increasing children's access to an education that views the child as a capable, creative learner, fosters the expression of their hundred languages, and ensures access to participation rights.

STUDY ABROAD AS A VEHICLE FOR FACILITATING CHILDREN'S RIGHTS

Because teachers are among the principal influencers in the child's microsystem (Bronfenbrenner, 1977; 1979; 1986) they have a fundamental responsibility to nurture children's rights. Training for this begins in pre-service teacher education programs and continues through in-service teacher professional development. Study abroad offers participants a rich, hands-on international experience that bridges theory and practice (Benavides et al., 2022; Macy et al., 2025; Pipitone, 2018; Vatalaro et al., 2015; Zhang et al., 2019. These cross-cultural exchanges can inspire effective strategies to address the complex challenges children encounter, promoting their holistic well-being. According to Carter (2016), "...hundreds and hundreds of North American educators have delved deep into studying the theories and pedagogical practices of their Reggio counterparts, transforming their own thinking and practices, and becoming an inspiration for others" (p. 26). When pre-service and practicing teachers explore other worlds, they begin to imagine other possibilities for ensuring the rights of children are met.

Study Abroad With Pre-Service Teachers

Study abroad is an example of an experiential learning model for pre-service teachers. Study abroad supports learning within a global context. Contextual and temporal factors which influence the development of pre-service teachers through global experiences will be discussed next.

Contextual

The environment could be a factor in the way teacher preparation programs create learning opportunities for their future educators. Contextual considerations in human development were a result of the ecological systems theory where Bronfenbrenner stressed the importance of the environment (Bronfenbrenner, 1977; 1979; 1986). Learning from the environment has multiple dimensions, as noted by Nguyen (2024), "one aspect that makes the Reggio Emilia approach so successful is that it is rooted deeply within its societal context and community" (p. 2). The study abroad experience context should be one consideration because involvement could create impactful learning, making a mark in the lives of the people who engage in global education (Haines et al., 2021; Kuh, 2008; Morley et al., 2019).

Learning to become a teacher from traveling abroad may be a strategy for retention. A high impact experience for students, like short- and long-term study abroad, can lead to stronger retention and graduation rates (Malmgren & Galvin 2008; Metzger, 2006; Tinto, 2010). Study abroad programs for undergraduate students have been shown to lead to retention and higher levels of graduation rates in students who participate in global experiential learning (Biraimah & Jotia, 2013; Brownell & Swaner, 2009; Costello, 2015; Dewey et al., 2013; Di Maggio, 2016; Dunn et al., 2014).

Career preparation for serving students from diverse cultural and linguistic backgrounds may be another outcome of college-age study abroad programs. Teachers need to be ready for diverse classrooms for which global experiential learning could provide experience (Norris & Gillespie, 2009). Study abroad could also promote global citizenship in college students (Klein & Wikan, 2019; Veltri, 2012). When students participate in a study abroad program in a different country, they are the minority. Deeper cultural understandings and empathy may result after participating in study abroad (Leggett, 2020; Vezzali et al., 2015; Zhang et al., 2019).

Researchers have studied motivation for study abroad (Nyaupane et al., 2011; Salyers et al., 2015). People at various stages of their career could be motivated to embark on journeys to discovery on location outside of their country of origin. Undergraduate experience may be different from graduate students (Linder & McGaha, 2013). Social change could be an outcome for people engaged in global education (Pipitone, 2018). Deeper understanding of complex pedagogy is another possible outcome from people who engage in experiential learning (Sanders-Smith & Cordoba, 2022). Pre-service teachers could experience different degrees of knowledge and understanding from study abroad experiences (Mo et al., 2021).

Temporal

Temporal considerations in human development were a result of the ecological systems theory in which Bronfenbrenner proposed multiple layers of influence on human development (Bronfenbrenner, 1977; 1979; 1986). He called one of the layers of influence the *chronosystem*, which is the way in which time impacts both the individual and the environment in which the individual lives. The element of time is observed by pre-service teachers and could be a factor in the way teacher preparation programs create learning opportunities for their pre-service teachers. According to Nguyen (2004), "it required teachers to learn new abilities and be willing to risk failure to try new ideas, give more of their time, collaborate with one another, and critique one another" (p. 18). Youngmin Mo and colleagues (2021) found that the time spent in study abroad learning communities made a meaningful difference in how professionals perceived their self-efficacy. In a research study published in *Global Education Review*, researchers found similar trends of gains in professionalism when analyzing 47 studies with pre-service teachers in study abroad experiences (Morley et al., 2019).

There are short- and long-term study abroad experiences. The Institute of International Education (2019) states that short term study abroad is defined as one to eight weeks in duration. In a short-term study abroad to Finland, pre-service teachers learned on location for ten days (Zhang et al., 2019). There are also long-term study abroad experiences where the duration could be a month or longer. Student teaching could be an example of a long-term study abroad (Quezada, 2004). A semester-long student teaching experience could have long term results for undergraduate students (DeGraaf et al., 2013; Franklin, 2010). Long term impacts can also be found with short term study abroad experiences (Castañeda & Zirger, 2011; Donnelly-Smith, 2009; Fischer, 2009; He et al., 2017; Lenz & Wister, 2008; Shiveley & Misco, 2015; Vatalaro et al., 2015; Witkowsky & Mendez, 2018).

Therefore, duration or length of study abroad should be a consideration. Some topics to consider related to temporal elements are:

- How much time spent in another country makes a meaningful difference in what is gained?
- Is there a recommended amount of time that is best and under what conditions?
- Does time make a difference for study abroad experiences?
- Is a longer amount of time spent on study abroad better (Dwyer, 2004)?

Contextual and temporal factors can influence study abroad experiences. Through study abroad, pre-service teachers learn on location (Benavides et al., 2022; Macy et al., 2025; Pipitone, 2018; Vatalaro et al., 2015; Zhang et al., 2019). High-impact practices through experiential learning can make a meaningful difference in the journey of a professional from the years before they enter the workforce until long after they have been serving in their profession. Observing authentic school settings in which the agentic teacher empowers children to have agency in the classroom (NCCA, 2025; Ruscoe et al., 2018), pre-service teachers are better able to connect classroom learning to concrete examples for nurturing children's participation rights (UN, 1989). Transforming the global perspective of pre-service teachers can expose them to diverse cultures, ways of thinking, and models for supporting children's growth and development (Vatalaro et al., 2015). This, in turn, can increase their commitment to supporting the rights of all children.

OUR REGGIO-INSPIRED JOURNEY

Adapting the Approach globally in Reggio-inspired settings can strengthen the role of the agentic educator (NCCA, 2025; Ruscoe et al., 2018) and the democratic parent with a shared goal of supporting the right of the child to be an active participant in their community, school, and family life (APA, 2018; Sanvictores & Mendez, 2022; Tiwari, 2022). This begins with a thorough understanding of the Approach by these stakeholders who directly interact with children. We are: a retired university senior lecturer, a former university researcher and lecturer, a doctoral student, a university early learning center director, and a professor who all have backgrounds in early childhood development and education. We have taught and implemented Reggio-inspired practices in various ways, including teaching in pre-professional early childhood theory and creative activity courses as well as implementation of Reggio-inspired practices in early learning classrooms.

Our Reggio Emilia-inspired path moved beyond learning from books to hands-on experiential learning through a study abroad trip in 2012 with pre-service teachers. As with any journey, some of us have participated in more trips to Reggio Emilia than others. As we picked up passengers along the way, learners have become leaders, expanding the study abroad experience to travelers across the United States. In true Reggio Emilia Approach fashion, we started this long-term project and our focus evolved as our knowledge, interests, and passion for serving children and families in our local communities grew. This journey, viewed from the perspective of the child's microsystem (Bronfenbrenner, 1977; 1979; 1986) is represented in Figure 1. Through our combined experiences we have led seven professional trips to Reggio Emilia, Italy including: three designed primarily for pre-service teachers, two designed for distinct groups of in-service professionals, and two designed for a mixed group of pre- and in-service professionals (Levin et al., 2023; Macy et al., 2025; Vatalaro et al., 2015).

Figure 1. The Child's Microsystem and the Role of Study Abroad in Enhancing Collaboration Within a Child's Global World

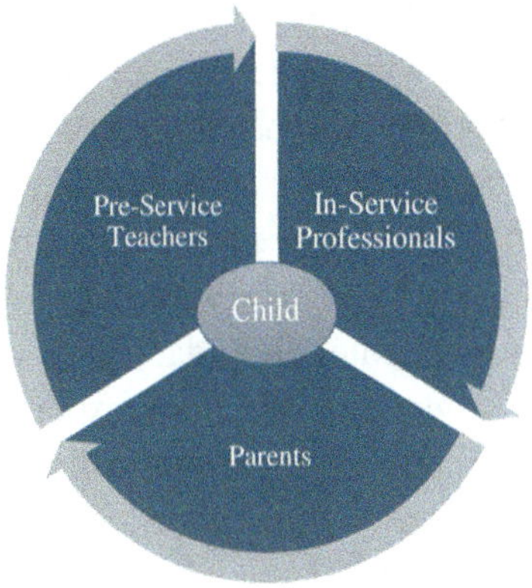

Pre-Service Teacher Training
Study abroad offers pre-service teachers the opportunity to learn on location, transforming their textbook of knowledge about theory and practice to concrete understanding of the Approach.
"[The most rewarding aspect of study abroad in Reggio Emilia] was witnessing with my own eyes children ages 4-6 creating clay sculptures that could rival—or beat—anything that I could do...If we let kids construct their own knowledge, they will" (Vatalaro et al., 2015, p. 48).

In-Service Professional Development
Study abroad can serve as a form of professional development, providing in-service professionals with understanding of how to transform their current practice and more quickly incorporate new knowledge into their interactions with children, parents, and colleagues than a pre-service teacher can.
"You see what you're already doing at your center. You see what you already have in practice, and then you see small bits of things that you can put into practice when you get back to your center, and that to me is part of professional development" (Levin et al., 2023).

Professional Delegations with Pre- and In-Service Professionals
Outcomes from professional abroad trips are further strengthened when pre-service teachers and in-service professionals travel abroad together as a professional delegation. In this model, new and experienced professionals can learn from and be inspired by one another.
"I realized too like how different but amazing it was to be with like other people that are already teachers or professors or older teachers because...it's nice being around my classmates and stuff, but...it was really, really nice to be able to connect with people who have been doing this for a long time and had so many pieces of advice for us" (Macy et al., 2025, p. 12).

Parents are the primary influence in the child's microsystem, but they often do not have the theoretical knowledge or practical application for activities that best support a child-centered, democratic approach to learning and parenting. A study trip with in-service professionals and parents may help foster mutual respect and deep co-construction of knowledge better than a traditional parent teacher organization can.
"[A parent] wanted [the teacher] to implement dotted lines for [her child] to learn how to form letters correctly. I discussed...that I would encourage exploration and self-expression...I used various materials such as sand trays, paintbrushes, and sticks for [the child] to freely experiment with writing and letter formation...when [the child] was leaving to adventure to kindergarten, her mother was astonished at the progress [the child] had made at our school...[the child] now forms all upper- and lower-case letters, she could easily write three-to-five-word sentences" (S. Turner, personal communication, September 15, 2025).

Pre-Service Teachers Learn On Location

Our first study abroad trip to Reggio Emilia was coordinated and planned with a university study abroad office, who made most of the arrangements. Included in the activities were classroom observations; discussions with teachers, directors, and atelieristas (educators who specialize in promoting children's 100 languages through creativity, critical thinking, project work, and research) (Edwards et al., 2012); a presentation at the Loris Malaguzzi International Center; and a hands-on activity at the creative recycling center Remida. There were 13 participants who were primarily pre-service teachers, five of whom responded in detail to qualitative directed reflective journal prompts pre-departure to Italy, mid-program, and post-arrival back to the United States as well as a pre- and post-evaluation of culture, values, language (Vatalaro et al., 2015).

We found participants increased their content knowledge of the Approach and used their new-found knowledge to present their experiences in their courses and at professional conferences after returning to the United States. Perhaps equally as important as content knowledge, participants gained appreciation for Italian culture and values. They reflected on how they wanted to support a similar appreciation for diverse cultures in their future classrooms. As outsiders to Italian culture and language, participants were required to learn how to adapt to activities that came easy to them in their home country such as shopping for groceries and ordering food at a restaurant. These experiences could be reflected upon as they entered the teaching profession and worked with immigrant students and families. Participants' reflections are certainly encouraging for the implementation of children's rights, particularly as it relates to allowing for the celebration of diversity in the classroom.

Training our future teachers to embrace the Approach was an important first step in our journey. Unfortunately, we realized a major potential roadblock. Once university students moved into the profession, there was often school administration push-back for implementing Reggio-inspired practices. As Okken and colleagues (2019) found, the impact of study abroad on practice once teachers enter the profession can be limited by school-specific factors not aligning with the implementation of practices observed abroad. These factors include the school's chosen curriculum, school district policies, and state legislation. One participant in our pre-professional study abroad group (Vatalaro et al., 2015) specifically reflected that she did not feel she could infuse Reggio-inspired practices in the rigid American school system. Similar attitudes were reported by Seipel and Seeger's (2024) undergraduate pre-service teachers after study abroad to Reggio Emilia who "felt a lack of support and guidance as a new teacher in being able to incorporate the philosophical beliefs into their classrooms" (p. 1).

Learning Abroad With In-Service Professionals

After three study abroad trips to Reggio Emilia, we decided to try to navigate around the lack of confidence and ability new teachers felt in implementing Reggio-inspired practices (Seipel & Seeger, 2024; Vatalaro et al., 2015) and design trips for in-service professionals. This included practicing teachers, early learning center administrators, and professionals from agencies serving children and families. Our hope in designing in-service professional study trips was to grow Reggio-inspired practices that began with leaders and decision-makers. In-service professional abroad trips are not as common of a model as pre-service teacher trips with university students, however there is compelling evidence that in-service professional development abroad can produce similar outcomes of increasing the global perspectives and cultural competence of participants with the added benefit of professionals being able to immediately infuse what was learned into their practice (Festervand & Tillery, 2001; He et al., 2017).

For this in-service professional trip, because we were not taking university students, the university study abroad office was not used. Leveraging the contacts we made during previous trips, we were able to design an experience we felt would most benefit in-service professionals. Many of the activities were similar to the pre-service teachers' experiences. However, the lens was different. The professionals participating in the first in-service group were selected due to their expertise and role as early intervention leaders in their work settings. A relationship of collaborative thought partners was formed with these professionals. With the perspective of early intervention at the core of this study group, discussions and observations gave a first-hand look at truly seeing the special rights of children as the foundation of the Approach. We could connect the hundred languages of children to this concept because we saw in practice how the environment, materials, and teachers influence participation and engagement in learning for all children.

The second study trip for in-service professionals primarily included early childhood administrators in community preschools and university lab schools. They viewed the trip in the context of implementation at a broader level and thought of how to leverage this experience to receive support and funding to infuse Reggio-inspired practices in their work communities. While some of the professionals were further along in their journey to implement these practices in their work environment, the ongoing, collaborative discussions were designed to be mutually beneficial in sharing ideas and making connections with the knowledge they gained from observing the Approach in Reggio Emilia and being immersed in Italian culture. In addition to highly valuing the ability to collaborate with other professionals, participants reflected on the viewpoint of the child and how the Approach provided support for teachers to create meaningful learning experiences for the child to explore the world around them (Levin et al., 2023). One of our practicing teacher participants stated, "it was a reminder that we have to always justify the importance of early childhood and developmentally appropriate practices in [the United States]. In [Reggio Emilia] they recognize and appreciate the value of it and they support these practices" (Levin et al., 2023). This expanded view of the child yields more opportunities for supporting children's right to fully participate in their school experiences and use their 100 languages to learn and grow in educational settings (Edwards et al., 2012; UN, 1989).

Professional Delegations With Pre- and In-Service Professionals

There was immeasurable value in focusing on leaders and decision-makers for a professional study trip. However, just as children in Reggio Emilia learn from exploration and collaboration, we were also learning and constructing new knowledge from the different types of study trips to Reggio Emilia. Within our travel group, one of our leaders was retiring and another was training to continue this journey. After two trips with in-service professionals and a new perspective, we began to ask: what was the best way to go back and train our staff in Reggio-inspired practices, and how do we counteract pushback from staff? A new type of professional "delegation" (Macy et al., 2025) emerged with intentional inclusion of both pre- and in-service professionals. Much of the data collected were similar to our previous trips (e.g., surveys, journals, focus groups). Monthly pre-travel meetings were added for participants to build a stronger foundation of the Approach and begin to co-learn from each other before the trip began.

Both the environment (i.e., living and learning in Reggio Emilia) and the social interactions between participants that occurred formally and informally resulted in deep reflective practice. Pre-service teachers found it beneficial to learn alongside seasoned professionals who can scaffold knowledge more than a fellow university student. In-service professionals felt the delegation "reignit[ed] passion for early childhood" (Macy et al., 2025, p. 12), helping them overcome the fatigue that occurs when they are bogged down by regulations in their schools and classrooms. This model has the potential to help strengthen the bonds between university students and those already in the field, which opens the door to a willingness for newer and experienced professionals to co-construct knowledge, working together to advocate for a child-centered approach utilizing documentation of learning in ways that support and honor children's participation rights (UN, 1989).

REIMAGINING PARENT INVOLVEMENT WITH REGGIO-INSPIRED EDUCATION

When discussing partners in a child's well-being, Bronfenbrenner uses the term linkages to describe interactions between influences from the microsystem, such as family and school (Sadownik & Jevtić, 2023). We found there is immense benefit to living and learning in Reggio Emilia that results in shifts in thinking about developmentally appropriate practices and the importance of interaction between community, school, and family. In our experience, trips with pre-service teachers and in-service professionals are valuable steps in the process of supporting the rights of the child, but leave out a core pillar of the Approach and a system that directly impacts the child's world: their parents. Reviewing qualitative data we collected from both pre-service teachers and in-service professionals (Levin et al., 2023; Macy et al., 2025; Vatalaro et al., 2015), parents were mentioned in the context of observations from around the city as well as ways in which parents welcomed visitors to schools. We did not see deep reflection about ways in which our travelers could meaningfully incorporate Reggio-inspired inclusion of parents in the school learning community that would foster participation rights for parents and their children.

A parent is the child's first teacher and has a primary influence over how well their child succeeds in school (White, 1981). As discussed earlier in this chapter, Bronfenbrenner's ecological systems theory (1977; 1979; 1986) views the child through the lens of each system interacting with the child throughout a lifetime. When a child enters preschool, this is also a parent's first foray into the school setting in their role as a parent, thus connecting systems: the family and school. The Reggio Emilia Approach views these as partnerships. Bronfenbrenner views these as influences. Neither has the perspective that family and school are separate, competing entities.

A longitudinal examination of different types of parent involvement indicated that high levels of parents participating in the school (i.e., school-based involvement) and contact between teachers and parents (i.e., home-school communication) in kindergarten positively impacts reading achievement scores in the third grade (Anthony & Ogg, 2019). The philosophy of the Approach involves a deep commitment to both school-based involvement and home-school communication. In Reggio Emilia schools, parent involvement is viewed as a form of civic engagement (Landi & Pintus, 2022) where parents support the education of every child in the school (Gandini, 1993). The child, parent, and teacher are active "protagonists" working together to form open, supportive home and school partnerships.

A Reggio Emilia school environment involves deep collaboration with families to learn about and support their children's interests and skills while inviting family members to share their talents and resources with the school (Edwards et al., 2012).

Just as we respect the unique qualities a child brings into the classroom, we need to respect the individual qualities of parents. Allowing parents to utilize their time, knowledge, skills, and interests encourages an involvement in the school, fostering a proactive parent-school relationship. This requires the school to provide many different types of opportunities for parents to participate in the school community (Brown, 1995).

In Reggio-inspired adaptations, parent involvement often hinges on the photographic and written documentation of children's growth and learning that is displayed and shared with parents (Alaçam, 2025; Chng et al., 2022; Harris, 2021; Lim & Cho, 2019). While shared documentation in Reggio-inspired schools might be a mechanism for home-school communication, it has not always been the best option for deeper levels of school-based involvement. For example, Alaçam (2025) found that teachers at a Reggio-inspired school believed including children in the documentation process increased child participation and included the child's voice and perspective, but when documentation was digitized and uploaded in online spaces it excluded children from seeing their efforts. Parents received the documentation and often reflected on their child's learning with other family members, but did not participate in the process to co-construct reflections on child's development and learning with teachers. There was also a disconnect between what parents wanted to see and what educators were including in the documentation.

Reflections on parent involvement in Reggio-inspired programs indicate that home-school communication via shared documentation is not enough. There should be a positive reciprocal relationship between parents and teachers where parents feel welcomed and encouraged to be physically present and involved in the classroom and around the school (Smith, 2014). Additionally, teachers must be willing to understand the cultural backgrounds, skills, and needs of each child through consistent communication and collaboration with parents (Liu & Sulaimani, 2022).

One university lab school recognized that the Reggio-inspired approach to learning was new to most families joining the school community. They wanted to implement a system to engage the families in understanding that the school could be a model for viewing children as "idea generators, concept builders, and collaborators" (Parnell et al., 2018, p. 23). Once parents have foundational knowledge of the Approach, societal pressure about academic achievement can still be a hurdle for them. A director at another Reggio-inspired university preschool often encounters parents who are concerned after their children did not test well on kindergarten acceptance assessments given by public and private schools. After these assessments, parents want to see more worksheets being used in the classroom. In these instances, open dialogue between parents, teachers, and school administration is crucial (S. Turner, personal communication, September 15, 2025).

In our experience, when teachers can clearly and simply articulate the benefits of a child-centered, play-based, hands-on learning environment by offering a portfolio to include numerous examples of their child achieving state learning standards, parents become more comfortable with the Approach. At the end of the school year, child care personnel also see a shift in parents' language. Instead of only focusing on academic knowledge, parents discuss the child being ready socially and emotionally as well. Parents describe the school as a place where children are given space to grow in an environment that is magical, nurturing, and inspiring. Equally as important, one child in this Reggio-inspired school described it as "a special place with my chosen family" (S. Turner, personal communication, September 15, 2025). This provides a safe space for children to be an active participant in their school activities. The parent-school partnership encourages democratic parenting that promotes the UNCRC (UN, 1989) and the UN SDGs (2015).

BEYOND A PARENT TEACHER ORGANIZATION: FORMING AN EDUCATIONAL PARTNERSHIP

Although parents and teachers are two main influencers in a child's microsystem (Bronfenbrenner, 1977; 1979; 1986), inherently there is a power imbalance between the school and the parent (Krijnen et al., 2022; Oostdam & Hooge 2013; Sadownik & Jevtić, 2023). Traditionally, teachers have knowledge through education and credentials that they impart upon both children and parents, but too often they fail to consider what can be learned from the child and the parent. When parents are invited into schools through formal systems like a parent teacher organization (PTO) or professional learning community (PLC), it may still be difficult to overcome the school's hierarchy, which in turn can create unsuccessful parent-teacher collaborations and discourage parent involvement (Krijnen et al., 2022; Oostdam & Hooge 2013; Sadownik & Jevtić, 2023).

School staff may approach the PLC as parents having a deficit rather than something they can contribute to the school community (Oostdam & Hooge 2013; Sadownik & Jevtić, 2023). Parents may not persist in the PTO, partly because the school holds itself as more knowledgeable than parents, which can limit parent inclusion and voice in a PTO or PLC (Krijnen et al., 2022). To understand how to effectively involve parents and the community in schools, there is a need for research on which strategies work for specific populations (Eden et al., 2024). There must be open dialogue with teachers and parents to continue to nurture and strengthen the bonds in this chosen family.

PACKING OUR BAGS FOR A PARENT-TEACHER EDUCATIONAL PARTNERSHIP: PLAN OF ACTION

After seven trips to Reggio Emilia we are proposing a new type of professional delegation that includes parents and teachers learning and living together in Reggio Emilia for one week. We want to form a more meaningful "educational partnership" between parents and teachers where the two groups mutually and actively work together to form educational and social opportunities that improve the classroom and school environment (Oostdam & Hooge, 2013). We are advocating for a more immersive level of parent inclusion in schools where parents and teachers from various socio-economic and cultural backgrounds go on a journey together to co-construct their knowledge of Reggio-inspired practices implemented in early learning centers. Seeing first-hand how schools in Reggio Emilia include families and the larger community can create a stronger understanding of how each system can interact with each other to strengthen a child's global world. Our vision is that they will co-construct their experiences and form a strong parent-teacher partnership that can then involve the communities in which they live, thus shifting the conversation to a proactive, shared perspective of democratic parenting and teaching.

We strive to leverage our existing contacts, relationships, and knowledge of activities and schools in and around Reggio Emilia to develop a new roadmap for implementation of Reggio-inspired practices. We believe this proposed model will interconnect the microsystems of home, school, and community (Bronfenbrenner, 1977; 1979; 1986). Our intention is to recruit parents and teachers from diverse communities across the United States to ensure inclusion of participants with different perspectives and capitalize on grants and community partnerships to assist in funding this experience.

This educational partnership (Oostdam & Hooge, 2013) will loosely follow Macy and colleagues' model (2025) for structuring a Reggio Emilia professional delegation. Table 1 provides an overview of the planned pre- and post-trip activities designed to develop a shared vision for a long-term parent and teacher collaboration. We anticipate starting this new Reggio-inspired journey by recruiting parent and teacher participants in the months leading up to the beginning of a new school year. At the beginning of the school year, we propose a group meeting to create a parent and teacher shared vision for this journey. In following the Reggio Emilia model, we would gather information about the interests, skills, and needs of the group so we can form a partnership that is unique to the group and not a "one size fits all" model.

We are cognizant that we could easily fall into the role of university faculty and disrupt the balance of power. With pre-service teachers and in-service professionals, we would typically assign readings from published books and journal articles for participants to review to gain a better understanding of the Reggio Emilia philosophy. In designing this new model, we plan to provide information through the lens of the participant. While understanding the Approach is important, rather than assigning lengthy readings, we might instead show videos that clearly and simply describe the Approach such as a CNN news report on Reggio Emilia schools in the United States (Gabli, 2013). We would also add shorter-form articles written for parents and teachers to understand the basic tenets of the Approach such as Gandini's (1993) publication in *Young Children* about the fundamentals of the Approach. In all instances in which we share knowledge about Reggio Emilia and the Approach with participants, we strive to ensure we are aligning discussions with their experiences and perspectives. The intent of these sessions is to create a framework for an exchange of ideas and respectful discussion, rather than a university lecture.

We will place particular emphasis on documentation because, through photos of children and children's quotes about their activities, we can make learning visible. Moreover, we can make direct connections to participants' lives because adults often use similar documentation through the photos on their phone, voice notes, and digital or handwritten notes. To avoid issues that have been identified in the literature about documentation (Alaçam, 2025; Chng et al., 2022; Harris, 2021; Lim & Cho, 2019), we want to create a collaborative dialogue between parents and teachers regarding documentation so parents are able to meaningfully understand their child's knowledge, skills, and development through teachers' documentation. This understanding is reciprocal as teachers also need to gain knowledge of how to present documentation in a way parents can understand how an artifact reflects children's growth, development, and learning.

To reinforce the concept of documentation, we plan to discuss how participants can document their own learning experiences in Reggio Emilia. This may look different for each participant who draws on their own 100 languages while engaging in this partnership. Some participants may want to journal daily and others may want to take notes during group discussions. We anticipate most participants will want to take photos, but the focus of their photos may look different based on their interests and what stands out to them. These different forms of documentation will contribute to the collaborative vision of this educational partnership and will allow parents and teachers to understand different ways in which children's participation can be encouraged at home, in school, and in the community.

Ideal "Itinerary"

With previous groups, we typically designed a 10-day study abroad. With this group, we are proposing a one-week trip so parents and teachers are not away from their jobs and families for an extended period of time. Participants in our other groups (Levin et al., 2023; Macy et al., 2025; Vatalaro et al., 2015) found value in being immersed in Italian culture. We plan to continue cultural immersion with this group of participants, which includes staying in a small family-owned hotel, eating in locally-owned restaurants, buying food in a grocery store, using public transportation, taking an Italian language class, and participating in a group cooking class. In addition to formal school visits, we will encourage participants to observe children and families in the community (e.g., riding bikes, in the park, in piazzas, in the grocery store, buying and eating gelato). After the first day of community observation, parent-teacher dyads within the group will identify a community activity to document throughout this journey. In assigning dyads we hope to identify similarities and differences in what a parent focuses on and what a teacher focuses on, with the aim of understanding each other's perspective and creating a joint vision of documentation.

In our combined trips to Reggio Emilia, we have visited several diverse types of schools and educational experiences. We have a general understanding of what might be conducive to a parent-teacher educational journey. We are proposing visits to three schools that exemplify various aspects of the Approach and include infant/toddler and preschool-age classrooms. In 2012 the Emilia Romagna region, particularly in and around Reggio Emilia, experienced devastating earthquakes that destroyed homes, schools, and businesses. One of our school visits would focus on learning about coming together after a natural disaster and involving families and the community in rebuilding and shaping the school. The second visit would include an observation at a traditional Reggio Emilia school that provides a concrete example of children moving and learning freely in different areas around the school. The third visit would include a school that does not fall under the municipality of Reggio Emilia, but implements the Approach. Although a school like this would still embody the language and culture of the Approach, it may provide an example of adapting a program outside of the traditional model. After every observation, each school arranges time for discussion and questions from the group with a pedagogista and teachers. At the third school, we hope to arrange an opportunity for a small group of school parents to be part of this discussion so that our participants can learn more about the Reggio-inspired parent perspective.

There are other educational experiences we believe parents and teachers would benefit from experiencing together. Early in the week, we plan for visits to the Loris Malaguzzi International Center and the creative recycling center Remida. Both serve as resources for teachers and students in the Reggio Emilia community as well as international visitors. At the Malaguzzi Center participants will interact with an atelierista who will present information about the 100 languages and ateliers. Participants will then experience a hands-on learning activity where they will assume the lens of a child. This will allow participants to understand how child-centered learning experiences can be facilitated and enriched by a teacher or parent. At Remida, participants will learn how local businesses contribute to classroom materials and gain a deeper understanding of how unwanted materials can be repurposed for children's exploration. Although these materials are typically available for use in the classroom, parents can also begin to understand how simple, low- or no-cost materials can be used meaningfully with children at home. In visiting the Malaguzzi Center and Remida early in the trip, participants can make stronger connections as they see these practices and materials used in the classroom.

We would plan a final community-based visit to the Civic Museum of Reggio Emilia to learn how a local museum opens its doors to collaborate with children, teachers, and families. We want our participants to begin thinking about how to use similar places in their communities to engage children in open-ended discoveries. These three experiences will help participants broaden their thinking beyond home-school collaborations to expand into the child's microsystem of the community (Bronfenbrenner, 1977; 1979; 1986).

Table 1. Proposed Schedule for a Parent-Teacher Education Abroad Partnership

Month	Topic
May-July	Recruitment of participants
August	Creating a shared vision: parent and teacher connections
September	Introduction to the Reggio Emilia Approach
October	Documentation: making learning visible
November	Discussion with a Reggio Emilia tour coordinator and trip logistics
December	Putting all the pieces together
January	Week-long trip to Reggio Emilia
February	Post-Italy reflections and forming a Reggio-inspired parent-teacher project
March	Educational partnership meetings/checks-ins
April	Educational partnership meetings/checks-ins
May	Final thoughts/wrap up

WE WENT TO REGGIO EMILIA, NOW WHAT?

After every trip to Reggio Emilia, we ask "now what?" This, perhaps, is why we have reimagined the study abroad experience from pre-service teachers to two distinct groups of in-service professionals to a mix of pre- and in-service professionals to this novel idea of a parent-teacher educational partnership. All of the experiences proposed in this chapter will hopefully provide a hands-on, minds-on experience for how parents and teachers can collaborate as central protagonists in democratic, child-centered learning that protects the rights of the child to participate and use their voice at home, school, and in the community.

When the trip to Italy comes to an end we plan for this educational partnership to continue meeting through at least the end of the school year. During this time, parents and teachers will collaborate on a Reggio-inspired project based on the interests of their children. The topic will be generated from the group, but examples could be a parent or teacher having a baby, children's interest in taking pictures, rainstorms, the beach, or children's growing interest in symbols, shapes, letters, and numbers. Parents and teachers will continue to co-construct what is being done at home and what is being done at school. Additionally, we will help guide our participants in being ambassadors for Reggio-inspired practices, sharing their knowledge and experiences with other parents, teachers, and their local communities.

CONCLUSION

In this chapter we reflect on the ways in which children's rights (UN, 1989) are met through addressing the systems in which they are most influenced (Bronfenbrenner, 1977; 1979; 1986)). Study abroad programs for pre-service teachers and in-service professionals play a critical role in adopting the Reggio Emilia Approach in the United States. We propose taking this a step further by inviting parents and teachers on a study trip in which they can co-construct knowledge of children's rights and the Approach.

At the culmination of this year-long educational partnership, we hope to reduce the power imbalance between teachers and parents (Krijnen et al., 2022; Oostdam & Hooge 2013; Sadownik & Jevtić, 2023) by helping them use the same "language" when talking about children's interests, skills, growth, development, and knowledge. We want to honor both parents' rights and children's rights (Quennerstedt, 2009). We hope participants will have a shift in their thinking of how they view children and a better understanding of the rights and the many languages of the child (Edwards et al., 2012; UN, 1989). We want participants to think of a child not just in relation to the requirements of school or society (e.g., meeting basic needs for provision and protection; following a set curriculum to achieve rigid learning standards), but as a "citizen of the present" (Rinaldi, 2020, p. 12) who, in a democratic system, has voice and agency over the experiences in which they are directly impacted (Hart, 1992; Lundy, 2007; Sanvictores & Mendez, 2022; Tiwari, 2022). We want parents and teachers to work together to be both child protectors and child liberators (Dillen,

2006). We want to foster an environment where parents and teachers support the education of every child in the school (Gandini, 1993), not just their own children or children in their own classroom. Our journey is one where we strive to strengthen connections in the microsystem between family, school, and the community (Bronfenbrenner, 1977; 1979; 1986), introducing these protagonists to other worlds and other possibilities. In doing so, our goal is to expand the child's global world. After all, "the hundred is there" (Edwards et al., 2012).

REFERENCES

Acencio, E., & Cordero, H. (2023). Parental styles and their impact on affective development in early childhood. *Revista Iberoamericana De Educación*, *7*(1), 1–12. DOI: 10.31876/rie.v6i1.241

Alaçam, N. (2025). The role of pedagogical documentation in child and parent participation: An investigation of educator and parent perspectives in a Reggio Emilia-inspired preschool. *European Early Childhood Education Research Journal*, 1–18. Advance online publication. DOI: 10.1080/1350293X.2025.2508319

Ali, N., Ullah, A., Khan, A. M., Khan, Y., Ali, S., Khan, A. B., Khan, A., Din, M. U., Ullah, R., Khan, U. N., Aziz, T., & Ahmad, M. (2023). Academic performance of children in relation to gender, parenting styles, and socioeconomic status: What attributes are important. *PLoS One*, *18*(11), 1–30. DOI: 10.1371/journal.pone.0286823 PMID: 37967095

American Psychological Association. (2018). Democratic parenting. In *APA dictionary of psychology*. https://dictionary.apa.org/democratic-parenting

Anthony, C. J., & Ogg, J. (2019). Parent involvement, approaches to learning, and student achievement: Examining longitudinal mediation. *School Psychology*, *34*(4), 376–385. DOI: 10.1037/spq0000282 PMID: 31294595

Bagnato, S. J., & Ho, H. Y. (2006). High stakes testing with preschool children: Violation of professional standards for evidence based practice in early childhood intervention. *KEDI Journal of Educational Policy*, *3*(1), 23–43.

Barblett, L., Knaus, M., & Barratt-Pugh, C. (2016). The pushes and pulls of pedagogy in the early years: Competing knowledge and the erosion of play-based learning. *Australasian Journal of Early Childhood*, *41*(4), 36–43. DOI: 10.1177/183693911604100405

Bassok, D., Latham, S., & Roem, A. (2016). Is kindergarten the new first grade? *AERA Open*, *2*(1), 1–31. DOI: 10.1177/2332858415616358 PMID: 26942210

Benavides, A. W., Freed, A., & Huffling, L. D. (2022). Study Abroad Programs at the Vanguard for Education for Sustainable Development: A Teacher Education Case Study. In Öztürk, M. (Ed.), *Engagement with Sustainable Development in Higher Education. Sustainable Development Goals Series*. Springer., DOI: 10.1007/978-3-031-07191-1_9

Biraimah, K. L., & Jotia, A. L. (2013). The longitudinal effects of study abroad programs on teachers' content knowledge and perspectives: Fulbright-Hays group projects abroad in Botswana and Southeast Asia. *Journal of Studies in International Education, 17*(4), 433–454. DOI: 10.1177/1028315312464378

Bronfenbrenner, U. (1977). Toward an experimental ecology of human development. *The American Psychologist, 32*(7), 513–531. DOI: 10.1037/0003-066X.32.7.513

Bronfenbrenner, U. (1979). *The ecology of human development: Experiments by nature and design*. Harvard University Press. DOI: 10.4159/9780674028845

Bronfenbrenner, U. (1986). Ecology of the family as a context for human development: Research perspectives. *Developmental Psychology, 22*(6), 723–742. DOI: 10.1037/0012-1649.22.6.723

Brown, K. P. (1995). *Developing strategies to encourage and improve parent participation in an early childhood program adapting the Reggio Emilia approach to early childhood* (Publication No. 1768) [Master's thesis, University of Dayton]. eCommons University of Dayton. https://ecommons.udayton.edu/graduate_theses/1768

Brownell, J. E., & Swaner, L. E. (2009). High-impact practices: Applying the learning outcomes literature to the development of successful campus programs. *Peer Review : Emerging Trends and Key Debates in Undergraduate Education, 11*(2), 26–30.

Bruyere, E., & Garbarino, J. (2010). The ecological perspective on the human rights of children. In Kamerman, S. B., Phipps, S., & Ben-Arieh, A. (Eds.), *From child welfare to child well-being: An international perspective on knowledge in the service of policy making* (pp. 137–154). Springer., DOI: 10.1007/978-90-481-3377-2_9

Carlsson-Paige, N., McLaughlin, G. B., & Almon, J. W. (2015). *Reading instruction in Kindergarten: Little to gain and much to lose*. Alliance for Childhood and Defending the Early Years. https://deyproject.files.wordpress.com/2015/01/readinginkindergarten_online-1.pdf

Carter, M. (2016, November/December). Study tours reveal a new world of ideas: An interview with Eliana Elias. *Exchange*, •••, 26–31. https://hub.exchangepress.com/wp-content/uploads/2024/09/5023226.pdf

Castañeda, M. E., & Zirger, M. L. (2011). Making the most of the "new" study abroad: Social capital and the short-term sojourn. *Foreign Language Annals, 44*(3), 544–564. DOI: 10.1111/j.1944-9720.2011.01146.x

Chng, A., Waniganayake, M., & Andrews, R. (2022). Inviting inquiry on pedagogical documentation in Singapore: Perspectives of parents and teachers. *European Early Childhood Education Research Journal, 30*(2), 296–308. DOI: 10.1080/1350293X.2022.2046837

Costello, J. (2015). Students' stories of studying abroad: Reflections upon return. *Journal of International Students, 5*(1), 50–59. DOI: 10.32674/jis.v5i1.442

DeGraaf, D., Slagter, C., Larsen, K., & Ditta, E. (2013). The long-term personal and professional impacts of participating in a study abroad program. *Frontiers: The Interdisciplinary Journal of Study Abroad, 23*(1), 42–59. DOI: 10.36366/frontiers.v23i1.328

Dewey, D. P., Ring, S., Gardner, D., & Belnap, R. K. (2013). Social network formation and development during study abroad in the Middle East. *System, 41*(2), 269–282. DOI: 10.1016/j.system.2013.02.004

Di Maggio, L. M. (2016). *An analysis of study abroad as a factor to increase student engagement and reduce dropouts in higher education institutions* (Publication No. 10108237) [Doctoral Dissertation, Saint Peter's University]. ProQuest Dissertations and Theses Global. https://search.proquest.com/openview/1ec4cb1a9cf21a765ced5f333fe7c99b/1?pq-origsite=gscholar&cbl=18750

Dillen, A. (2006). Children between liberation and care: Ethical perspectives on the rights of children and parent-child relationships. *International Journal of Children's Spirituality, 11*(2), 237–250. DOI: 10.1080/13644360600797230

Donnelly-Smith, L. (2009). Global learning through short-term study abroad. *Peer Review : Emerging Trends and Key Debates in Undergraduate Education, 11*(4), 12–15.

Dunn, A. H., Dotson, E. K., Cross, S. B., Kesner, J., & Lundahl, B. (2014). Reconsidering the local after a transformative global experience: A comparison of two study abroad programs for preservice teachers. *Action in Teacher Education, 36*(4), 283–304. DOI: 10.1080/01626620.2014.948227

Dwyer, M. M. (2004). More is better: The impact of study abroad program duration. *Frontiers: The Interdisciplinary Journal of Study Abroad, 10*(1), 151–163. DOI: 10.36366/frontiers.v10i1.139

Edwards, C., Gandini, L., & Forman, G. (Eds.). (2012). *The hundred languages of children: The Reggio Emilia experience in transformation* (3rd ed.). Praeger.

Festervand, T. A., & Tillery, K. R. (2001). Short-term study-abroad programs–A professional development tool for international business faculty. *Journal of Education for Business*, *2*(77), 106–111. DOI: 10.1080/08832320109599058

Fischer, K. (2009, February 20). Short study-abroad trips can have lasting effect, research suggests. *Chronicle of Higher Education*. https://www.chronicle.com/article/short-study-abroad-trips-can-have-lasting-effect-research-suggests-117376/

Fisher, P. A., & Lombardi, J. (2025). *The new ecology of early childhood: Revisiting Bronfenbrenner's theory in the context of contemporary challenges and opportunities* [Working paper]. Stanford Center on Early Childhood, Stanford University. https://earlychildhood.stanford.edu/new-ecology-early-childhood-revisiting-bronfenbrenners-theory-context-contemporary-challenges-and

Franklin, K. (2010). Long-term career impact and professional applicability of the study abroad experience. *Frontiers: The Interdisciplinary Journal of Study Abroad*, *19*(1), 169–190. DOI: 10.36366/frontiers.v19i1.279

Gabli, S. (2013, March 24). *CNN news reports on Reggio Emilia Italy early childhood schools in the US* [Video]. YouTube. https://youtu.be/XVv5ZL9nlgs?si=h38ZvLZldQf36cPX

Gandini, L. (1993, November). Fundamentals of the Reggio Emilia approach to early childhood education. *Young Children*, *49*(1), 4–8. https://www.jstor.org/stable/42725533

Guy-Evans, O. (2025). *Bronfenbrenner's ecological systems theory*. Simply Psychology. https://www.simplypsychology.org/bronfenbrenner.html

Haines, S. J., Strolin-Goltzman, J., & Dinis, R. J. J. (2021). Odyssey in the Azores: A US travel-study course preparing teachers for the magic of the profession. *Teaching and Teacher Education, 106.Article, 103430*, 1–10. DOI: 10.1016/j.tate.2021.103430

Harmon, F., & Viruru, R. (2018). Debunking the myth of the efficacy of "push-down academics": How rigid, teacher-centered, academic early learning environments disempower young children. *Journal of Family Strengths*, *18*(1), 11. Advance online publication. DOI: 10.58464/2168-670X.1390

Harris, H. A. (2021). Parental choice and perceived benefits of Reggio Emilia inspired classrooms. *Early Child Development and Care*, *191*(1), 123–135. DOI: 10.1080/03004430.2019.1608194

Hart, R. A. (1992). *Children's participation from tokenism to citizenship, Innocenti Essays* (No. 4). UNICEF International Child Development Centre. https://unesdoc.unesco.org/ark:/48223/pf0000171538

He, Y., Lundgren, K., & Pynes, P. (2017). Impact of short-term study abroad program: Inservice teachers' development of intercultural competence and pedagogical beliefs. *Teaching and Teacher Education, 66,* 147–157. DOI: 10.1016/j.tate.2017.04.012

Institute of International Education. (2019). *Open Doors Fast Facts 2010-2019.* Open Doors Report on International Educational Exchange. https://opendoorsdata.org/wp-content/uploads/2020/11/Open-Doors-Fast-Facts-2010-2019.pdf

Klein, J., & Wikan, G. (2019). Teacher education and international practice programmes: Reflections on transformative learning and global citizenship. *Teaching and Teacher Education, 79,* 93–100. DOI: 10.1016/j.tate.2018.12.003

Krijnen, E., van Steensel, R., Meeuwisse, M., & Severiens, S. (2022). Aiming for educational partnership between parents and professionals: Shared vision development in a professional learning community. *School Community Journal, 32*(1), 265–300. https://www.adi.org/journal/2022ss/KrijnenEtAlSS22.pdf

Kuh, G. D. (2008). *High-impact educational practices: What they are, who has access to them, and why they matter.* Association of American Colleges and Universities. https://dgmg81phhvh63.cloudfront.net/content/user-photos/Publications/PDFs/E-HIGHIMP.pdf

Landi, L., & Pintus, A. (2022). A critical approach to the Reggio Emilia Approach. *Educazione. Giornale di Pedagogia Critica, 11*(1), 107–125. https://iris.unimore.it/retrieve/1861203e-e021-42ee-b42a-d20195c206c9/216-713-1-PB.pdf

Lavrič, M., & Naterer, A. (2020). The power of authoritative parenting: A cross-national study of effects of exposure to different parenting styles on life satisfaction. *Children and Youth Services Review, 116,* 105274. Advance online publication. DOI: 10.1016/j.childyouth.2020.105274

Leggett, N. (2020). A fish out of water: Developing intercultural understanding of students in higher education. *The Australian Journal of Teacher Education, 45*(12), 43–56. DOI: 10.14221/ajte.202v45n12.3

Lenz, W., & Wister, J. (2008, May/June). Short-term abroad with long-term benefits. *International Educator, 17*(3), 84–87.

Levin, J. N., Brasel, N. H., & Macy, M. (2023). [Unpublished raw data from a qualitative examination of how a team of professionals re-envisioned early childhood with a study abroad to Reggio Emilia].

Lim, S., & Cho, M.-H. (2019). Parents' use of mobile documentation in a Reggio Emilia-inspired school. *Early Childhood Education Journal, 47*(4), 367–379. DOI: 10.1007/s10643-019-00945-5

Linder, S., & McGaha, J. (2013). Building on successes: Reflections from two approaches to study abroad for undergraduate and graduate students. *The Educational Forum, 77*(3), 379–389. DOI: 10.1080/00131725.2013.792900

Lipsey, M. W., Farran, D. C., & Durkin, K. (2018). Effects of the Tennessee prekindergarten program on children's achievement and behavior through third grade. *Early Childhood Research Quarterly, 45*(4), 155–176. DOI: 10.1016/j.ecresq.2018.03.005

Lundy, L. (2007). 'Voice' is not enough: Conceptualising Article 12 of the United Nations Convention on the Rights of the Child. *British Educational Research Journal, 33*(6), 972–942. DOI: 10.1080/01411920701657033

Macy, M., Harshbarger, D., Burke, K., & Neukirch, E. (2025). Experiential learning in Reggio Emilia, Italy: Reflections from in-service and pre-service professionals. *Journey of Early Childhood Teacher Education*. Advance online publication. DOI: 10.1080/10901027.2025.2493175

Malmgren, J., & Galvin, J. (2008). Effects of study abroad participation on student graduation rates: A study of three incoming freshman cohorts at the University of Minnesota, Twin Cities. *NACADA Journal, 28*(1), 29–42. DOI: 10.12930/0271-9517-28.1.29

Mayall, B. (2000). The sociology of childhood in relation to children's rights. *International Journal of Children's Rights, 8*(3), 243–259. DOI: 10.1163/15718180020494640

Metzger, C. A. (2006). Study abroad programming: A 21st century retention strategy? *The College Student Affairs Journal, 25*(2), 164–175.

Mo, Y., Appel, M., Kim, J. W., & Lee, W. (2021). Pre-service teachers' international study experiences or in-service teachers' professional learning communities: What comes into play in Finnish teachers' self-efficacy in multicultural classrooms? *Teachers and Teaching, 27*(7), 602–624. DOI: 10.1080/13540602.2021.1983535

Morley, A., Braun, A. M. B., Rohrer, L., & Lamb, D. (2019). Study abroad for pre-service teachers: A critical literature review with considerations for research and practice. *Global Education Review, 6*(3), 4–29. https://ger.mercy.edu/index.php/ger/article/view/521/394

National Council for Curriculum and Assessment. (2025, January 15). Aistear blog #1: The principles of early learning and development. Author. https://ncca.ie/en/updates-and-events/latest-news/2025/january/aistear-blog-1/

Nguyen, P. K. (2024). *Exploring the integration of Reggio Emilia-inspired practices in U.S. early childhood settings* (Publication No. 148) [Honors undergraduate theses, University of Central Florida]. Showcase of Text, Archives, Research & Scholarship. https://stars.library.ucf.edu/hut2024/148

Norris, E. M., & Gillespie, J. (2009). How study abroad shapes global careers. Evidence from the United States. *Journal of Studies in International Education, 13*(3), 382–397. DOI: 10.1177/1028315308319740

Nyaupane, G. P., Paris, C. M., & Teye, V. (2011). Study abroad motivations, destination selection and pre-trip attitude formation. *International Journal of Tourism Research, 13*(3), 205–217. DOI: 10.1002/jtr.811

Okken, G. J., Jansen, E. P. W. A., Hofman, W. H. A., & Coelen, R. J. (2019). Beyond the 'welcome-back party': The enriched repertoire of professional teacher behaviour as a result of study abroad. *Teaching and Teacher Education, 86. Teaching and Teacher Education, 102927*, 1–11. DOI: 10.1016/j.tate.2019.102927

Oostdam, R., & Hooge, E. (2013). Making the difference with active parents; forming educational partnerships between parents and schools. *European Journal of Psychology of Education, 28*(2), 337–351. DOI: 10.1007/s10212-012-0117-6

Parnell, W., Justice, E., & Patrick, L. P. (2018). Extended family and friends in young children's education. *Young Children, 73*(4), 20–27. https://www.naeyc.org/resources/pubs/yc/sep2018/engaging-extended-family-friends

Pećnik, N., Matić, J., & Milaković, A. T. (2016). Fulfillment of the child's participation rights in the family and the child's psychosocial adjustment: Children's and parent's views. *Revija za Socijalnu Politiku, 23*(3), 399–421. DOI: 10.3935/rsp.v23i3.1382

Pipitone, J. M. (2018). Place as pedagogy: Toward study abroad for social change. *Journal of Experiential Education, 41*(1), 54–74. DOI: 10.1177/1053825917751509

Quennerstedt, A. (2009). Balancing the rights of the child and the rights of parents in the Convention on the Rights of the Child. *Journal of Human Rights, 8*(2), 162–176. DOI: 10.1080/14754830902897270

Quezada, R. L. (2004). Beyond educational tourism: Lessons learned while student teaching abroad. *International Education Journal, 5*(4), 458–465.

Rinaldi, C. (2020). The child as a citizen: Holder of rights and competent. The Reggio Emilia educational experience. *Miscellanea Historico-luridica, 19*(1), 11–22. DOI: 10.15290/mhi.2020.19.01.01

Ruscoe, A., Barblett, L., & Barratt-Pugh, C. (2018). Sharing power with children: Repositioning children as agentic learners. *Australasian Journal of Early Childhood, 43*(3), 63–71. DOI: 10.23965/AJEC.43.3.07

Sadownik, A. R., & Jevtić, A. V. (Eds.). (2023). *(Re)theorising more-than-parental involvement in early childhood education and care: Vol. 40. International perspectives on early childhood education and development*. Springer. DOI: 10.1007/978-3-031-38762-3

Salyers, V., Carston, C. S., Dean, Y., & London, C. (2015). Exploring the motivations, expectations, and experiences of students who study in global settings. *Journal of International Students, 5*(4), 368–382. DOI: 10.32674/jis.v5i4.401

Sanders-Smith, S. C., & Cordoba, T. E. (2022). Study abroad as a means of unpacking pedagogical complexity in context. *Early Childhood Education Journal, 50*(6), 1059–1069. DOI: 10.1007/s10643-021-01238-6

Sanvictores, T., & Mendez, M. D. (2022). *Types of parenting styles and effects on children*. StatPearls Publishing.

Seipel, S. A., & Seeger, V. (2024). Impact of the Reggio Emilia approach through short term study abroad and the lenses of Lundy's model: Space, voice, audience, and influence. *Educational Considerations, 49*(3), 1–19. DOI: 10.4148/0146-9282.2372

Shiveley, J., & Misco, T. (2015). Long-term impacts of short-term study abroad: Teacher perceptions of preservice study abroad experiences. *Frontiers: The Interdisciplinary Journal of Study Abroad, 26*(1), 107–120. DOI: 10.36366/frontiers.v26i1.361

Smith, S. C. (2014). Parent engagement in a Reggio Emilia-inspired Head Start program. *Early Childhood Research & Practice, 16*(1 & 2), 1–11. https://ecrp.illinois.edu/v16n1/smith.html

Tinto, V. (2010). From theory to action: Exploring the institutional conditions for student retention. In Smart, J. C. (Ed.), *Higher education: Handbook of theory and practice* (pp. 51–89). Springer., DOI: 10.1007/978-90-481-8598-6_2

Tiwari, A. P. (2022). Authoritative parenting: The best style in children's learning. *American Journal of Education and Technology, 1*(3), 18–21. DOI: 10.54536/ajet.v1i3.687

Tomanović-Mihajlović, S. (2000). Young people's participation within the family: Parents' accounts. *International Journal of Children's Rights, 8*(2), 151–167. DOI: 10.1023/A:1008700320881

Tripon, C. (2024). Nurturing sustainable development: The interplay of parenting styles and SDGs in children's development. *Children (Basel, Switzerland), 11*(6), 695–713. DOI: 10.3390/children11060695 PMID: 38929274

United Nations. (1989). *Convention on the rights of the child.* Author. https://www.ohchr.org/sites/default/files/crc.pdf

United Nations. (2015). *Transforming our world: The 2030 agenda for sustainable development* (A/RES/70/1). https://www.un.org/ga/search/view_doc.asp?symbol=A/RES/70/1&Lang=E

Vatalaro, A., Szente, J., & Levin, J. (2015). Transformative learning of pre-service teachers during study abroad in Reggio Emilia, Italy: A case study. *The Journal of Scholarship of Teaching and Learning, 15*(2), 42–55. DOI: 10.14434/josotl.v15i2.12911

Veltri, B. T. (2012). Educator abroad: Teaching (insegnare) and learning (imparare) with Italian children. *Social Studies and the Young Learner, 24*(4), 23–26. https://www.socialstudies.org/system/files/publications/articles/yl_240423.pdf

Vezzali, L., Crisp, R. J., Stathi, S., & Giovannini, D. (2015). Imagined intergroup contact facilitates intercultural communication for college students on academic exchange programs. *Group Processes & Intergroup Relations, 18*(1), 66–75. DOI: 10.1177/1368430214527853

Voicu, C., Anghel, A., & Savu-Cristescu, M. (2015). Parent education for children's rights. *Procedia: Social and Behavioral Sciences, 191*, 1707–1712. DOI: 10.1016/j.sbspro.2015.04.433

White, B. (1981). Education for parenthood. *Journal of Education, 163*(3), 205–218. DOI: 10.1177/002205748116300303

Witkowsky, P., Mendez, S. L., & Arminio, J. (2018). Influence of a short-term study abroad experience on professional competencies and career aspirations of graduate students in student affairs. *Journal of College Student Development, 59*(6), 769–775. DOI: 10.1353/csd.2018.0073

Youngmin, M., & Appel, M. (2021). Pre-service teachers' international study experiences or in-service teachers' professional learning communities: What comes into play in Finnish teachers' self-efficacy in multicultural classrooms? *Teachers and Teaching, 27*(7), 602–624. DOI: 10.1080/13540602.2021.1983535

Zhang, B., Szente, J., & Levin, J. (2019). Early childhood pre-professionals' experience in a study abroad program to Finland: Evaluation of professional growth, and personal and cultural gains. *International Journal for the Scholarship of Teaching and Learning*, *13*(2), 1–5. DOI: 10.20429/ijsotl.2019.130216

Chapter 11

Enacting Children's Rights Through Reggio Emilia-Inspired Practices In Türkiye: The Quilt-Making Project

Hatice Zeynep Inan
http://orcid.org/0000-0001-6247-7857
Sam Houston State University, USA

Melissa Dawn Gatlin
http://orcid.org/0009-0002-1656-5658
Sam Houston State University, USA

Aysenur Gungor-Kircadag
http://orcid.org/0009-0005-5511-7999
Naturel Forest Preschool and Primary School, Turkey

ABSTRACT

This study presents the Quilt-Making Project carried out in a Reggio Emilia-inspired school (second grade; n = 21). It examines how children's rights, particularly participation, expression, collaboration, play, inquiry, and cultural life, were enacted through the project. Document analysis of pedagogical records including children's voices, classroom observations, and educator reflections traced the five-week process as students investigated the distinction between art and craft, explored materials, and collaborated with families and local artisans to produce a handmade quilt. Children's inquiry drove the project, shaping its direction and generating hands-on opportunities for interdisciplinary learning. Reggio Emilia principles provide a robust framework

DOI: 10.4018/979-8-3373-3431-8.ch011

for actualizing children's rights, sustaining democratic participation and cultural heritage while achieving beyond standards. Ultimately, the project demonstrates how playful, culturally situated, and ecologically attuned environments transform curiosity into civic participation and embed children's rights into daily practice.

INTRODUCTION

This chapter presents how Reggio Emilia-inspired educators can implement a quilt making project that executes children's rights through interdisciplinary perspectives. It integrates multiple educational subjects (e.g., literacy, mathematics, science), ethics, ecology, material culture, and Nature Based Learning [NBL], enacting children's rights through sustained, multimodal investigation. The story illustrates a real-world application of the Reggio Emilia philosophy. Children act as protagonists, while the curriculum is co-constructed through documentation, dialogue, and community encounters. The hundred languages are honored through making, storytelling, and research in the Quilt-Making Project.

The chapter emphasizes the importance of cultural interpretations and local adaptations in global contexts. In this story, quilting is treated as living heritage in Türkiye. Educators adapt quilting to the classroom's linguistic and cultural community while connecting this community to broader ecological and ethical questions. Children's daily experiences and questions drive the Quilt-Making Project. Learning standards are documented as outcomes, not starting points, demonstrating how inquiry-led projects meet requirements without narrowing practice. The following illustrates project-based learning rooted in children's lived experiences and inquiries.

> *On the way back from a school trip, one of the second-grade students made a comment about art: "You know what? Some people can't say 'sanat' [art]; they say 'zanat' [mispronunciation blending 'sanat' and 'zanaat'] instead." The teacher responded, "Maybe they mean 'zanaat' [craft]?" This prompted the children to ask, "What is craft?" We told them, "Let's explore this together when we get off the bus."*

This small Turkish linguistic puzzle sparked a sustained inquiry at a Reggio Emilia-inspired, forest-based primary school in Türkiye and led to the launch of the Quilt-Making Project. As children explored quilts, which are part of their cultural heritage, and other textiles, their questions multiplied: What goes inside a quilt? Where did this fabric come from? Who grew the cotton? Eventually their inquiry took an ethical turn: Do sheep feel pain when they're sheared for their wool? Such questions lie at the heart of the Reggio Emilia approach, inquiry-rooted in children's strong instinct to explore and recognized as a right in the Reggio tradition (Malaguzzi, 1993; Municipality of Reggio Emilia, Infant-Toddler Centers and

Preschools, 1995/1998). This inquiry sparks motivated, hands-on exploration and helps the youngest learners build meaningful connections and understand how the world works (Axelsson, 2022; Baker et al., 2021; Inan et al., 2010; Manera, 2022; Rinaldi, 1998; Westerberg & Vandermaas-Peeler, 2021). This inquiry-based, rights-driven approach stands in contrast to more traditional forms of education that have not always prioritized children's agency in shaping their own learning (Greene & Nixon, 2020), a principle that is an essential right of the child.

CHILDREN'S RIGHTS

Global discussions of children's rights in early childhood education often have centered on protections such as keeping children safe from harm, neglect, and exclusion. These protections are essential, yet children's rights extend beyond protection to include opportunities adults and institutions should provide. In Reggio Emilia schools, the environment is considered the "third teacher" (Gandini, 1998). Therefore, the environment should not only be safe and secure, protecting children from harm, but also open and inviting, provoking inquiry and creating spaces where children can interact with materials collaboratively and engage in hands-on experiences that support and sustain child agency.

Realizing children's rights requires creating conditions across pedagogy, community, and relationships that enable children to develop and express their capabilities (Hanson et al., 2014). For young children, these rights include, but are not limited to, expressing ideas, influencing decisions, participating in culturally relevant activities, and experiencing joy and belonging through play, as affirmed by Malaguzzi (1993), Municipality of Reggio Emilia, Infant-Toddler Centers and Preschools (1998), and the United Nations Convention on the Rights of the Child [UNCRC] (UN, 1989, Articles. 12 & 31). Nevertheless, young children's perspectives remain underrepresented in the research literature, partly due to the misconception that they have limited capacity to communicate their thoughts (Arnott et al., 2024). As a result, the work of advancing rights-affirming pedagogy frequently falls to classroom teachers engaged in action research and reflective practice.

In this Quilt-Making Project, educators in Türkiye advocated for children's rights, drawing from the Reggio Emilia philosophy in which projects emerge from children's inquiries and experiences, such as *The Amusement Park for Birds* (Forman & Gandini, 1994). This Quilt-Making Project shows how early childhood classrooms can braid inquiry, cultural heritage, nature, and children's lived experience into an emergent curriculum within a Reggio Emilia-inspired framework. Moreover, it illustrates how children's questions about nature, craft, materials, and animal welfare can seed academically rich, place-based investigations that teachers align to standards as natural outcomes, rather than as starting points. An inquiry-based, rights-driven approach matters amid mounting pressures in Türkiye for standardization and efficiency that risk narrowing early learning to what is most easily measured and constraining many children's rights, namely

- to be recognized as subjects of rights and active participants;
- to have their rich inborn potential acknowledged;
- to realize and expand that potential through relationships, affection, trust, and a desire to learn;
- to an educational stance that privileges inquiry and constructive strategies over direct transmission; and
- to develop creative intelligence and free thought, as outlined by Malaguzzi (1993), the founding figure of the Reggio Emilia approach.

Using a Reggio lens, this chapter adopts a rights-respecting stance: Children's participation, expression, collaboration, play, inquiry, and access to cultural life are children's entitlements (Malaguzzi, 1993; Municipality of Reggio Emilia, Infant-Toddler Centers and Preschools, 1998). In this framing, listening and reciprocity are modalities through which rights are enacted daily: Voices are documented, revisited, and negotiated in community (Lundy, 2007; Rinaldi, 2011). The critical belief that the child possesses rights is the foundation on which the Reggio Emilia approach is built (Hewett, 2001). Malaguzzi framed children's rights within a triad of children-parents-teachers and explicitly discussed the rights of all three protagonists (Malaguzzi, 1993). Because children do not learn in isolation, parents and teachers are partners in learning. It is therefore fitting that their rights are addressed alongside children's, although this remains uncommon in many contexts. While the Quilt-Making Project considered parents' and teachers' rights, this chapter focuses only on children's rights.

Moreover, since Türkiye ratified the UNCRC in 1995, thereby committing to uphold the children's rights, among others, to express views, to play, and to participate in cultural and artistic life as elaborated in Articles 12 and 31 (UN, 1989), this chapter treats those rights as daily entitlements enacted through the Quilt-Making Project, fully convergent with the rights articulated in the Reggio tradition. Viewed through both the UNCRC and the Reggio Emilia tradition, this chapter demonstrates how the Quilt-Making Project cultivated a learning environment in which children's rights were not only acknowledged but actively upheld. Within this stance, children's rights constituted the foundation of the work: Collaboration and reciprocity were prioritized, and inquiry and interest emerged organically rather than being predetermined. Sustained project work naturally generates cross-disciplinary learning, while the hundred languages of children, specifically play and arts, allow for multiple modes of expression and participation, as documented in prior research (e.g., Inan et al., 2010).

The Quilt-Making Project also illustrates how a Reggio-inspired approach naturally dovetails with NBL, an increasingly prominent strand in Turkish early childhood education and an approach defined as teaching and learning, indoors or outdoors, through direct engagement with nature (Warden, 2018), by fostering connections between the natural world and children's everyday lives (Uluay, 2024). Beyond this alignment, Reggio Emilia's guiding principles extend NBL further. For example, Reggio Emilia's inherent flexibility allows for seamless integration of multiple subjects, including technology, art, math, science, social sciences, language, and literacy within a single, coherent project; and it remains responsive to emerging issues as they arise. Moreover, because Reggio Emilia is always reinterpreted within each local context, schools outside Italy are rightly called "Reggio-inspired" rather than replicas. This local adaptation preserves cultural identity and helps countries avoid the pitfalls of wholesale adoption of foreign curricular models (Zhang et al., 2025), while simultaneously creating rich, context-responsive learning environments in which children's rights are enacted through substantive projects from quilting to ecosystem studies and beyond.

THEORETICAL FRAMEWORK

> *"Someone may think that we set ourselves overly ambitious objectives, but this is a suspicion that the children immediately dispelled. Each of them, with their different identities, participated as much as they liked, as much as they were able to gather their experiences into words and thoughts (we don't know from where, because nowadays the places in which children learn are more numerous than in the past), moving toward meaning, sometimes fleeting, sometimes more lucid, with an unsuspected and extraordinarily vital maturity and competence in expressing their rights." (Malaguzzi et al., 1995/1998, pp. 11-12).*

This recognition of children's intrinsic competence and their right to participate meaningfully in learning processes underpins the present study's theoretical framing. Grounded in the Reggio Emilia tradition, this study works with seven interlocking commitments:

- a strong image of all children, regardless of ability or diagnosis, reframed as *bambini con diritti speciali* (children with special rights, a Reggio Emilia term emphasizing rights rather than deficits) rather than children with special needs (Landini & Colacino, 2023; Malaguzzi, 1994);

- *progettazione*, an emergent curriculum animated by children's questions and sustained through project work (Katz, 1993; Rankin, 1997; Rinaldi, 1998);
- co-construction of knowledge through dialogue and relationships among school, families, community, and the material world (Childress, 2020; Malaguzzi, 1993; Rinaldi, 1998);
- the environment as a third teacher that invites inquiry (Gandini, 1998);
- educators as listeners, co-researchers, and provocateurs (Aydemir Özalp & Inan, 2021; Rinaldi, 1998);
- documentation and pedagogical listening as tools for reflection and assessment (Gandini, 2004); and
- recognition of the hundred languages of children: multiple, equally valued modes of expression (Edwards et al., 1993, 2012; Rinaldi, 2011; Vecchi, 2010).

Building on Rinaldi's "Pedagogy of Listening" (2011), educators in this school treated listening as an ethical, relational, and political stance that foregrounded children's voices and cultivated reciprocity in educator-child partnerships.

This chapter also draws on Vygotsky's sociocultural theory and children's rights frameworks (Malaguzzi, 1993; Municipality of Reggio Emilia, Infant-Toddler Centers and Preschools, 1998; UN, 1989). The Vygotskian perspective situates learning in social interaction, tools, and language, emphasizing how meanings are co-constructed through guided participation and cooperation (Vygotsky, 1978). Following the Vygotskian perspective, in Reggio-inspired settings, collective inquiry and documentation function as cultural tools that mediate children's thinking and make learning visible (Inan et al., 2010; Wilson et al., 2013). In this view, projects like the Quilt-Making Project can be understood as sociocultural activities in which tools, symbols, words, and relationships mediate children's participation and transform everyday practices into shared cultural knowledge. From this perspective, visible classrooms emphasize that learning is not only purposeful and social but also emotional, empowering, and representational (Wilson et al., 2013).

Moreover, the Heads-Hearts-Hands-on (3Hs) Education model offers a rights-based lens for showing how Reggio-inspired educators can realize children's rights by fulfilling the whole child. This model emphasizes that body, spirit, and mind should all be engaged; Head, Heart, and Hand represent inquiry, interest-based, and physical engagement (Inan & Inan, 2015; Inan et al., 2010). It shows how thinking, feeling, and doing intertwine in Reggio Emilia-inspired practice.

The project also intersects with NBL, understood as experiences in and with nature, including materials, plants, animals, and water, that support academic learning, personal development, and environmental awareness connected to local culture and place (Jordan & Chawla, 2019; Larimore, 2019). NBL helps center children's memories, emotions, language, and ethical concerns (Jordan & Chawla, 2019; Larimore, 2019). Evidence from Reggio-inspired contexts suggests that NBL activities can strengthen communication and social skills while nurturing respectful relationships with the more-than-human world and feelings of safety and connectedness (Omidvar et al., 2019; Osgood & Ødegård, 2022; Uluay, 2024). Since the study site is a Reggio Emilia-inspired, forest-based primary school and NBL profoundly shapes early childhood education practice across Türkiye, an NBL lens helps to interpret this Reggio Emilia-inspired Quilt-Making Project as well.

Taken together, children's rights frameworks, Vygotsky's sociocultural theory, the 3Hs Education model, and NBL form a coherent rights-based lens for interpreting sustained, context-responsive projects grounded in Reggio Emilia principles.

METHODOLOGY

This qualitative study employed Document Analysis as its primary research method. More specifically, it utilized Bowen's (2009) systematic three-step procedure for reviewing and interpreting existing documents to generate empirical insights: (a) superficial scanning, (b) close reading, and (c) interpretation (Bowen, 2009; Ozkan, 2019). Specifically, the study critically examined written, visual, and video-based documentation produced in a Reggio Emilia-inspired primary school in Türkiye. These project-generated records traced the unfolding of the five-week Quilt-Making Project in a second-grade classroom ($n = 21$; ages 8-9). The project began with seven children whose shared interest in craft catalyzed the work; although all students eventually participated, these seven co-directed the process.

Document Analysis

The research team drew on both insider and outsider perspectives, integrating practitioner expertise with scholarly analysis. Document Analysis proceeded inductively, following Bowen's (2009) three-stage process. Initially, the school conducted a "superficial examination" and "close reading" (Bowen, 2009, p.32) of all project documents, de-identified the data, and summarized materials including the following:

- children's voices, such as transcripts of dialogues (e.g., "What is craft?"; "Do sheep feel pain when sheared?");
- multimodal records such as atelier displays, classroom observations, field trip notes, video recordings, and photographs;
- children's artifacts such as drawings, writing samples, quilt panel sketches, and a 40-patch quilt; and

- reflections such as accounts from teachers and visiting artisans.

Subsequently, the university researchers interpreted the summary project documentation provided by the school and of materials disseminated on social media, through iterative analytic cycles in order to situate the project narrative within the broader literature on Reggio Emilia-inspired pedagogy, children's rights, and nature-based learning. This process continued until informational and analytic needs were fully addressed. Collectively, the documents illuminated the story of engagement with ancestral crafts, hands-on work with wool and fiberfill, community encounters, and collaborative quilt construction. In this chapter, the researchers report the summary of the project narratively to trace the project's emergence, development, and conclusion and to highlight how educators used standards as tools for documentation and accountability rather than as curricular starting points. Parental consent was obtained by the school for photographs, and pseudonyms are used for students in this chapter to protect their privacy.

Context

The project took place at a Reggio Emilia-inspired primary school in Türkiye, situated at the edge of a forest. Founded as a Reggio Emilia-inspired preschool and later expanded to Grades K-4, its mission is to enact the Turkish National Curriculum in nature and in life, extending learning beyond the classroom to neighborhood markets, seashores, and museums while honoring children's curiosity. Its democratic school culture empowers students to select curriculum topics and enrichment activities (e.g., art, music, sewing, cooking, sports, and dance).

Project facilitation and analysis were supported by a highly trained team: the school pedagogista *(provocateur)*, classroom teacher (*documenter*), and art teacher (*atelierista*). The school's philosophy is rooted in the Reggio Emilia approach, as the educators received Reggio Emilia training in both Italy and Türkiye from Reggio Children. They also received Reggio Emilia training from one of the study's researchers in the past, creating a strong connection between the research team and the school.

The school team also developed professionally through workshops in Finnish forest school pedagogy (learning in nature), Finland-centered mathematics education, play therapy, music, and philosophical storytelling. Together, these Reggio Emilia-inspired educators wove sociocultural, rights-respecting, and NBL frameworks into a co-constructed classroom atelier that honored children as protagonists and used documentation as both learning and assessment. They maintained a deep commitment to project work rooted in children's cultural and natural contexts, co-

constructed classroom life around their interests and needs, and explicitly upheld children's rights and democratic participation.

Below, the project summary, translated from Turkish into English by the bilingual researcher, is presented with particular attention to how shared experiences, cultural participation, and intergenerational knowledge foster community-building and the co-construction of meaning. This inquiry-driven narrative weaves teachers' and children's voices, documentation excerpts, and educator reflections to trace the arc from an initial question, "Is art the same as craft?", to the collaborative making of a quilt. This story would not be possible without classroom teacher Hakan conducting the documentation, art teacher Esra managing the atelier, and pedagogista Aysenur provoking the children's inquiry and interests.

Results

Earlier in the chapter an exerpt from the children's inspirational conversation that led to the Quilt Making Project was shared with the reader to inform the connection between child wonder and practice in the classroom. This quote is repeated below as a reminder that children's voice inspired the project.

Is Art the Same As Craft? How Did This Question Arise?

On the way back from a school trip, one of the second-grade students made a comment about art: "You know what? Some people can't say 'sanat' [art]; they say 'zanat' [mispronunciation blending 'sanat' and 'zanaat'] instead.' The teacher responded, "Maybe they mean 'zanaat' [craft]?" This prompted the children to ask, "What is craft?" We told them, "Let's explore this together when we get off the bus."

Let's First Recall the Different Forms of Art!

The children started naming various types of art they knew, and we took note of their responses. We noticed that some art forms are auditory, some are visual, and others are dramatic, and the children grouped them accordingly (see Figure 1).

Figure 1. Building a Shared Taxonomy of Art and Craft on the Classroom Chalkboard

Note. Left panel: The text on the chalkboard reads "Types of Art: Auditory (Music); Visual (Painting, Sculpture, Architecture); Dramatic/Performing (Theater, Animation, Dance, Ballet, Opera)" Right panel: The text on the chalkboard reads "Types of Craft: Carpenter".

The children then shared which of these art forms they liked, had taken classes in, or had experienced themselves.

> Teacher Hakan: Writing poetry, like writing stories and novels, is part of the literary arts.
> Elowyn: I love painting. That's an art form, too.
> Fatma: I really enjoy going to the cinema. Could we go again with the school?
> Ata: I like cartoons. If we go, let's watch a cartoon this time. Is animation also considered art?
> Teacher Hakan: Yes, animation is an original work created by combining drawings. Today, with technology, the variety of visual arts has expanded.
> Eren: Weren't some of these art forms nonexistent in the past?
> Teacher Hakan: As materials and techniques have evolved over time, new art forms have emerged.
> Pedagogista Aysenur: For example, do you think the clay projects we made are art?

Dilara: Yes. I really enjoy making them. I've seen them in a museum, too.
Meryem: We have the same pottery at school that they have in the museum. We even made yogurt in it.
Pedagogista Aysenur: But we bought that pot, and there were many identical ones. If every work by an artist is supposed to be unique, are these pots artworks?

WHAT ARE THE TYPES OF CRAFT?

We discussed professions that require manual skills such as tailoring, carpentry, jewelry-making, and pottery. If what these professionals do isn't considered art, what is it called?

This discussion led us to an introduction to the definition and varieties of craft. Artists and craftspeople can use the same materials, so why are they named differently? For instance, both might use wood, paint, or fabric. However, an artist typically creates a unique, one-of-a-kind piece, whereas a craftsperson can produce multiples of the same product. Does the quantity produced matter? An artist is naturally gifted from birth, while a craftsperson learns the trade through training. The children learned these distinctions by visiting and talking with a local carpenter and tailor.

Thus, we introduced the topic by defining "craft" and giving examples of its various forms.

Pedagogista Aysenur: Actually, both a ceramic artist and a potter use the same materials. So why do we call one an artist and the other a craftsperson?
Eren: Because an artist creates one-of-a-kind works, while a potter makes many identical pieces.
Melis: Potters don't hold exhibitions; they sell their wares in shops.
Berke: Then potters must earn more money.
Dilara: No way. Potter's pieces are cheap; an artist's work sells for much more.
Berke: But the potter has so many pieces. I think that's more valuable.
Yavuz: I read that a single painting can sell for millions. I'd rather have one famous painting than a whole pile of pots.
Teacher Hakan: So an artist produces a unique work, while a craftsperson produces multiples of the same item. Does the number produced matter, then?
Dilay: A ceramic artist makes one piece; a potter makes many. The potter sells theirs in a shop. But I don't understand: If Yayoi Kusama is an artist, why are the bags, shoes, and clothes she designed sold in stores?
Pedagogista Aysenur: Yes, we discussed this in art class when we studied Yayoi Kusama's collaboration with Louis Vuitton and how she created designs for

Louis Vuitton brand. There, she was working as a designer; her designs were exhibited and sold in boutiques. Design is also considered art.
Melis: Then is a tailor an artist, too?
Pedagogista Aysenur: If you like, we could go to the tailor in our neighborhood and ask them that question.

VISITING THE TAILOR IN OUR NEIGHBORHOOD!

We visited the neighborhood tailor to answer the children's questions (see Figure 2).

Figure 2. Visiting the Neighborhood Tailor

Note. Children examine fabrics, tools, and techniques while learning that most shop work involves repairs and alterations rather than making new garments.

The students examined the fabrics and tools in his shop. The tailor explained that he mainly does simple repairs, such as mending tears, hemming pant legs, and taking in skirts, rather than making new garments from scratch.

> Tailor: In the past, people came to have clothes, custom made. Now, they buy ready-to-wear items, and I only handle basic alterations.
> Diana: Did you go to school for this?
> Tailor: When I was in primary school, I used to go to a tailor after school to learn the trade. I learned by helping out, without ever attending a vocational school.
> Berke: I would never go to work after school. I'd rather stay home.
> Tailor: In my day, there was a master-apprentice system. We learned by working alongside a skilled craftsman.
> Melis: How old were you?
> Tailor: I was in third grade, about 10 or 11 years old.
> Meryem: Did you ever play?
> Tailor: We didn't have as many toys as you do. We were focused on learning a profession.

After the visit, the children returned to school and reflected, "We're glad we go home after school. We'd rather play than learn a trade as an apprentice from a master."

> Teacher Hakan: As you've seen, this tailor learned his trade by training alongside a master. From whom do artists learn their craft?
> Taskin: Yayoi had visions of polka dots and fishing nets. No one taught her. She painted her dreams.
> Gordon: Frida painted countless self-portraits because, lying in bed and seeing herself in the mirror, she had no other outlet. She was too ill to attend school.
> Teacher Hakan: To develop creativity, a person needs the freedom to discover themselves. If everything were taught step by step, every outcome would look the same, just like factory-made pottery.

While the second graders were exploring art and craft, the first graders mentioned they wanted to have a pajama party. Excited by the idea, the second graders chimed in, "We want one too!"

As they expressed a desire to host a pajama party, we asked what they thought would be needed for such an event. They said they wanted to watch cartoons, eat popcorn, and sleep in pajamas on a floor mattress. They also mentioned needing a quilt. We suggested that, if they wished, we could visit a local quilt master and make a quilt together. Since we had been exploring types of craft, this was a timely and engaging topic for the children.

> Pedagogista Aysenur: Since you want a pajama party, what do you need?
> Deren: Pajamas.
> Fatma: I'd like a nightgown.
> Eren: Can we watch cartoons, too?
> Dilay: Popcorn would be great.
> Meryem: If only we had a quilt, we could lie down and sleep.
> Berke: How will we sleep without pillows?
> Meryem: We could use the pillows from the studio.
> Yavuz: But we don't have a quilt.
> Pedagogista Aysenur: What if we sew our own quilt?
> Children: Okay, but how do we make one?
> Pedagogista Aysenur: Let's all bring unused fabric scraps from home. Then we'll decide together what to do with them.

But If We Were to Make Our Own Quilt, What Should It Be Like? What Would We Need?

The children decided to bring leftover fabric from home to make the quilt (see Figure 3).

Figure 3.Measuring, Cutting, and Piecing

Note. Children cut equal-sized squares from assorted scraps and began stitching them side by side to form a shared quilt top.

The fabric scraps brought from home were small pieces and none were sufficient on their own to make a quilt. So we decided to join the scraps together and discussed what would be needed to make a quilt (see Figure 4).

Figure 4. Planning Our Quilt

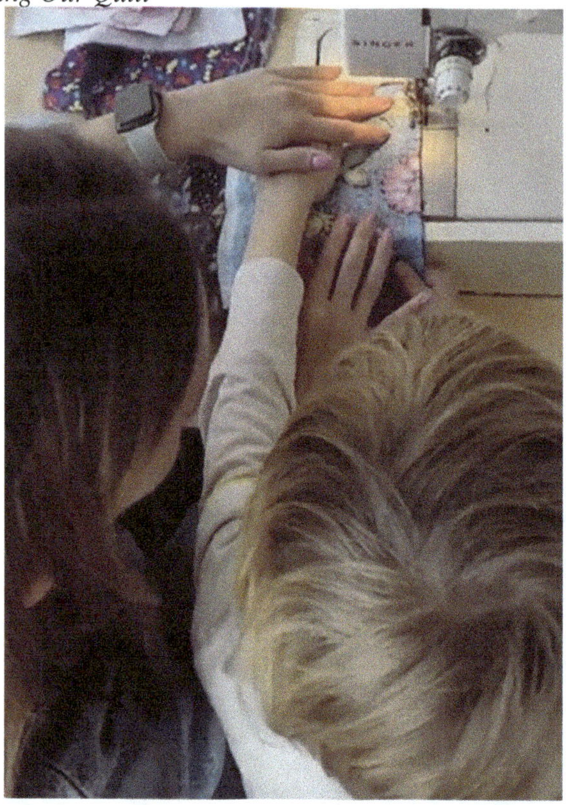

The students measured and cut the materials into equal-sized squares at school. They ended up with a variety of textures and colors. We decided to sew them side by side to create a large quilt top. Through this process, they also experienced the craft of tailoring (see Figure 5).

Figure 5. A Student Machine-Stitching Quilt Panels During the Making Phase

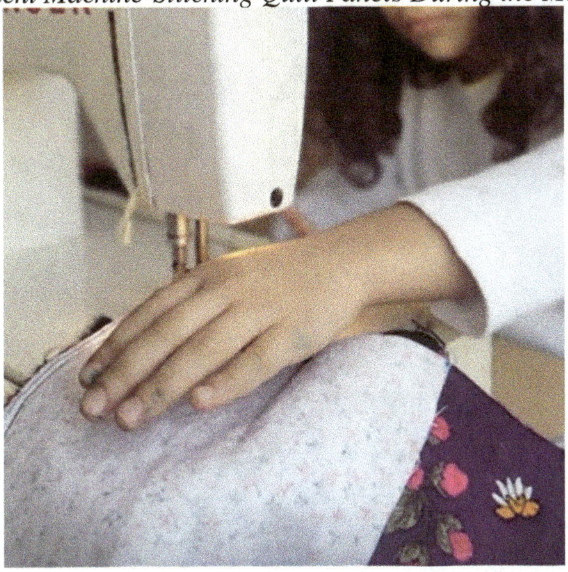

When they successfully sewed the quilt top, the result was very colorful. Each child's scrap fabric became part of a whole. We told them that this patchwork technique is called "40-patch." Through this activity, we experienced firsthand how being together enriches life.

What Goes Inside a Quilt?

The children shared what materials they thought could be used to fill a quilt:

> Eren: It can be made with sheep's wool. When the wool grows long, it's cut and is used to make quilts.
> Mirabella: You need large pieces of fabric.
> Norah: You can use fiberfill. Is fiber made from cotton?
> [We researched the materials used in fiberfill.]
> Selim: You can use cotton, too.

One child's question, "Don't sheep feel pain?", was set aside to explore in more depth the following day. We started to examine the materials that could be used to fill quilts via an overhead projector (see Figure 6).

Figure 6. Exploring Cotton and Wool on a Overhead Projector With Light and Shadow

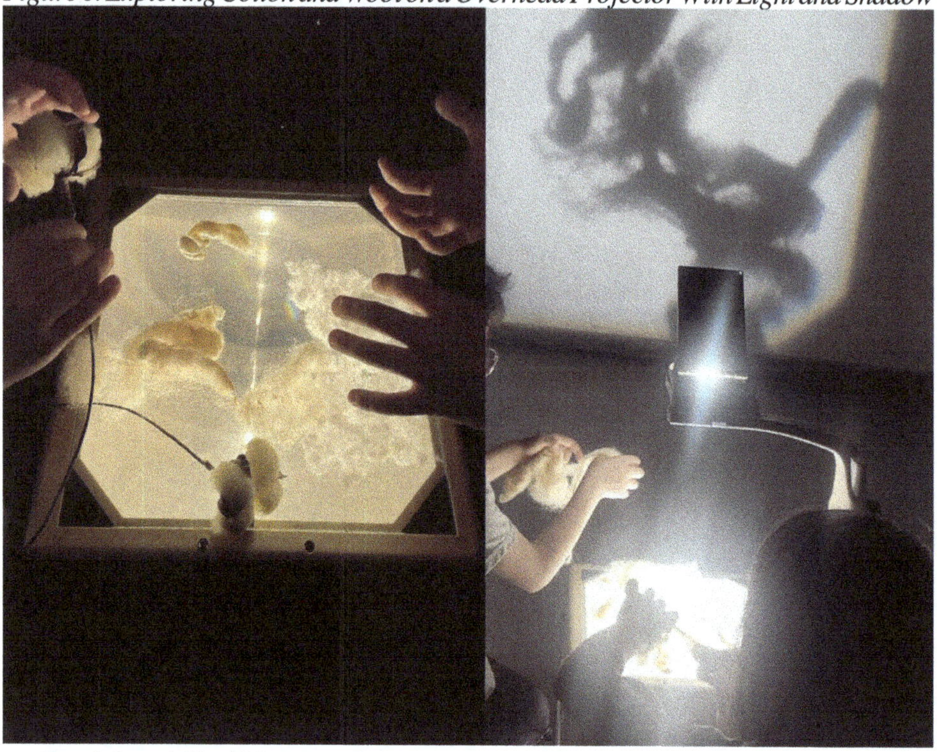

Note. Left panel: The children are exploring cotton on an overhead projector. Right panel: The children are exploring wool on an overhead projector.

The children pulled and separated wool with their hands and questioned the color differences.

One child, Ali, asked, "Is the black wool darker because it's expired?"

When Ali asked that question, the children laughed: Of course, sheep can be different colors. Dilek noticed that fiberfill and cotton felt very different and found it fascinating that cotton comes from a plant. They also learned that fiberfill isn't made from a natural material. Excitedly, they tried planting cotton seeds in the school garden but discovered that cotton won't grow in our climate, showing them that not every plant can thrive everywhere.

The students discovered that different colors of wool come from different breeds of sheep and that even animals like llamas and goats can provide usable wool.

Doesn't It Hurt the Sheep?

The next day, in response to one child's question, we brought the children's book *Rebel Sheep Melo* by Nihan Kaya to class. The children were intrigued and decided we should read it. In the story, Melo is a sheep who loves her wool so much that she runs off into the forest rather than having it sheared. As her fleece grows, she becomes a huge ball of wool, shocking the other animals who have never seen anything like her. When the story ended, Teacher Hakan asked, "Did you know this book was inspired by a true story?"

> Fatma: What do you mean? Was there a real sheep named Melo?
> Teacher Hakan: Actually, the sheep's name was Shrek, and the events took place in New Zealand.
> Hardy: But Shrek isn't a sheep! That's the cartoon character!
> Teacher Hakan: The farmers who found her six years later gave her that nickname after the film character.
> Hifzi: Is there a picture of Shrek the sheep?
> Teacher Hakan: Let's look online together.

We then researched Shrek's story, how she escaped being sheared and survived for six years in a cave. By the time she was found, her fleece had grown so excessively that it restricted her movement and endangered her health. Rescuers determined she needed to be sheared for her own well-being. The child who had asked, "Doesn't it hurt the sheep to be sheared?" concluded, "I'm glad they found her. She really did need her wool cut, and it was for her health."

VISITING THE QUILT MASTER!

It was time to visit the quilt master. He told the children that, like the tailor they had met, he had begun apprenticing under a master craftsman as a young boy. He then explained that traditional handmade quilting was gradually being forgotten, supplanted by factory-made quilts that are both faster to produce and far less expensive. When the children asked about filling materials, some proposed wool, others cotton, and a few suggested synthetic fiberfill.

He said the children could most easily sew a quilt with fiberfill. Quilting with other materials is more difficult. He laid the fabric inside out on the ground and scattered fiberfill over it. Then he handed a stick to the children one by one and said, "Now beat it!" (see Figure 7).

> Melis: Beating isn't a good thing to do.
> Alec: Are we going to be violent with the fiberfill?

Figure 7. "Beating" the Fiberfill

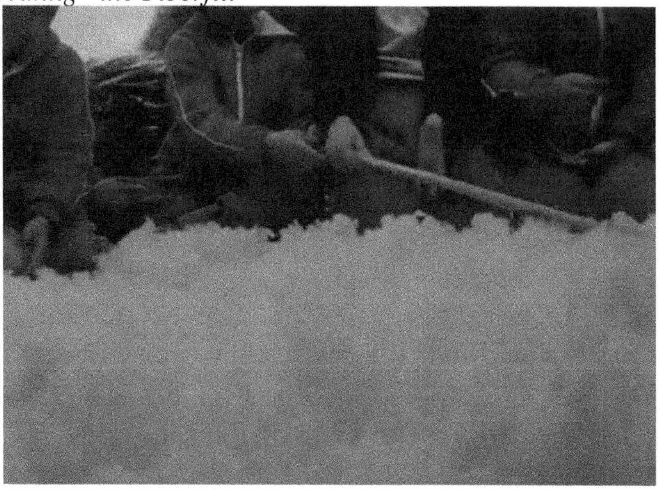

The children were puzzled by the word "beat." The master explained that it's a technical term in the profession. The children took turns hitting the fiberfill with the stick, which fluffed up the material. They spread it evenly across the fabric. Then the master flipped the fabric over to trap the fiberfill inside the quilt. It was time to sew. The filling needed to be stitched down to keep it from shifting. The master put on a thimble and explained what it was for and how it protected his finger. The children began sewing the quilt one by one (see Figure 8). They were very happy to take on a task normally done by an adult.

Figure 8. Preparing the Filling and Stitching With the Master

Once the quilt was complete, the children thanked the master and returned to school. We had leftover cotton and wool filling from old pillows originally intended for the quilt. Since our school follows NBL's ecological approach and aligns with the Zero Waste project, instead of composting leftovers, we repurposed them into cushions for our seating corner (see Figure 9), using unused pillowcases from dowry chests.

Figure 9. Sustainability in Action: Cushions Made From Repurposed Materials

The students selected a day for their pajama party and, on that day, watched the cartoon they had chosen, dressed in their pajamas and snuggled under the quilt they had made from the 40-piece patchwork, while enjoying popcorn.

Ethical and sustainable material usage formed a central thread in the Quilt-Making Project, emphasizing the children's rights of expression and participation through shared decision-making that promoted one of the tenets of Reggio Emilia and NBL-caring for the environment. Table 1 shows how the project operationalized these values through the 7Rs (i.e., Rethink, Refuse, Reduce, Reuse, Repair, Repurpose/Upcycle, and Recycle/Compost), adapted from Potting et al. (2017).

Table 1. Eco-Friendly Quilt-Making Project: 7R and Class Decisions

7R	Action in Quilt-Making Project
Rethink	Instead of purchasing new fabric for our quilt, we chose to repurpose unused fabrics from families' homes. We informed children and parents about this choice, emphasizing sustainability over consumption.
Refuse	The quilt workshop began as part of a pajama party where children would watch cartoons while eating popcorn. We intentionally avoided single-use materials (plastic plates/cups). Popcorn was served in porcelain bowls. When children asked, "Aren't we going to use cardboard containers for popcorn?" we discussed the environmental damage caused by disposable materials and how long they take to decompose. We reminded them that our school also avoids disposable cups by using a water dispenser system. Another child suggested using old paper, but the group decided this would not be hygienic.
Reduce	For the quilt filling, we considered using old cotton/wool pillows. However, the quilt maker explained that these materials would make the quilt too firm, making it difficult for children to sew. Therefore, we had to use fiberfill, though we tried to keep its use to a minimum. The quilt maker explained this decision to the children, helping them understand the balance between practicality and sustainability.
Reuse	We made use of old fabrics and did not buy any new ones. By stitching together small fabric scraps, we created a large double-sized piece of fabric. The children realized that a tiny piece, when combined with others, could become part of a larger whole.
Repair	Instead of buying a ready-made quilt from a store, we decided to repair and reuse old fabrics, allowing the children to actively participate in the process.
Repurpose/ Upcycle	Rather than simple recycling, this project applied upcycling, turning old materials into something of greater value.
Recycle/Compost	Although our school has a composting area, we could not compost the leftover fabrics because, despite being cotton, they contained dye and patterns. We explained this to the children and decided to save the scraps for future projects.

Ultimately, what began with one child's remark about "zanat" / "sanat" grew into an experiential study of art versus craft. Curiosity kept students highly engaged and joyful. On one hand, fueled by their curiosity and sustained interest, the children remained highly motivated and fully engaged, learning joyfully throughout the process. As educators, we were delighted to have fostered such deep, lasting learning. As Table 2 outlines, the project met Grade 2 expectations and reached Grade 3 outcomes. It showcases integrated learning: braiding literacy, math, science, arts, and sustainability into one coherent, standards-evidenced project.

Table 2. Examples From the Activities and Corresponding Turkish National Curriculum Standards

Children's questions / activities	Related MoNE learning outcomes (Grades 2/3)	Subjects
Designing and sewing quilt panels (40-patch); Measurement used during visits to a quilt-maker and a tailor.	M.2.3.1.2. Recognizes standard units of length and explains their uses.[a]	Mathematics
While discussing what is needed for a pajama party, children decided a quilt was necessary and discussed what they would need to obtain/make it.	G.2.1.1. Finds various solutions to problems encountered while creating a visual artwork.[a]	Visual arts
When they decided to sew a quilt, they chose to use leftover materials (scraps).	HB.2.6.4. Contributes to the recycling of consumed materials.[b]	Life studies
When the quilt-maker explained how to sew the quilt, the children followed the oral instructions.	T.2.1.7. Follows oral instructions.[a]	Language arts
Visiting a neighborhood tailor and quilt-maker; observing tools; having conversations about their professions, the children identified historical/period differences.	HB.3.2.1. Compares the characteristics of elder family members' childhoods with those of their own childhood.[a]	Life studies
Began with "What is craft? Is art the same as craft?" → Brainstorming and categorizing art versus craft; exploring quilt fillings (wool, cotton, fiberfill) → "Doesn't it hurt sheep?" Then planted cotton seeds in the garden → discovered cotton won't grow in our climate. While discussing which material to choose for quilting, they reviewed cotton's growth stages.	F.3.6.1.2. Presents the results of observations on a plant's life cycle.[a]	Science

Note. MoNE = Ministry of National Education.

[a] The items in the MoNE's learning-outcomes list fall short of the broader gains achieved in our Reggio Emilia-inspired project.

[b] MoNE documents focus on recycling; our project goes further, incorporating other Rs like upcycling.

DISCUSSION

The Quilt-Making Project moved beyond a linguistic puzzle to enact children's rights in daily classroom life. It offers a compelling blueprint for a shift, showing how teaching intentionality, documentation, and relational pedagogy can bring children's rights to life within the fabric of classroom practice. Rather than treating rights as an abstract concept, educators supported participation, cultural identity, play, and voice through the hands-on, inquiry-based project inspired by the Reggio Emilia philosophy. Drawing from UN (1989), particularly Articles 12 (to be heard) and 31 (to play and culturally participate), this project demonstrated how pedagogical practices rooted in Reggio Emilia philosophy can embed children's rights into everyday learning. Children were not passive participants in the project but co-constructors of meaning whose questions influenced the direction of their work. Following the children's curiosity, the teacher created space for them to shape their learning, make meaningful contributions to the community, and engage deeply with the process through their cultural heritage. These exchanges reflect the intent of Article 12, which calls for student perspectives to shape the direction of learning, ensuring their voices are valued in the process (UN, 1989, Arts. 12 & 31). Echoing Malaguzzi (1993), educators treated children as rights-bearing protagonists with rich potential realized through relationships and inquiry-centered, creative pedagogy.

A single offhand question, "Is art the same as craft?", ignited a five-week inquiry that braided children's agency, cultural heritage, nature, and ethical reasoning within a Reggio Emilia-inspired pedagogy. In this project, questions served as the engine of the curriculum: Children's observations and dialogues set the course, while teachers listened, documented, and co-researched alongside them, as in the Reggio Emilia tradition (Edwards et al., 1993, 2012; Gandini, 1998, 2004; Rinaldi, 1998, 2012). Such a project honored the child as a competent protagonist and reframed standards as outcomes documented after inquiry rather than prescribed beginnings. In doing so, it resisted the narrowing effects of efficiency-driven schooling and affirmed children's rights to participation, expression, play, collaboration, inquiry, and cultural life, rights articulated in the Reggio tradition (Malaguzzi, 1993; Municipality of Reggio Emilia, Infant-Toddler Centers and Preschools, 1998).

Participation went beyond having a token voice; instead, the children were co-constructors of the project and had genuine influence. Teachers organized space and audience to ensure authentic encounters, allowing children's ideas to reshape plans and decisions, thereby enacting Article 12 (Lundy, 2007; UN, 1989). Agency was visible when students defined problems, planned actions, and redistributed roles. For example, they conversed with a neighborhood tailor, compared artistic and craft practices, and decided how to design and stitch a 40-patch quilt. Documentation made learning visible, functioning as a cultural tool that mediated thinking and collaboration (Vygotsky, 1978; Wilson et al., 2013). These moves align with Reggio's image of the child and with Turkish practitioners' accounts of teachers as listeners, co-researchers, and provocateurs (Aydemir Özalp & Inan, 2021; Gandini, 2004; Rinaldi, 1998, 2012), while recognizing inclusion as special rights in community (Landini & Colacino, 2023). Framed by Vygotskian social constructivism and the hundred languages, the classroom became a space where children collaboratively constructed the meaning of craft through exploration, social interaction, and multiple forms of representation, rather than by receiving pre-digested facts (e.g., Edwards et al., 1993, 2012; Greene & Nixon, 2020).

Throughout the Quilt-Making Project, children were offered a safe, invitational space where their ideas, questions, and concerns were genuinely heard and acted upon. When students worried about sheep shearing, for example, the class extended the inquiry by reading a story and researching animal care, folding their concern directly into the next day's work. In keeping with Reggio Emilia's emergent curriculum, participation was treated as multimodal (e.g., spoken words, drawings, gestures, and making) with teachers acting as co-researchers rather than mere listeners, a stance consistent with prior findings (Arnott et al., 2024; Lundy, 2007). The project advanced through a chain of child-posed questions, with teachers iteratively reshaping plans, while hands-on tasks such as designing lively quilt patterns and filling the quilt with fiber allowed children to materialize their thinking as joyful learning. Aligned with Article 31 of the UN Convention (1989), play, culture, and artistic creation were not diversions but the learning itself. The synergy of Reggio Emilia principles with NBL fostered a child-centered environment where inquiry and creativity flourished in and with the natural world, while supporting sustainability through the 7R.

The project's aesthetic and material dimensions also mattered. Children developed a nuanced understanding of material origins and processes like cotton cultivation, dyeing, and shearing, and clearly distinguished handmade from mass-produced work. As they traced textile histories, family heritage gained prominence and artistry was treated not as a luxury but as a way of thinking and knowing (Manera, 2022; Vecchi, 2010). Mathematical reasoning (measurement, patterning) and disciplinary literacy (terminology, process recounting) emerged organically and were later mapped to standards across literacy, mathematics, technology, arts, and science. These findings parallel prior research (Inan et al., 2010; Westerberg & Vandermaas-Peeler, 2021). In this way, 3Hs learning (Inan & Inan, 2015) operated simultaneously: Inquiry, interest-based, and physical engagement intertwined throughout the Quilt-Making Project.

Grounded in the 3Hs Education model (Inan & Inan, 2015) and a whole-child framework, classroom processes in the Quilt-Making Project illustrated how emotion, reasoning, and material exploration interweave. By attending to children's intellectual curiosities (e.g., "What is craft?"), ethical inquiries (e.g., "Does shearing hurt sheep?"), and physical work (manipulating wool and fiberfill, stitching quilt panels), the Quilt-Making project enacted a holistic approach that affirmed each student's right to engage mentally, emotionally, and physically in learning, honoring the whole child and supporting rights to participate, explore, and create.

NBL was not an add-on but a throughline. Students handled wool, compared it with cotton and fiberfill, and even planted cotton seeds in the school garden, discovering that not every plant grows everywhere. Such experiences situated knowledge in place and relationship, consistent with NBL's evidence base and with Reggio Emilia-inspired work that ties learning to local ecologies (Jordan & Chawla, 2019; Larimore, 2019; Omidvar et al., 2019; Uluay, 2024). Through curiosity, care, and observation, children explored independently. Nature was the place where they felt grounded and connected; it was also the intersection between where children were and where they were from, a lived context that binds memory, relationship, and culture. This coupling of culture and nature echoes classic Reggio projects, such as *The Amusement Park for Birds*, in which children's questions catalyze design, ethics, animal care, and community encounter (Forman & Gandini, 1994; Warden, 2018).

During the Quilt-Making Project, students collected fabric from home, "many pieces, one quilt," creating a living archive that spanned generations and grounded a shared narrative of belonging, community, and citizenship. Within a Reggio Emilia-inspired NBL framework, the culminating pajama popcorn party beneath the finished quilt became an authentic performance of understanding: Children explained sewing techniques, traced material journeys, and reflected on sustainability, labor, and care. In this sense, the work evolved into a rich collaboration across culture, care, and place, guided by the 7R: Rethink, Refuse, Reduce, Reuse, Repair, Recycle/Compost, and Repurpose/Upcycle.

Ethical reasoning emerged naturally from children's inquiries, especially around animal welfare ("Does shearing hurt sheep?"). Through research and story (e.g., *Rebel Sheep Melo*) and hands-on material study, children recognized that humane shearing supports animal welfare, linking empathy with ecological understanding, consistent with prior findings (Omidvar et al., 2019; Osgood & Ødegård, 2022). Such moments illustrate how rights to culture and participation can be realized through play, making, and dialogue, not just through policy statements (UN, 1989). This study reveals that children's sense of justice and equality, the maturity of their judgment, and their genuine responsibility and solidarity show they are more capable than adults assume; across borders, they deserve to be better understood and respected for their true worth. This trajectory parallels Malaguzzi et al.'s (1998) observation that children reveal ethical and civic capacities that exceed adult expectations. Children also show how teachers' relational responsiveness, including listening, reframing, and acting on children's concerns, nurtures democratic habits and civic imagination (Childress, 2020; Rinaldi, 2011).

At the same time, this case surfaces a persistent systems-level tension: There remains a gap between the vision and implementation of children's rights in education (Jerome et al., 2015). Early childhood education degrees often emphasize cognitive and behavioral domains while giving limited explicit preparation in rights-based pedagogy; without such preparation, enactment risks being superficial (Robson, 2016; Zanatta & Long, 2021). As Curtis (1996) warned, cursory treatment undermines substantive dialogue about participation, equity, and advocacy. The Quilt-Making Project offers a concrete counterexample and a practice-based blueprint: Teaching intentionality, pedagogical documentation, and community-anchored progettazione make rights visible in daily routines. This blueprint aligns with calls to challenge the status quo in early childhood education by centering justice-oriented, culturally sustaining practice (Souto-Manning, 2021) and with evidence that families actively seek Reggio Emilia-inspired programs for their holistic benefits (Harris, 2021). It also illustrates how Reggio is always locally reinterpreted, or "glocalized," rather than replicated wholesale, enabling cultural integrity while sustaining children's rights (Zhang et al., 2025).

Collaboration was evident throughout the Quilt-Making Project. From planning the material to working together to sew, children realized that their contributions mattered for reaching a shared goal. It was through the children's shared inquiry that allowed for such a space for agency, collaboration, cultural identity, and joyful learning. The Quilt-Making Project began with a child's question, unfolded through relationships, and culminated in celebration. Along the way, it stitched together agency, heritage, emotion, and artistry, showing how classrooms can become living expressions of democracy and belonging. When teachers listen pedagogically, design responsively, and document transparently, children's rights are not abstract ideals but daily practices: Voices shape decisions, play and culture are the curriculum, and learning is constructed through many languages of expression (Edwards et al., 1993, 2012; Lundy, 2007; UN, 1989). In short, Reggio Emilia-inspired and nature-attuned progettazione can turn curiosity into citizenship, questions into creations, and classrooms into communities, here realized one 40-patch quilt at a time.

Finally, this study underscores the professional stance required to hold inquiry and accountability together. Teachers used documentation to align emergent learning with standards, without letting standards drive the learning. They treated the environment as a third teacher, curated materials as aesthetic and conceptual provocations, and partnered authentically with families and local artisans, in line with the Reggio tradition (Edwards et al., 1993, 2012; Gandini, 1998, 2004; Inan et al., 2010; Katz, 1993; Rankin, 1997; Vecchi, 2010). In doing so, they enacted a rights-affirming charter recognizable across Reggio's history: Children are subjects of rights, rich in potential, and entitled to relationships, play, and creative thought (Malaguzzi, 1993; Municipality of Reggio Emilia, Infant-Toddler Centers and Preschools, 1998).

IMPLICATIONS

These outcomes underscore the need to preserve classroom spaces where children can pose complex questions, express themselves in multiple modalities, participate actively in cultural and social life, collaborate within and beyond the school, engage deeply with the natural world, and experience intrinsic satisfaction and joy rather than being driven by extrinsic rewards. The project challenges efficiency-driven curricula that mute such inquiry. Reggio Emilia-inspired work not only strengthens children's agency and holistic development but also equips teachers to cultivate a more connected, compassionate, and courageous pedagogy.

Educators who employ Reggio Emilia-inspired curricula will gain the following:

- ways to honor cultural and linguistic heritage as a living resource that enriches early learning environments and connects families, community, and curriculum;
- strategies for co-constructing curricula from children's observations and interests, using documentation and dialogue to sustain inquiry;
- pedagogical uses of craft (i.e., quilting) to integrate science, technology, engineering, and mathematics and to resist one-size-fits-all standardization;
- reflections on teacher agency in designing emotionally and socially meaningful experiences that protect time for play, curiosity, and care; and
- insights into Reggio Emilia-inspired NBL work that intersects with children's moral reasoning, ethics of care for animals and materials, and storytelling.

CONCLUSION

In this school, children's initial curiosity set the direction; their decisions shaped the process; and their labor and voices were central to the outcome. Crucially, the Quilt-Making Project was not simply about making an object but about making meaning together. The culminating pajama party under the handmade quilt was not merely a celebration; it affirmed value, effort, and shared meaning, rendering participation visible as a right rather than a reward.

Rooted in a single classroom, this chapter illustrates how small, emergent, rights-based projects can travel across cultures and systems, offering scalable, context-responsive ways to enact children's rights without narrowing practice. Thus, the chapter offers concrete cases, tools, and frameworks for preparing educators to listen closely, document thoughtfully, and design inquiry-based, nature-based, reflective practice. It models how to integrate cultural heritage, sustainability, and narrative-rich learning in ways that resist narrow accountability pressures while meeting required outcomes. Centering children's rights and participation, it illustrates how early childhood educators can preserve the richness of children's emotional, cultural, and social lives amid intensifying standardization. Ultimately, the chapter affirms educators' professional agency in defending the early years as a space for creativity, belonging, and justice as rights of children.

REFERENCES

Arnott, L., Mevawalla, Z., & Wall, K. (2024). Starting from pedagogy: Supporting children's ethical and playful involvement in early childhood research. *International Journal of Early Years Education, 32*(4), 791–795. DOI: 10.1080/09669760.2024.2440234

Axelsson, S. (2022). *The original learning approach: Weaving together playing, learning, and teaching in early childhood.* Redleaf Press.

Aydemir Özalp, T., & Inan, H. Z. (2021). The process of being a teacher at a Reggio Emilia-inspired preschool: A phenomenological study. *ENAD Journal of Qualitative Research in Education, 27*, 155–181. DOI: 10.14689/enad.27.8

Baker, S. T., Le Courtois, S., & Eberhart, J. (2021). Making space for children's agency with playful learning. *International Journal of Early Years Education, 31*(2), 372–384. DOI: 10.1080/09669760.2021.1997726

Bowen, G. A. (2009). Document analysis as a qualitative research method. *Qualitative Research Journal, 9*(2), 27–40. DOI: 10.3316/QRJ0902027

Childress, T. (2020). Putting relationships first: Using principles from Reggio Emilia to be responsive to our students. *Childhood Education, 96*(6), 46–53. DOI: 10.1080/00094056.2020.1846386

Curtis, M. K. (1996). Free speech and its discontents: The rebellion against general propositions and the danger of discretion. *Wake Forest Law Review, 31*, 419.

Edwards, C., Gandini, L., & Forman, G. (1993). Introduction. In C. Edwards, L. Gandini, & G. Forman (Eds.), *The hundred languages of children: The Reggio Emilia approach to early childhood education* (pp. 3–18). Ablex Publishing.

Edwards, C., Gandini, L., & Forman, G. (2012). Introduction. In C. Edwards, L. Gandini, & G. Forman (Eds.), *The hundred languages of children: The Reggio Emilia experience in transformation* (3rd ed., pp. 5-26). Praeger.

Forman, G., & Gandini, L. (1994). *The amusement park for birds* [Video]. Reggio Children.

Gandini, L. (1998). Educational and caring spaces. In C. Edwards, L. Gandini, & G. Forman (Eds.), *The hundred languages of children: The Reggio Emilia approach—Advanced reflections* (2nd ed., pp. 161–178). Ablex Publishing.

Gandini, L. (2004). Foundations of the Reggio Emilia approach. In Hendrick, J. (Ed.), *Next steps toward teaching the Reggio way: Accepting the challenge to change* (2nd ed., pp. 13–26). Pearson/Merrill/Prentice Hall.

Greene, S., & Nixon, E. (2020). *Children as agents in their worlds: A psychological–relational perspective*. Routledge., DOI: 10.4324/9781315625911

Hanson, K., Poretti, M., & Darbellay, F. (2014). Children's rights between normative and empirical realms. In Stoecklin, D., & Bonvin, J.-M. (Eds.), *Children's rights and the capability approach* (pp. 233–252). Springer., DOI: 10.1007/978-94-017-9091-8_12

Harris, H. A. (2021). Parental choice and perceived benefits of Reggio Emilia inspired programs. *Early Child Development and Care, 191*(1), 123–135. DOI: 10.1080/03004430.2019.1608194

Hewett, V. M. (2001). Examining the Reggio Emilia approach to early childhood education. *Early Childhood Education Journal, 29*(2), 95–100. DOI: 10.1023/A:1012520828095

Inan, H. Z., & Inan, T. (2015). 3Hs education: Examining hands-on, heads-on, and hearts-on early childhood science education. *International Journal of Science Education, 37*(12), 1974–1991. DOI: 10.1080/09500693.2015.1060369

Inan, H. Z., Trundle, K. C., & Kantor, R. (2010). Understanding natural sciences education in a Reggio Emilia–inspired preschool. *Journal of Research in Science Teaching, 47*(10), 1186–1208. DOI: 10.1002/tea.20375

Jerome, L., Emerson, L., Lundy, L., & Orr, K. (2015). *Teaching and learning about child rights: A study of implementation in 26 countries*. UNICEF. https://www.unicef.org/media/63086/file/UNICEF-Teaching-and-learning-about-child-rights.pdf

Jordan, C., & Chawla, L. (2019). A coordinated research agenda for nature-based learning. *Frontiers in Psychology, 10*, 766. Advance online publication. DOI: 10.3389/fpsyg.2019.00766 PMID: 31065246

Katz, L. (1993). What can we learn from Reggio Emilia? In C. Edwards, L. Gandini, & G. Forman (Eds.), *The hundred languages of children: The Reggio Emilia approach to early childhood education* (pp. 19–37). Ablex Publishing.

Landini, A., & Colacino, M. (2023). Inclusione e politiche di valorizzazione della persona: Dalla prospettiva internazionale al contesto della città di Reggio Emilia [Inclusion and policies for the enhancement of the person: From an international perspective to the context of the city of Reggio Emilia]. *Annali online della Didattica e della Formazione Docente, 15*(25), 117–131.

Larimore, R. A. (2019). *Preschool beyond walls: Blending early childhood education and nature-based learning*. Gryphon House.

Lundy, L. (2007). "Voice" is not enough: Conceptualising Article 12 of the United Nations Convention on the Rights of the Child. *British Educational Research Journal, 33*(6), 927–942. DOI: 10.1080/01411920701657033

Malaguzzi, L. (1993). Una carta per tre diritti. [A charter of rights] In *The hundred languages of children* [Exhibition catalogue]. Reggio Children.

Malaguzzi, L. (1994). Your image of the child: Where teaching begins. *Child Care Information Exchange, 96*, 52–61.

Malaguzzi, L., Castagnetti, M., Rubizzi, L., & Vecchi, V. (1998). Introductory note. In Municipality of Reggio Emilia, Infant–Toddler Centers and Preschools (Ed.), *A journey into the rights of children* (L. Morrow, Trans.; 5th ed., pp. 11–12). Reggio Children. (Original work published 1995)

Manera, L. (2022). Art and aesthetic education in the Reggio Emilia approach. *Education 3–13, 50*(4), 483–493. https://doi.org/DOI: 10.1080/03004279.2022.2052230

Municipality of Reggio Emilia, Infant–Toddler Centers and Preschools. (1998). *A journey into the rights of children* (L. Morrow, Trans.; 5th ed.; The Unheard Voice of Children, No. 3). Reggio Children. (Original work published 1995)

Omidvar, N., Wright, T., Beazley, K., & Séguin, D. (2019). Examining children's indoor and outdoor nature exposures and nature-related pedagogic approaches of teachers at two Reggio Emilia preschools in Halifax, Canada. *Journal of Education for Sustainable Development, 13*(2), 215–241. DOI: 10.1177/0973408219872066

Osgood, J., & Ødegård, N. (2022). Crafting granular stories with child-like embodied, affective and sensory encounters that attune to the world's differential becoming. *Australian Journal of Environmental Education, 38*(1), 85–101. DOI: 10.1017/aee.2022.11

Ozkan, U. B. (2019). *Eğitim bilimleri araştırmaları için doküman inceleme yöntemi* [Document analysis methodology for research in educational sciences]. Pegem Akademi.

Potting, J., Hekkert, M., Worrell, E., & Hanemaaijer, A. (2017). *Circular economy: Measuring innovation in product chains*. PBL Netherlands Environmental Assessment Agency. https://www.pbl.nl/en/publications/circular-economy-measuring-innovation-in-product-chains

Rankin, B. (1997). Education as collaboration: Learning from and building on Dewey, Vygotsky, and Piaget. In Hendrick, J. (Ed.), *First steps toward teaching the Reggio way* (pp. 70–83). Prentice-Hall.

Rinaldi, C. (1998). Projected curriculum constructed through documentation—*Progettazione*: An interview with Lella Gandini. In C. Edwards, L. Gandini, & G. Forman (Eds.), *The hundred languages of children: The Reggio Emilia approach—Advanced reflections* (2nd ed., pp. 113–125). Ablex Publishing.

Rinaldi, C. (2011). The pedagogy of listening: The listening perspective in Reggio Emilia. In Edwards, C. P., Gandini, L., & Forman, G. E. (Eds.), *The hundred languages of children: The Reggio Emilia experience in transformation* (3rd ed., pp. 233–246). Praeger., DOI: 10.5040/9798400667664.ch-013

Robson, J. (2016). Early years teachers and young children's rights: The need for critical dialogue. *Research in Teacher Education, 6*(1), 6–11. https://doi.org/DOI: 10.15123/PUB.5091

Souto-Manning, M. (2021). *The critical turn in early childhood education: Challenging the status quo*. Teachers College Press.

Uluay, G. (2024). Nature-based learning in early childhood education. In *Transforming early childhood education: Technology, sustainability, and foundational skills for the 21st century* (pp. 247–260). Özgür Yayın-Dağıtım.

United Nations. (1989). *Convention on the rights of the child*. Office of the United Nations High Commissioner for Human Rights. https://www.ohchr.org/sites/default/files/crc.pdf

Vecchi, V. (2010). *Art and creativity in Reggio Emilia: Exploring the role and potential of ateliers in early childhood education*. Routledge. DOI: 10.4324/9780203854679

Vygotsky, L. S. (1978). *Mind in society*. Harvard University Press.

Warden, C. (2018, February). *Nature pedagogy: A common thread connecting nature-based settings worldwide*. Natural Start Alliance. https://naturalstart.org/resources/articles/nature-pedagogy-common-thread-connecting-nature-based-settings-worldwide

Westerberg, L., & Vandermaas-Peeler, M. (2021). How teachers, peers, and classroom materials support children's inquiry in a Reggio Emilia-inspired preschool. *Early Child Development and Care, 191*(7–8), 1259–1276. DOI: 10.1080/03004430.2021.1881075

Wilson, D. G., Krechevsky, M., Mardell, B., & Rivard, M. (2013). *Visible learners: Promoting Reggio-inspired approaches in all schools*. Wiley.

Zanatta, F., & Long, S. (2021). Rights to the front: Child rights-based pedagogies in early childhood degrees. *Journal of Early Childhood Education Research, 10*(1), 139–165.

Zhang, Q., Yin, J., & Jiang, K. (2025). Glocalization of early childhood curriculum: An ethnographic study on the integration of the Reggio Emilia approach into the Chinese kindergarten curriculum. *Asia Pacific Education Review, 26*(1), 49–60. DOI: 10.1007/s12564-023-09851-3

ADDITIONAL READINGS

Inan, H. Z. (2009). Science education in preschool: How to assimilate the Reggio Emilia pedagogy in a Turkish preschool. *Asia-Pacific Forum on Science Learning and Teaching Education*, 10(2), Article 14.

Inan, H. Z. (2021). Reggio Emilia-ilhamlı okullarda kaynaştırma eğitimi: Meta-etnografik bir araştırma. [Inclusive education in Reggio Emilia–inspired preschools: A meta-ethnographic study]. *Early Childhood Research Journal, 5*(1), 5–43. DOI: 10.24130/eccd-jecs.1967202151284

Inan, H. Z. (2021). Understanding the Reggio Emilia–inspired literacy education: A meta-ethnographic study. *International Journal of Curriculum and Instruction, 13*(1), special issue, 68–92.

Inan, H. Z. (2021). Challenges of distance/online and face-to-face education in the new normal: Experiences of Reggio Emilia-Inspired early childhood educators in Turkey. *Pedagogical Research, 6*(1), em0086. Advance online publication. DOI: 10.29333/pr/9304

Inan, H. Z. (2022). Sustainability of early childhood education inspired by the Reggio Emilia approach during the emergency times: A phenomenographic research. *International Journal on Lifelong Education and Leadership, 8*(1), 36–48. DOI: 10.25233/ijlel.1094854

Compilation of References

Abdelfattah, M. (2015). Realizing a progressive pedagogy: A comparative case study of two Reggio Emilia preschools in San Francisco. *Universal Journal of Educational Research, 3*(12), 1074–1086. DOI: 10.13189/ujer.2015.031217

Acencio, E., & Cordero, H. (2023). Parental styles and their impact on affective development in early childhood. *Revista Iberoamericana De Educación, 7*(1), 1–12. DOI: 10.31876/rie.v6i1.241

Adams, M. J. (1990). *Beginning to read: Thinking and learning about print.* MIT Press.

Africa Reggio Emilia Alliance (AREA). (n.d.). *Reggio Emilia and SA's liberation struggle.* Retrieved from Africa Reggio Emilia Alliance - promoting inspired education from birth to 99: https://reggio.co.za/reggio-emilia-and-sas-liberation-struggle/

Africa Reggio Emilia Alliance. (2017). Tiziana's 2017 visit. Insights, answers and advice. Au-thor. https://reggio.co.za/wp-content/uploads/2017/12/tiziana-filippini-2017-visit-to-sa-insights-answers-advice.pdf

Alaçam, N., & Olgan, R. (2025). How do child portfolios enable assessment? Content analysis of portfolios from a Reggio Emilia-inspired preschool and a university preschool in Türkiye and the United States. *Education 3-13, 53*(5), 756-767. DOI: 10.1080/03004279.2023.2220339

Alaçam, N. (2025). The role of pedagogical documentation in child and parent participation: An investigation of educator and parent perspectives in a Reggio Emilia-inspired preschool. *European Early Childhood Education Research Journal,* •••, 1–18. DOI: 10.1080/1350293X.2025.2508319

Ali, N., Ullah, A., Khan, A. M., Khan, Y., Ali, S., Khan, A. B., Khan, A., Din, M. U., Ullah, R., Khan, U. N., Aziz, T., & Ahmad, M. (2023). Academic performance of children in relation to gender, parenting styles, and socioeconomic status: What attributes are important. *PLoS One*, *18*(11), 1–30. DOI: 10.1371/journal.pone.0286823 PMID: 37967095

Aljabreen, H. (2020). Montessori, Waldorf, and Reggio Emilia: A comparative analysis of alternative models of early childhood education. *International Journal of Early Childhood*, *52*(3), 337–353. DOI: 10.1007/s13158-020-00277-1

Allport, G. W. (2004). *The nature of prejudice*. Basic Books.

American Psychological Association. (2018). Democratic parenting. In *APA dictionary of psychology*. https://dictionary.apa.org/democratic-parenting

Andrews, J. E., Carnine, D. W., Coutinho, M. J., Edgar, E. B., Forness, S. R., Fuchs, L. S., Jordan, D., Kauffman, J. M., Patton, J. M., Paul, J., Rosell, J., Rueda, R., Schiller, E., Skrtic, T. M., & Wong, J. (2000). Bridging the Special Education Divide. *Remedial and Special Education*, *21*(5), 258–267. DOI: 10.1177/074193250002100501

Anthony, C. J., & Ogg, J. (2019). Parent involvement, approaches to learning, and student achievement: Examining longitudinal mediation. *School Psychology*, *34*(4), 376–385. DOI: 10.1037/spq0000282 PMID: 31294595

Aries, P. (1962). Centuries of. *Childhood*, •••, 71.

Armbruster, B. B., Lehr, F., Osborn, J., O'Rourke, R., Beck, I., Carnine, D., & Simmons, D. (2001). *Put reading first*. National Institute for Literacy, National Institute of Child Health and Human Development, US Department of Education. https://www.nichd.nih.gov/publications/product/239

Arnott, L., Mevawalla, Z., & Wall, K. (2024). Starting from pedagogy: Supporting children's ethical and playful involvement in early childhood research. *International Journal of Early Years Education*, *32*(4), 791–795. DOI: 10.1080/09669760.2024.2440234

Arseven, A. (2014). The Reggio Emilia approach and curriculum development process. *International Journal of Academic Research*, *6*(1), 166–171. Advance online publication. DOI: 10.7813/2075-4124.2014/6-1/B.23

Association for Middle Level Education. (2023). *Middle schoolers must play*. https://www.amle.org/middle-schoolers-must-play/

Avetisyan, M., & Konjoyan, H. (2023). A Comparative Analysis Between Traditional and Alternative Early Childhood Education, such as the Maria Montessori Method, Reggio Emilia Pedagogical Approach. *Armenian Journal of Special Education, 7*(2), 65–77. DOI: 10.24234/se.v7i2.8

Axelsson, S. (2022). *The original learning approach: Weaving together playing, learning, and teaching in early childhood.* Redleaf Press.

Aydemir Özalp, T., & Inan, H. Z. (2021). The process of being a teacher at a Reggio Emilia-inspired preschool: A phenomenological study. *ENAD Journal of Qualitative Research in Education, 27*, 155–181. DOI: 10.14689/enad.27.8

Azzolini, D., Mantovani, D., & Santagati, M. (2019). Italy: Four emerging traditions in immigrant education studies. In P. A. J. Stevens & A. G. Dworkin (Eds.), *The Palgrave handbook of race and ethnic inequalities in education*. Palgrave Macmillan. DOI: 10.1007/978-3-319-94724-2_17

Bagnato, S. J., & Ho, H. Y. (2006). High stakes testing with preschool children: Violation of professional standards for evidence based practice in early childhood intervention. *KEDI Journal of Educational Policy, 3*(1), 23–43.

Baker, F. S. (2015). Reflections on the Reggio Emilia approach as inspiration for early childhood teacher education in Abu Dhabi, UAE. *Early Child Development and Care, 185*(6), 982–995. DOI: 10.1080/03004430.2014.974036

Baker, M., & Ryan, J. (2021). Playful provocations and playful mindsets: Teacher learning and identity shifts through playful participatory research. *International Journal of Play, 10*(1), 6–24. DOI: 10.1080/21594937.2021.1878770

Baker, M., & Salas Davila, G. (2018). Inquiry is play: Playful participatory research. *YC Young Children, 73*(5), 64–71. https://www.naeyc.org/resources/pubs/yc/nov2018/inquiry-is-play-playful-participatory-research

Baker, S. T., Le Courtois, S., & Eberhart, J. (2021). Making space for children's agency with playful learning. *International Journal of Early Years Education, 31*(2), 372–384. DOI: 10.1080/09669760.2021.1997726

Balfour, B. (2022). Early childhood education, politics, and memory: Tracing social imaginaries in Reggio Emilia schools' diaries of the 1970s. *Paedagogica Historica, 58*(1), 19–31. DOI: 10.1080/00309230.2020.1769143

Balfour, B. J. V. (2016). Feminist tales of teaching and resistance: Reimagining gender in early childhood education (Reggio Emilia, Italy). *Gender and Education, 28*(3), 445–457. DOI: 10.1080/09540253.2016.1167176

Barad, K. (2003). Posthumanist Performativity: Toward an Understanding of How Matter Comes to Matter. *Signs (Chicago, Ill.)*, *28*(3), 801–831. DOI: 10.1086/345321

Barblett, L., Knaus, M., & Barratt-Pugh, C. (2016). The pushes and pulls of pedagogy in the early years: Competing knowledges and the erosion of play-based learning. *Australasian Journal of Early Childhood*, *41*(4), 36–43. DOI: 10.1177/183693911604100405

Barbour, N. E., & Shalilee, B. D. (1998). Gifted education meets Reggio Emilia: Visions for curriculum in gifted education for young children. *Gifted Child Quarterly*, *42*(4), 228–237. DOI: 10.1177/001698629804200406

Barclay, H. (2025, October). Principal of Mimosa School and PhD Fellow Research Reggio Childhood Studies. (S. Browne, Interviewer)

Barrett, M. (Ed.). (2013). *Interculturalism and multiculturalism: similarities and differences*. Council of Europe Publishing.

Bassok, D., Latham, S., & Roem, A. (2016). Is kindergarten the new first grade? *AERA Open*, *2*(1), 1–31. DOI: 10.1177/2332858415616358 PMID: 26942210

Bateson, G. (1979). *Mind and Nature: A necessary unity*. Dutton.

Bateson, P., & Martin, P. (2013). *Play, playfulness, creativity and innovation*. Cambridge University Press. DOI: 10.1017/CBO9781139057691

Bayer, J., & Bárd, P. (2020). *Hate speech and hate crime in the EU and the evaluation of online content regulation approaches*. European Parliament.

Beach, P. (2025). Research on early literacy in Reggio and Montessori classrooms: A scoping review. *Journal of Early Childhood Literacy*, *25*(3), 694–722. DOI: 10.1177/14687984231186090

Beach, P., & Bolden, B. (2019). Word painting: Using a musical technique to enhance vocabulary. *The Reading Teacher*, *72*(6), 750–754. https://www.jstor.org/stable/26801678. DOI: 10.1002/trtr.1780

Becker, S. (2016). Developing pedagogy for the creation of a school makerspace: Building on constructionism, design thinking, and the Reggio Emilia approach. *The Journal of Educational Thought (JET). Revue de la Pensée Éducative*, *49*(2), 192–209. DOI: 10.55016/ojs/jet.v49i2.46293

Bekemans, L. (2013). Educational challenges and perspectives in multiculturalism vs. interculturalism: Citizenship education for intercultural realities? In Barrett, M. (Ed.), *Interculturalism and multiculturalism: Similarities and differences* (pp. 169–187). Council of Europe.

Beltchenko, L. (2016). Intellectual pursuits of young children through picture book literacy, focusing on Italian preschools. *Gifted Child Today, 39*(3), 145–153. https://doi-org.proxy.queensu.ca/10.1177/1076217516644. DOI: 10.1177/1076217516644636

Benavides, A. W., Freed, A., & Huffling, L. D. (2022). Study Abroad Programs at the Vanguard for Education for Sustainable Development: A Teacher Education Case Study. In Öztürk, M. (Ed.), *Engagement with Sustainable Development in Higher Education. Sustainable Development Goals Series.* Springer., DOI: 10.1007/978-3-031-07191-1_9

Better Start National Early Years Quality Development Service. (n.d.). What is the role of the inclusion co-ordinator? Author. https://aim.gov.ie/app/uploads/2021/05/AIM-role-of-the-inclusion-co-ordinator.pdf

Bianchi, G. (2020). *Sustainability competences: A systematic literature review.* https://op.europa.eu/publication/manifestation_identifier/PUB_KJNA30555ENN

Biesta, G. J. (2011). *Learning democracy in school and society: Education, lifelong learning, and the politics of citizenship.* Springer Science & Business Media. DOI: 10.1007/978-94-6091-512-3

Biraimah, K. L., & Jotia, A. L. (2013). The longitudinal effects of study abroad programs on teachers' content knowledge and perspectives: Fulbright-Hays group projects abroad in Botswana and Southeast Asia. *Journal of Studies in International Education, 17*(4), 433–454. DOI: 10.1177/1028315312464378

Bobbio, A. (2007). *I diritti sottili del bambino. Implicazioni pedagogiche e prospettive formative per una nuova cultura dell'infanzia.* Armando Editore.

Bodrova, E., & Leong, D. J. (2015). Vygotskian and post-Vygotskian views on children's play. *American Journal of Play, 7*(3), 371–388.

Bonacini, L., & Girardi, R. (Eds.). (2021). *Annuario della scuola reggiana. Anno scolastico 2021-2022.* Provincia di Reggio Emilia.

Bond, V. L. (2013). Follow and facilitate: What music educators can learn from the Reggio Emilia approach. *General Music Today, 27*(1), 24–28. DOI: 10.1177/1048371313480798

Bond, V. L. (2015). Created in context: A comparative case study of the use of music in two Reggio Emilia-inspired schools. *Early Childhood Education Journal, 43*(2), 119–126. DOI: 10.1007/s10643-014-0639-4

Bond, V. L. (2015). Sounds to share: The state of music education in three Reggio Emilia–inspired North American preschools. *Journal of Research in Music Education, 62*(4), 462–484. DOI: 10.1177/0022429414555017

Bonfield, T., & Horgan, K. (2016). *Learning to teach: Teaching to learn.* Gill Education.

Bonnett, M. (2002). Education for sustainability as a frame of mind. *Environmental Education Research, 8*(1), 9–20. DOI: 10.1080/13504620120109619

Borda, O. F. (2001). Participatory (Action) Research in Social. *Handbook of action research: Participative inquiry and practice*, 27.

Bowen, G. A. (2009). Document analysis as a qualitative research method. *Qualitative Research Journal, 9*(2), 27–40. DOI: 10.3316/QRJ0902027

Bowyer, R. (2025, August). Soul Action School Principal and Foundation Phase Teacher . (S. Browne, Interviewer)

Braidotti, R. (2013). *The Posthuman.* Polity Press.

Breen, F., Ring, E., Stapleton, S., & Kelleher, S. (2018). LINC programme: Enabling leadership for inclusion through an innovative competency-based blended adult continuing professional learning programme. The Adult Learner 2018, 99-115. https://www.aontas.com/assets/resources/Adult-Learner-Journal/AONTAS-Adult-Learner-Journal-2018.pdf

Broderick, A. (2015). *The long and winding road to equality and inclusion for persons with disabilities. The united nations convention on the rights of persons with disabilities.* Intersentia.

Bronfenbrenner, U. (1977). Toward an experimental ecology of human development. *The American Psychologist, 32*(7), 513–531. DOI: 10.1037/0003-066X.32.7.513

Bronfenbrenner, U. (1979). *The ecology of human development: Experiments by nature and design.* Harvard University Press.

Bronfenbrenner, U. (1986). Ecology of the family as a context for human development: Research perspectives. *Developmental Psychology, 22*(6), 723–742. DOI: 10.1037/0012-1649.22.6.723

Broström, S. (2017). Curriculum in preschool: Adjustment or a possible liberation? *Nordic Journal of Studies in Educational Policy, 3*(1), 19–28.

Brown, K. P. (1995). *Developing strategies to encourage and improve parent participation in an early childhood program adapting the Reggio Emilia approach to early childhood* (Publication No. 1768) [Master's thesis, University of Dayton]. eCommons University of Dayton. https://ecommons.udayton.edu/graduate_theses/1768

Browne, J. (2017). Tizianna Filippini 2017 visit to SA insights answers advice. Johannesburg: Africa Reggio Emilia Alliance (AREA).

Browne, T. (2025, September). Co-Founder and Co-Ordinator of the Africa Reggio Emilia Alliance (AREA). (A. a. Sarah Browne, Interviewer)

Brownell, J. E., & Swaner, L. E. (2009). High-impact practices: Applying the learning outcomes literature to the development of successful campus programs. *Peer Review : Emerging Trends and Key Debates in Undergraduate Education, 11*(2), 26–30.

Brown, S., & Vaughan, C. (2009). *Play: How it shapes the brain, opens the imagination, and invigorates the soul.* Avery.

Bruner, J. (1996). *The culture of education.* Harvard University Press. DOI: 10.4159/9780674251083

Bruner, J. (1997). Celebrating divergence: Piaget and Vygotsky. *Human Development, 40*(2), 63–73. DOI: 10.1159/000278705

Bruner, J. S. (2003). *Making Stories: Law, Literature, Life.* Harvard University Press.

Brussoni, M., Gibbons, R., Gray, C., Ishikawa, T., Sandseter, E. B. H., Bienenstock, A., & Tremblay, M. S. (2015). What is the relationship between risky outdoor play and health in children? *International Journal of Environmental Research and Public Health, 12*(6), 6423–6454. DOI: 10.3390/ijerph120606423 PMID: 26062038

Bruyere, E., & Garbarino, J. (2010). The ecological perspective on the human rights of children. In Kamerman, S. B., Phipps, S., & Ben-Arieh, A. (Eds.), *From child welfare to child well-being: An international perspective on knowledge in the service of policy making* (pp. 137–154). Springer., DOI: 10.1007/978-90-481-3377-2_9

Burghardt, G. M. (2011). Defining and recognizing play. In Pellegrini, A. D. (Ed.), *The Oxford handbook of the development of play* (pp. 9–18). Oxford University Press.

Byrne, M., Schroeter, K., Carter, S., & Mower, J. (2009). The professional portfolio: An evi-dence-based assessment method. *Journal of Continuing Education in Nursing, 40*(12), 542–552. https://journals.healio.com/doi/10.3928/00220124-20091119-07

Cagliari, P., Castagnetti, M., Giudici, C., Rinaldi, C., Vecchi, V., & Moss, P. (2016). *Loris Malaguzzi and the schools of Reggio Emilia: A selection of his writings and speeches, 1945-1993.* Routledge., DOI: 10.4324/9781315778631

Capra, F. (2005). *Ecoalfabeto. L'orto dei bambini*. Stampa Alternativa.

Capra, F., & Luisi, P. L. (2014). *The Systems View of Life: A Unifying Vision* (1st ed.). Cambridge University Press., DOI: 10.1017/CBO9780511895555

Carle, E. (1987). *The very hungry caterpillar*. Philomel Books.

Carle, E. (2007). *The tiny seed*. Neugebauer Press.

Carlsson-Paige, N., McLaughlin, G. B., & Almon, J. W. (2015). *Reading instruction in Kindergarten: Little to gain and much to lose*. Alliance for Childhood and Defending the Early Years. https://deyproject.files.wordpress.com/2015/01/readinginkindergarten_online-1.pdf

Carter, M. (2016, November/December). Study tours reveal a new world of ideas: An interview with Eliana Elias. *Exchange*, •••, 26–31. https://hub.exchangepress.com/wp-content/uploads/2024/09/5023226.pdf

Castañeda, M. E., & Zirger, M. L. (2011). Making the most of the "new" study abroad: Social capital and the short-term sojourn. *Foreign Language Annals*, *44*(3), 544–564. DOI: 10.1111/j.1944-9720.2011.01146.x

Cavanaugh, D. M., Clemence, K. J., Teale, M. M., Rule, A. C., & Montgomery, S. E. (2017). Kindergarten scores, storytelling, executive function, and motivation improved through literacy-rich guided play. *Early Childhood Education Journal*, *45*(6), 831–843. DOI: 10.1007/s10643-016-0832-8

Centre for Early Childhood Development and Education. (2006). Síolta: The national quality framework for early childhood education. Author. Síolta

Chafel, J. A. (1991, April). The play of children: Developmental processes and policy implications. []. New York: Kluwer Academic Publishers-Human Sciences Press.]. *Child and Youth Care Forum*, *20*(2), 115–132. DOI: 10.1007/BF00756693

Cheatham, J. P., & Allor, J. H. (2012). The influence of decodability in early reading text on reading achievement: A review of the evidence. *Reading and Writing*, *25*(9), 2223–2246. DOI: 10.1007/s11145-011-9355-2

Chicken, S. (2023). 'Doing Reggio?' Exploring the complexity of 'curriculum' migration through a comparison of Reggio Emilia, Italy and the EYFS, England. *Global Studies of Childhood*, *13*(4), 322–340. DOI: 10.1177/20436106211068041

Children's Rights Alliance. (2025). Report card 2025. Author. https://childrensrights.ie/wp-content/uploads/2025/02/FINAL-Report-Card-2025.pdf

Childress, T. (2020). Putting relationships first: Using principles from Reggio Emilia to be responsive to our students. *Childhood Education*, *96*(6), 46–53. DOI: 10.1080/00094056.2020.1846386

Chiwamba, S. V. (2016). Investigation on the applicability of Reggio Emilia Approach in teaching early childhood education: An intensive comparison between China and Tanzania. DOI: 10.5539/jedp.v6n2p29

Chng, A., Waniganayake, M., & Andrews, R. (2022). Inviting inquiry on pedagogical documentation in Singapore: Perspectives of parents and teachers. *European Early Childhood Education Research Journal*, *30*(2), 296–308. DOI: 10.1080/1350293X.2022.2046837

Claxton, G. (2008). *What's the point of school? Rediscovering the heart of education*. Oneworld.

Clément, G., & Jones, L. (2015). *Piccola pedagogia dell'erba. Riflessioni sul giardino planetario*. DeriveApprodi.

Cochran-Smith, M., & Lytle, S. L. (2009). *Inquiry as stance: Practitioner research for the next generation*. Teachers College Press.

Comune di Reggio Emilia . (1977, June 27). Foto storica Sudafrica. *Reggio Emilia, 27.06.1977 – Corteo cittadino contro il colonialismo e l'apartheid*. Reggio Emilia, Italy: Comune di Reggio Emilia .

Comune di Reggio Emilia . (n.d.). Foto storica Sudafrica. *Rea Silvia, la seconda nave della solidarietà italiana parte da Livorno l'16.03.1984 ed è diretta a Luanda, Maputo e Dar es Salam.* Comune Di Reggio Emilia.

Corte, E., Giudici, C., & De Poi, S. (A cura di). (2022). *Un pensiero in festa: le metafore visive nei processi di apprendimento dei bambini*. Reggio Children.

Costello, J. (2015). Students' stories of studying abroad: Reflections upon return. *Journal of International Students*, *5*(1), 50–59. DOI: 10.32674/jis.v5i1.442

Council of Europe. (2008). *The White Paper on intercultural dialogue – Living together as equals with dignity.* Council of Europe.

Council of Europe. (2016). *Competences for a democratic culture. Living together as equals in culturally diverse and democratic societies*. Council of Europe Publishing.

Craft, A. (2013). Childhood in a digital age: Creative play. *British Journal of Educational Studies*, *61*(1), 123–141.

Curtis, M. K. (1996). Free speech and its discontents: The rebellion against general propositions and the danger of discretion. *Wake Forest Law Review*, *31*, 419.

Cutcher, A. (2013). Art spoken here: Reggio Emilia for the big kids. *International Journal of Art & Design Education*, *32*(3), 318–330. DOI: 10.1111/j.1476-8070.2013.12028.x

D'Souza, K. (2024, October 18). *Nature's classroom: Why preschoolers need more time outdoors*. EdSource. https://edsource.org/2024/learning-amid-the-leaves-why-preschoolers-need-more-time-outdoors/720758#:~:text=Yet%2C%20that's%20the%20exception%20to,attention%20spans%20and%20frayed%20nerves

Dahlberg, G., & Moss, P. (2005). *Ethics and politics in early childhood education*. Routledge.

Dahlberg, G., Moss, P., & Pence, A. (2013). *Beyond quality in early childhood education and care: Languages of evaluation* (3rd ed.). Routledge. DOI: 10.4324/9780203371114

Dahl, R. (1961). *James and the giant peach*. Knopf.

Dar, A. (2025). A critical perspective on children's right to play. In Llobet, V., Reynaert, D., Imoh, A.T.-D., & Vandenhole, W. (Eds.). *Critical Children's Rights Studies: A Research Companion (1st ed.)*, 255-267. Routledge. DOI: 10.4324/9781003510284-18

Davis, J. (2009). Revealing the research 'hole' of early childhood education for sustainability: A preliminary survey of the literature. *Environmental Education Research, 15*(2), 227–241. DM 35/2020 [Decreto Ministeriale n.35 del 22 giugno 2020]. *Linee guida per l'insegnamento dell'educazione civica, ai sensi dell'articolo 3 della legge 20 agosto 2019, n. 92.* Italian Ministry of Education and Merit.DOI: 10.1080/13504620802710607

DeGraaf, D., Slagter, C., Larsen, K., & Ditta, E. (2013). The long-term personal and professional impacts of participating in a study abroad program. *Frontiers: The Interdisciplinary Journal of Study Abroad*, *23*(1), 42–59. DOI: 10.36366/frontiers.v23i1.328

Department of Basic Education - Republic of South Africa. (2022). *Implications for ECD shift to Basic Education.* Retrieved from Basic Education - Department of Basic Education South Africa: https://www.education.gov.za/ECDFunctionShift2021.aspx

Department of Basic Education - Republic of South Africa. (2025, February 18). *DBE briefs Portfolio Committee on ECD and Grade R as the new compulsory grade.* Retrieved from Department of Basic Education - Republic of South Africa: https://www.education.gov.za/ArchivedDocuments/ArchivedArticles/ECDandGradeRasthenewcompulsorygradeR.aspx

Department of Basic Education. (2024). https://thrivebyfive.co.za/findings-enrolled-children/. Retrieved from Thrive by Five Index: https://thrivebyfive.co.za/wp-content/uploads/2025/09/TB5-Main-Report_FINAL.pdf

Department of Children and Youth Affairs. (2015). National strategy on children and young people's participation in decision-making, 2015 – 2020. Author. https://assets.gov.ie/24462/48a6f98a921446ad85829585389e57de.pdf

Department of Children and Youth Affairs. (2016). Diversity, equality and inclusion charter and guidelines for early childhood care and education. Author. diversity-equality-and-inclusion-charter-and-guidelines-for-early-childhood-care-and-e.pdf

Department of Children and Youth Affairs. (2019) An end of year one review of the access and inclusion model (AIM). Author. https://aim.gov.ie/app/uploads/2021/05/AIM-end-of-year-one-review.pdf

Department of Education. (2023). Statistical bulletin – July 2023. Author. https://www.gov.ie/pdf/?file=https://assets.gov.ie/263000/f2932136-6191-4e56-9af0-5b315e85702f.pdf#page=null

Department of Education. (2025). A guide to early years education inspection. Author. https://assets.gov.ie/static/documents/a-guide-to-early-years-education-inspection-eyei-updated-january-2025.pdf

Dewey, D. P., Ring, S., Gardner, D., & Belnap, R. K. (2013). Social network formation and development during study abroad in the Middle East. *System*, *41*(2), 269–282. DOI: 10.1016/j.system.2013.02.004

Dewey, J. (1910). *How we think.* D.C. Heath & Co. DOI: 10.1037/10903-000

Dewey, J. (1938). *Experience and education.* Macmillan.

Di Maggio, L. M. (2016). *An analysis of study abroad as a factor to increase student engagement and reduce dropouts in higher education institutions* (Publication No. 10108237) [Doctoral Dissertation, Saint Peter's University]. ProQuest Dissertations and Theses Global. https://search.proquest.com/openview/1ec4cb1a9cf21a765ced5f333fe7c99b/1?pq-origsite=gscholar&cbl=18750

Di Rocco, E. (2024). Sostenibilità è creare (buoni) legami. In Augelli, A. (Ed.), *Dello scarto e del recupero: Orientamenti di educazione alla sostenibilità* (pp. 120–124). Franco Angeli.

Diamond, A. (2013). Executive functions. *Annual Review of Psychology, 64*(1), 135–168. DOI: 10.1146/annurev-psych-113011-143750 PMID: 23020641

Diana Municipal Preschool. (2001). *Forme aformate.*

Dillen, A. (2006). Children between liberation and care: Ethical perspectives on the rights of children and parent-child relationships. *International Journal of Children's Spirituality, 11*(2), 237–250. DOI: 10.1080/13644360600797230

DM 183/2024 [Decreto Ministeriale n.183 del 7 settembre 2024]. *Adozione delle Linee guida per l'insegnamento dell'educazione civica.* Italian Ministry of Education and Merit.

Dodd-Nufrio, A. T. (2011). Reggio Emilia, Maria Montessori, and John Dewey: Dispelling teachers' misconceptions and understanding theoretical foundations. *Early Childhood Education Journal, 39*(4), 235–237. DOI: 10.1007/s10643-011-0451-3

Donnelly-Smith, L. (2009). Global learning through short-term study abroad. *Peer Review : Emerging Trends and Key Debates in Undergraduate Education, 11*(4), 12–15.

Dunn, A. H., Dotson, E. K., Cross, S. B., Kesner, J., & Lundahl, B. (2014). Reconsidering the local after a transformative global experience: A comparison of two study abroad programs for preservice teachers. *Action in Teacher Education, 36*(4), 283–304. DOI: 10.1080/01626620.2014.948227

Dwyer, M. M. (2004). More is better: The impact of study abroad program duration. *Frontiers: The Interdisciplinary Journal of Study Abroad, 10*(1), 151–163. DOI: 10.36366/frontiers.v10i1.139

Eckhoff, A., & Spearman, M. (2009). Rethink, reimagine, reinvent: The Reggio Emilia approach to incorporating reclaimed materials in children's artworks. *Art Education, 62*(2), 10–16. DOI: 10.1080/00043125.2009.11519007

Edwards, C., Gandini, L., & Foreman, G. (Eds.). (1998). *The hundred languages of children.* The Reggio Emilia Approach. Advanced Reflections. Ablex Publishing Corporation.

Edwards, C., Gandini, L., & Forman, G. (1993). Introduction. In C. Edwards, L. Gandini, & G. Forman (Eds.), *The hundred languages of children: The Reggio Emilia approach to early childhood education* (pp. 3–18). Ablex Publishing.

Edwards, C., Gandini, L., & Forman, G. (2012). Introduction. In C. Edwards, L. Gandini, & G. Forman (Eds.), *The hundred languages of children: The Reggio Emilia experience in transformation* (3rd ed., pp. 5-26). Praeger.

Edwards, C. P., & Gandini, L. (2018). The Reggio Emilia approach to early childhood education. In Roopnarine, J. P., Johnson, J. E., Flannery Quinn, S., & Patte, M. M. (Eds.), *Handbook of international perspectives on early childhood education* (pp. 365–378). Routledge., DOI: 10.4324/9781315562193-26

Edwards, C., & Gandini, L. (2020). The Reggio Emilia approach to early childhood education. In Roopnarine, J. L., Johnson, J. E., Flannery Quinn, S., & Patte, M. M. (Eds.), *Handbook of interna-tional perspectives on early childhood education* (pp. 365–378). Routledge.

Edwards, C., Gandini, L., & Forman, G. (Eds.). (2012). *The hundred languages of children: The Reggio Emilia experience in transformation* (3rd ed.). Praeger.

Edwards, S. (2005). Children's learning and developmental potential: Examining the theoretical informants of early childhood curricula from the educator's perspective. *Early Years Journal of International Research and Development, 25*(1), 67–80. DOI: 10.1080/09575140500043161

Elliott, E. M. (2005). Changing perspectives in early childhood education: Recasting the Reggio Emilia approach. *Journal of Early Childhood Teacher Education, 25*(2), 153–163. DOI: 10.1080/1090102050250208

Emerson, A. M., & Linder, S. M. (2021). A review of research of the Reggio Inspired approach: An integrative re-framing. *Early Years Journal of International Research and Development, 41*(4), 428–442. DOI: 10.1080/09575146.2019.1591350

European Agency for Special Needs and Inclusive Education. (2017a). *Inclusive early child-hood education: New insights and tools – Contributions from a European study. (M, Kyri-azopoulou, P. Bartolo, E. Björck-Åkesson* (Giné, C., & Bellour, F., Eds.). Author., https://www.european-agency.org/sites/default/files/IECE_Synthesis _Report_2017.pdf

European Agency for Special Needs and Inclusive Education. (2017b) Inclusive early child-hood education self-reflection tool. (E. Björck-Åkesson, M, Kyriazopoulou, C. Giné & P. Barto-lo, (Eds)). Author. https://www.european-agency.org/sites/default/files/IECE%20Environment%20Self-Reflection%20Tool.pdf

European Agency for Special Needs and Inclusive Education. (2025). *Teacher professional learning in Finland and Ireland: Findings report* (Symeonidou, S., Topalli, P. Z., Bilgeri, M., Svarinskaite, R., & Kefallinou, A., Eds.). Author., https://www.european-agency.org/sites/default/files/Findings_Report_on_Teacher_Professional_Learning.pdf

European Commission. Joint Research Centre. (2022). *GreenComp, the European sustainability competence framework*. Publications Office of the European Union. https://data.europa.eu/doi/10.2760/13286

European Commission/EACEA/Eurydice. (2025). Key data on early childhood education and care in Europe 2025: Eurydice report. OECD, 2001.

Eurostat. (2025). *Eurostat Regional Yearbook: 2025 edition*. Publication Office of the European Union.

Fabbi, C. (2022, October). The Reggio Emilia approach - quotation on the rights of the child. Johannesburg, Gauteng, South Africa.

Feliu-Torruella, M., Fernández-Santín, M., & Atenas, J. (2021). Building relationships between museums and schools: Reggio Emilia as a bridge to educate children about heritage. *Sustainability (Basel)*, *13*(7), 3713. DOI: 10.3390/su13073713

Fernández Santín, M., & Feliu Torruella, M. (2017). Reggio Emilia: An essential tool to develop critical thinking in early childhood. *Journal of New Approaches in Educational Research*, *6*(1), 50–56. DOI: 10.7821/naer.2017.1.207

Fernández-Santín, M., & Feliu-Torruella, M. (2020). Developing critical thinking in early childhood through the philosophy of Reggio Emilia. *Thinking Skills and Creativity*, *37*, 100686. DOI: 10.1016/j.tsc.2020.100686

Ferrari, A., & Giacopini, E. (2005). *Remida day: Muta... menti* (1st ed., Engl. version). Reggio Children.

Ferri, G. (Ed.). (with Malaguzzi, L., Castagnetti, M., Rubizzi, L., & Vecchi, V.). (1995). *In viaggio coi diritti delle bambine e dei bambini: Autori i bambini stessi: bambine e bambini fra i 5 e i 6 anni della scuola "Diana" = A journey into the rights of children: as seen by children themselves: 5 and 6 year-old children of the "Diana" school* (L. Morrow, Trans.). Reggio Children.

Festervand, T. A., & Tillery, K. R. (2001). Short-term study-abroad programs–A professional development tool for international business faculty. *Journal of Education for Business*, *2*(77), 106–111. DOI: 10.1080/08832320109599058

Firlik, R. J. (1994). Reggio Emilia, Italy Preschools: The Synergies of Theory and Practice.

First National Bank (FNB) and Innovation Edge, i. c. (2022). *Thrive By Five Index Report - Revised 2022.* First National Bank (FNB) and Innovation Edge, in collaboration with the DBE, and is supported by the United States Agency for International Development (USAID) and ECD Measure.

Fischer, K. (2009, February 20). Short study-abroad trips can have lasting effect, research suggests. *Chronicle of Higher Education.* https://www.chronicle.com/article/short-study-abroad-trips-can-have-lasting-effect-research-suggests-117376/

Fisher, P. A., & Lombardi, J. (2025). *The new ecology of early childhood: Revisiting Bronfenbrenner's theory in the context of contemporary challenges and opportunities* [Working paper]. Stanford Center on Early Childhood, Stanford University. https://earlychildhood.stanford.edu/new-ecology-early-childhood-revisiting-bronfenbrenners-theory-context-contemporary-challenges-and

Foerch, D. F., & Iuspa, F. (2016). The internationalization of the Reggio Emilia philosophy. *Contrapontos, 16*(2), 321–350. DOI: 10.14210/contrapontos.v16n2.p321-350

Fondazione Reggio Children. Play Explore Research Reggio Emilia conference proceedings, 2024, Reggio Emilia, Edizioni Junior

Forman, G., & Gandini, L. (1994). *The amusement park for birds* [Video]. Reggio Children.

Fortunati, A. (2010a). Children's identity and the quality of ECEC services. In: *Early Childhood Education and Care Services in the European Union Countries. Proceedings of the ChildONEurope Seminar and integrated review.* Istituto degli Innocenti.

Fortunati, A. (2010b). Italy. Public Policies. In: M. Cochran & R. S. New *(Eds.), Early childhood education. An international encyclopedia, vol. 4.* Praeger Publishers.

Fortunati, A. (2010c). Italy. Quality. In: M. Cochran & R. S. New (Eds.), *Early Childhood Education. An International Encyclopedia* (Vol. 4). Praeger Publishers.

Fortunati, A. (1998). *Il mestiere dell'educare. Bambini, educatori e genitori nei nidi e nei nuovi servizi per l'infanzia e la famiglia.* Edizioni Junior.

Fortunati, A. (2006). *The education of young children as a community project. Children, teachers and parents in the infant-toddler centers and the new early childhood services.* Edizioni Junior.

Fortunati, A. (2014). *San Miniato's approach to the education of children. Children's protagonism, family participation and community responsibility toward a curriculum of possibilities.* ETS.

Fortunati, A. (2016b). *Can design be sustainable? No, design must be sustainable.* Exchange Magazine.

Fortunati, A. (Ed.). (2016a). *Towards a curriculum open to possibilities. Children's protagonism and education. Thoughts, actions, tools.* La Bottega di Geppetto.

Fortunati, A. (Ed.). (2020). *Trust, opportunity, time. Looking at, imagining, building the future with children's eyes.* La Bottega di Geppetto.

Fortunati, A., & Catarsi, E. (Eds.). (2012). *The Tuscan Approach to early childhood education.* Edizioni Junior.

Fortunati, A., & Pagni, B. (Eds.). (2018). *Children and the revolution of diversities.* La Bottega di Geppetto.

Fortunati, A., & Pucci, A. (Eds.). (2019). *Together, unique and different. New ideas from the Tuscan Approach to children's education.* Istituto degli Innocenti.

Fortunati, A., & Tognetti, G. (Eds.). (2017). *Towards a curriculum open to possibilities. Children's protagonism and education. MP4.* La Bottega di Geppetto.

Franklin, K. (2010). Long-term career impact and professional applicability of the study abroad experience. *Frontiers: The Interdisciplinary Journal of Study Abroad, 19*(1), 169–190. DOI: 10.36366/frontiers.v19i1.279

Freeman, R. (2011). Reggio Emilia, Vygotsky, and family childcare: Four American providers describe their pedagogical practice. *Child Care in Practice, 17*(3), 227–246. DOI: 10.1080/13575279.2011.571236

Freire, P. (1970). *Pedagogy of the oppressed.* Herder and Herder.

Gabli, S. (2013, March 24). *CNN news reports on Reggio Emilia Italy early childhood schools in the US* [Video]. YouTube. https://youtu.be/XVv5ZL9nlgs?si=h38ZvLZldQf36cPX

Gandini, L. (1998). Educational and caring spaces. In C. Edwards, L. Gandini, & G. Forman (Eds.), *The hundred languages of children: The Reggio Emilia approach—Advanced reflections* (2nd ed., pp. 161–178). Ablex Publishing.

Gandini, L. (2008). Introduction to the fundamental values of the education of young children in Reggio Emilia. Northern American Reggio Emilia Alliance. https://www.reggioalliance.org/wp-content/uploads/2021/08/INTRODUCTION-EDITED-FOR-BOOK-rev-LG-10-20-08.pdf

Gandini, L. (2012). The atelier: A conversation with Vea Vecchi. In C. Edwards, L. Gandini & G. Foreman (Eds.), The hundred languages of children: The Reggio Emilia experience trans-formation (3rd ed.) (pp. 303-316). Prager.

Gandini, L. (1993, November). Fundamentals of the Reggio Emilia approach to early childhood education. *Young Children, 49*(1), 4–8. https://www.jstor.org/stable/42725533

Gandini, L. (2004). Foundations of the Reggio Emilia approach. In Hendrick, J. (Ed.), *Next steps toward teaching the Reggio way: Accepting the challenge to change* (2nd ed., pp. 13–26). Pearson/Merrill/Prentice Hall.

Gandini, L. (2012). *The Hundred languages of children: The Reggio Emilia experience in transformation.* Praeger.

Gandini, L., & Kaminsky, A. (2005). Remida, the creative recycling center in Reggio Emilia: An interview with Elena Giacopini, Graziella Brighenti, Arturo Bertoldi, and Alba Ferrari. *Innovations in Early Education: The International Reggio Exchange, 12*(3), 1–13.

Gardner, H. (1993). *Multiple intelligences: The theory in practice.* Basic Books.

Giamminuti, S., Cagliari, P., Giudici, C., & Strozzi, P. (2024). *The role of the pedagogista in Reggio Emilia: Voices and Ideas for a Dialectic Educational Experience.* Routledge., DOI: 10.4324/9781003181026

Giamminuti, S., & Merewether, J. (2023). The Reggio Emilia atelier as a place of disruption: Remaking pedagogical alliances through aesthetics and experimentation. *Pedagogies, 18*(4), 746–766. DOI: 10.1080/1554480X.2022.2106233

Giamminuti, S., Merewether, J., & Blaise, M. (2023). Aesthetic-ethical-political movements in professional learning: Encounters with feminist new materialisms and Reggio Emilia in early childhood research. In *Non-Linear Perspectives on Teacher Development* (pp. 240–252). Routledge., DOI: 10.4324/9781003372097-16

Gilman, S. (2007). Including the child with special needs: Learning from Reggio Emilia. *Theory into Practice, 46*(1), 23–31. DOI: 10.1080/00405840709336545

Ginsburg, K. R. (2007). The importance of play in promoting healthy child development and maintaining strong parent–child bonds. *Pediatrics, 119*(1), 182–191. DOI: 10.1542/peds.2006-2697 PMID: 17200287

Giovannini, E. (2018). *L'utopia sostenibile*. Laterza.

Giudici, C., Barchi, P., & Rinaldi, C. (Eds.). (2011). *Making learning visible: Children as individual and group learners*. Reggio Children.

Glassman, M. (2001). Dewey and Vygotsky: Society, experience, and inquiry in educational practice. *Educational Researcher, 30*(4), 3–14. DOI: 10.3102/0013189X030004003

Gouzouasis, P., & Yanko, M. (2018). Learning stories and Reggio Emilia-inspired pedagogical documentation: Formative methods of assessment for the elementary school music classroom. In *Handbook of cultural studies and education* (pp. 486–502). Routledge., DOI: 10.4324/9781351202398-30

Government of Ireland. (2018). First 5: A whole of government strategy for babies, young chil-dren and their families. Government Publications Office. https://assets.gov.ie/31184/62acc54f4bdf4405b74e53a4afb8e71b.pdf

Government of Ireland. (2024a). Aistear: the early childhood curriculum framework. Author. https://curriculumonline.ie/getmedia/1e9e4eff-5d44-4950-bfa6-a28f43895d3f/Aistear-FW-ENG.pdf

Government of Ireland. (2024b). Aistear – Guidance for good practice. Author. https://curriculumonline.ie/getmedia/f2932ad8-326d-4cb7-9d6c-09bc138f9a8a/Aistear-G-ENG.pdf

Greene, S., & Nixon, E. (2020). *Children as agents in their worlds: A psychological–relational perspective*. Routledge., DOI: 10.4324/9781315625911

Guattari, F. (2005). The three ecologies. *Continuum*.

Guerra, M., & Zuccoli, F. (2012). Finished and Unfinished Objects: Supporting Children's Creativity Through Materials. *Procedia: Social and Behavioral Sciences, 51*, 721–727. DOI: 10.1016/j.sbspro.2012.08.231

Gül Hazar, R., & Yilmaz, A. (2025). Using a teacher portfolio as a professional development tool for Turkish early childhood teachers. *Journal of Early Childhood Teacher Education*, •••, 1–22. DOI: 10.1080/10901027.2025.2581790

Guo, K., & Rouse, E. (2025). Searching for evidence-based practice: A qualitative meta-synthesis of the research on Reggio Emilia practices in Australian early years settings. *Australian Journal of Education, 69*(1), 58–78. DOI: 10.1177/00049441241302831

Guy-Evans, O. (2025). *Bronfenbrenner's ecological systems theory.* Simply Psychology. https://www.simplypsychology.org/bronfenbrenner.html

Hadley, E. B., Dickinson, D. K., Hirsh-Pasek, K., & Golinkoff, R. M. (2019). Building semantic networks: The impact of a vocabulary intervention on preschoolers' depth of word knowledge. *Reading Research Quarterly, 54*(1), 41–61. DOI: 10.1002/rrq.225

Haines, S. J., Strolin-Goltzman, J., & Dinis, R. J. J. (2021). Odyssey in the Azores: A US travel-study course preparing teachers for the magic of the profession. *Teaching and Teacher Education, 106. Article, 103430*, 1–10. DOI: 10.1016/j.tate.2021.103430

Hanson, K., Poretti, M., & Darbellay, F. (2014). Children's rights between normative and empirical realms. In Stoecklin, D., & Bonvin, J.-M. (Eds.), *Children's rights and the capability approach* (pp. 233–252). Springer., DOI: 10.1007/978-94-017-9091-8_12

Haraway, D. (2008). *When species meet.* University of Minnesota Press.

Haraway, D. (2016). *Staying with the trouble: Making kin in the Chthulucene.* Duke University Press.

Harmon, F., & Viruru, R. (2018). Debunking the myth of the efficacy of "push-down academics": How rigid, teacher-centered, academic early learning environments disempower young children. *Journal of Family Strengths, 18*(1), 11. Advance online publication. DOI: 10.58464/2168-670X.1390

Harris, H. A. (2021). Parental choice and perceived benefits of Reggio Emilia inspired programs. *Early Child Development and Care, 191*(1), 123–135. DOI: 10.1080/03004430.2019.1608194

Hart, R. A. (1992). *Children's participation from tokenism to citizenship, Innocenti Essays* (No. 4). UNICEF International Child Development Centre. https://unesdoc.unesco.org/ark:/48223/pf0000171538

Heath, S. B. (1982). What no bedtime story means: Narrative skills at home and school. *Language in Society, 11*(1), 49–76. DOI: 10.1017/S0047404500009039

Heckman, J. J. (2013). *Giving kids a fair chance.* MIT Press.

Henningsen, M. (2013). Making sense of experience in preschool: Children's encounters with numeracy and literacy through inquiry. *South African Journal of Childhood Education, 3*(2), 41–55. DOI: 10.4102/sajce.v3i2.39

Hesterman, S. (2011). Extending Reggio Emilia principles in the middle school context: A western Australian case study. *Educational Practice and Theory, 33*(1), 73–91. DOI: 10.7459/ept/33.1.05

Hewett, V. M. (2001). Examining the Reggio Emilia approach to early childhood education. *Early Childhood Education Journal, 29*(2), 95–100. DOI: 10.1023/A:1012520828095

He, Y., Lundgren, K., & Pynes, P. (2017). Impact of short-term study abroad program: Inservice teachers' development of intercultural competence and pedagogical beliefs. *Teaching and Teacher Education, 66*, 147–157. DOI: 10.1016/j.tate.2017.04.012

Hirsh-Pasek, K. (2009). A mandate for playful learning in preschool: Applying the scientific evidence.

Hočevar, A., Šebart, M. K., & Štefanc, D. (2013). Curriculum planning and the concept of participation in the Reggio Emilia pedagogical approach. *European Early Childhood Education Research Journal, 21*(4), 476–488. DOI: 10.1080/1350293X.2013.845437

Hong, S. B., Shaffer, L., & Han, J. (2017). Reggio Emilia inspired learning groups: Relationships, communication, cognition, and play. *Early Childhood Education Journal, 45*(5), 629–639. DOI: 10.1007/s10643-016-0811-0

Hoover, W. A., & Gough, P. B. (1990). The simple view of reading. *Reading and Writing, 2*(2), 127–160. DOI: 10.1007/BF00401799

Howden, L. (2025, Septemeber). The Reggio Emilia approach at St Mary's School for Girls. (S. Browne, Interviewer)

Hulme, I. (n.d.). Co-Founder, Teacher and Pedagogista of Forest House School . (S. Browne, Interviewer)

Hunsburger, W. (2015). A Reggio Emilia-Inspired Pedagogy of Listening. *Listening to Teach: Beyond Didactic Pedagogy, 15*, 15–23. Advance online publication. DOI: 10.1515/9781438458335-002

İnan, H. (2022). Sustainability of early childhood education inspired by the Reggio Emilia Approach during the emergency times: A phenomenographic research. *International Journal on Lifelong Education and Leadership, 8*(1), 36–48. DOI: 10.25233/ijlel.1094854

Inan, H. Z. (2021). Challenges of Distance/Online and Face-to-Face Education in the New Normal: Experiences of Reggio Emilia-Inspired Early Childhood Educators in Turkey. *Pedagogical Research, 6*(1), em0086. Advance online publication. DOI: 10.29333/pr/9304

Inan, H. Z., & Inan, T. (2015). 3Hs education: Examining hands-on, heads-on, and hearts-on early childhood science education. *International Journal of Science Education, 37*(12), 1974–1991. DOI: 10.1080/09500693.2015.1060369

İnan, H. Z., & Kayir, G. (2015). Reggio Emilia Inspired Projects Conducted in a Preschool: An Action Research. *Journal of International Social Research, 8*(38), 733. Advance online publication. DOI: 10.17719/jisr.20153813682

Inan, H. Z., Trundle, K. C., & Kantor, R. (2010). Understanding natural sciences education in a Reggio Emilia-inspired preschool. *Journal of Research in Science Teaching, 47*(10), 1186–1208. DOI: 10.1002/tea.20375

Ingold, T. (2021). *Corrispondenze* (N. Perullo, Trans.). Cortina.

Institute of International Education. (2019). *Open Doors Fast Facts 2010-2019.* Open Doors Report on International Educational Exchange. https://opendoorsdata.org/wp-content/uploads/2020/11/Open-Doors-Fast-Facts-2010-2019.pdf

Inter-departmental Group. (2015). Supporting access to the early childhood care and education (ecce) programme for children with a disability. Author. https://aim.gov.ie/app/uploads/2021/05/Inter-Departmental-Group-Report-launched-Nov-2015.pdf

International Play Association. (1989). *Declaration of the Child's Right to Play.* International Play Association.

IPCC. (2023). IPCC 2023: Summary for Policymakers. In: *Climate Change 2023: Synthesis Report. Contribution of Working Groups I, II, and III to the Sixth Assessment Report of the Intergovernmental Panel on Climate Change* [Core Writing Team, H. Lee and J. Romero (eds.)]. IPCC, Geneva, Switzerland (pp. 1-34). DOI: 10.59327/IPCC/AR6-9789291691647

Istoreco Reggio Emilia - Reggio Africa Archives - Bruna Soncini Ganapini Archives - Comune di Reggio Emilia. (1997, June 1997). Pact of Solidarity . Reggio Emilia, Emilia-Romangna, Italy: Istoreco Reggio Emilia - Reggio Africa Archives.

Istoreco Reggio Emilia - Reggio Africa Archives - Bruna Soncini Ganapini Archives - Comune di Reggio Emilia. (n.d.). *Second Solidarity Ship. Reggio Emilia.* Istoreco Reggio Emilia - Reggio Africa Archives - Bruna Soncini Ganapini Archives - Comune di Reggio Emilia.

Jerome, L., Emerson, L., Lundy, L., & Orr, K. (2015). *Teaching and learning about child rights: A study of implementation in 26 countries.* UNICEF. https://www.unicef.org/media/63086/file/UNICEF-Teaching-and-learning-about-child-rights.pdf

Johnson, R. (2000). Colonialism and cargo cults in early childhood education: Does Reggio Emilia really exist? *Contemporary Issues in Early Childhood*, *1*(1), 61–78. DOI: 10.2304/ciec.2000.1.1.8

Johnston, O., Wildy, H., & Shand, J. (2023). Teenagers learn through play too: Communicating high expectations through a playful learning approach. *Australian Educational Researcher*, *50*(3), 921–940. DOI: 10.1007/s13384-022-00534-3

Jones, M., & Shelton, M. (2011). *Developing your portfolio. Enhancing your learning and showing your stuff: A guide for the early childhood student or professional* (2nd ed.). Routledge.

Jordan, C., & Chawla, L. (2019). A coordinated research agenda for nature-based learning. *Frontiers in Psychology*, *10*, 766. Advance online publication. DOI: 10.3389/fpsyg.2019.00766 PMID: 31065246

Justice, L. M., & Pullen, P. C. (2003). Promoting the development of language and literacy in children at risk: A comparison of two early interventions. *Journal of Educational Psychology*, *95*(2), 368–379.

Katz, L. (1993). What can we learn from Reggio Emilia? In C. Edwards, L. Gandini, & G. Forman (Eds.), *The hundred languages of children: The Reggio Emilia approach to early childhood education* (pp. 19–37). Ablex Publishing.

Kaynak-Ekici, K. B., İmir, H. M., & Temel, Z. F. (2021). Learning invitations in Reggio Emilia approach: A case study. *Education 3-13*, *49*(6), 703-715. DOI: 10.1080/03004279.2020.1775272

Kemmis, S., Heikkinen, H. L., Fransson, G., Aspfors, J., & Edwards-Groves, C. (2014). Mentoring of new teachers as a contested practice: Supervision, support and collaborative self-development. *Teaching and Teacher Education*, *43*, 154–164. DOI: 10.1016/j.tate.2014.07.001

Kinney, L., & Wharton, P. (2007). *An encounter with Reggio Emilia: Children's early learning made visible*. Routledge., DOI: 10.4324/9780203937143

Kinney, L., & Wharton, P. (2015). *An encounter with Reggio Emilia: Children and adults in transformation*. Routledge., DOI: 10.4324/9781315750309

Klein, J., & Wikan, G. (2019). Teacher education and international practice programmes: Reflections on transformative learning and global citizenship. *Teaching and Teacher Education*, *79*, 93–100. DOI: 10.1016/j.tate.2018.12.003

Kołodziejski, M., & Butvilas, T. (2021). Creativity and parental involvement in early childhood education in the Reggio Emilia approach and philosophy. *Edukacja Elementarna w Teorii i Praktyce, 16*(3 (61), 103-112. DOI: 10.35765/eetp.2021.1661.07

Korczak, J. (1967). *Selected works of Janusz Korczak* (Lewin, A., Trans.). Foreign Languages Publishing House. (Original work published in Polish)

Krijnen, E., van Steensel, R., Meeuwisse, M., & Severiens, S. (2022). Aiming for educational partnership between parents and professionals: Shared vision development in a professional learning community. *School Community Journal, 32*(1), 265–300. https://www.adi.org/journal/2022ss/KrijnenEtAlSS22.pdf

Kuh, G. D. (2008). *High-impact educational practices: What they are, who has access to them, and why they matter.* Association of American Colleges and Universities. https://dgmg81phhvh63.cloudfront.net/content/user-photos/Publications/PDFs/E-HIGHIMP.pdf

La Cecla, F., & Vitone, L. (2013). *Non è cosa. Vita affettiva degli oggetti - Non siamo mai stati soli. Oggetti e disegni*. Elèuthera.

Lally, J. R. (2006). Metatheories of childrearing. In J.R. Lally, P.L. Mangione and D. Greenwald (Eds.), 20 essays on infant/toddler development and learning (pp. 7–14). WestEd.

Lancy, D. F. (2015). *The anthropology of childhood. Cherubs, chattels, changelings* (3rd ed.). Cambridge University Press.

Landi, L., & Pintus, A. (2022). A critical approach to the Reggio Emilia Approach. *Educazione. Giornale di Pedagogia Critica, 11*(1), 107–125. https://iris.unimore.it/retrieve/1861203e-e021-42ee-b42a-d20195c206c9/216-713-1-PB.pdf

Landini, A., & Colacino, M. (2023). Inclusione e politiche di valorizzazione della persona: Dalla prospettiva internazionale al contesto della città di Reggio Emilia [Inclusion and policies for the enhancement of the person: From an international perspective to the context of the city of Reggio Emilia]. *Annali online della Didattica e della Formazione Docente, 15*(25), 117–131.

Landini, A. (2022). La scuola che abita al museo: Dall'emergenza all'immersione nella cultura, per innovare spazi e contesti dell'apprendimento. *IUL Research, 3*(6), 206–219. DOI: 10.57568/iulres.v3i6.349

Landrigan, P. J., Dunlop, S., Treskova, M., Raps, H., Symeonides, C., Muncke, J., Spring, M., Stegeman, J., Almroth, B. C., Chiles, T. C., Cropper, M., Deeney, M., Fuller, L., Geyer, R., Karasik, R., Mafira, T., Mangwiro, A., Matias, D. M., Mulders, Y., & Rocklöv, J. (2025). The Lancet Countdown on health and plastics. *Lancet*, *406*(10507), 1044–1062. Advance online publication. DOI: 10.1016/S0140-6736(25)01447-3 PMID: 40769171

Lang, J. R. (2007). *How to succeed with education for sustainability*. Curriculum Corp.

Lanphear, J., & Vandermaas-Peeler, M. (2017). Inquiry and intersubjectivity in a Reggio Emilia–inspired preschool. *Journal of Research in Childhood Education*, *31*(4), 597–614. DOI: 10.1080/02568543.2017.1348412

Larimore, R. A. (2019). *Preschool beyond walls: Blending early childhood education and nature-based learning*. Gryphon House.

Latour, B. (2004). *Politics of nature: How to bring the sciences into democracy*. Harvard University Press. DOI: 10.4159/9780674039964

Lavrič, M., & Naterer, A. (2020). The power of authoritative parenting: A cross-national study of effects of exposure to different parenting styles on life satisfaction. *Children and Youth Services Review*, *116*, 105274. Advance online publication. DOI: 10.1016/j.childyouth.2020.105274

Leadership for INClusion in the Early Years Consortium. (2016-2025). Blogs. Author. https://lincprogramme.ie/linc-programme-blogs/

Leadership for INClusion in the Early Years Consortium. (2019). Interim evaluation of the leadership for inclusion in the early years (LINC) programme (Ring, E., Kelleher, S., Kelleher, S., Heeney, T., McLoughlin, M., Kearns, A., Stafford, S., Skehill, S., Campion, K., Comerford, D., & O'Sullivan, L.). Mary Immaculate College, Limerick, Ireland. https://acrobat.adobe.com/link/track?uri=urn%3Aaaid%3Ascds%3AUS%3Ad8c95d7d-2d75-40a8-9f65-b6582908c08d

Leadership for INClusion in the Early Years Consortium. (2022). The Role of INclusion Coordi-nator (INCO). Mary Immaculate College, Limerick, Ireland. https://aim.gov.ie/app/uploads/2022/08/Role-of-the-INclusion-COordinator-2022.pdf

Leadership for INClusion in the Early Years Consortium. (2024). Final evaluation of phase one of the leadership for inclusion in the early years (LINC) programme 2016-2020 (Kelly, L., Ring, E., Heaney, S., O'Sullivan, L., Fortune, N., Heeney, T., Kerrins, L., Stafford, P., & Thompson, H). Mary Immaculate College, Limerick, Ireland. Web-version-of-LINC-Evaluation-Report-2-page-view-1.pdf

Leadership for INClusion in the Early Years Consortium. (2025a). Leading from within: Devel-oping a professional portfolio for inclusion in the early years. A celebration of the leadership for inclusion in the early years (LINC) Programme graduates and their inspiring contributions to the lives of children and families (Heaney, S., Butterly, C., Horgan, K., Ring, E., O'Byrne, A., Donnellan, A., Harte, P., Madden, L., Joyce, M. &Thompson, H.). Mary Immaculate College, Limerick, Ireland. https://lincprogramme.ie/linc-programme-research/

Leadership for INClusion in the Early Years Consortium. (2025b). An interim evaluation of the leadership for inclusion in the early years continuing professional development (LINC + CPD) programme 2021-2023 (Kelly, L., Kerrins, L., Stafford, P., Heaney, S., Butterly, C., Heeney, T., Ring, E., O'Sullivan, L., Fortune, N., Kearns, A. & Thompson, H.), Mary Immaculate College, Limerick, Ireland. https://lincprogramme.ie/wp-content/uploads/2025/04/Interim-Evaluation-of-the-LINC-CPD-Programme-2021-2023.pdf

Legge (1971). n. 1044. Piano quinquennale per l'istituzione di asili-nido comunali con il concorso dello Stato [Five-year plan for the establishment of municipal nursery schools with State contribution]. *Gazzetta Ufficiale*, No. 316. https://www.normattiva.it/uri-res/N2Ls?urn:nir:stato:legge:1971-12-06;1044

Legge (2016). n. 232. Bilancio di previsione dello Stato per l'anno finanziario 2017 e bilancio pluriennale per il triennio 2017-2019 [State budget for the 2017 financial year and multi-year budget for the 2017-2019 three-year period]. *Gazzetta Ufficiale*, No. 297. https://www.normattiva.it/uri-res/N2Ls?urn:nir:stato:legge:2016-12-11;232@originale

Leggett, N. (2020). A fish out of water: Developing intercultural understanding of students in higher education. *The Australian Journal of Teacher Education*, *45*(12), 43–56. DOI: 10.14221/ajte.202v45n12.3

Lenz, W., & Wister, J. (2008, May/June). Short-term abroad with long-term benefits. *International Educator*, *17*(3), 84–87.

Lester, S., & Russell, W. (2008). *Play for a change: Play, policy and practice: A review of contemporary perspectives*. Play England.

Lester, S., & Russell, W. (2010). *Children's right to play: An examination of the importance of play in the lives of children worldwide*. Bernard van Leer Foundation.

Levin, J. N., Brasel, N. H., & Macy, M. (2023). [Unpublished raw data from a qualitative examination of how a team of professionals re-envisioned early childhood with a study abroad to Reggio Emilia].

Lgs, D. (2017). n. 65. Istituzione del sistema integrato di educazione e di istruzione dalla nascita sino a sei anni, a norma dell'articolo 1, commi 180 e 181, della legge 13 luglio 2015, n. 107 [Establishment of the integrated education and training system from birth up to six years, pursuant to article 1, paragraphs 180 and 181, of Law No. 107 of July 13, 2015]. *Gazzetta Ufficiale*, No. 112. https://www.normattiva.it/uri-res/N2Ls?urn:nir:stato:decreto.legislativo:2017;065

Lgs, D. (2022). n. 149. Attuazione della legge 26 novembre 2021, n. 206, recante delega al Governo per l'efficienza del processo civile e per la revisione della disciplina degli strumenti di risoluzione alternativa delle controversie e misure urgenti di razionalizzazione dei procedimenti in materia di diritti delle persone e delle famiglie nonché in materia di esecuzione forzata [Implementation of Law No. 206 of November 26, 2021, delegating the Government to improve the efficiency of civil proceedings and revise the discipline of alternative dispute resolution, and urgent measures to streamline proceedings concerning personal and family rights as well as enforcement proceedings]. *Gazzetta Ufficiale*, No. 243. https://www.normattiva.it/uri-res/N2Ls?urn:nir:stato:decreto.legislativo:2022-10-10;149!vig=2022-11-02

Lillard, A. S., Lerner, M. D., Hopkins, E. J., Dore, R. A., Smith, E. D., & Palmquist, C. M. (2013). The impact of pretend play on children's development: A review of the evidence. *Psychological Bulletin*, *139*(1), 1–34. DOI: 10.1037/a0029321 PMID: 22905949

Lim, S., & Cho, M.-H. (2019). Parents' use of mobile documentation in a Reggio Emilia-inspired school. *Early Childhood Education Journal*, *47*(4), 367–379. DOI: 10.1007/s10643-019-00945-5

Linder, S., & McGaha, J. (2013). Building on successes: Reflections from two approaches to study abroad for undergraduate and graduate students. *The Educational Forum*, *77*(3), 379–389. DOI: 10.1080/00131725.2013.792900

Lindsay, G. (2015). Reflections in the mirror of Reggio Emilia's soul: John Dewey's foundational influence on pedagogy in the Italian educational project. *Early Childhood Education Journal*, *43*(6), 447–457. DOI: 10.1007/s10643-015-0692-7

Lino, D. M., & Parente, C. (2018). Play and learning in early childhood education: The contribution of High Scope, Reggio Emilia, and Montessori Pedagogical approaches. In *Early childhood education from an intercultural and bilingual perspective* (pp. 147-163). IGI Global. DOI: 10.4018/978-1-5225-5167-6.ch010

Lipsey, M. W., Farran, D. C., & Durkin, K. (2018). Effects of the Tennessee prekindergarten program on children's achievement and behavior through third grade. *Early Childhood Research Quarterly*, *45*(4), 155–176. DOI: 10.1016/j.ecresq.2018.03.005

Logaridis, L., Tranter, K., & Siegrist, L. (2012). Make it meaningful! Emergent literacy in the kindergarten years. *The Early Childhood Educator*. https://playfullyinspireddotcom1.wordpress.com/2014/04/13/make-it-meaningful/

Lonigan, C. J., & Shanahan, T. (2009). Developing early literacy: Report of the National Early Literacy Panel. Executive summary. A scientific synthesis of early literacy development and implications for intervention. *National Institute for Literacy*. https://files.eric.ed.gov/fulltext/ED508381.pdf

Lücker-Babel, M. F. (2008). Il diritto ad esprimere opinioni e ad essere ascoltato. In Belotti, V., & Ruggiero, R. (Eds.), *Vent'anni d'infanzia: Retorica e diritti dei bambini dopo la Convenzione dell'ottantanove* (pp. 157–172). Guerini e Associati.

Lundy, L. (2007). 'Voice' is not enough: Conceptualising Article 12 of the United Nations Convention on the Rights of the Child. *British Educational Research Journal, 33*(6), 972–942. DOI: 10.1080/01411920701657033

Lundy, L., Murray, C., Smith, K., & Ward, C. (2024). Young children's right to be heard on the quality of their education: Addressing potential misunderstandings in the context of early childhood education. *British Educational Research Journal, 00*, 1–15. DOI: 10.1002/berj.3968

MacDonald, M. (2011). Review of Kathy Hall et al. loris malaguzzi and the Reggio Emilia experience. *Studies in Philosophy and Education, 2010*(6), 631–639. Advance online publication. DOI: 10.1007/s11217-011-9224-0

Macy, M., Harshbarger, D., Burke, K., & Neukirch, E. (2025). Experiential learning in Reggio Emilia, Italy: Reflections from in-service and pre-service professionals. *Journey of Early Childhood Teacher Education*. Advance online publication. DOI: 10.1080/10901027.2025.2493175

Mages, W. K. (2016). Taking inspiration from Reggio Emilia: An analysis of a professional development workshop on fostering authentic art in the early childhood classroom. *Journal of Early Childhood Teacher Education, 37*(2), 175–185. DOI: 10.1080/10901027.2016.1165763

Magnusson, L. O. (2024). 'Look, my name! I can write'–Literacy events and digital technology in the preschool atelier. *Journal of Early Childhood Literacy, 24*(2), 253–275. DOI: 10.1177/14687984211058943

Malaguzzi, L. (1990). Speech at the international conference on the rights and potentials of children and adults. In P. Cagliari, M. Castagnetti, C. Giudici, C. Rinaldi, V. Vecchi, & P. Moss (Eds.), *Loris Malaguzzi and the schools of Reggio Emilia* (pp. 396–397). Routledge.

Malaguzzi, L. (1993). History, ideas, and basic philosophy: An interview with Lella Gandini. In C. Edwards, L. Gandini, & G. Forman (Eds.), *The hundred languages of children: The Reggio Emilia approach to early childhood education* (pp. 9–16). Ablex Publishing.

Malaguzzi, L. (1993a). A charter of rights. Reggio Children. https://www.reggiochildren.it/assets/Uploads/RC-100LM-CartaDiritti-3.pdf

Malaguzzi, L. (1994). Your image of the child: Where teaching begins. In C. Edwards, L. Gandini, & G. Forman (Eds.), *The hundred languages of children: The Reggio Emilia approach—Advanced reflections* (pp. 1–10). Ablex Publishing.

Malaguzzi, L. (1996). *The hundred languages of children: The Reggio Emilia approach—Advanced reflections* (C. Edwards, L. Gandini, & G. Forman, Eds.). Ablex Publishing.

Malaguzzi, L. (1998). History, ideas, and basic philosophy: An interview with Lella Gandini. In C. Edwards, L. Gandini, & G. Forman (Eds.), *The hundred languages of children: The Reggio Emilia approach—Advanced reflections* (2nd ed., pp. 49–97). Ablex Publishing.

Malaguzzi, L. (2012) No way. The hundred is there. In In C. Edwards, L. Gandini, & G. Forman (Eds.), The hundred languages of children: The Reggio Emilia experience in transformation (3rd ed.) (pp. 2-3). Praeger.

Malaguzzi, L. (2016). *Loris Malaguzzi and the schools of Reggio Emilia: A selection of his writings and speeches, 1945–1993* (P. Cagliari, M. Castagnetti, C. Giudici, C. Rinaldi, V. Vecchi, & P. Moss, Eds.). Routledge.

Malaguzzi, L., Castagnetti, M., Rubizzi, L., & Vecchi, V. (1998). Introductory note. In Municipality of Reggio Emilia, Infant–Toddler Centers and Preschools (Ed.), *A journey into the rights of children* (L. Morrow, Trans.; 5th ed., pp. 11–12). Reggio Children. (Original work published 1995)

Malaguzzi, L. (1987). *The hundred languages of children exhibition catalogue.* Reggio Children.

Malaguzzi, L. (1993). For an education based on relationships. *Young Children, 49*(1), 9–12.

Malaguzzi, L. (1993). *Una carta per tre diritti.*

Malaguzzi, L. (1993). Una carta per tre diritti. [A charter of rights] In *The hundred languages of children* [Exhibition catalogue]. Reggio Children.

Malaguzzi, L. (1993b). For an education based on relationships (translated by Lella Gandini). *Young Children, 49*(1), 9–12.

Malaguzzi, L. (1994). Your image of the child: Where teaching begins. *Child Care Information Exchange, 96*, 52–61.

Malaguzzi, L. (1995). A Charter of Rights. In Malaguzzi, L. (Ed.), *A Journey into the Rights of Children: As Seen by the Children Themselves* (pp. 67–69). Reggio Children Srl.

Malaguzzi, L. (2012). No Way. The hundred is there. In Edwards, C., Gandini, L., & Forman, G. (Eds.), *The Hundred Languages of Children: The Reggio Emilia Experience in Transformation* (p. 3). ABC-CLIO.

Malmgren, J., & Galvin, J. (2008). Effects of study abroad participation on student graduation rates: A study of three incoming freshman cohorts at the University of Minnesota, Twin Cities. *NACADA Journal, 28*(1), 29–42. DOI: 10.12930/0271-9517-28.1.29

Manera, L. (2022). Art and aesthetic education in the Reggio Emilia Approach. Education 3- 13, 50(4), 483-493. https://doi.org/DOI: 10.1080/03004279.2022.2052230

Manera, L. (2022). The Reggio Emilia Approach to Early Childhood Education. An Analysis to Its Inclusive Perspectives and Their Relationships to Aesthetic Aspects. In *Fostering Inclusion in Education: Alternative Approaches to Progressive Educational Practices* (pp. 145–153). Springer International Publishing., DOI: 10.1007/978-3-031-07492-9_7

Mardell, B., Ryan, J., Krechevsky, M., Baker, M., Schulz, T. S., & Liu-Constant, Y. (2023). *A pedagogy of play: Supporting playful learning in classrooms and schools*. Project Zero.

Martins, M. A., & Silva, C. (2006). The impact of invented spelling on phonemic awareness. *Learning and Instruction, 16*(1), 41–56. DOI: 10.1016/j.learninstruc.2005.12.005

Maureen, I. Y., van der Meij, H., & de Jong, T. (2020). Enhancing storytelling activities to support early (digital) literacy development in early childhood education. *International Journal of Early Childhood, 52*(1), 55–76. DOI: 10.1007/s13158-020-00263-7

Mayall, B. (2000). The sociology of childhood in relation to children's rights. *International Journal of Children's Rights, 8*(3), 243–259. DOI: 10.1163/15718180020494640

Maynard, T., & Chicken, S. (2010). Through a different lens: Exploring Reggio Emilia in a Welsh context. *Early Years Journal of International Research and Development, 30*(1), 29–39. DOI: 10.1080/09575140903443000

McCormick Smith, M., & Chao, T. (2018). Critical science and mathematics early childhood education: Theorizing Reggio, play, and critical pedagogy into an actionable cycle. *Education Sciences, 8*(4), 162. DOI: 10.3390/educsci8040162

McNally, S. A., & Slutsky, R. (2017). Key elements of the Reggio Emilia approach and how they are interconnected to create the highly regarded system of early childhood education. *Early Child Development and Care, 187*(12), 1925–1937. DOI: 10.1080/03004430.2016.1197920

Metzger, C. A. (2006). Study abroad programming: A 21st century retention strategy? *The College Student Affairs Journal, 25*(2), 164–175.

Ministero dell'istruzione e del merito. (2024). *Linee guida per l'insegnamento dell'educazione civica.*

Moreno, C. (2025). *La città dei 15 minuti: Per una cultura urbana democratica.* ADD Editore.

Morley, A., Braun, A. M. B., Rohrer, L., & Lamb, D. (2019). Study abroad for preservice teachers: A critical literature review with considerations for research and practice. *Global Education Review, 6*(3), 4–29. https://ger.mercy.edu/index.php/ger/article/view/521/394

Morris, J. (1991). *Pride against prejudice: Transforming attitudes to disability: A personal poli-tics of disability.* Women's Press.

Mortari, L. (2020). Educazione ecologica (1st ed.). GLF editori Laterza.

Mortari, L. (1994). Educating ourselves to think with a view to 'ecologically inhabiting the earth' in the light of the thought of Hannah Arendt. *Australian Journal of Environmental Education, 10*, 91–111. DOI: 10.1017/S0814062600003116

Mortari, L. (2017). La materia vivente e il pensare sensibile: Per una filosofia ecologica dell'educazione. *Mimesis.*

Moss, P. (2015). *Transformative change and real utopias in early childhood education: A story of democracy, experimentation and potential.* Routledge.

Moss, P. (2016). Loris Malaguzzi and the schools of Reggio Emilia: Provocation and hope for a renewed public education. *Improving Schools, 19*(2), 167–176. DOI: 10.1177/1365480216651521

Moss, P. (2019). *Alternative narratives in early childhood: An introduction for students and practitioners*. Routledge.

Mo, Y., Appel, M., Kim, J. W., & Lee, W. (2021). Pre-service teachers' international study experiences or in-service teachers' professional learning communities: What comes into play in Finnish teachers' self-efficacy in multicultural classrooms? *Teachers and Teaching*, *27*(7), 602–624. DOI: 10.1080/13540602.2021.1983535

Mubonderi, F. (2025, July). Grade 00 Teacher at Capstone College. (S. Browne, Interviewer)

Municipality of Reggio Emilia, Infant–Toddler Centers and Preschools. (1998). *A journey into the rights of children* (L. Morrow, Trans.; 5th ed.; The Unheard Voice of Children, No. 3). Reggio Children. (Original work published 1995)

Murris, K., & Reynolds, R. A. (2018). Reggio Emilia inspired philosophical teacher education in the Anthropocene: Posthuman child and the family (tree). DOI: 10.18357/jcs.v43i1.18262

Murris, K. (2017). Reading two rhizomatic pedagogies diffractively through one another: A Reggio inspired philosophy with children for the postdevelopmental child. *Pedagogy, Culture & Society*, *25*(4), 531–550. DOI: 10.1080/14681366.2017.1286681

National Council for Curriculum and Assessment. (2009). Aistear: the early childhood curricu-lum framework. Author. Aistear (2009) | Curriculum Online

National Council for Curriculum and Assessment. (2025). Aistear (2024) as a rights-based ear-ly childhood curriculum framework. Author. aistear-as-a-rights-based-early-childhood-curriculum-framework.pdf

National Council for Curriculum and Assessment. (2025, January 15). Aistear blog #1: The principles of early learning and development. Author. https://ncca.ie/en/updates-and-events/latest-news/2025/january/aistear-blog-1/

new Charter of Values of the Reggio Children Foundation. https://www.youtube.com/watch?v=rfHdTlaf_8U

New, R. S. (2007). Reggio Emilia as cultural activity theory in practice. *Theory into Practice*, *46*(1), 5–13. DOI: 10.1080/00405840709336543

Nguyen, P. K. (2024). *Exploring the integration of Reggio Emilia-inspired practices in U.S. early childhood settings* (Publication No. 148) [Honors undergraduate theses, University of Central Florida]. Showcase of Text, Archives, Research & Scholarship. https://stars.library.ucf.edu/hut2024/148

Norris, E. M., & Gillespie, J. (2009). How study abroad shapes global careers. Evidence from the United States. *Journal of Studies in International Education, 13*(3), 382–397. DOI: 10.1177/1028315308319740

Nxumalo, F., Gagliardi, L. M., & Won, H. R. (2020). Inquiry-based curriculum in early childhood education. In *Oxford research encyclopedia of education.* DOI: 10.1093/acrefore/9780190264093.013.1064

Nyaupane, G. P., Paris, C. M., & Teye, V. (2011). Study abroad motivations, destination selection and pre-trip attitude formation. *International Journal of Tourism Research, 13*(3), 205–217. DOI: 10.1002/jtr.811

O'Sullivan, L., & Ring, E. (2023). On the path to developing a high-quality inclusive preschool system in the Irish context: Outcomes from a systemic focus on structural and process quality dimensions. In H. Şenol, H. (Ed.), Recent perspectives on preschool education and care (pp.1-22). IntechOpen. https://www.intechopen.com/chapters/88601

O'Sullivan, L., & Ring, E. (2026). *Play from the inside out: Theory, research and practice per-spectives.* Peter Lang.

Ocampo, M. L. (2004, September 9). *Leland Standford Junior University.* Retrieved from Standford.edu: https://web.stanford.edu/~jbaugh/saw/Lizet_Education_Inequity.html

OECD. (2001). *Starting strong: Early childhood education and care.* OECD Publishing., DOI: 10.1787/9789264192829-

OECD. (2021). *Starting Strong VI: Supporting Meaningful Interactions in Early Childhood Education and Care.* OECD Publishing. https://doi.org/DOI: 10.1787/f47a06ae-en

Okken, G. J., Jansen, E. P. W. A., Hofman, W. H. A., & Coelen, R. J. (2019). Beyond the 'welcome-back party': The enriched repertoire of professional teacher behaviour as a result of study abroad. *Teaching and Teacher Education, 86. Teaching and Teacher Education, 102927*, 1–11. DOI: 10.1016/j.tate.2019.102927

Omidvar, N., Wright, T., Beazley, K., & Seguin, D. (2019). Examining children's indoor and outdoor nature exposures and nature-related pedagogic approaches of teachers at two Reggio-Emilia preschools in Halifax, Canada. *Journal of Education for Sustainable Development, 13*(2), 215–241. DOI: 10.1177/0973408219872066

Oostdam, R., & Hooge, E. (2013). Making the difference with active parents; forming educational partnerships between parents and schools. *European Journal of Psychology of Education, 28*(2), 337–351. DOI: 10.1007/s10212-012-0117-6

Organisation for Economic Cooperation and Development. (2019). *OECD learning compass 2030: A series of concept notes*. Organisation for Economic Co-operation and Development. https://www.oecd.org/education/2030-project/learning-compass-2030/

Organisation for Economic Co-operation and Development. (2023). Equity and inclusion in ed-ucation. Finding strength through diversity. Author. https://www.oecd.org/en/publications/2023/01/equity-and-inclusion-in-education_e8cfc768.html

Osgood, J., & Ødegård, N. (2022). Crafting granular stories with child-like embodied, affective and sensory encounters that attune to the world's differential becoming. *Australian Journal of Environmental Education, 38*(1), 85–101. DOI: 10.1017/aee.2022.11

Ozkan, U. B. (2019). *Eğitim bilimleri araştırmaları için doküman inceleme yöntemi* [Document analysis methodology for research in educational sciences]. Pegem Akademi.

Pacini-Ketchabaw, V., Taylor, A., & Blaise, M. (2016). Decentering the Human in Multispecies Ethnographies. In *Posthuman Research Practices in Education* (pp. 149–167). Palgrave Macmillan UK.

Panksepp, J. (2010). The affective neuroscience of play: The joyful discovery of self. *American Journal of Play, 2*(3), 315–337, 245–277.

Paoli, E. S. (2023). Comunità/gioco. In Consiglio nazionale degli architetti, pianificatori, paesaggisti e conservatori (Eds.), *Abitare il Paese – La cultura della domanda. Attivare comunità educanti: Nuove generazioni, partecipazione, città* (Anno scolastico 2023/2024). CNAPPC.

Paoli, E. S., & Ronzoni, R. (2025). Come un'ape. Dialoghi tra naturale e digitale per una visione ecologica in ambito educativo. *FRC news, 1*, 28–29.

Parker, R., & Thomsen, B. S. (2019). *Learning through play at school: A study of playful integrated pedagogies that foster children's holistic skills development in the primary school classroom*. LEGO Foundation.

Parnell, W., Justice, E., & Patrick, L. P. (2018). Extended family and friends in young children's education. *Young Children, 73*(4), 20–27. https://www.naeyc.org/resources/pubs/yc/sep2018/engaging-extended-family-friends

Passarelli, A. (2022). Report relativo alla raccolta e all'analisi dei dati sulle famiglie frequentanti l'Istituto Comprensivo "Alessandro Manzoni": Anagrafica, relazioni, soddisfazione e bisogni. In Ferrari, E., Landini, A., & Righi, L. (Eds.), *Pace fra le culture. Ricerche e azioni per il dialogo interreligioso e interculturale tra famiglie, studenti e insegnanti dell'I.C. "A. Manzoni" di Reggio Emilia* (pp. 63–89). Fscire Press.

Pećnik, N., Matić, J., & Milaković, A. T. (2016). Fulfillment of the child's participation rights in the family and the child's psychosocial adjustment: Children's and parent's views. *Revija za Socijalnu Politiku*, *23*(3), 399–421. DOI: 10.3935/rsp.v23i3.1382

Pellis, S. M., & Pellis, V. C. (2009). *The playful brain: Venturing to the limits of neuroscience*. Oneworld.

Peterson, H. (2023). Scribbling in early childhood: Why do young children make marks? *Exchange*, *270*, •••. https://hub.exchangepress.com/articles-on-demand/3182/

Piaget, J. (1952). *The origins of intelligence in children* (Cook, M., Trans.). International Universities Press. (Original work published 1936) DOI: 10.1037/11494-000

Piasta, S. B. (2023). The science of early alphabet instruction. In Cabell, S. Q., Neuman, S. B., & Terry, N. P. (Eds.), *Handbook on the science of early literacy* (pp. 83–94). Guilford Publications.

Piazza, G. (A c. Di). (2001). *Le fontane: Da un progetto per la costruzione di un luna park degli uccellini = The fountains: from a project for the construction of an amusement park for birds* (L. Morrow, Trad.). Reggio Children.

Pignataro, P. (2014). *La pedagogia relazionale di Loris Malaguzzi*. FrancoAngeli.

Pipitone, J. M. (2018). Place as pedagogy: Toward study abroad for social change. *Journal of Experiential Education*, *41*(1), 54–74. DOI: 10.1177/1053825917751509

Potting, J., Hekkert, M., Worrell, E., & Hanemaaijer, A. (2017). *Circular economy: Measuring innovation in product chains*. PBL Netherlands Environmental Assessment Agency. https://www.pbl.nl/en/publications/circular-economy-measuring-innovation-in-product-chains

Pyle, A., Prioletta, J., & Poliszczuk, D. (2018). The play-literacy interface in full-day kindergarten classrooms. *Early Childhood Education Journal*, *46*(1), 117–127. DOI: 10.1007/s10643-017-0852-z

Quality and Qualifications Ireland. (2021) National framework of qualifications. Author. https://www.qqi.ie/Articles/Pages/National-Framework-of-Qualifications-(NFQ).aspx

Queiros, P. (n.d.). Head of School and Music Atelierista - Petra's EduPlay. (S. Browne, Interviewer)

Quennerstedt, A. (2009). Balancing the rights of the child and the rights of parents in the Convention on the Rights of the Child. *Journal of Human Rights*, *8*(2), 162–176. DOI: 10.1080/14754830902897270

Quezada, R. L. (2004). Beyond educational tourism: Lessons learned while student teaching abroad. *International Education Journal*, *5*(4), 458–465.

Rand, M., & Morrow, L. (2021). The contribution of play experiences in early literacy: Expanding the science of reading. *Reading Research Quarterly*, *56*(S1), S239–S248. DOI: 10.1002/rrq.383

Rankin, B. (1997). Education as collaboration: Learning from and building on Dewey, Vygotsky, and Piaget. In Hendrick, J. (Ed.), *First steps toward teaching the Reggio way* (pp. 70–83). Prentice-Hall.

Reggio Children (Ed.). (2021). Perché i bambini non siano invisibili. *Rechild, December 2021.*

Reggio Children Srl P.IVA 01586410357. (2022). *Investigating natural phenomena - at home with the Reggio Emilia approach - school goes home*. Retrieved from Reggio Children S.r.l: https://www.reggiochildren.it/en/athomewiththereggioapproach/investigating-natural-phenomena/

Reggio Children Srl P.IVA 01586410357. (2022). *Reggio Emilia Approach - 100 Languages*. Retrieved from Reggio Children: https://www.reggiochildren.it/en/reggio-emilia-approach/100-linguaggi-en/

Reggio Children. (1997). *The amusement park for birds: A project from the infant-toddler centers and preschools of Reggio Emilia*. Reggio Children.

Reggio Children. (2014). *Planetary Messages.* https://vimeo.com/394903249

Resnick, M. (2017). *Lifelong kindergarten: Cultivating creativity through projects, passion, peers, and play*. MIT Press. DOI: 10.7551/mitpress/11017.001.0001

Rigney, L. I., & Kelly, S. (2023). Reterritorialising pedagogies of listening: Bringing into dialogue culturally responsive pedagogies with Reggio Emilia principles. *Discourse (Abingdon)*, *44*(1), 147–161. DOI: 10.1080/01596306.2021.1961688

Rigney, L. I., & Rinaldi, C. (2023). Teaching in cultural and linguistic super-diverse Australian classrooms: A north–south exploration of Reggio Emilia. In *Affirming the Rights of Emergent Bilingual and Multilingual Children and Families* (pp. 209–225). Routledge., DOI: 10.4324/9781003294405-19

Riley-Ayers, S. (2013). Supporting language and literacy development in quality preschools. In Barone, D. M., & Mallette, M. H. (Eds.), *Best practices in early literacy instruction* (pp. 58–78). The Guilford Press.

Rinaldi, C. (1998). Projected curriculum constructed through documentation—*Progettazione*: An interview with Lella Gandini. In C. Edwards, L. Gandini, & G. Forman (Eds.), *The hundred languages of children: The Reggio Emilia approach—Advanced reflections* (2nd ed., pp. 113–125). Ablex Publishing.

Rinaldi, C. (1999). *L'ascolto visibile.* Comune di Reggio Emilia. https://books.google.it/books?id=HxQjjwEACAAJ

Rinaldi, C. (2001). The pedagogy of listening: The listening perspective from Reggio Emilia. *Innovations in Early Education: The International Reggio Exchange, 8*(4).

Rinaldi, C. (2022). *Quality education, a global challenge.* Video presentation of the

Rinaldi, C. (2025, April 10). Open Questions on Education [Conference Keynote]. Retrieved from https://www.frchildren.org/en/news-and-events/news/post/carla-rinaldis-open-questions-education

Rinaldi, C. (2001). A pedagogy of listening: The listening perspective from Reggio Emilia. *Innovations in Early Education: The International Reggio Exchange, 8*(4), 1–4.

Rinaldi, C. (2006). *In dialogue with Reggio Emilia: Listening, researching and learning*. Routledge.

Rinaldi, C. (2009). *Dialogue with Reggio Emilia: Listening, Researching and Learning*. Routledge.

Rinaldi, C. (2012). The pedagogy of listening. The listening perspective of Reggio Emilia. In *The Hundred Languages of Children: The Reggio Emilia experience in transformation* (3rd ed., pp. 233–246). Praeger.

Rinaldi, C. (2018). The space of childhood. In Ceppi, G., & Zini, M. (Eds.), *Children, spaces, re-lations. Metaproject for an environment for young children* (pp. 114–120). Reggio Children.

Rinaldi, C. (2020). The child as a citizen: Holder of rights and competent. The Reggio Emilia educational experience. *Miscellanea Historico-luridica, 19*(1), 11–22. DOI: 10.15290/mhi.2020.19.01.01

Rinaldi, C. (2021). *In dialogue with Reggio Emilia*. Routledge. DOI: 10.4324/9780367854539

Rinaldi, C. (2021). *In dialogue with Regio Emilia. Listening, researching and learning* (2nd ed.). Routledge.

Rinaldi, C. (2022). *Charter "Quality Education, a Global Challenge"*. Fondazione Reggio Children.

Ring, E. (2021). Introduction: Looking towards a new era of leading education for all from the inside out: The potential of a bioecological lens in creating early childhood experiences where diversity becomes the norm. In E. Ring, L. O'Sullivan, L., M. Ryan, & P. Daly (Eds.), Leading inclusion from the inside out: A handbook for parents and early childhood teachers in early learning and care, primary and special school settings (pp. 3-27). Peter Lang.

Ring, E., & O'Sullivan, L. (2025). Play, learning and teaching in a redeveloped primary curricu-lum. National Council for Curriculum and Assessment. https://ncca.ie/en/resources/play-learning-and-teaching-in-a-redeveloped-primary-curriculum/

Ring, E., Grey, T., O'Sullivan, L., Corbett, M., Sheerin, J., & Heeney, T. (2019). Universal de-sign guidelines for early learning and care settings: Literature review. The Government Publica-tions Office. https://aim.gov.ie/app/uploads/2021/05/universal-design-guidelines-for-elc-settings-literature-review-2.pdf

Ring, E. (2024). *Special education in an independent Ireland 1922-2022. Insights from a jour-ney through the century*. National Council for Special Education., ncse.ie/wp-content/uploads/2024/09/Emer_Ring_Special_Education_Independent_Ireland_NCSE2024.pdf

Ring, E., & Breen, F. (2017). *Changing lives: The transformative possibilities of blended learn-ing: Initial findings from a national programme in Ireland. In the Future of Education Confer-ence Proceedings* (7th ed.). Libreria Universitaria.

Ring, E., & O'Sullivan, L. (2019). Creating spaces where diversity is the norm. *Childhood Education, 95*(2), 29–39. DOI: 10.1080/00094056.2019.1593758

Robinson, D., Gowers, S., Codina, G., Artess, J., Delgado Fuenes, M.A., Mycock, K., Qyreshi, S., Shepherd, R., IFF Research., & Ní Luanaigh, A. (2022). End-of-year three evaluation of the access and inclusion model: Full technical and research Report. University of Derby, Institute of Education. https://assets.gov.ie/281416/efef74fb-04d6-4f8b-ba80-f7af48c6d8b1.pdf

Robinson, K., & Robinson, K. (2021). *IMMAGINA CHE... Come creare un futuro migliore per tutti*. Erickson.

Robson, J. (2016). Early years teachers and young children's rights: The need for critical dialogue. *Research in Teacher Education, 6*(1), 6–11. https://doi.org/DOI: 10.15123/PUB.5091

Rodari, G. (1973). *Grammatica della fantasia: introduzione all'arte di inventare storie*. Einaudi.

Rodari, G. (2023). *Grammatica della fantasia. Introduzione all'arte di inventare storie. 50 anni*. Einaudi Ragazzi.

Rogers, S. (2010). Play and pedagogy: A conflict of interests? In *Rethinking play and pedagogy in early childhood education* (pp. 13–26). Routledge., DOI: 10.4324/9780203839478

Rouse, E. (2023). 'If you don't feel respect then morally, it just takes a lot out of everything you're doing": Learning in a pedagogical approach inspired by Reggio Emilia middle years school settings. *Australian Educational Researcher, 50*(4), 1089–1104. DOI: 10.1007/s13384-022-00538-z

Ruscoe, A., Barblett, L., & Barratt-Pugh, C. (2018). Sharing power with children: Repositioning children as agentic learners. *Australasian Journal of Early Childhood, 43*(3), 63–71. DOI: 10.23965/AJEC.43.3.07

Sadownik, A. R., & Jevtić, A. V. (Eds.). (2023). *(Re)theorising more-than-parental involvement in early childhood education and care: Vol. 40. International perspectives on early childhood education and development*. Springer. DOI: 10.1007/978-3-031-38762-3

Saldaña, J. (2013). *The coding manual for qualitative researchers*. Sage Publications.

Salyers, V., Carston, C. S., Dean, Y., & London, C. (2015). Exploring the motivations, expectations, and experiences of students who study in global settings. *Journal of International Students, 5*(4), 368–382. DOI: 10.32674/jis.v5i4.401

Samuelsson, I. P., Sheridan, S., & Williams, P. (2006). Five preschool curricula—Comparative perspective. *International Journal of Early Childhood, 38*(1), 11–30. DOI: 10.1007/BF03165975

Sanders-Smith, S. C., & Cordoba, T. E. (2022). Study abroad as a means of unpacking pedagogical complexity in context. *Early Childhood Education Journal, 50*(6), 1059–1069. DOI: 10.1007/s10643-021-01238-6

Sani, A. N. H., Mahmudah, S., & Muhammad, A. A. (2022). The Concept of Merdeka Belajar in Early Childhood: Comparative Study of Reggio Emilia and Ki Hajar Dewantara's Thoughts. *JOYCED: Journal of Early Childhood Education, 2*(2), 156–175. DOI: 10.14421/joyced.2022.22-06

Sanson A, Bellemo M. (2021). Children and youth in the climate crisis. *BJPsych Bull. Aug;45*(4), (pp. 205-209). DOI: 10.1192/bjb.2021.16

Sanvictores, T., & Mendez, M. D. (2022). *Types of parenting styles and effects on children.* StatPearls Publishing.

Saracho, O. N., & Evans, R. (2022). Early childhood education pioneers and their curriculum programs. In *The Influence of Theorists and Pioneers on Early Childhood Education* (pp. 159–166). Routledge., DOI: 10.4324/9781003120216-14

Save The Children. (2025). *Born into the Climate Crisis 2: An unprecedented life: Protecting children's rights in a changing climate.* https://resourcecentre.savethechildren.net/pdf/Born-into-the-Climate-Crisis-2.-An-Unprecedented-Life-Protecting-Childrens-Rights-in-A-Changing-Climate.pdf

Schneider, B. H., Manetti, M., Frattini, L., Rania, N., Santo, J. B., Coplan, R. J., & Cwinn, E. (2014). Successful transition to elementary school and the implementation of facilitative practices specified in the Reggio-Emilia philosophy. *School Psychology International, 35*(5), 447–462. DOI: 10.1177/0143034313511003

Schön, D. A. (1983). *The reflective practitioner.* Basic Books.

Schwanenflugel, P. J., & Knapp, N. F. (2015). *The psychology of reading: Theory and applications.* Guilford Publications.

Seipel, S. A., & Seeger, V. (2024). Impact of the Reggio Emilia approach through short term study abroad and the lenses of Lundy's model: Space, voice, audience, and influence. *Educational Considerations, 49*(3), 1–19. DOI: 10.4148/0146-9282.2372

Shiveley, J., & Misco, T. (2015). Long-term impacts of short-term study abroad: Teacher perceptions of preservice study abroad experiences. *Frontiers: The Interdisciplinary Journal of Study Abroad, 26*(1), 107–120. DOI: 10.36366/frontiers.v26i1.361

Smidt, S. (2012). *Introducing Malaguzzi: Exploring the life and work of Reggio Emilia's founding father.* Routledge., DOI: 10.4324/9780203111857

Smith-Gilman, S. (2015). Culture matters: The arts, the classroom environment, and a pedagogy of EntewateNikonri: Sake: A study in a first nations pre-school. *Canadian Review of Art Education, 42*(2), 53–68. DOI: 10.26443/crae.v42i2.1

Smith, L. T. (2021). *Decolonizing methodologies: Research and indigenous peoples*. Bloomsbury Publishing. DOI: 10.5040/9781350225282

Smith, S. C. (2014). Parent engagement in a Reggio Emilia-inspired Head Start program. *Early Childhood Research & Practice*, *16*(1 & 2), 1–11. https://ecrp.illinois.edu/v16n1/smith.html

Snow, C. E. (2017). *Early literacy development and instruction: An overview*. The Routledge International Handbook of Early Literacy Education. DOI: 10.4324/9781315766027-2

Soler, J., & Miller, L. (2003). The struggle for early childhood curricula: A comparison of the English Foundation Stage Curriculum, Te Wha riki and Reggio Emilia. *International Journal of Early Years Education*, *11*(1), 57–68. DOI: 10.1080/0966976032000066091

Soncini, I. (2012). The inclusive community. In C. Edwards, L. Gandini, & G. Forman (Eds.), The hundred languages of children: The Reggio Emilia experience in transformation (3rd ed.) (pp.187-211). Praeger.

Sorin, R. (2005). Changing images of childhood: Reconceptualising early childhood practice. *International Journal of Transitions in Childhood*, *1*(1), 12–21. https://citeseerx.ist.psu.edu/document?repid=rep1&type=pdf&doi=9594881ae4f396a654957f719b1bb4e3589d0819

Souto-Manning, M. (2021). *The critical turn in early childhood education: Challenging the status quo*. Teachers College Press.

Souto-Manning, M., & James, N. (2008). A multi-arts approach to early literacy and learning. *Journal of Research in Childhood Education*, *23*(1), 82–95. DOI: 10.1080/02568540809594647

Spaggiari, M. (2024, April). Reggio Emilia approach quotation on the Environment. Reggio Emilia, Emilia-Romagna, Italy.

Sparks, R. L., Patton, J., & Murdoch, A. (2014). Early reading success and its relationship to reading achievement and reading volume: Replication of 10 years later. *Reading and Writing*, *27*(1), 189–211. DOI: 10.1007/s11145-013-9439-2

Spencer, R. A., Joshi, N., Branje, K., Murray, N., Kirk, S. F., & Stone, M. R. (2021). Early childhood educator perceptions of risky play in an outdoor loose parts intervention. *AIMS Public Health*, *8*(2), 213–228. DOI: 10.3934/publichealth.2021017 PMID: 34017887

Spiteri, J. (2025). Climate anxiety in early childhood: A state-of-the-art review. *Journal of Childhood. Education and Society*, *6*(2), 230–248.

St Mary's School. (2025, October). *St Mary's School Waverley*. Retrieved from St Mary's School Waverley: https://www.stmarysschool.co.za/

Stanley, C. T., Petscher, Y., & Catts, H. (2018). A longitudinal investigation of direct and indirect links between reading skills in kindergarten and reading comprehension in tenth grade. *Reading and Writing*, *31*(1), 133–153. DOI: 10.1007/s11145-017-9777-6

Sterling, S. (2003). *Whole Systems Thinking as a Basis for Paradigm Change in Education: Explorations in the Context of Sustainability*. University of Bath.

Stone, J. E. (2012). A Vygotskian commentary on the Reggio Emilia approach. *Contemporary Issues in Early Childhood*, *13*(4), 276–289. DOI: 10.2304/ciec.2012.13.4.276

Strong-Wilson, T., & Ellis, J. (2007). Children and place: Reggio Emilia's environment as third teacher. *Theory into Practice*, *46*(1), 40–47. DOI: 10.1080/00405840709336547

Strong-Wilson, T., & Kind, S. (2013). *Reggio Emilia, the image of the child and the child's voice in the classroom.* Routledge.

Sturloni, S. (2022). *Lasciate che vi parli di foglie: Educatori e bambini alla scoperta di un mondo insospettabile*. Junior.

Suggate, S., Schaughency, E., McAnally, H., & Reese, E. (2018). From infancy to adolescence: The longitudinal links between vocabulary, early literacy skills, oral narrative, and reading comprehension. *Cognitive Development*, *47*, 82–95. DOI: 10.1016/j.cogdev.2018.04.005

Sutton-Smith, B. (1997). *The ambiguity of play*. Harvard University Press.

Swann, A. C. (2008). Children, objects, and relations: Constructivist foundations in the Reggio Emilia approach. *Studies in Art Education*, *50*(1), 36–50. DOI: 10.1080/00393541.2008.11518754

Taylor, A. (2013). *Reconfiguring the natures of childhood.* Routledge. DOI: 10.4324/9780203582046

Taylor, A., Pacini-Ketchabaw, V., & Blaise, M. (2012). Children's Relations to the More-Than-Human World. *Contemporary Issues in Early Childhood*, *13*(2), 81–85. DOI: 10.2304/ciec.2012.13.2.81

Taylor, A., Zakharova, T., & Cullen, M. (2021). Common Worlding Pedagogies: Opening Up to Learning with Worlds. *Journal of Childhood Studies*, *46*(4), 74–88. DOI: 10.18357/jcs464202120425

Teachers, B. C. (2025, July). Bekezela Creche Interview - a Reggio Emilia inspired creche and research project. (S. Browne, Interviewer)

Tedeschi, M. (2016). Il pensiero ecologico nell'esperienza educativa del Comune di Reggio Emilia. In G. Bonini & R. Pazzagli, *Paesaggio nel piatto. Storia del paesaggio agrario italiano* (VII) (pp. 231-233). Istituto Alcide Cervi.

The LEGO Foundation. (2017a). *What we mean by: Learning through play (Version 1.2)*. Billund: The LEGO Foundation. https://cms.learningthroughplay.com/media/vd5fiurk/what-we-mean-by-learning-through-play.pdf

The LEGO Foundation. (2017b). *Learning through play: What does it mean?* Billund: LEGO Foundation. https://www.lego.com/cdn/cs/sustainability/assets/blt7aaec03836d94291/LtP_What_Is_It_-_Parents_PDF.pdf

The Presidency of the Republic of South Africa. (2025, October). *Giuseppe Soncini (Posthumous)*. Retrieved from The Presidency Republic of South Africa: https://www.presidency.gov.za/giuseppe-soncini-posthumous

Theodotou, E., & Aden, F. (2019). Reggio Emilia and the arts approach: Two exceptional examples of multimodal learning in early years. *Journal of Global Education and Research*, *3*(2), 158–167. DOI: 10.5038/2577-509X.3.2.1050

Thibodeau, R. B., Gilpin, A. T., Brown, M. M., & Meyer, B. A. (2016). The effects of fantastical pretend-play on the development of executive functions: An intervention study. *Journal of Experimental Child Psychology*, *145*, 120–138. DOI: 10.1016/j.jecp.2016.01.001 PMID: 26835841

Thornton, L., & Brunton, P. (2015). *Understanding the Reggio approach: Early years education in practice*. Routledge., DOI: 10.4324/9781315744018

Tijnagel-Schoenaker, B. (2018). The Reggio Emilia Approach… The Hundred Languages. *Prima Educatione*, *1*, 139. DOI: 10.17951/pe.2017.1.139

Tinto, V. (2010). From theory to action: Exploring the institutional conditions for student retention. In Smart, J. C. (Ed.), *Higher education: Handbook of theory and practice* (pp. 51–89). Springer., DOI: 10.1007/978-90-481-8598-6_2

Tiwari, A. P. (2022). Authoritative parenting: The best style in children's learning. *American Journal of Education and Technology*, *1*(3), 18–21. DOI: 10.54536/ajet.v1i3.687

Tomanović-Mihajlović, S. (2000). Young people's participation within the family: Parents' accounts. *International Journal of Children's Rights*, *8*(2), 151–167. DOI: 10.1023/A:1008700320881

Torgesen, J. K., & Mathes, P. G. (1998). *What every teacher should know about phonological awareness*. Florida Department of Education, Division of Schools and Community Education, Bureau of Instructional Support and Community Services. https://www.fullertonsd.org/cms/lib/CA50010905/Centricity/Domain/1993/PA-_what_you_should_know_.pdf

Trawick-Smith, J. (2014). The physical play and motor development of young children: A review of literature and implications for practice. In Roopnarine, J. L., & Johnson, J. E. (Eds.), *Approaches to early childhood education* (6th ed., pp. 213–234). Pearson.

Tripon, C. (2024). Nurturing sustainable development: The interplay of parenting styles and SDGs in children's development. *Children (Basel, Switzerland)*, *11*(6), 695–713. DOI: 10.3390/children11060695 PMID: 38929274

Tsing, A. L., Gan, E., Swanson, H. A., & Bubandt, N. (A c. Di). (2017). *Arts of living on a damaged planet*. University of Minnesota Press.

Turner, T., & Wilson, D. G. (2009). Reflections on documentation: A discussion with thought leaders from Reggio Emilia. *Theory into Practice*, *49*(1), 5–13. DOI: 10.1080/00405840903435493

Uluay, G. (2024). Nature-based learning in early childhood education. In *Transforming early childhood education: Technology, sustainability, and foundational skills for the 21st century* (pp. 247–260). Özgür Yayın-Dağıtım.

UN Committee on the Rights of the Child. (2019). *Concluding observations on the combined 5th and 6th periodic reports of Italy: Committee on the Rights of the Child (CRC/C/ITA/CO/5-6)*. United Nations. https://tbinternet.ohchr.org/_layouts/15/treatybodyexternal/Download.aspx?symbolno=CRC%2fC%2fITA%2fCO%2f5-6&Lang=en

UNESCO. (2006). *Guidelines on intercultural education*. UNESCO.

UNESCO. (2015a). *Recommendation on Adult Learning and Education*. UNESCO.

UNESCO. (2015b). *International Charter of Physical Education, Physical Activity, and Sport*. UNESCO.

UNESCO. (2017). *Education for Sustainable Development Goals: Learning objectives*. UNESCO., DOI: 10.54675/CGBA9153

UNICEF, & UNESCO. (2007). *A human rights-based approach to education for all: A framework for the realization of children's right to education and rights within education*. UNICEF; UNESCO.

UNICEF. (2021). *Sfere di influenza: un'analisi dei fattori che condizionano il benessere dei bambini nei paesi ricchi*. United Nations.

United Nations Committee on the Rights of the Child. (2013). *General comment No. 17 on the right of the child to rest, leisure, play, recreational activities, cultural life and the arts (Article 31) (CRC/C/GC/17)*. United Nations. https://digitallibrary.un.org/record/778539?ln=en

United Nations Committee on the Rights of the Child. (2023). Concluding observations on the combined fifth and sixth periodic reports of Ireland. Author. https://tbinternet.ohchr.org/_layouts/15/treatybodyexternal/SessionDetails1.aspx?SessionID=2600&Lang=en

United Nations Committee on the Rights of the Child. (2023). *General Comment No. 26 on Children's Rights and the Environment, with a special focus on climate change—Version for Children*. United Nations.

United Nations Educational. Scientific & Cultural Organisation. (1994). The Salamanca state-ment and framework for action on special needs education. Adopted by the World Conference on Special Needs Education: Access and Quality, Salamanca, Spain, 7-10 June 1994. Author. https://unesdoc.unesco.org/ark:/48223/pf0000098427

United Nations General Assembly. (1959). *Declaration of the Right of the Child*. UN General Assembly.

United Nations General Assembly. (1989). *Convention on the Rights of the Child*. United Nations, Treaty Series, vol. 1577, p. 3. https://www.ohchr.org/en/instruments-mechanisms/instruments/convention-rights-child

United Nations General Assembly. (1989). *Convention on the Rights of the Child*. United Nations.

United Nations. (1948). Universal declaration of human rights. Author. https://www.un.org/en/about-us/universal-declaration-of-human-rights

United Nations. (1948). *Universal declaration of human rights*. https://www.un.org/en/about-us/universal-declaration-of-human-rights

United Nations. (1959). Declaration of the rights of the child. Author. https://digitallibrary.un.org/record/195831?ln=en&v=pdf

United Nations. (1989). *Convention on the rights of the child.* Adopted and opened for signature and ratification by General Assembly resolution 44/25, 20 November 1989. https://www.ohchr.org/en/instruments-mechanisms/instruments/convention-rights-child

United Nations. (1989). Convention on the rights of the child. Author. https://www.ohchr.org/sites/default/files/crc.pdf

United Nations. (1989). *Convention on the rights of the child.* Office of the United Nations High Commissioner for Human Rights. https://www.ohchr.org/sites/default/files/crc.pdf

United Nations. (1989). *Convention on the Rights of the Child.* United Nations. https://www.ohchr.org/en/instruments-mechanisms/instruments/convention-rights-child

United Nations. (2006). Convention on the rights of persons with disabilities. Author. https://treaties.un.org/doc/Publication/CTC/Ch_IV_15.pdf

United Nations. (2015). *Transforming our world: The 2030 agenda for sustainable development* (A/RES/70/1). https://www.un.org/ga/search/view_doc.asp?symbol=A/RES/70/1&Lang=E

United Nations. (2015). Transforming Our world: The 2030 agenda for sustainable develop-ment. UN Doc A/RES/70/1. Author. Document Viewer

United Nations. (2025). The sustainable development agenda. Author. https://www.un.org/sustainabledevelopment/development-agenda/

Vakil, S., Freeman, R., & Swim, T. J. (2003). The reggio Emilia approach and inclusive early childhood programs. *Early Childhood Education Journal, 30*(3), 187–192. Advance online publication. DOI: 10.1023/A:1022022107610

Vallberg Roth, A. C., & Månsson, A. (2011). Individual development plans from a critical didactic perspective: Focusing on Montessori-and Reggio Emilia-profiled preschools in Sweden. *Journal of Early Childhood Research, 9*(3), 247–261. DOI: 10.1177/1476718X10389148

Valodia, I. (2023, September 14). *South Africa can't crack the inequality curse. Why, and what can be done.* Retrieved from The Conversation -: https://theconversation.com/south-africa-cant-crack-the-inequality-curse-why-and-what-can-be-done-213132?utm_medium=email&utm_campaign=Latest%20from%20The%20Conversation%20for%20September%2014%202023%20-%202736927673&utm_content=Latest%20from%20The%20Conv

Vatalaro, A., Szente, J., & Levin, J. (2015). Transformative learning of pre-service teachers during study abroad in Reggio Emilia, Italy: A case study. *The Journal of Scholarship of Teaching and Learning*, *15*(2), 42–55. DOI: 10.14434/josotl.v15i2.12911

Vea Vecchi, A.-T. (1998). "The Role of the Atelierista: An Interview with Lella Gandini.". In L. G. edited by Carolyn Edwards, *In The Hundred Languages of Children: The Reggio Emilia Approach – Advanced Reflections, 2nd edition* (pp. 139 - 147). Norwood, New Jersey, United States of America: Ablex Publishing.

Vecchi, V. (2010). *Art and creativity in Reggio Emilia: Exploring the role and potential of ateliers in early childhood education*. Routledge. DOI: 10.4324/9780203854679

Veltri, B. T. (2012). Educator abroad: Teaching (insegnare) and learning (imparare) with Italian children. *Social Studies and the Young Learner*, *24*(4), 23–26. https://www.socialstudies.org/system/files/publications/articles/yl_240423.pdf

Vezzali, L., Crisp, R. J., Stathi, S., & Giovannini, D. (2015). Imagined intergroup contact facilitates intercultural communication for college students on academic exchange programs. *Group Processes & Intergroup Relations*, *18*(1), 66–75. DOI: 10.1177/1368430214527853

Višnjić-Jevtić, A., Sadownik, A. R., & Engdahl, I. (2021). Introducing human rights for children. In Višnjić-Jevtić, A., Sadownik, A. R., & Engdahl, I. (Eds.), *Young children in the world and their rights* (pp. 1–16). Springer Nature Switzerland AG.

Voicu, C., Anghel, A., & Savu-Cristescu, M. (2015). Parent education for children's rights. *Procedia: Social and Behavioral Sciences*, *191*, 1707–1712. DOI: 10.1016/j.sbspro.2015.04.433

Vygotsky, L. S. (1978). *Mind in society*. Harvard University Press.

Vygotsky, L. S. (1978). *Mind in society: The development of higher psychological processes* (Cole, M., John-Steiner, V., Scribner, S., & Souberman, E., Eds. & Trans.). Harvard University Press.

Waks, L. J. (Ed.). (2015). *Listening to teach: Beyond didactic pedagogy*. Suny Press., DOI: 10.1515/9781438458335

Wallace, R., Tolley, E., & Vonk, M. (2021). *Immigrant minorities index*. School of Policy Studies, Queen's University.

Warden, C. (2018, February). *Nature pedagogy: A common thread connecting nature-based settings worldwide*. Natural Start Alliance. https://naturalstart.org/resources/articles/nature-pedagogy-common-thread-connecting-nature-based-settings-worldwide

Webb-Williams, J., Kennedy-Behr, A., & Graham, A. (2021). *Play in early adolescence*. University of South Australia. https://www.unisa.edu.au/research/.../play-in-early-adolescence/

Weisberg, D. S., Hirsh-Pasek, K., & Golinkoff, R. M. (2013). Guided play: Where curricular goals meet a playful pedagogy. *Mind, Brain and Education : the Official Journal of the International Mind, Brain, and Education Society*, *7*(2), 104–112. DOI: 10.1111/mbe.12015

Westerberg, L., & Vandermaas-Peeler, M. (2021). How teachers, peers, and classroom materials support children's inquiry in a Reggio Emilia-inspired preschool. *Early Child Development and Care*, *191*(7–8), 1259–1276. DOI: 10.1080/03004430.2021.1881075

Wexler, A. (2004). A theory for living: Walking with Reggio Emilia. *Art Education*, *57*(6), 13–19. DOI: 10.1080/00043125.2004.11653571

White, B. (1981). Education for parenthood. *Journal of Education*, *163*(3), 205–218. DOI: 10.1177/002205748116300303

Whitebread, D., Basilio, M., Kuvalja, M., & Verma, M. (2012). *The importance of play: A report on the value of children's play with a series of policy recommendations*. University of Cambridge.

Wien, C. A., & Dudley-Marling, C. (1998). Limited vision: The Ontario curriculum and outcomes-based learning. *Canadian Journal of Education/Revue canadienne de l'education*, 405-420. DOI: 10.2307/1585755

Wilson, D. G., Krechevsky, M., Mardell, B., & Rivard, M. (2013). *Visible learners: Promoting Reggio-inspired approaches in all schools*. Wiley.

Witkowsky, P., Mendez, S. L., & Arminio, J. (2018). Influence of a short-term study abroad experience on professional competencies and career aspirations of graduate students in student affairs. *Journal of College Student Development*, *59*(6), 769–775. DOI: 10.1353/csd.2018.0073

Wood, E. (2014). The play–pedagogy interface in contemporary debates. In L. Brooker, M. Blaise, & S. Edwards (Eds.), *The SAGE handbook of play and learning in early childhood* (pp. 145–156). SAGE. DOI: 10.4135/9781473907850.n15

Wood, J., Thall, T., & Parnell, E. C. (2015). The move: Reggio Emilia-inspired teaching. *Complicity: An International Journal of Complexity and Education, 12*(1). Advance online publication. DOI: 10.29173/cmplct24241

Wyness, M. (2019). *Childhood and society* (3rd ed.). RedGlobe Press.

You, H. (2014). Learning from Learning Environments: The Effects of the Reggio Emilia Approach in Early Childhood Education Centers. *Creativity in Educational Research and Practice*, 95-109. DOI: 10.1163/9781848883086_010

Zanatta, F., & Long, S. (2021). Rights to the front: Child rights-based pedagogies in early childhood degrees. *Journal of Early Childhood Education Research, 10*(1), 139–165.

Zapata-Barrero, R. (2017). Interculturalism in the post-multicultural debate: A defence. *Comparative Migration Studies, 5*(14). [1] The Italian Ministry of Education is referred to by different names depending on the period: *Ministero della Pubblica Istruzione* (MPI) in 1994 and in 2007, *Ministero dell'Istruzione, dell'Università e della Ricerca* (MIUR) in 2006, and *Ministero dell'Istruzione* (MI) in 2022. This section will use these acronyms to refer to the Ministry.

Zhang, B., Szente, J., & Levin, J. (2019). Early childhood pre-professionals' experience in a study abroad program to Finland: Evaluation of professional growth, and personal and cultural gains. *International Journal for the Scholarship of Teaching and Learning, 13*(2), 1–5. DOI: 10.20429/ijsotl.2019.130216

Zhang, Q., Yin, J., & Jiang, K. (2025). Glocalization of early childhood curriculum: An ethnographic study on the integration of the Reggio Emilia approach into the Chinese kindergarten curriculum. *Asia Pacific Education Review, 26*(March), 49–60. DOI: 10.1007/s12564-023-09851-3

Zosh, J. M., Hopkins, E. J., Jensen, H., Liu, C., Neale, D., Hirsh-Pasek, K., Solis, S. L., & Whitebread, D. (2017). *Learning through play: a review of the evidence (white paper)*. The LEGO Foundation.

About the Contributors

Marisa Galliano Macy is a full professor in the College of Education in the School of Teacher Education at the University of Wyoming. She holds the John P. Ellbogen Foundation Professorship of Early Childhood Education. Macy has more than 25 years of experience as an educator. She started her career as a special education teacher in Washington, and she has served in teaching and research roles at a number of higher education institutions, including the University of Oregon, Penn State University, University of Texas, El Paso, University of Central Florida, University of Nebraska Kearney where she held the Cille and Ron Williams endowed chair of Early Childhood Education, as well as community chair for the Buffett Early Childhood Institute. Macy, a Seattle native, earned a bachelor's degree in English at the University of Washington and a post baccalaureate in K–12 special education from St. Martin's College in Olympia, Washington. She received master's and doctorate degrees in special education with early childhood special education and early intervention from the University of Oregon. Macy completed the Certificate in Early Education Leadership from the Graduate School of Education at Harvard.

Emer Ring is Dean of Education, (Early Childhood and Teacher Education) at Mary Immaculate College (MIC), Limerick. Emer previously worked as a teacher of children in the early years and as teacher supporting neurodivergent children in mainstream provision. She has also worked in the Department of Education's Inspectorate in Ireland and as Head of Department of Reflective Pedagogy and Early Childhood Studies at MIC. Emer's research interests include education law; inclusion; early childhood; child voice; autism; play and pedagogy and she has researched and published widely in these areas.

Alessandra Landini is the Principal of the I.C. A. Manzoni in Reggio Emilia, with a PhD in Human Sciences, thesis in Physics Education from the Department of Education and Human Sciences at the University of Modena and Reggio Emilia, and a Master Degree in Organization and Management of Multicultural

School Institutions from Alma Mater, Bologna. Her scientific education research project studies a vertical science curriculum based on storytelling and the use of metaphor, between early childhood and secondary school. Adjunct Professor in Special Pedagogy at UNIMORE, as a General Didactics' expert, she provides integrative teaching activities at the university. She collaborates with the "Metaphor and Narrative in Science" research center. Other areas of research focus on the use of narrative formative evaluation for ECE, primary and secondary schools and on teacher training as a community of practice that cultivates educational co-responsibility by co-designing and integrating innovative didactic in school and museum settings. Since 2020, she has been studying a Vertical curriculum of Heritage and Citizenship K-13, which leads teachers and students to immerse themselves in the city's territory and its cultural heritage and School leaders to express diffused leadership by the school institution contributing to the creation, development and sustainability of learning democratic ecosystems. She is a Member of the Board of Directors of Preschools and Infant-toddler Centres, Istituzione of the Municipality of Reggio Emilia. In A.A. 2025-26 she is a Fulbrighter, SIR in residence, at Millersville University of Pennsylvania, USA.

* * *

Ashraf Alam is an Assistant Professor at Alliance University, Bangalore. Dr. Ashraf has been distinguished as one of the World's Top 2% Scientists by Stanford University and Elsevier. His prolific academic output includes over sixty SCOPUS-indexed publications and more than one hundred conference presentations at esteemed national and international academic forums. He earned his Ph.D. in Education from the IIT Kharagpur. His research has been disseminated through elite academic platforms, including Elsevier, Springer, Taylor & Francis, Wiley, Routledge, Sage, Emerald, and IEEE, and addresses a remarkably diverse array of topics including but not limited to pedagogical theories, educational administration, educational psychology, educational sociology, educational policy, technology-integrated learning, mathematics education, educational philosophy, educational technology, teacher education, and AI/ML in learning environments.

Pamela Beach is an Associate Professor of Language and Literacy at the Faculty of Education, Queen's University, Canada. Pamela completed her MA in Child Study and Education at the Dr. Eric Jackman Institute of Child Study, University of Toronto and her PhD in Developmental Psychology and Education at the Ontario Institute for Studies in Education, University of Toronto. Pamela has a decade of elementary classroom experience, teaching a range of grades and subject areas from pre-kindergarten to seventh grade. Her background as an early years and elementary teacher has influenced her research which centres on the dissemination of research-informed literacy practices.

Rosalba Bortolotti is a highly experienced and dedicated pedagogist with over 30 years of experience in early childhood education, pedagogical research, and project work innovation. A past owner of a progressive preschool that functioned as a learning hub for educators, her school became known for its study tours, workshops, and retreats that introduced educators to reflective and inquiry-based practices. Rosalba is the author a tomato story in Beautiful Stuff from Nature (Gandini & Topal) and creator of the Acorn Mini Books (2004–2015; republished 2025), a curated collection documenting Acorn School's work and topic areas-ranging from children's encounters with materials, food, and nature to the evolving relationship among educators, families and community. As a part-time professor in the School of Early Childhood Education and chair of the York Region Nature Collaborative, Rosalba continues to advocate for pedagogies of care, sustainability, and the rights of children and educators. Her ongoing work includes consulting, mentoring, and leading professional learning across Canada and beyond through Acorn Collaborative (founder) Inspired by her visits to Reggio Emilia and long-standing inquiry into material thinking, Rosalba explores how educators and children can build deeper relationships with open-ended materials, food, and the natural world. Her work reflects a lifelong commitment to fostering democratic, ethical, and environmentally responsive education that honours children as capable citizens and co-researchers in learning.

Sarah Browne is an atelierista, presenter, and the social media curator for the Africa Reggio Emilia Alliance (AREA). She is currently the resident atelierista at Reddam House Waterfall Early Learning School and coordinates the Reggio Emilia approach professional development at the school and is part of their Social Media Team. Sarah is passionate about the Reggio Emilia approach and promoting the rights of every child in every context. Sarah renamed her workspace, the Everywhere Atelier, a Reggio Emilia inspired laboratory of research, and aims to ensure that the culture of the atelier diffuses throughout the school and beyond like the fragrance of perfume.

Kelcie Burke is a doctoral student in the Department of Child, Youth, and Family Studies at the University of Nebraska–Lincoln, specializing in Child Development and Early Childhood Education. A Nebraska native, she earned a Bachelor of Science in Early Childhood and Family Advocacy with a minor in Special Education and a Master of Arts in Education in Curriculum and Instruction with an emphasis in Early Childhood from the University of Nebraska at Kearney. Burke's research explores play-based development, teacher practices, and authentic assessment to support high-quality early childhood education. She serves as a graduate assistant and lead teacher at the Ruth Staples Child Development Laboratory, a nature and play based Reggio inspired program.

Mara Davoli worked as an atelierista in Reggio Emilia's early childhood system (1973–2007) and contributed to landmark exhibitions like I cento linguaggi dei bambini. Her extensive career includes collaborations with the University of Modena and Reggio Emilia (2000–2007) and the Rosa Sensat Association in Barcelona (since 2008). Since 2012, she has served as a trainer for the Municipality of Correggio, focusing on educational design and expressive languages. A frequent contributor to specialized publications, she has co-curated several books, including Reggio tutta: Una guida dei bambini alla città, and for Edizioni Junior, Ri-abitare i luoghi and L'atelier che rigenera. She also edited the Italian edition of Carla Rinaldi's In dialogo con Reggio Emilia. She currently serves as a consultant for the Fondazione Reggio Children – Centro Loris Malaguzzi.

Eloisa Di Rocco has been working since 2012 for the Reggio Children Foundation as an atelierista and coordinator of Remida, the Creative Recycling Center. In 2025, she defended her doctoral thesis in Reggio Childhood Studies at the University of Modena and Reggio Emilia, entitled "Listening to matter: The Reggio Emilia Approach in the Anthropocene Era." She conducts research on the dialogue between the Pedagogy of Listening, at the heart of the Reggio Emilia approach, and environmental studies, waste studies, and waste pedagogies from a post-human perspective.

Maria Barbara Donnici has been working with Fondazione Reggio Children since 2012, holding various roles over time. She currently coordinates the Play Explore Research (P.E.R.) project, a global platform promoting the value of play, exploration, and research as essential dimensions of learning and social change. P.E.R. advocates for the right to play and the right to quality education for all. She holds a degree in Foreign Languages and Literatures and a PhD in Reggio Childhood Studies. Her research investigates the transition from a transmissive educational model to one that emphasizes the playful dimension as a more effective and inclusive approach to teaching and learning. Maria Barbara has authored and co-authored articles and publications in Italy and abroad, and has presented her work at international conferences, contributing to scholarly discussions on innovative, research-based approaches to education.

Elisa Ferrari is a pedagogista with extensive experience in coordinating and supervising national and international educational projects at Fondazione Reggio

Children. Over the years, Elisa has gained solid expertise in co-design processes and engagement with public and private entities. Elisa's strengths include teamwork, problem-solving, and leadership. Her educational background includes a Master's degree in Pedagogical Sciences, emphasizing her commitment to pedagogical development. Additionally, Elisa is actively involved in educational research, with a focus on combating educational poverty and contributing to the advancement of innovative teaching and learning strategies in fragile non-formal contexts.

Aldo Fortunati is the President of BOTTEGA DI GEPPETTO – International Research and Documentation Center on Childhood Gloria Tognetti, (San Miniato, Pisa), a Professor at the University of Florence and the National Representative of Italy at World Forum Foundation (USA). From 1999 until his retirement in 2025, he served as the Director of the Documentation, Research, and Training Department at the Istituto degli Innocenti in Florence. He graduated in Philosophy at Sapienza University of Rome and Specialized in Developmental Psychology at the Institute of Education, University of London; he began his research activity at the National Research Council (CNR) in Rome. His biography combines research interests in child development with fieldwork for innovative education services and the coordination of policy monitoring in the Tuscany Region, on behalf of the Italian Government, and in Latin American countries. His bibliography includes books translated into English, Spanish, and Portuguese, and articles published in national and international journals.

Melissa Dawn Gatlin is an academic and researcher whose work emphasizes community engagement in early childhood education. Her interest in bridging academic learning with real-world issues promotes equity, empathy, and responsibility among future educators.

Lisa Goddard is a PhD Fellow in Reggio Childhood Studies at the University of Modena and Reggio Emilia, Italy. Her research currently focuses on posthuman playful pedagogies for early childhood education in the ecological crisis. Lisa holds an MSc in Applied Linguistics from the University of Edinburgh, an MEd in Early Childhood Education from Boston University, and a BA in Language and Social Behavior from Brown University. Throughout her career, she has served as an early childhood educator in Reggio-inspired settings, teacher educator, curriculum developer and coach for Boston (USA) toddler teachers implementing a play-based approach, and pedagogista in Italy and the US, and now facilitates an international practitioner inquiry group to explore play and Reggio-inspired values in education in the Anthropocene.

Aysenur Gungor-Kircadag is the founder and school director of a Reggio Emilia-inspired Naturel Forest Preschool and Primary School in Türkiye. She brings a rich practice-based perspective as both a leader and facilitator in a learning community where the rights of the child are actively upheld and celebrated through daily pedagogical practice.

Hatice Zeynep Inan is a professor at Sam Houston State University and researcher in early childhood education specializing in the Reggio Emilia approach. Since 2002, her research has focused on how this philosophy supports inclusive, participatory, and rights-based practices in early childhood education. She has authored numerous scholarly publications on Reggio Emilia-inspired education. Dr. Inan has supervised theses and led research projects related to early childhood education while collaborating with and supporting early childhood and primary education institutions internationally.

Judith N. Levin recently retired from the University of Central Florida (UCF) as a Senior Lecturer in the Early Childhood Development and Education program where she served as program coordinator and taught undergraduate, masters, and doctoral courses. Levin earned her Bachelor's degree in Elementary Education at the University of Florida, Master's degree in Counselor Education at UCF, and Doctorate degree in Child and Youth Studies at Nova Southeastern University. Her research includes a longitudinal study examining the influence of high-quality preschool experiences on children living in poverty. She has also worked on a variety of projects with Sesame Workshop, including upcoming seasons of Sesame Street. She continues her work presenting at professional conferences and providing training for early childhood professionals and parents. Levin has taken multiple groups of pre-service students on study abroad to Reggio Emilia, Italy and Finland and co-coordinated two trips with early childhood professionals to Reggio Emilia.

Benedetta Melloni is a PhD candidate in Reggio Childhood Studies at the University of Modena and Reggio Emilia, in partnership with the Reggio Children Foundation. Her research focuses on intercultural dialogue and inclusion in primary education, analyzing policies, educational practice, and perceptions across formal and non-formal settings. Her multidisciplinary career began in 2012 with roles at both the European Commission and the European Parliament in Brussels and Luxembourg. She subsequently spent five years at Engineering International Belgium and Engineering Ingegneria Informatica, where she managed projects and drafted R&D proposals focused on Smart Cities and Smart Communities. Since 2018, she has been with the Reggio Children Foundation, where she integrates her expertise in EU project design into her role as International Research Strategist.

Lisha O'Sullivan is Head of the Department of Reflective Pedagogy and Early Childhood Studies and Senior Lecturer in Early Childhood Education, at Mary Immaculate College, Limerick, Ireland. Lisha is a qualified play therapist and lectures at undergraduate and post-graduate levels and engages in a wide range of research focused on the role of play in development, playful learning and teaching, inclusive education, and playful participatory research methods.

Alfonso Trillicoso is an elementary school teacher holding a degree in Modern Humanities with a focus on contemporary history. In addition to co-authoring articles on digital educational innovation, he currently teaches science at the "A. Bergonzi" State Elementary School in Reggio Emilia. At the "A. Manzoni" Comprehensive School, he serves as the Digital Learning Coordinator, leading training initiatives for both digital literacy and STEAM education. Notably, during the pandemic, he participated in an experimental heritage pedagogy project that involved conducting classes directly within the "A. Spallanzani" Civic Museum in Reggio Emilia.

Suzette Turner is a Childcare Director and Adjunct Instructor at the University of Central Florida. She earned her Ph.D. in Curriculum and Instruction from Saint Louis University, specializing in Early Childhood Education. With more than 35 years of hands-on experience, Dr. Turner has led numerous initiatives focused on improving outcomes for young children. She has served as Principal Investigator on several federal and state childcare grants, supporting innovative programs for early learning. She often presents at conferences on Conscious Discipline, the Project Approach, Reggio Emilia and the transformative power of early education.

Angela Vatalaro received her B.S. (2008), M.Ed. (2010), and Ph.D. (2015) in Early Childhood Education from the University of Central Florida (UCF). She previously worked as an Associate in Research in the College of Behavioral and Community Sciences at the University of South Florida where she conducted program evaluation and research on state, federal, and private foundation grants in the areas of home visitation, child welfare, systems of care, mental health and wellbeing of men and boys of color, and housing sustainability. She most recently served as a Visiting Lecturer at UCF in the Early Childhood Development and Education Program. She has participated in several study abroad trips, including: one to England; three to Reggio Emilia, Italy; and one to Finland.

Index

Symbols

A

B

C

D

E

F

H

S

T

U

www.ingramcontent.com/pod-product-compliance
Lightning Source LLC
LaVergne TN
LVHW062327300926
849161LV00007B/1599